Spatializing Practices of Regional Organizations during Conflict Intervention

I0888343

This book studies relevant actors and practices of conflict intervention by African regional organizations and their intimate connection to space-making, addressing a major gap regarding what actually happens within and around these organizations.

Based on extensive empirical research, it argues that those intervention practices are essentially spatializing practices, based on particular spatial imaginations, contributing to the continuous construction and formatting of regional spaces as well as to ordering relations between different regional spaces. Analyzing the field of developing practices of conflict intervention by the Economic Community of West African States (ECOWAS) and the African Union (AU), the book contributes a new theory-oriented analytical approach to study African regional organizations (ROs) and the complex dynamics of African peace and security, based on insights from Critical Geography. As such, it helps to close an empirical gap with regard to the 'internal' modes of operation of African ROs as well as the lack of their theorization. It demonstrates that, contrary to most accounts, intervention practices of African ROs have been diverse and complexly interrelated, involving different actors within and around these organizations, and that they are essentially tied to space-making.

This book will be of key interest to students and scholars of African Politics, Governance, Peace and Security Studies, International or Regional Organizations and more broadly to Comparative Regionalism, International Relations and International Studies.

Jens Herpolsheimer is a post-doctoral researcher at the Research Centre Global Dynamics, Leipzig University, Germany.

Routledge Studies in African Politics and International Relations
Series Editor: *Daniel C. Bach, Emile Durkheim Centre for Comparative Politics and Sociology, Sciences Po Bordeaux, France.*

Regionalism in Africa
Genealogies, Institutions and Trans-State Networks
Daniel C. Bach

China's Aid to Africa
Does Friendship Really Matter?
Zhangxi Cheng and Ian Taylor

African Border Disorders
Addressing Transnational Extremist Organizations
Edited by Olivier J. Walther and William F.S. Miles

Political Trust and the Politics of Security Engagement
China and the European Union in Africa
Benjamin Barton

Human Rights and the Judicialisation of African Politics
Peter Brett

The Finances of Regional Organisations in the Global South
Follow the Money
Edited by Ulf Engel and Frank Mattheis

African Foreign Policies
Selecting Signifiers to Explain Agency
Edited by Paul-Henri Bischoff

Regional Economic Communities and Peacebuilding in Africa
Lessons from ECOWAS and IGAD
Edited by Victor Adetula, Redie Bereketeab and Cyril Obi

Spatializing Practices of Regional Organizations during Conflict Intervention
The Politics of ECOWAS and the African Union
Jens Herpolsheimer

Spatializing Practices of Regional Organizations during Conflict Intervention

The Politics of ECOWAS and the African Union

Jens Herpolsheimer

Routledge
Taylor & Francis Group
LONDON AND NEW YORK

First published 2021
by Routledge
2 Park Square, Milton Park, Abingdon, Oxon OX14 4RN

and by Routledge
52 Vanderbilt Avenue, New York, NY 10017

Routledge is an imprint of the Taylor & Francis Group, an informa business

British Library Cataloguing-in-Publication Data
A catalogue record for this book is available from the British Library

Library of Congress Cataloging-in-Publication Data
Names: Herpolsheimer, Jens, author.
Title: Spatializing practices of regional organizations during conflict intervention: the politics of ECOWAS and the African Union / Jens Herpolsheimer.
Other titles: Routledge studies on African politics and international relations.
Description: Abingdon, Oxon; New York, NY: Routledge, 2021. |
Series: Routledge studies in African politics and international relations |
Includes bibliographical references and index.
Identifiers: LCCN 2020044948 (print) | LCCN 2020044949 (ebook) |
ISBN 9780367618032 (hardback) | ISBN 9781003106647 (ebook)
Subjects: LCSH: African Union–Political activity. |
Economic Community of West African States–Political activity. |
African cooperation. | Peace-building–Africa.
Classification: LCC JQ1873.5.R43 H47 2021 (print) |
LCC JQ1873.5.R43 (ebook) | DDC 327.6–dc23
LC record available at https://lccn.loc.gov/2020044948
LC ebook record available at https://lccn.loc.gov/2020044949

ISBN: 978-0-367-61803-2 (hbk)
ISBN: 978-0-367-61807-0 (pbk)
ISBN: 978-1-003-10664-7 (ebk)

Typeset in Times New Roman
by Newgen Publishing UK

Contents

List of figures vi
Acknowledgments vii
List of acronyms ix

1 Introduction: spatializing practices in AU and ECOWAS interventions 1

2 A spatial approach to African Peace and Security 34

3 Establishing 'reach': ECOWAS and AU intervention practices 'from afar' 62

4 Establishing 'presence': ECOWAS and AU intervention practices 'on the ground' 103

5 Regional security policies: spatial imaginations and spatial formatting 145

6 Contested relations: spatial ordering during conflict interventions 173

7 Conclusion: spatializing the study of African Peace and Security 202

Appendix 213
Index 221

Figures

1.1 AU intervention practices, 2006–18 10
1.2 ECOWAS intervention practices, 2000–18 11
3.1 AU PSC Meetings and other meetings of AU actors on conflict situations, 2006–18 72
3.2 Meetings of the ECOWAS Authority on conflict situations, 2000–18 75
4.1 Visits of AU actors to conflict sites, 2006–18 105
4.2 Visits of ECOWAS actors to conflict sites, 2000–18 106

Acknowledgments

First of all, this book would not have been possible without the continuous encouragement, support and understanding of my family, especially my wife Sara and our sons Karl and Artur. I am infinitely grateful for their belief in my abilities, as well as their sacrifices in favor of my always time- and attention-consuming research and writing process. I take none of it for granted.

Furthermore, I am deeply indebted to numerous colleagues and friends who over the years have provided invaluable intellectual and personal inspiration, constructive criticism and support in various ways. I have been most fortunate to be a part of the Collaborative Research Center (SFB 1199) "Processes of Spatialization under the Global Condition", based at Leipzig University. Generously funded by the German Research Foundation (DFG), the SFB 1199 has allowed me to conduct research and write this book in a setting of rare scholarly freedom combined with invaluable mutual academic exchanges across multiple disciplines, research fields and areas, with a shared interest in space-making. Without the intellectual and financial support of the SFB 1199, this book – based on true multi-sited field research and taking place at the intersections of different academic fields – would not have become what it is. In particular, I want to thank Steffi Marung, Antje Dietze, Geert Castryck and Katja Naumann for always being available and ready to give advice and valuable comments on various drafts. I am also grateful for the stimulating scholarly exchanges and valuable advice by Matthias Middell and the immense administrative support provided to my research by Ute Rietdorf and Martina Keilbach.

Although probably doing injustice to many others who have helped me along the way, I nevertheless want to foreground a few people who have played an extraordinary role in the process leading to this book. First, I want to thank Ulf Engel for encouraging me to take on this challenge, providing a framework that allowed for rich academic experiences and a maximum of academic freedom, to develop my ideas and capabilities as a researcher, while always being available when I needed guidance or support. Moreover, I am deeply grateful to have shared the experience of working together, doing research and writing a dissertation with my colleague Katharina Döring. I have learned a lot from her and her open mind, reflexivity, support and friendship have helped me to navigate the vicissitudes of doing interdisciplinary research in 'messy' research environments. In addition, several research assistants have supported my work over the years. In particular, Eva Ommert, Rüdiger Lauberbach and Skollan Elisabeth Warnck have offered invaluable and tireless support at various stages of this book project. Likewise, several fellow scholars have offered invaluable reflection, commented on different stages of this book and provided advice. In particular, I want to thank Rita Abrahamsen, Linnéa Gelot, Jan Bachmann, Joshua Forrest, Vincent Foucher, Toni Haastrup and Clionadh Raleigh for engaging with this project from an 'outside' perspective. I would also like to thank the two anonymous reviewers for their insightful and constructive comments. Equally important have been the many people who have supported my research in different places in Africa. I am immensely grateful to all the people who have agreed to talk to me during numerous interviews and personal conversations, spending some of their scarce time and energy. It is greatly appreciated.

Acronyms

1999 Mechanism	Protocol Relating to the Mechanism for Conflict Prevention, Management, Resolution, Peacekeeping and Security
2001 Supplementary Protocol	Protocol A/SP1/12/01 on Democracy and Good Governance Supplementary to the Protocol Relating to the Mechanism for Conflict Prevention, Management, Resolution, Peacekeeping and Security
ACCORD	African Centre for the Constructive Resolution of Disputes
ACDEG	African Charter on Democracy, Elections and Governance
ACP	African, Caribbean and Pacific Group of States
AfDB	African Development Bank
AFISMA	African-led International Support Mission to Mali
ANT	actor-network theory
APF	African Peace Facility
APSA	African Peace and Security Architecture
ARB	Africa Research Bulletin
ASF	African Standby Force
AU	African Union
AU PSC	African Union Peace and Security Council
AU PSD	African Union Peace and Security Department
AUC	African Union Commission
AULO	AU liaison office
AULO-GB	AU liaison office in Guinea-Bissau
CAR	Central African Republic
CCDS	ECOWAS Committee of Chiefs of Defense Staff

CEWS	AU Continental Early Warning System
CISSA	Committee of Intelligence and Security Services of Africa
CMD	AU Conflict Management Division
CMPCRD	AU Conflict Management and Post-Conflict Reconstruction Division
COAFR	Africa Working Party of the EU Council
CPAPS	Commissioner for Political Affairs, Peace and Security
CPEWD	AU Conflict Prevention and Early Warning Division
CPLP	Community of Portuguese-Speaking Countries (Comunidade dos Países de Língua Portuguesa)
CSDP	EU Common Security and Defense Policy
CSSDCA	Conference on Security, Stability, Development and Cooperation in Africa
DCAF	Geneva Center for the Democratic Control of Armed Forces
DDR	demobilization, disarmament and reintegration
DEA	US Drug Enforcement Agency
DG DEVCO	Directorate General for International Cooperation and Development (of the EU Commission)
DPA	Department of Political Affairs
DPAPS	ECOWAS Department for Political Affairs, Peace and Security
DSSR	defense and security sector reform
ECDPM	European Centre for Development Policy Management
ECOMIB	ECOWAS Standby Force Mission in Guinea-Bissau
ECOMOG	ECOWAS Cease-fire Monitoring Group
ECOWARN	ECOWAS Early Warning System
ECOWAS	Economic Community of West African States
ECPF	ECOWAS Conflict Prevention Framework
EDF	European Development Fund
EEAS	European External Action Service
EIDHR	European Instrument for Democracy and Human Rights
EOM	election observation mission

ESDP	European Security and Defense Policy
ESF	ECOWAS Standby Force
EU	European Union
EU SSR	EU Security Sector Reform Mission
EU SSR-GB	EU Security Sector Reform Mission to Guinea-Bissau
EWD	ECOWAS Early Warning Directorate
GDP	gross domestic product
GIZ	German Society for International Cooperation (Deutsche Gesellschaft für Internationale Zusammenarbeit)
ICG	International Contact Group
ICG-GB	International Contact Group for Guinea-Bissau
IcSP	EU Instrument contributing to Stability and Peace
IMF	International Monetary Fund
INEP	National Study and Research Institute of Guinea-Bissau (Instituto Nacional de Estudos e Pesquisa)
IPA	International Peace Academy
IPI	International Peace Institute
IR	International Relations
ISC	AU Intelligence and Security Committee
ISS	Institute for Security Studies (Pretoria, Addis Ababa and Dakar)
ISSAT	International Security Sector Advisory Team
ITF-PCRD	AU Interdepartmental Task Force on Post-Conflict Reconstruction and Development
JAM	joint assessment mission
KAIPTC	Kofi Anan Peacekeeping and Training Center
LGDH	Guinean League for Human Rights (Liga Guineense para os Direitos Humanos)
MICEMA	ECOWAS Mission in Mali (Mission de la CEDEAO au Mali)
MINUSMA	UN Integrated Multidimensional Stabilization Mission in Mali (Mission multidimensionnelle intégrée des Nations Unies pour la stabilisation au Mali)
MISSANG	Angolan Security Mission in Guinea-Bissau

MoU	Memorandum of Understanding
MSC	ECOWAS Mediation and Security Council
NEC	National Electoral Commission
NGO	non-governmental organization
OAU	Organization of African Unity
OECD	Organization for European Cooperation and Development
OIF	International Organization of the Francophonie
P5 of Guinea-Bissau	Permanent Five of Guinea-Bissau
PAIGC	African Party for the Independence of Guinea-Bissau and Cabo Verde (Partido Africano para a Independência da Guiné e Cabo Verde)
PALOP	African Countries with Portuguese as an Official Language (Países Africanos de Língua Oficial Portuguesa)
PCRD	post-conflict reconstruction and development
PRC	AU Permanent Representatives Committee
PSC	Peace and Security Council
PSC Protocol	Protocol Relating to the Establishment of the Peace and Security Council
PSD	Peace and Security Department
RCG-GB	Regional Contact Group for Guinea-Bissau
REC	Regional Economic Community
RIP	regional indicative program
RM	regional mechanism
RO	regional organization
SRCC	Special Representative of the Chairperson of the AU Commission
SRPC	Special Representative of the President of the ECOWAS Commission
SRSG	Special Representative of the UN Secretary General
SSR	security sector reform
STCDSS	Specialized Technical Committee on Defense, Safety and Security
T/PCCs	troop- and police-contributing countries
TOC	transnational organized crime
UCG	unconstitutional change of government

UEMOA	West African Economic and Monetary Union (Union Economique et Monétaire Ouest Africaine)
UK	United Kingdom of Great Britain and Northern Ireland
UN	United Nations
UN PBC	UN Peacebuilding Commission
UNDP	UN Development Program
UNIOGBIS	UN Integrated Peace-Building Support Office in Guinea-Bissau
UNOAU	UN Office to the AU
UNODC	UN Office on Drugs and Crime
UNSC	UN Security Council
UNSG	UN Secretary General
US	United States (of America)
US DOJ	US Department of Justice
USAID	US Agency for International Development

1 Introduction

Spatializing practices in AU and ECOWAS interventions

Introduction

Since the late 1990s, African regional organizations (ROs) have emerged as key actors, responding to violent conflicts on the African continent – famously framed as 'African solutions to African problems' (among many, e.g., Mays 2003; Coleman 2011; Abatan and Spies 2016). International policy makers, practitioners and academics have hailed them as the missing link in an emerging global 'architecture' for peace and security. During the 1990s, they appeared as a possible answer to serious problems in the UN peacekeeping system. Since then, African ROs have been important, in particular in situations and operations in which the UN and Western states have been unwilling or unable to risk the lives of their own personnel or citizens, but also as a 'laboratory' for peacekeeping norms and practices (Tardy and Wyss 2014, 1–4).

Two African ROs have especially stood out in this regard: the Economic Community of West African States (ECOWAS) and the African Union (AU), which became the successor organization of the Organization of African Unity (OAU) in 2002. Since the early 1990s, both organizations have developed elaborate legal foundations, normative frameworks and operational mechanisms to deal with conflict in their respective regions. What is more, both have repeatedly deployed peacekeeping forces to some of the most violent conflicts in Africa (e.g., Liberia, Sierra Leone, Sudan and Somalia). Testifying to the continued elevated importance of these organizations for peace and security on the continent, but increasingly also beyond it, the UN Secretariat and the EU Commission have developed ever closer relations with both the AU and ECOWAS commissions (e.g., cf. UN DPA 2018; EU Commission 2018; ECOWAS Commission 2018, 2020).

At the same time, African ROs have been the target of harsh and persistent criticism. Most strikingly, this has centered on an apparent gap between rhetoric and implementation, between high aspirations and intentions declared in foundational documents, and actual results of ECOWAS and AU conflict management and peacekeeping efforts. Next to a lack of human and material resources and capacity, among other things, observers have criticized the lack of political will on the part of member states, as well as a lack of clear objectives, coordination and adequate leadership (cf. Vines 2013, 106–108). In addition, coordination and cooperation between the AU and the Regional Economic Communities (RECs), which constitute the pillars of the African Peace and Security Architecture (APSA), have been judged insufficient (cf. Vines 2013, 101ff.; see also Nathan et al. 2015).

Here, apparently, high expectations and ambitions have met 'realities on the ground' (cf. European Court of Auditors 2018, 33ff.).[1] However, what exactly these 'realities' are still evades deeper understanding. While a variety of detailed empirical studies deal with specific conflicts and interventions,[2] large parts of the academic literature studying African ROs have focused on what these appear (not) to be or what they should be (see below). In contrast, both empirically and theoretically, few scholars have focused on what African ROs actually do or how they do it (i.e., how they 'work', cf. Chabal and Daloz 1999). As a result, still very little is known about their 'internal' modes of operation in practice.[3] In addition, despite ubiquitous spatial references and terminology – e.g., 'state', 'territory', 'region', 'architecture', 'cross-border', 'transnational' – the overwhelming majority of the literature on African Peace and Security has overlooked 'space' as an analytical category. Consequently, the connection between conflict intervention and space-making in Africa (and beyond it) remains largely unexplored.[4]

Against this backdrop, this book takes a close look at what happens 'inside' African ROs during conflict intervention, asking *how different actors at African ROs have intervened in conflict situations and how these interventions have related to space-making*. Consequently, studying intervention practices and their spatializing effects, I argue that these are essentially spatializing practices and that only if 'space' is included, as an analytical category, is it possible to make sense more fully of the complex dynamics developing around conflict intervention in Africa. The spatial approach developed to this end offers a new theory-oriented analytical lens that productively bridges insights from International Relations (IR), International Studies, Global Studies and Critical Geography. Therefore, in this book, space is conceptualized as socially constructed and relational. It is the result of multiple, heterogeneous and continuous interactions and social interrelations between different actors, but is also a category of thought that enables sense-making and meaning-making and allows people to act upon and change social 'realities'. In this way, space is always political, involving relations of power, and politics are often spatial (cf. Massey 2005, 9; discussed in more detail in Chapter 2).

Empirically, the book comprises an in-depth study of intervention practices of ECOWAS and AU actors in response to various conflict situations in their respective regions, with special emphasis on their interventions in Guinea-Bissau. The example of the latter, so far underrepresented in scholarly literature, provides a unique prism to engage with the developing field of practices of conflict intervention by African ROs. Combined with a comprehensive review of official ECOWAS and AU documents, it demonstrates that, contrary to most accounts, intervention practices of African ROs have been diverse and complexly interrelated, involving different kinds of actors, and are essentially tied to space-making.

To the partly overlapping fields of IR, International Studies and Global Studies, this book contributes by both narrowing down an empirical gap, specifically regarding African actors and African agency 'within' African ROs as well as between different African ROs and other regional and international actors, reflecting upon their 'internal' modes of operation and complex interactions in African peace and security dynamics. At the same time, the spatial approach employed to this end also allows us to theorize how, especially during conflict interventions, different actors *make space*, specifically 'regions', at different, interconnected sites, using different practices. Thereby, this book contributes to a better understanding of the roles of African ROs, and different actors therein, in pursuing specific regionalisms (i.e., spatial-political projects) as part of 'regional' and 'trans-regional' (if not 'global') ordering efforts.

Setting the stage for this endeavor, the remainder of this introduction first reviews the state of the art before, second, further explaining and substantiating the main argument of the book. Subsequently, it reflects upon sources, methods and methodological challenges, before introducing the prism, interventions in Guinea-Bissau following the coup d'état in April 2012, that allows me to study basic sets of ECOWAS and AU intervention practices in detail. Finally, it provides an outline of the remaining chapters.

The contours of African Peace and Security as a research field

African Peace and Security denotes a developing interdisciplinary research field that has the African Peace and Security Architecture (APSA) as its central reference point and specifically studies the role of African ROs therein, along with several other actors, including, for example, different self-identified 'African' and 'non-African' state actors, civil society organizations and think tanks. While drawing on and often relating to academic literature on UN peacekeeping and/or peacebuilding, scholars of African Peace and Security pursue a specific interest in African actors and African agency.

Despite offering valuable insights, large parts of the existing literature in that field can be described by three interrelated characteristics, which have come to limit a more in-depth understanding of African ROs in African peace and security dynamics – especially, however, during conflict interventions. First, due to a very practical orientation, much of this literature has been primarily descriptive and to some extent also prescriptive. Second, and closely related, while often based in conventional IR approaches, the overwhelming majority of this literature has remained largely disconnected from theoretical debates in IR and International Studies (cf. Tieku, Obi and Scorgie-Porter 2014, 4; Tieku 2019b, 3), especially more recent innovative approaches. Third, many contributions treat African ROs either as unitary actors or as solely driven by their member states, all while overly focusing on military peacekeeping. The following considerations briefly reflect upon the contributions and limitations of existing research, in line with the empirical focus of this book, primarily focusing on literature dealing with ECOWAS and the AU.[5]

Practical orientation, descriptive and prescriptive literature

To date, large parts of the extensive body of literature on conflict interventions by African ROs are primarily descriptive. Many contributions provide information on the formal setup and mandate of African ROs in peace and security. Therefore, the institutional setup of the AU and the African Peace and Security Architecture, its legal and normative framework and its state of implementation, including some significant achievements as well as key problems, are well known (e.g., Engel and Porto 2010, 2014; Vines 2013; Bah et al. 2014; Makinda, Okumu and Mickler 2016; Dersso 2016a). The same applies to the 'security architecture' of ECOWAS (e.g., Bah 2005; Hartmann 2010; Bolaji 2011; Cowell 2011; Iwilade and Agbo 2012; Maiangwa 2016). In addition, an enormous amount of scholarly literature has dealt with the operationalization of the African Standby Force, and the different African or African-led peacekeeping missions (e.g., Tardy and Wyss 2014; de Coning, Gelot and Karlsrud 2016; Darkwa 2017; Onditi and Okoth 2017), as well as the missions of the ECOWAS Cease-fire Monitoring Group (ECOMOG) and its successor the ECOWAS Standby Force (ESF) (e.g., Adebajo 2002b; Kabia 2009; Obi 2009; Arthur 2010; Jaye 2016). In this, UN–AU and UN–RO relations in peacekeeping in Africa have also received much attention (e.g., Aning 2005; Boulden 2013; Williams and Boutellis 2014).

In addition, much of the descriptive literature has a very strong practical orientation, mostly concerned with 'problem solving'. On the one hand this is due to the fact that contributions are either produced by 'think tanks' (among many more, e.g., ACCORD, ISS, KAIPTC, DCAF, ECDPM, ICG, IPI),[6] whose organizational mandates are primarily concerned with policy advice.[7] On the other hand, many of the scholars that publish in academic journals or edited volumes hold 'double identities' as academic researchers and practitioners or consultants, working or having worked for (or with) one or several organizations that they write about. Therefore, their publications have often aimed to provide recommendations and policy advice, as well (e.g., Aning and Atuobi 2009; Cravinho 2009; Wane et al. 2010; Bah et al. 2014). Consequently, evaluations and assessments have often resulted in binary constructions such as 'success' or 'failure', 'challenges' and 'potentials'. Moreover, many of these studies are implicitly or explicitly normative and prescriptive. While sometimes providing a lot of empirical details, these publications have been concerned more with what African ROs are not or are not doing (i.e., apparent 'deficits' and 'dysfunctions'), as well as what African ROs should or should not be doing, and how to 'fix' them. They have given much less attention to *what they actually do and how they do it*.

In other words, this literature has reached its limits in explaining and theorizing how exactly different regional actors operate in (everyday) practice, especially beyond formal procedures and military peacekeeping, and how this translates into conflict intervention practices and specific outcomes of policy implementation, which are often mixed and sometimes surprising (e.g., cf. Engel 2017b). Moreover, how exactly African ROs interact with each other, as well as with other ROs or international actors, remains under-researched. In particular, how these relations actually play out in practice, and how they are continuously contested and renegotiated, is still insufficiently understood. Finally, despite pervasive spatial references, such as, for example, 'state', 'region' and 'architecture', these accounts hardly reflect on the role and relevance of space. Thereby, these contributions overlook how efforts by African ROs to manage peace and security in Africa are intimately connected to the construction, formatting and ordering of space.

Theoretical disconnects and incipient theorization

To some extent also following from the strong practical orientation of literature on African Peace and Security, described above, a large portion of scholarly contributions have been disconnected from theoretical debates in IR and International Studies. Although many of them are more or less explicitly based in conventional, mostly realist IR approaches, only a few have actively pursued theoretical ambitions. Especially more recent innovative theoretical approaches in IR and International Studies, so far, have not yet been received, with very few exceptions (see Chapter 2). The following paragraphs very briefly review incipient efforts to increase the level of theorization in the research field, which may be roughly grouped into theoretical approaches concerned with (i) regional and interregional relations and (ii) with 'norms' and 'culture'.

Regional and interregional relations. This includes efforts to conceptualize and research African ROs as 'collective security mechanisms' (Abass 2000), 'regional security systems' (Francis 2006; see also Aning 2000), 'multilayered security communities' (Franke 2008; see also Bah 2005), and Africa's evolving security architecture as a 'security regime complex' (Brosig 2013, 2015) or 'peace and security regime' (Engel and Porto 2013). It also includes studies that offer theoretical frameworks around the concepts of 'security regionalism' (e.g., Francis 2006; Kabia 2009; Gandois 2014), 'regional security governance' (e.g., cf. Babarinde 2011; Jackson 2012), or 'regional security orders' (e.g., cf. Keller 1997). Relations between the UN and African ROs (mostly the AU, however) have been dealt with in the theoretical framework of 'interorganizational relations' (e.g., Welz 2016, 2018; Wondemagegnehu 2017). Relations between African ROs and the EU have been theorized in terms of 'interregionalism' (e.g., Pirozzi and Litsegård 2018; Plank 2017; Engel 2018a).

These contributions have added significantly to the understanding of the complexity of regional security dynamics in Africa, their embeddedness in transnational and continental linkages and the prominent role of and interaction with actors such as the UN and the EU. However, these theoretical efforts seem to be mainly concerned with describing and defining what African ROs and their 'security architectures' *are*, as well as identifying forms or types of cooperation, giving less attention to what they actually *do* and *how they do it* and how relations between different actors and organizations work in (everyday) practice. In addition, many contributions continue to portray African ROs (and others) as 'unitary actors', leaving aside or overlooking the multiple, interrelated actors within these organizations and across them (cf. Döring and Herpolsheimer 2021 (forthcoming)). Moreover, these approaches have firmly established regional thinking in African Peace and Security literature, both in terms of 'problems' and 'solutions', and show a central concern with the place of 'regions' in current international relations and processes of ordering, potentially taking place at a global scale (e.g., cf. Katzenstein 2005; Acharya 2007, 2018). However, the actual spaces that emerge from these processes and how they are made and remade through different practices remains largely unreflected, apparently being taken for granted in much of these debates (for two exceptions, see Bach 2016 and Söderbaum 2016).

'Norms' and 'culture'. Another rather vibrant strand of literature with theoretical ambition has focused on norms in African ROs, studying their emergence, evolution, as well as diffusion or convergence (e.g., Dembinski and Schott 2013; Zähringer 2013; Darkwa and Attuquayefio 2014). A similar interest has been behind the theoretical framework of 'governance transfer' (e.g., Leininger 2015 and Hartmann and Striebinger 2015). Some scholars have applied the concept of 'norm entrepreneur' to direct attention to the specific actors behind these processes (e.g., Souaré 2014; Murithi 2016). Others have sought to explain the behavior of African ROs in response to security concerns using the theoretical concept of 'security culture' (e.g., Williams 2007; Williams and Haacke 2008; Bischoff 2014).

These contributions have provided valuable insights into the normative dimensions of the peace and security efforts of African ROs. While advocating for the importance of 'process' and the significance of 'behavioral norms', these academic efforts to improve our understanding of African ROs in African peace and security have again mainly focused on states (or state elites) as the main relevant actors behind African security cultures, combined, once more, with a somewhat contradictory tendency to refer to their organizations as unitary actors. Therefore, many of these works overlook some important dynamics in the emergence of these norms (e.g., processes, practices and actors, both state and non-state; cf. Engel 2013), and fail to fully account for when and how they are applied, as well as how they remain subject to competing interpretation and essential contestation (cf. Witt 2013).

Beyond states, unitary actors and military peacekeeping

From the above, it becomes clear that vast parts of the literature on African Peace and Security, on the one hand, continue to be state-centric and/or treat African ROs as unitary actors (i.e., 'the AU' or 'ECOWAS' did this or that). This has resulted in the neglect and oversight of multiple, interrelated actors at work within and across African ROs, both state and non-state. On the other, military peacekeeping has been overrepresented in that literature, diverting attention from various other intervention practices. However, more recently, several scholars have begun working towards overcoming some of these limitations.

Aiming to open the 'black box' of actors 'inside' African ROs, several scholars have started to investigate the 'internal' logics and modes of operation of the AU and, to a lesser extent, ECOWAS. For example, a few studies have taken closer looks at the AU Peace and Security Council (e.g., Cilliers and Sturman 2004; Williams 2009; Ukeje and Ako 2017) and the AU Permanent Representative Council (e.g., Lisakafu 2016). Nevertheless, most of them still focus on the role of member states and their respective, and often unknown, state interests within these AU organs (notable exceptions include Dersso 2016b; Hardt 2016; Tieku 2019a). Less-researched organs of the AU and APSA include the AU Panel of the Wise (e.g., Murithi and Mwaura 2010; Gomes Porto and Ngandu 2014, 2015). Research on the role of non-state actors, informal rules and everyday practices at the AU Commission has only recently begun to develop more momentum (e.g., Tieku 2011, 2016, 2019a; Engel 2013, 2017a, 2018b; Hardt 2014, 2016). Some of these authors have also pursued explicit theoretical ambitions (discussed in Chapter 2). In comparison, the ECOWAS Commission has received much less attention regarding the same issues (limited exceptions are Cernicky 2008; Ismail 2015; Bossuyt 2016; Bappah 2018; Gänzle, Trondal and Kühn 2018).

More recently, non-military intervention practices have also received increased attention, especially mediation (e.g., Engel 2012; Zartman 2016; Khadiagala 2016; Nathan 2017), and to some extent also early warning (e.g., Wane et al. 2010; Wulf and Debiel 2010; Noyes and Yarwood 2013) and post-conflict reconstruction (e.g., Ismail 2008; Tadesse 2010; Carvalho, de Coning and Ahere 2016). However, despite a broadening empirical base, a more detailed and theoretically guided understanding of actors and *even more basic practices* (underlying these efforts) is still missing. Moreover, studies that take a look at the larger 'fields' of intervention – that is, simultaneously considering different actors, different practices and their interrelations – are still rare (cf. Welz 2016, 568).

While all of these studies have contributed hugely to improve knowledge and understanding of African ROs and African peace and security dynamics, much more empirical evidence and theorization is required, regarding the AU, but even more importantly regarding other African ROs, such as ECOWAS. What is more, with very few exceptions (see Chapter 2), 'space' has been neglected almost completely as an analytical category and a basic empirical dimension of African peace and security and conflict interventions by African ROs.

Therefore, summing up the above, this book addresses, first, an empirical gap regarding concrete intervention processes, with regard to the multiple, interrelated actors involved, as well as regarding different intervention practices and 'internal' modes of operation of African ROs. Second, this book draws attention to the neglected, but important, spatial dimensions of African ROs' peace and security efforts and in particular their conflict interventions. To this end, it introduces a theoretically guided 'spatial approach' – drawing inspiration from more recent innovative theoretical advances in IR and International Studies, as well as from the academic fields of Global Studies and Critical Geography (see Chapter 2) – which simultaneously directs attention to empirical gaps in the literature and contributes towards increased theorization of African ROs and their peace and security efforts.

Multiple and entangled intervention practices and their spatializing effects

To identify and study the main intervention practices of African ROs, using a spatial approach, which I explain in more detail in Chapter 2, this book follows a two-pronged methodological approach. First, it draws on an in-depth study of ECOWAS and AU interventions in Guinea-Bissau, with special emphasis on responses to the coup d'état of April 2012, as a prism to identify, analyze and historicize key intervention practices and their spatializing effects, since the late 1990s and early 2000s (see below). Here, the spatial approach enables a fresh look, undercutting and looking beneath common labels that actors at African ROs and researchers have accorded to their intervention practices (e.g., 'mediation', 'post-conflict reconstruction' and 'early warning'), identifying the underlying, basic sets of intervention practices rather consistently employed by ECOWAS and AU actors over time.

Interested in how space influences actors at African ROs and their interventions, as well as how their practices relate to space-making, the spatial approach enables us to see that these basic practices, often considered 'weak' or irrelevant, are in fact key in constructing, formatting and ordering regional spaces as well as complex relations between different actors involved in African peace and security dynamics. Allowing us to follow these actors and their practices, the spatial approach also brings to the fore that these actors have not only intervened at the conflict site as such, commonly referred to as 'on the ground', but also from various other, interconnected sites, that is, 'from afar'.

Summing up the identified sets of practices briefly, 'from afar', ECOWAS and AU actors have (i) produced conflict knowledge, (ii) convened meetings and discussed and (iii) issued public pronouncements (see Chapter 3). 'On the ground', they have (iv) dispatched diplomatic field missions (i.e., visits) and established liaison offices, (v) provided 'technical' support and (vi) deployed military and police peacekeeping missions (see Chapter 4). A practice employed both 'from afar' and 'on the ground', although in slightly different ways, has been (vii) the strategic engagement of other regional and international actors (see Chapter 6).

Second, to assess whether these sets of intervention practices have not only applied to conflict in Guinea-Bissau but across different conflict situations, elaborations in this book are based on a comprehensive exploratory review of official documents, specifically AU PSC communiqués and activity reports of the PSC to the AU Assembly – since 2006, when the PSC started working more consistently (see Chapter 3) – as well as final communiqués of the ECOWAS Authority and annual reports of the ECOWAS Commission – since 2000, following the establishment of the ECOWAS conflict management mechanism (see Chapter 5). Figures 1.1 and 1.2 map the results of this exploratory review qualitatively and in a slightly simplified fashion. They group political and technical missions into the category 'visits', for example, ranging from workshops to election observation to diplomatic missions. Public communication is not listed separately as pronouncements closely, although not completely, link to 'meetings'. In Figure 1.1, 'other meetings' refer to any non-PSC meetings that involved AU actors and discussed the conflict situation. In Figure 1.2, 'meetings' comprise meetings of the ECOWAS Authority and the MSC (at different levels) as well as other meetings. The hatched areas indicate the years where reports were only partially available or not available. In addition, in Chapters 3 and 4 respectively, additional quantitative mappings zoom in on the practices of meetings and visits at the AU.[8]

While these figures invite detailed discussion and wide-ranging analysis, their purpose in this book is to demonstrate that, first, ECOWAS and AU intervention practices have been multiple, involving more than just military and police peacekeeping, which is not even the most important intervention practice. Moreover, second, these practices have been applied relatively consistently over time, and often simultaneously in one place, but also across different conflicts in West/Africa. Put differently, they have been entangled and complementary rather than competing.

Only implicit in these mappings, but argued and explained across subsequent chapters in more detail, these intervention practices have essentially also been spatializing practices, enabling and contributing to space-making by African actors during conflict interventions. Above all, they do so by linking different conflicts to regional security concerns and policies, discussing them at the regional level (i.e., 'bringing the conflict to the region') and subsequently enabling and communicating regional action on the conflict situation (i.e., 'bringing the region to the conflict') (see Chapters 3 and 4). Both result in dense social interaction and the construction of connections between different actors and places. What is more, during these interventions, beyond conflict management, regional actors simultaneously pursue more general objectives. On the one hand, based on particular spatial imaginations, they seek to develop and consolidate regional security policies, thereby formatting regional spaces (see Chapter 5). On the other hand, moments of conflict interventions provide opportunities to strategically engage other regional and international actors, both to mobilize support and coordinate efforts, and to contest and renegotiate relationships among those actors in spatial

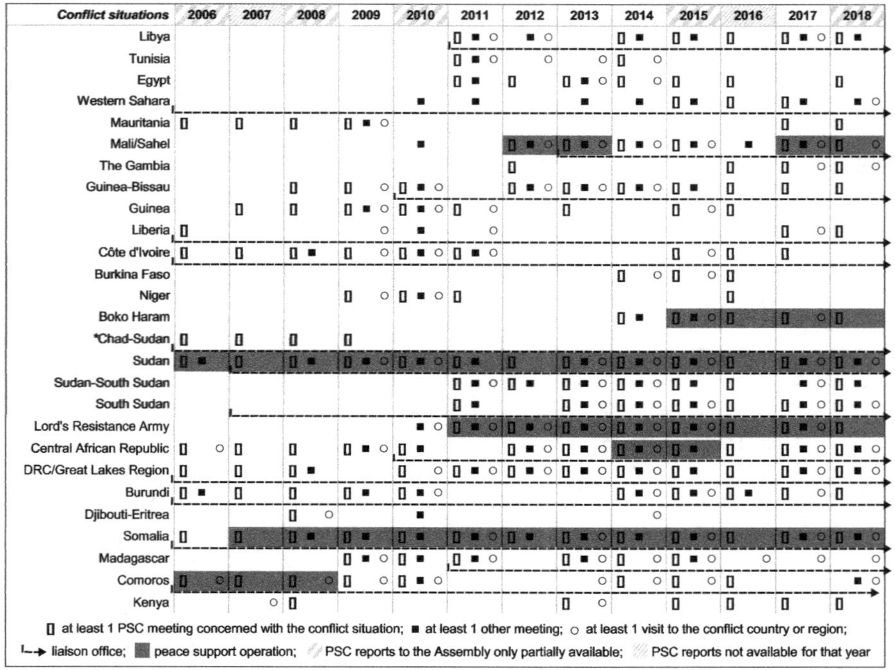

Figure 1.1 AU intervention practices, 2006–18

Notes: Liaison offices have been compiled based on information provided by Global Peace Operations Review (see https://peaceoperationsreview.org/maps/africa/). Peace support operations have been compiled based on Williams (2013). The indicated peace support operation in Mali are AFISMA and the G5 Sahel Joint Force. For Boko Haram the Multinational Joint Task Force is indicated. *The liaison office is located in Chad.

Source: *(cc) BY-NC-ND Jens Herpolsheimer, Skollan Elisabeth Warnck*

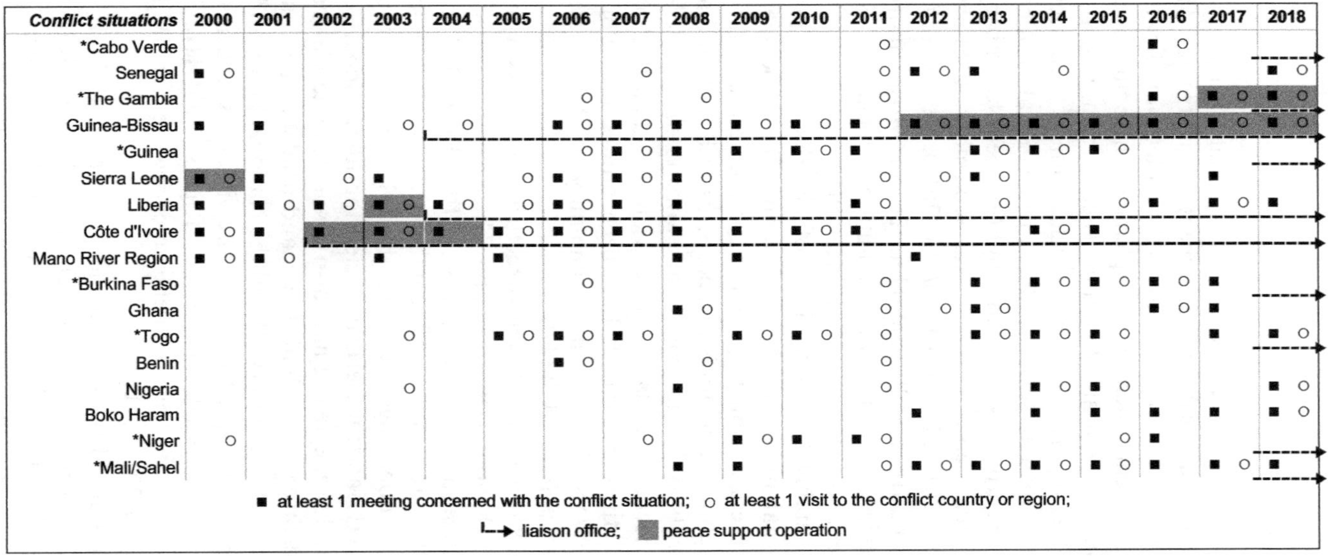

Figure 1.2 ECOWAS intervention practices, 2000–18

Notes: The dotted line indicates that these liaison offices may have been closed intermittently. *These countries have ECOWAS liaison offices, but the available information does not allow to say since when exactly.

Source: *(cc) BY-NC-ND Jens Herpolsheimer, Skollan Elisabeth Warnck*

terms (ordering *by* space) and/or to establish specific spatial orders (ordering *of* space) (see Chapter 6).

Sources and methods

In this book, I draw on three kinds of sources and related qualitative methods of data collection and analysis: official documents, semi-structured interviews, and reports and news articles produced by media outlets or policy think tanks. In a few instances, academic literature complements these three main sources. Some of these sources are available online, such as a large part of official documents as well as reports and news articles. Others have been accessed during subsequent research stays at the organizational headquarters of ECOWAS (Abuja, February/March 2017 and October/November 2018) and the AU (Addis Ababa, September 2016 and September 2018) as well as in Bissau (March/April 2017), Dakar (April/May 2017), New York (November 2017 and December 2018) and Brussels (June 2018).[9] Most importantly, this has included interviews, field notes and additional documents collected or accessed in libraries and archives at these locations.

First, based on archival research, I use official documents produced by different international and regional organizations. These documents include most importantly press statements, meeting communiqués, final reports and declarations, and annual and topical reports, as well as founding treaties, protocols, agreements and other basic framework texts. To a lesser degree, they also include meeting agendas and records, memoranda and background reports. Above all, these documents have been produced and/or published by actors at ECOWAS, the AU, the Community of Portuguese-Speaking Countries (CPLP), the EU and the UN.

Second, the book draws on 170 semi-structured interviews with 145 interview partners and field notes (see Appendix). These have been conducted with various representatives of ECOWAS, the AU, CPLP, EU and UN. Moreover, I have interviewed representatives of member states (i.e., diplomatic staff) and development or donor agencies (e.g., the US Agency for International Development (USAID) and the German Society for International Cooperation (GIZ)). Finally, to a lesser extent, I have also conducted interviews and talked to analysts and researchers of think tanks and academic institutions (e.g., the Institute for Security Studies (ISS) and the National Study and Research Institute of Guinea-Bissau (INEP)), as well as civil society leaders in Guinea-Bissau (e.g., Guinean League for Human Rights (LGDH)). The great majority of these interviews have been elite interviews (e.g., cf. Mikecz 2012; Brinkmann and Kvale 2015, 171).

Third, reports produced by different media outlets and think tanks have been used to fill in information, complementing or further substantiating the information gathered from official documents and during research stays and interviews. Most important, in that regard, have been reports produced by the International Crisis Group (ICG, based in Brussels, with an additional office in Dakar) and the ISS (based in Pretoria, South Africa, with additional offices in Addis Ababa and Dakar).

Methodological challenges

Doing research on and at African ROs, specifically at ECOWAS and the AU, constitutes a challenge for multiple reasons, resulting in different practical and methodological problems, which often receive little or no methodological reflection in existing publications on African Peace and Security. For example, information about the extent, kind and limitations of sources and material underlying the presented accounts and narratives often remains concealed. While unable to overcome these problems completely, in the following, I want to briefly reflect upon some of these issues, in order to at least alleviate some of them and increase the transparency of my research practice.

This book presents a qualitative, interpretive study (cf. Yanow and Schwartz-Shea 2009). As such it confronts a world that is "complex and messy", which is often inadequately reflected in existing research, and therefore requires researchers "to think, to practise, to relate, and to know in new ways" (Law 2004, 2). The 'spatial approach' presented in this book is a step in that direction, offering both a new epistemological (i.e., a new way of thinking and speaking about conflict interventions of African ROs) and ontological perspective (i.e., space as a central empirical dimension of African peace and security dynamics). Whereas Chapter 2 outlines the methodological and theoretical characteristics of that approach in detail, the following briefly addresses a few more general methodological questions.

Conducting research at African ROs, I have been constantly confronted with a variety of information provided in official documents and during interviews, but also through personal conversations and observations 'on the ground'. Out of these, I have tried to reconstruct relevant events, dynamics and processes, and come up with more or less coherent narratives of 'what actually happened' and 'why'. However, this not only requires a lot of caution, as various changing and often obscure personal or organizational motivations, interests, strategies and agendas, choices, decisions and so on are at play; it usually also leaves questions unanswered and aspects unaccounted for. Moreover, sometimes confidential or inside information (e.g., stories or rumors of varying plausibility) may put into question parts of the carefully crafted accounts and narratives. This raises the question of how close one can actually get to 'what actually happened'. In addition to diverging accounts and information, several factors may come into play that are usually not part of academic research and narratives, at least not in IR or International Studies, such as, for example, 'private' emotions, passions, intuitions, fears and betrayals (Law 2004, 2–3).

To give an example, publicly available official documents often do not mention the source, content and kind of information that fed into them, representing a stylized version that fuses knowledge with specific messages (discussed in Chapter 3). On the other hand, interviews at the headquarters of the AU and ECOWAS allow access to knowledge about specific conflict situations that is circulating among staff. However, it is often hard to trace how it got there (e.g., personal channels of information, 'external' influences). More importantly, information gathered for this book on conflict in Guinea-Bissau, between 2016 and 2019, has been 'post-hoc' for the situation in 2012. Some relevant actors at the time were no longer working in their former positions. What is more, even for those interviewees that were around at the time, it is not clear exactly what information they had back then, and what they learned or rationalized only later.

All of this is impossible to capture in any objective and completely consistent way.[10] The only way to do research in this kind of 'messy' environment is to move as close as possible, zooming in on specific instances, actors, practices and processes and to follow them across time and space.[11] In that way, it becomes possible to attain a better understanding of how different actors make sense and give meaning, based on different kinds of knowledge, ideas and practices that inform their action and how they communicate them to others. Consequently, the best that research in such settings can do is to produce a close description and provide a particular interpretation of the findings that allows us to make some interesting observations and ask interesting questions.

Accepting the absence of complete objectivity, and a certain 'messiness' of methods, qualitative approaches become scientific through constant self-reflexivity (e.g., cf. Mellor 2001; Yanow and Schwartz-Shea 2009). That means reflecting on and making transparent, as much as possible, the researcher's own positionality – in my case, for example, being a white, male, academic, German national in his thirties – as well as underlying assumptions and choices. Most importantly, this includes being open about sources and methods (see above). It also includes reflection upon the role of the researcher him or herself, as part of the research environment – specifically the ways in which he or she may influence and to some extent also co-produce the object of study (e.g., cf. Law 2004, 5, 10 and 12; see also Mellor 2001; Yanow and Schwartz-Shea 2009).

Related to the positionality and role of the researcher, but also a more general methodological challenge, has been access to sources, material and information. First, on a very practical level, access to both interview partners and documents has been limited and unequal for varying reasons and not always in any obvious fashion. Reasons here may range from 'technical' (e.g., relating to different, often limited resources, capacities and infrastructures) to 'political' (e.g., diplomatic sensitivities or general secrecy) to 'ethical' (e.g., to protect certain groups or individuals).This condition partly also explains the content and focus of much of the existing literature (see above), largely based on more- or less-detailed analyses of publicly available official documents. Second, on a metatheoretical level, the question emerges of how to access knowledge and information that may be rather implicit and/or unconscious.

In Chapter 2, I offer an answer to this question with regard to knowledge and information about space.

Finally, the use of theory and theoretical ambition in this book comes closest to what social scientists call 'grounded theory'. On the one hand, it highlights the continuous and intimate interaction between empirical research and theory building. On the other hand, it emphasizes the 'usefulness' of theory as measured against its ability to help make sense of concrete empirical observations (cf. Darian-Smith and McCarty 2017, 85–6; see also Yanow and Schwartz-Shea 2009).

The prism of interventions in Guinea-Bissau

In this book, I use ECOWAS and AU interventions in Guinea-Bissau, especially but not exclusively those following the coup d'état in April 2012, as a prism to study intervention practices of African ROs more generally, and their spatializing effects in detail. Therefore, it does not constitute a 'case study' in the common understanding of the term in Political Science. Instead, it exemplifies an emerging field of practices by African ROs in African peace and security dynamics, which is characterized by multiple, entangled actors and practices that simultaneously respond to different conflicts in their respective regions (see Figures 1.1 and 1.2), drawing on and connecting them to previous intervention experiences, regional security policies and political projects.[12] As I am going to outline in subsequent chapters, interventions in Guinea-Bissau have been deeply embedded in this context. While certainly not the only example worth detailed analysis, several factors justify the choice of Guinea-Bissau in this book, which I explain in the following. Moreover, this section also provides some context information on interventions in Guinea-Bissau, required for a better understanding of the considerations and elaborations in subsequent chapters.

Why interventions in Guinea-Bissau?

At least three important factors justify the focus on interventions in Guinea-Bissau in this book, all of which compound with a *surprising neglect* of the subject in the existing academic literature, especially regarding more recent interventions.[13] First, despite this neglect and its seeming 'marginality', in terms of economic and political weight,[14] Guinea-Bissau has received unparalleled attention by international media and politicians, at least for some time. Following reports about increasing drug trafficking through Guinea-Bissau, during the mid-2000s, the country spectacularly moved into the focus of public interest in Western states, becoming known as "Africa's" or even "the world's first narco-state" (e.g., Vulliamy 2008; O'Regan and Thompson 2013; Loewenstein 2016). Numerous media reports and policy briefs describe the country not only as a prime example, but as the "epicenter" of a seemingly new dynamic. Attention to Guinea-Bissau increased even more in 2013, when the US Drug Enforcement Agency arrested Guinea-Bissau's Navy chief, Bubo NaTchuto, in an undercover sting operation, charging him with 'narco-terrorism' (e.g., Lewis and Valdmanis 2013). The latter is a narrative framing that links income from illegal drug trafficking to terrorist activities in West Africa, the Sahel, and potential beyond both, as a source of funding (e.g., Lacher 2013).[15] This attention, and related spatial imaginations (see Chapter 5), have triggered various interventions in Guinea-Bissau, resulting in a *particularly dense setting of social interaction* among different regional and international actors.

Second, in this dense setting, African ROs have assumed leading roles, exercising *African agency* in a way that has stood out against other conflict interventions, making use of all of their available 'tools' for conflict intervention. Since the ECOWAS Monitoring Group (ECOMOG) missions in the 1990s and initial, tentative efforts of the ESF in the early 2000s, this once more also included the ECOWAS Mission in Guinea-Bissau (ECOMIB), deployed in 2012. This military and police peacekeeping force constituted the first African peacekeeping mission that was solely mandated and funded by an African RO for three full years. Therefore, the example offers rich insights about both the range of ECOWAS and AU intervention practices (see Chapters 3 and 4) as well as the role of African ROs in regional and 'global' peace and security (see Chapters 5 and 6). In particular, it illuminates the changing interactions and relationships between self-identified 'African' and 'non-African' actors on the one hand, and between the AU and the RECs on the other. Moreover, with the recent ECOWAS intervention in the Gambia since January 2017 in mind, Guinea-Bissau deserves scholarly attention as a potential turning point in ECOWAS intervention policies and practices.

Third, and intimately connected to all of the above, the conjuncture of different international and regional actors in a seemingly marginal place allows demonstration of the strength and added value of a spatial approach. This is because of the prominent and ubiquitous spatial references in the narratives that have accompanied conflict intervention in Guinea-Bissau. Therefore, different spatial imaginations are observable, which help to understand why and how different actors have intervened and interacted in Bissau. A spatial approach also allows us to make sense of the importance that organizational staffs have accorded to 'Guinea-Bissau' in different discourses and policy processes at ECOWAS and the AU, as well as at the EU, despite its seeming marginality (see Chapter 5).

Contextualizing interventions in Guinea-Bissau

The coup of 12 April 2012 in Guinea-Bissau has only been the most recent case of several violent changes of government in that country (e.g., 1999, 2003 and 2009) – as well as various alleged and attempted ones, military protests, uprisings and mutinies (e.g., 2004, 2007, 2008, 2010 and 2011). Thus, since its independence, Guinea-Bissau has continuously been plagued by what many observers have called 'political instability' (e.g., Ostheimer 2001; Ferreira 2004; Gibert 2009). It is worth noting, however, that since the early 2000s coups have been rather limited in their immediate effects, targeting only a very limited number of people, with limited violence and few casualties, leaving large parts of the population relatively unaffected, even more so outside the capital (cf. Bordonaro 2009). Consequently, it appears that what others call 'instability' has become 'normalcy' for many people in Guinea-Bissau, carrying on with their lives despite all hardship.[16]

To understand conflict and politics in Guinea-Bissau, it is necessary to reflect upon several general dynamics that have historically characterized politics in Guinea-Bissau. Above everything else, these have related, first, to the emergence and operating mode of the post-colonial state in Guinea-Bissau, as well as the key role played by the military in the independence struggle led by the African Party for the Independence of Guinea-Bissau and Cabo Verde (going by its Portuguese acronym PAIGC). Second, and closely related, central state institutions and political actors in Bissau have developed much stronger interlinkages with 'external' actors and institutions than with the rest of the country (i.e., the population at large, the 'hinterland'). This has resulted in massive external dependency, as well as continual factionalism and infighting for access to 'external' resources ('legal' and 'illegal'). Both of these dynamics have gone along with and have related to particular spatial arrangements. On the one hand, this refers to a state capital only ideationally and/or informally connected to an internationally recognized territory that central state actors physically govern or control only incompletely and sporadically. At the same time, actors in the capital are highly integrated into various networks of regional and trans-regional 'reach' (cf. Herpolsheimer 2019, 55ff.).

Most importantly, these networks link to different regional organizations. Guinea-Bissau is a member of the OAU/AU, ECOWAS, the CPLP and the International Organization of the Francophonie (OIF). Since 1998, actors at these organizations have intervened in response to coups d'état and military and political crises. Then, the war of 7 June 1998 triggered a diplomatic intervention by the CPLP, through Angolan and Portuguese diplomats, which in turn led ECOWAS actors to intervene more strongly, both diplomatically and eventually militarily, and to reassert their leadership role in West Africa (see Chapter 6). Likewise, OAU actors got involved, albeit only in a supporting role (see Chapters 3 and 4). In addition, the UN Security Council (UNSC) established a UN Peacebuilding Office in Bissau in 1999, which was later, in 2007, transformed into an 'integrated' office (UNIOGBIS) (cf. Herpolsheimer 2019, 194–5). During the mid-2000s, partly in response to reports about increased drug trafficking through Guinea-Bissau, EU actors have also stepped up their efforts to respond to 'political instability' in the country (see Chapter 5). Since then, all five organizations have closely followed events in Bissau, and intervened, at times cooperating at others competing with each other (see Chapters 5 and 6).

Of central relevance to conflict dynamics in Bissau became an Angolan military mission (MISSANG), deployed in early 2011 by the Angolan government, officially to support the SSR process and framed as a CPLP mission (see Chapter 6). This mission triggered serious tensions with factions of the Bissau-Guinean military, which saw the mission as a threat, enabling Prime Minister Gomes Junior to get rid of unwanted elements in the military. MISSANG therefore became one of the key drivers behind the coup d'état in 2012 (e.g., cf. ICG 2012a; Kohl 2013).

The coup of April 2012

On 12 April 2012, a self-proclaimed 'military command', composed of a group of generals and senior army officers, arrested the interim president, Raimundo Pereira, the prime minister, Carlos Gomes Junior, as well as the chief of the armed forces, António Indjai. Several high-level state representatives went into hiding; others were reported missing. After some initial confusion, it soon became clear that the events indeed constituted a coup d'état. They interrupted the presidential elections after the first – successful though inconclusive – round of voting (on 18 March), and aimed at removing the constitutional government, headed by Pereira and Gomes Junior (frontrunner in the ongoing elections), both members of the PAIGC. As it turned out, António Indjai, although initially arrested himself, was one of the ringleaders behind the coup. On 13 April, the 'military command' announced its terms for a transition government, and invited opposition parties for negotiations to form a National Transition Council supposed to run the country for a two-year transition period. A respective transition agreement was signed by the 'military command' and leaders of 20 opposition parties on 18 April, but not by the PAIGC (Herpolsheimer 2019, 63–4).

While a lot of continuity can be observed in the dynamics of the 2012 conflict in Guinea-Bissau, the situation has been a turning point. For one, it has hardened stances of some regional and international actors towards Guinea-Bissau, increasingly fed up with an apparently intransigent situation, defying all efforts by the international community to bring lasting 'stability' to the country. Moreover, it subsequently resulted in a contestation and reorganization of the roles and relations between different intervening actors and regional spaces (see Chapter 6).

International reactions to the coup of April 2012 in Guinea-Bissau

Reactions by regional and international actors to the coup of 12 April 2012 were swift and unanimous, initially reflecting a large consensus. Early statements by the ECOWAS Commission, AU Commission, CPLP Council of Ministers and EU Commission unanimously condemned the coup and called for the unconditional release of unlawfully detained officials and the immediate return to constitutional order. Moreover, they requested the completion of the interrupted electoral process, rejecting any illegitimate government established by unconstitutional means (cf. AU Commission 2012a; Conselho de Ministros da CPLP 2012; ECOWAS Commission 2012a; EU 2012). This position was subsequently also adopted by the UN Security Council (cf. UNSC 2012b). The World Bank, the African Development Bank and the EU Commission suspended their aid to Guinea-Bissau, except for some emergency assistance (cf. World Bank and African Development Bank 2012; EU 2012). The AU and the OIF suspended the membership of Guinea-Bissau (cf. AU PSC 2012; OIF 2012). Subsequently, the ECOWAS Authority, the EU Council and the UN Security Council imposed sanctions targeting individual members of the 'military command' (cf. ECOWAS Commission 2012b; EU Council 2012; UNSC 2012a).

However, this initial consensus was not maintained, most notably because ECOWAS actors changed their stance towards the coup leaders and the transitional organs, which the 'military command' had created, a couple of days after the coup. As a consequence, ECOWAS had to face the resistance of the remaining international actors that had been involved in Guinea-Bissau, in particular the CPLP. Although this resistance faded throughout 2012 – partly because the attention had shifted to other issues, such as the unfolding conflict in Mali – the West African RO still had to cope with a lack of external cooperation, financial assistance in particular, and failed to obtain international recognition for the transition organs and to have sanctions lifted. This situation prevailed until the successful elections in 2014 (Herpolsheimer 2019, 65–6).

Nevertheless, in the face of disengagement by many (more powerful) actors, through its proactive approach ECOWAS took the lead and managed to make some headway in the conflict. This included some concessions by the 'military command', most importantly the release of Pereira and Gomes Junior on 27 April. It also included the 'military command's' acceptance to hold fresh elections within 12 months, instead of 24 (i.e., the ECOWAS version of completing the electoral process; see ECOWAS Authority 2012, 7) and negotiations about the modalities of a "consensual transition" (ECOWAS Authority 2012, 7), resulting in the ECOWAS-brokered transition pact, signed on 16 May by 17 Guinean political parties, but not by the PAIGC (cf. UNSG 2012). Most importantly, however, ECOWAS managed to push the 'military command' to accept the deployment of the ECOWAS Standby Force (ESF) in Guinea-Bissau (ECOMIB), to replace MISSANG (see Chapter 4). The key role of ECOWAS was eventually acknowledged by most of the other international actors – appreciated especially by the AU Commission (2012b), and accepted first by the UN Security Council (UNSC 2012a) and later also by actors at the EU and the CPLP (see Chapter 6).

Developments since 2015

Starting in August 2015, with the dismissal of Prime Minister Domingos Simões Pereira by President José Mario Vaz, both elected in 2014, Guinea-Bissau entered another political crisis. This pitted the president against the parliament, rendering the government incapable of any action until February 2018. Constant pressure and relatively coordinated responses led by ECOWAS actors and supported by actors at the AU, CPLP, EU and UN resulted in the signing of the Conakry Agreement in September 2016, which subsequently became the key reference point for a concerted (although not always harmonious) effort to push for the appointment of a consensual prime minister and towards the next elections without renewed military interference. These efforts eventually bore fruits in February 2018 with the appointment of Aristides Gomes as consensual prime minister, after four non-consensual ones (one of them appointed twice). Following that, parliamentary elections in March 2019 and presidential elections in November and December 2019 marked the first peaceful transition in Guinea-Bissau, making Vaz the first democratically elected president to ever serve a full term in office (cf. Herpolsheimer 2019, 68–9).

Outline of the book

Following this introduction, Chapter 2 provides the main theoretical input for the book. It summarizes innovative approaches in IR, International Studies and Global Studies that are relevant to advancing the study of African Peace and Security. Most importantly, these have sought to direct attention to and theorize different actors, actual, everyday practices, entanglements and, though only to a very limited extent, space. The chapter reflects upon the extent to which these approaches have found their way into African Peace and Security literature, before introducing theoretical insights from Critical Geography, and a 'spatial approach' as a theoretically informed and theory-oriented approach to reconcile the different emphases of different approaches, focusing on actors, practices and entanglements, as well as to add 'space' as a new analytical dimension. Chapter 2 finishes by outlining how such a 'spatial approach' provides a new perspective on intervention practices, their spatializing effects – especially regarding the formatting of regional space and ordering relations between different regional spaces (spatial order) – and African peace and security dynamics more generally – allowing to capture and understand complex empirical dynamics more adequately and completely.

Based on the considerations developed in Chapter 2, I subsequently look at different intervention 'sites'. In this logic, Chapter 3 starts describing, historicizing and analyzing intervention practices of different actors at ECOWAS and the AU, for example, including staff of different organizational units, as well as different 'technical' and 'political' decision making organs. Looking in detail at those sets of practices, and the specific actors that apply them, the chapter begins developing in detail the central argument of this book, namely that those intervention practices have critical spatializing effects and are therefore essentially spatializing practices. These work to integrate a specific conflict situation into respective regional spaces, bringing regional actors together on the issue, and eventually regional views, policy and action to bear on local actors and politics. Moreover, the practices described in this chapter are all applied 'from afar' (i.e., different places outside the actual conflict site), thereby creating a network of relevant places that reaches far beyond the conflict situation.

Following this, Chapter 4 continues the description and analysis, taking a close look at intervention practices of ECOWAS and the AU 'on the ground'. Like the previous chapter, Chapter 4 identifies three main sets of practices, namely 'dispatching diplomatic field missions and establishing liaison offices', 'providing technical support' and 'military deployment'. It also traces their emergence across time and space. The chapter further develops the central argument of the book, linking all of those practices to the active construction of regional spaces. Through its detailed analysis it also further adds to a more complete picture of the complexity and diversity of intervention practices of African regional organizations trying to manage conflicts on the continent. Chapter 4 also highlights different kinds of African actors at work in these organizations, which include state actors but are by no means limited to those.

In this way, Chapters 3 and 4 address the gap in detailed knowledge about ECOWAS and AU practices of conflict intervention, in particular drawing on the example of interventions in Guinea-Bissau for illustration and additional explanation. Moreover, these chapters show how these practices have intimately related to space-making (i.e., the construction, formatting and ordering of space), and can thus also be considered 'spatializing practices'. Whereas Chapters 3 and 4 have studied efforts by different actors at ECOWAS and the AU to manage conflict directly in their member states, and their spatializing effects, Chapters 5 and 6 take a close look at other, more general objectives and political projects of actors at these organizations that have been pursued during conflict intervention, applying the described spatializing practices.

Therefore, Chapter 5 first reflects upon two of the main spatial imaginations that have triggered, framed and guided interventions in West Africa, which have been connected to specific regional and trans-regional security concerns, namely 'political instability' and 'narco-terrorism'. Second, looking through the prism of interventions in Guinea-Bissau, the chapter analyzes how actors at ECOWAS, the AU and the EU have sought to develop and consolidate specific regional security policies, thereby formatting their own regional spaces (i.e., 'internal formatting') or the regional spaces of other organizations (i.e., 'external formatting'). In this respect, it traces the emergence of certain policy processes at these organizations across different conflict situations.

Following this, Chapter 6 analyzes how actors at ECOWAS and the AU have strategically engaged other regional and international actors to mobilize support for their respective efforts and facilitate coordination. This constitutes another set of intervention practices, which has been applied both 'from afar' and 'on the ground'. Moreover, the chapter further reflects upon other, more general objectives that intervening actors have pursued beyond conflict management as such, linked to particular spatial-political projects, applying the spatializing practices described in this and previous chapters. Looking again through the prism of interventions in Guinea-Bissau, this chapter analyzes how actors at ECOWAS and the AU, during conflict interventions, have contested and negotiated relations among each other, as well as with other regional and international actors, such as, for example, the CPLP and the EU. It argues that these efforts have been essentially about spatial ordering, using 'space' as an argument to achieve a certain objective (ordering *by* space) and/or seeking to establish a specific spatial order (ordering *of* space).

Last, the book's conclusion (Chapter 7), picks up the main argumentative threads of the different chapters and brings them together. Based on this, it collects and synthesizes the book's main findings into a more complete picture of how the spatial analysis improves the understanding of the multiple and entangled actors and practices of conflict interventions by African ROs and their spatializing effects. Moreover, it sheds light on how these have related to efforts to construct, format and order space – through the different sets of spatializing practices analyzed in this book – and how different actors at ECOWAS and the AU have positioned themselves within wider spatial relations and spatial orders that are continuously negotiated and contested, made and remade among different regional and international actors during conflict interventions and around matters of peace and security in Africa. Finally, this chapter highlights this book's contribution to the fields of African Peace and Security as well as IR, International Studies and Global Studies, and spells out implications for future research on the subject.

Notes

1 Actors at ECOWAS and the AU commonly use the phrase 'on the ground'. While their motivations behind this particular choice of words may vary, I use it as a spatial marker, denoting physical 'presence' at the site of conflict, and in distinction to 'from afar', referring to the ability of different actors to establish their 'reach' over a conflict, e.g., from organizational headquarters (see also Chapters 2 and 3).

2 In this book I employ a very broad understanding of 'interventions', referring to any activities or practices that African ROs or other regional and international actors have pursued to deal with a particular conflict or crisis.

3 Here and in the following, I use single quotation marks to highlight specific concepts and raise awareness that specific terms are markers that different actors, including me as a researcher, use for different reasons and towards specific objectives, often to distinguish binary opposites (e.g., 'internal' versus 'external'; 'local' versus 'global'; 'technical' versus 'political'). As such they are part of different discourses, knowledge–power relations and subject to socio-political contestation.

4 In this book, I employ an understanding of 'practices' in line with that commonly used in the literature on 'international practices'. Thus, practices are "socially meaningful patterns of action, which, in being performed more or less competently, simultaneously embody, act out, and possibly reify background knowledge and discourse in and on the material world" (Adler and Pouliot 2011, 4) (see also Chapter 2).

5 ECOWAS and especially the AU have received most attention. However, valuable scholarly contributions also exist on conflict interventions of other African ROs, for instance, the Economic Community of Central African States (e.g., Meyer 2011; Welz 2016), the South African Development Community (e.g., Nathan 2006; Tavares 2011; Bischoff 2014) and the Inter-Governmental Authority on Development (e.g., Healy 2014; Elowson and Albuquerque 2016; Bereketeab 2019). While I do not refer to them systematically in the following, the considerations below also apply to these contributions.

6 ACCORD – African Centre for the Constructive Resolution of Disputes (based near Durban, South Africa), ISS – Institute for Security Studies (based in Pretoria, South Africa), KAIPTC – Kofi Annan Peacekeeping and Training Center (based in Accra, Ghana), DCAF – Center for the Democratic Control of Armed Forces (based in Geneva, Switzerland), ECDPM – European Centre for Development Policy Management (based in Maastricht, the Netherlands), ICG – International Crisis Group (based in Brussels, Belgium), IPI – International Peace Institute (based in New York, USA).

7 Among the numerous publications, e.g., see Odigie (2017); Aning, Okyere and Abdallah (2012); Ebo (2007); ICG (2011, 2012b); Desmidt and Hauck (2017); Boutellis and Williams (2013).

8 Systematic analysis of the mentioned official documents produced by ECOWAS and AU actors has been beset by a number of problems, for example, including differences and gaps in the availability of documents for the entire reporting period, inconsistent reporting practices in the available documents and difficulties in the clustering of conflict situations, due to their often transnational nature. For a detailed discussion of the potential and limitations of these exploratory mappings, see Herpolsheimer and Warnck (2020).

9 I have conducted a few additional interviews in Lisbon (February 2014 and November 2015) as well as in Ouagadougou (January 2017).

10 John Law, in this regard, refers to a "kaleidoscope of impressions and textures" that "reflects and refracts a world that in important ways cannot be fully understood as a specific set of determinate processes" – the world and its 'structures' are not only 'technically' complex, but also "necessarily exceed our capacity to know them" (Law 2004, 6).

11 Contrary to the now-popular method of 'process tracing' in Political Science (e.g., cf. Collier 2011; Siewert 2017), the reconstruction of concrete processes here does not aim to explain or establish 'causal mechanisms'. Instead, it aims to reconstruct specific historical trajectories, in order to understand these processes in their complexity, involving multiple, entangled actors and practices.

12 Although using slightly different terms, some have described this as a 'global case study method' (cf. Darian-Smith and McCarty 2017, 178ff.).

13 Analysis of interventions in Guinea-Bissau has mostly focused on the response by ECOWAS to the war of 1998/9, where it deployed ECOMOG III (e.g., cf. Adebajo 2002a; Kabia 2009; Obi 2009). To date, the little that is known about more recent efforts mainly comes from publications by the International Crisis Group (e.g., ICG 2008, 2009, 2012a). A few exceptions in scholarly literature, although limited in scope, include Yabi (2010); Kohl (2013); Aubyn (2013); and Hartmann (2013). Kohl (2014) and Uzoechina (2014) have dealt with SSR efforts in Guinea-Bissau by ECOWAS and other actors.

14 'Marginality', here, could refer to the country's small size (both territory and population). It could also refer to the country's low GDP per capita (ranking 188th out of 212 in 2017). Although Guinea-Bissau does possess valuable natural resources (e.g., oil, minerals, timber, fish), their exploitation, so far, has played only a minor role (cf. Central Intelligence Agency 2018).

15 Although parts of this narrative are supported by academic research, important aspects of it have been questioned, as discussed in Chapter 5 of this book.

16 Guinea-Bissau's economic performance has been poor, despite higher growth rates in recent years. Its population has suffered from poverty and a lack of basic services such as health care and education (e.g., cf. Barry et al. 2007). Highly indebted, Guinea-Bissau ranks among the lowest-scoring countries in the Human Development Index (177th out of 189 in 2017). Volatile agricultural production has repeatedly caused food insecurity (World Food Programme 2018). For more information about Guinea-Bissau's socio-economic development, see World Bank (2019).

References

Abass, Ademola. 2000. The New Collective Security Mechanism of ECOWAS: Innovations and Problems. *Journal of Conflict and Security Law* 5 (2): 211–29.

Abatan, Ella and Yolanda Spies. 2016. African Solutions to African Problems? The AU, R2P and Côte d'Ivoire. *South African Journal of International Affairs* 23 (1): 21–38. doi: 10.1080/10220461.2016.1153516.

Acharya, Amitav. 2007. The Emerging Regional Architecture of World Politics. *World Politics* 59 (4): 629–52. doi: 10.1353/wp.2008.0000.

———. 2018. *Constructing Global Order: Agency and Change in World Politics.* Cambridge: Cambridge University Press.

Adebajo, Adekeye. 2002a. *Building Peace in West Africa: Liberia, Sierra Leone, and Guinea-Bissau.* Boulder, CO: Lynne Rienner.

———. 2002b. *Liberia's Civil War: Nigeria, ECOMOG, and Regional Security in West Africa.* Boulder, CO: Lynne Rienner.

Adler, Emanuel and Vincent Pouliot. 2011. International Practices. *International Theory* 3 (1): 1–36. doi: 10.1017/S175297191000031X.

Aning, Emmanuel K. 2000. Towards the New Millennium: ECOWAS's Evolving Conflict Management System. *African Security Review* 9 (5–6): 50–63. doi: 10.1080/10246029.2000.9628081.

———. 2005. The Challenge of Civil Wars to Multilateral Interventions – UN, ECOWAS, and Complex Political Emergencies in West Africa: A Critical Analysis. *African and Asian Studies* 4 (1–2): 1–20. doi: 10.1163/1569209054547256.

Aning, Kwesi and Samuel Atuobi. 2009. Responsibility to Protect in Africa: An Analysis of the African Union's Peace and Security Architecture. *Global Responsibility to Protect* 1 (1): 90–113. doi: 10.1163/187598409X405505.

Aning, Kwesi, Frank Okyere and Mustapha Abdallah. 2012. *Addressing Emerging Security Threats in Post-Gaddafi Sahel and the ECOWAS Response to the Malian Crisis.* Policy Brief 1/May 2012. Accra: Kofi Annan International Peacekeeping Training Centre (KAIPTC).

Arthur, Peter. 2010. ECOWAS and Regional Peacekeeping Integration in West Africa: Lessons for the Future. *Africa Today* 57 (2): 2–24. doi: 10.2979/africatoday.57.2.2.

AU Commission. 2012a. "Press Release: The African Union Rejects the Ongoing Unconstitutional Manoeuvers in Guinea-Bissau", Addis Ababa, 14 April 2012.

———. 2012b. "Press Release: The AU Reaffirms its Support to the Efforts Aimed at Ensuring an Early Return to Constitutional Order", Addis Ababa, 11 May 2012.

AU PSC. 2012. "Communiqué (PSC/PR/COMM[CCCXVIII])", 318th Meeting, Addis Ababa, 17 April 2012.

Aubyn, Festus K. 2013. Managing Complex Political Dilemmas in West Africa: Ecowas and the 2012 Crisis in Guinea-Bissau. *Conflict Trends* 13 (4): 26–32.

Babarinde, Olufemi. 2011. The African Union and the Quest for Security Governance in Africa. In *The Security Governance of Regional Organizations*, eds Emil J. Kirchner and Roberto Dominguez, 273–99. New York: Routledge.

Bach, Daniel. 2016. *Regionalism in Africa: Genealogies, Institutions and Trans-State Networks.* New York: Routledge.

Bah, A. Sarjoh. 2005. From a Security Complex to a Security Community. *African Security Review* 14 (2): 77–83. doi: 10.1080/10246029.2005.9627357.

Bah, A. Sarjoh, Elizabeth Choge-Nyangoto, Solomon Dersso, Brenda Mofya and Tim Murithi. 2014. *The African Peace and Security Architecture: A Handbook.* Addis Ababa: Friedrich-Ebert-Stiftung, African Union.

Bappah, Habibu Y. 2018. ECOWAS Protagonists for Peace: An Internal Perspective on Policy and Community Actors in Peacemaking Interventions. *South African Journal of International Affairs* 25 (1): 83–98. doi: 10.1080/10220461.2018.1417905.

Barry, Boubacar-Sid, Edward G.E. Creppy, Estanislao Gacitua-Mario and Quentin Wodon. 2007. *Conflict, Livelihoods, and Poverty in Guinea-Bissau.* World Bank Working Paper 88. Washington, DC: The World Bank.

Bereketeab, Redie. 2019. Regional Economic Communities and Peacebuilding: The IGAD Experience. *South African Journal of International Affairs* 26 (1): 137–56. doi: 10.1080/10220461.2019.1596152.

Bischoff, Paul-Henri. 2014. How Much its Own and to What End? SADC and the Culture of Security and Regional Organisation in Southern Africa. In *Regional Organisations and Security: Conceptions and Practices*, eds Stephen Aris and Andreas Wenger, 59–78. London: Routledge.

Bolaji, Kehinde A. 2011. Adapting Traditional Peacemaking Principles to Contemporary Conflicts: The ECOWAS Conflict Prevention Framework. *African Conflict and Peacebuilding Review* 1 (2): 183–204. doi: 10.2979/africonfpeacrevi.1.2.183.

Bordonaro, Lorenzo I. 2009. Introduction: Guinea-Bissau Today – The Irrelevance of the State and the Permanence of Change. *African Studies Review* 52 (2): 35–46. doi: 10.1353/arw.0.0211.

Bossuyt, Jean. 2016. *The Political Economy of Regional Integration in Africa: The Economic Community of West African States (ECOWAS).* Brussels: ECDPM.

Boulden, Jane. 2013. *Responding to Conflict in Africa: The United Nations and Regional Organizations.* New York: Palgrave Macmillan.

Boutellis, Arthur and Paul D. Williams. 2013. *Peace Operations, the African Union, and the United Nations: Toward More Effective Partnerships.* New York: International Peace Institute.

Brinkmann, Svend and Steinar Kvale. 2015. *InterViews: Learning the Craft of Qualitative Research Interviewing*, 3rd edn. Los Angeles, CA: SAGE.

Brosig, Malte. 2013. Introduction: The African Security Regime Complex—Exploring Converging Actors and Policies. *African Security* 6 (3–4): 171–90. doi: 10.1080/19392206.2013.854088.

———. 2015. *Cooperative Peacekeeping in Africa: Exploring Regime Complexity.* London: Routledge.

Carvalho, Gustavo de, Cedric de Coning and John Ahere. 2016. *The African Union (AU) Post-Conflict Reconstruction and Development (PCRD) Framework: The First Ten Years.* Background Paper.

Central Intelligence Agency. 2018. The World Fact Book: Guinea-Bissau. Accessed April 17, 2019. www.cia.gov/library/publications/resources/the-world-factbook/geos/pu.html.

Cernicky, Jan. 2008. *Regionale Integration in Westafrika: Eine Analyse der Funktionsweise von ECOWAS und UEMOA.* Bonn: Scientia Bonnensis.

Chabal, Patrick and Jean-Pascal Daloz. 1999. *Africa Works: Disorder as Political Instrument.* London: James Currey.

Cilliers, Jakkie and Kathryn Sturman. 2004. Challenges Facing the AU's Peace and Security Council. *African Security Review* 13 (1): 97–104. doi: 10.1080/10246029.2004.9627276.

Coleman, Katharina P. 2011. Innovations in 'African Solutions to African Problems': The Evolving Practice of Regional Peacekeeping in Sub-Saharan Africa. *The Journal of Modern African Studies* 49 (4): 517–45. doi: 10.1017/S0022278X11000462.

Collier, David. 2011. Understanding Process Tracing. *PS: Political Science & Politics* 44 (4): 823–30. doi: 10.1017/S1049096511001429.

Conselho de Ministros da CPLP. 2012. "Resolução sobre a Situação na Guiné-Bissau", VIII Reunião Extraordinária, Lisbon, 14 April 2012.

Cowell, Frederick. 2011. The Impact of the ECOWAS Protocol on Good Governance and Democracy. *African Journal of International and Comparative Law* 19 (2): 331–42. doi: 10.3366/ajicl.2011.0015.

Cravinho, João G. 2009. Regional Organizations in African Security: A Practitioner's View. *African Security* 2 (2–3): 193–205. doi: 10.1080/19362200903362091.

Darian-Smith, Eve and Philip C. McCarty. 2017. *The Global Turn: Theories, Research Designs, and Methods for Global Studies.* Oakland, CA: University of California Press.

Darkwa, Linda. 2017. The African Standby Force: The African Union's Tool for the Maintenance of Peace and Security. *Contemporary Security Policy* 38 (3): 471–82. doi: 10.1080/13523260.2017.1342478.

Darkwa, Linda and Philip Attuquayefio. 2014. Analysis of Norm Diffusion in the African Union and the Economic Community of West African States. *African Conflict and Peacebuilding Review* 4 (2): 11–37. doi: 10.2979/africonfpeacrevi.4.2.11.

de Coning, Cedric, Linnéa Gelot and John Karlsrud, eds. 2016. *The Future of African Peace Operations: From the Janjaweed to Boko Haram.* London: Zed Books.

Dembinski, Matthias and Berenike Schott. 2013. Converging Around Global Norms? Protection of Civilians in African Union and European Union Peacekeeping in Africa. *African Security* 6 (3–4): 276–96. doi: 10.1080/19392206.2013.854085.

Dersso, Solomon A. 2016a. The APSA, Ten Years On: Mapping the Evolution of Regional Mechanisms for Conflict Management and Resolution. In *A Comprehensive Review of African Conflicts and Regional Interventions [CRACRI]*, ed. Festus B. Aboagye, 13–34. Addis Ababa: African Union Commission; APSTA Secretariat.

———. 2016b. *To Intervene or Not to Intervene? An Inside View of the AU's Decision-Making on Article 4(h) and Burundi.* Occasional Paper. Somerville, MA: World Peace Foundation.

Desmidt, Sophie and Volker Hauck. 2017. *Conflict Management Under the African Peace and Security Architecture (APSA)*. Discussion Paper 211. Maastricht: ECDPM.

Döring, Katharina P.W. and Jens Herpolsheimer. 2021 (forthcoming). Understanding Complex, Collective Actors at African Regional Organizations. In *Practises and Processes of Space-Making Under the Global Condition*, eds Steffi Marung and Ursula Rao. Munich: De Gruyter Oldenbourg.

Ebo, Adedeji. 2007. *Towards a Common ECOWAS Agenda on Security Sector Reform.* Policy Paper 23. Geneva: Geneva Centre for the Democratic Control of Armed Forces (DCAF).

ECOWAS Authority. 2012. "Final Communiqué", Extraordinary Summit of ECOWAS Heads of State and Government, Abuja, 26 April 2012.

ECOWAS Commission. 2012a. "Press Release: ECOWAS Reaction to Ongoing Coup Attempt in Guinea-Bissau (104/2012)", Abuja, 13 April 2012.

———. 2012b. "Press Release: ECOWAS Sanctions Guinea-Bissau after Failed Talks (124/2012)", Abuja, 1 May 2012.

———. 2018. "Press Release: ECOWAS, EU Reaffirm Commitment to Strengthen Cooperation", Abuja, 30 November 2018. Accessed 22 September 2020. https://www.ecowas.int/ecowas-un-restate-commitment-to-peace-security-and-stability-in-west-africa/.

———. 2020. "Press Release: ECOWAS, UN Restate Commitment to Peace, Security and Stability in West Africa", Abuja, 17 January 2020. Accessed 22 September 2020. https://www.ecowas.int/ecowas-un-restate-commitment-to-peace-security-and-stability-in-west-africa/.

Elowson, Camilla and Adriana L. d. Albuquerque. 2016. *Challenges to Peace and Security in Eastern Africa: The Role of IGAD, EAC and EASF.* FOI Memo 5634. Stockholm: FOI, Swedish Research Agency.

Engel, Ulf, ed. 2012. *New Mediation Practices in African Conflicts.* Leipzig: Leipziger Universitätsverlag.

———. 2013. The Changing Role of the AU Commission in Inter-African Relations: The Case of APSA and AGA. In *Africa in World Politics: Engaging a Changing Global Order*, eds John W. Harbeson and Donald Rothchild, 186–206. New York: Westview Press.

———. 2017a. The African Union's Peace and Security Architecture: From Aspiration to Operationalization. In *Africa in World Politics: Constructing Political and Economic Order*, eds John W. Harbeson and Donald Rothchild, 262–82. Boulder, CO: Westview Press.

———. 2017b. Trying to Understand the Implementation of APSA, or the Lack Thereof. Paper Presented at the Workshop African Security and Unbridled Militarization? New Approaches to African Peace and Security Governance of the Nordiska Afrikainsitutet, Uppsala, 21–23 November.

———. 2018a. An Emerging Inter-regional Peace and Security Partnership: The African Union and the European Union. In *Inter-Organisational Relations in International Security: Cooperation and Competition*, eds Stephen Aris, Aglaya Snetkov and Andreas Wenger, 170–87. London: Routledge.

———. 2018b. Knowledge Production on Conflict Early Warning at the African Union. *South African Journal of International Affairs* 25 (1): 117–32. doi: 10.1080/10220461.2018.1417902.

Engel, Ulf and João G. Porto, eds. 2010. *Africa's New Peace and Security Architecture: Promoting Norms, Institutionalizing Solutions.* Farnham: Ashgate.

———, eds. 2013. *Towards an African Peace and Security Regime: Continental Embeddedness, Transnational Linkages, Strategic Relevance.* Farnham: Ashgate.

———. 2014. Imagining, Implementing, and Integrating the African Peace and Security Architecture: The African Union's Challenges. *African Security* 7 (3): 135–46. doi: 10.1080/19392206.2014.945379.

EU. 2012. "Statement by the Spokesperson of EU High Representative Catherine Ashton on the Political Situation in Guinea-Bissau (A 171/12)", Brussels, 14 April 2012.

EU Commission. 2018. "Press Release: EU and African Union Commissions Step Up Their Cooperation to Support Young People, Jobs and Peace", Brussels, 23 May 2018. Accessed 1 May 2019. http://europa.eu/rapid/press-release_IP-18-3887_en.htm.

EU Council. 2012. "Council Imposes Sanctions on Coup Leaders in Guinea-Bissau (9412/12; Presse 187)", Brussels, 3 May 2012.

European Court of Auditors. 2018. *The African Peace and Security Architecture: Need to Refocus EU Support.* Special Report 20. Luxembourg: European Court of Auditors.

Ferreira, Patrícia M. 2004. Guinea-Bissau: Between Conflict and Democracy. *African Security Review* 13 (4): 45–56. doi: 10.1080/10246029.2004.9627317.

Francis, David J. 2006. *Uniting Africa: Building Regional Peace and Security Systems.* Aldershot: Ashgate.

Franke, Benedikt. 2008. Africa's Evolving Security Architecture and the Concept of Multilayered Security Communities. *Cooperation and Conflict* 43 (3): 313–40. doi: 10.1177/0010836708092839.

Gandois, Helene. 2014. Security Regionalism in West Africa: Conceptions and Practices. In Aris and Wenger, *Regional Organisations and Security*, 41–58.

Gänzle, Stefan, Jarle Trondal and Nadja S.B. Kühn. 2018. 'Not So Different After All': Governance and Behavioral Dynamics in the Commission of the Economic Community of West African States (ECOWAS). *Journal of International Organization Studies* 9 (1): 81–98.

Gibert, Marie V. 2009. The Securitisation of the EU's Development Agenda in Africa: Insights from Guinea-Bissau. *Perspectives on European Politics and Society* 10 (4): 621–37. doi: 10.1080/15705850903314882.

Gomes Porto, João and Kapinga Y. Ngandu. 2014. The African Union, Preventive Diplomacy, Mediation, and the Panel of the Wise: Review and Reflection on the Panel's First Six Years. *African Security* 7 (3): 181–206. doi: 10.1080/19392206.2014.952582.

———. 2015. *The African Union's Panel of the Wise: A Concise History.* Durban: ACCORD.

Hardt, Heidi. 2014. *Time to React: The Efficiency of International Organizations in Crisis Response.* New York: Oxford University Press.

———. 2016. From States to Secretariats: Delegation in the African Union Peace and Security Council. *African Security* 9 (3): 161–87. doi: 10.1080/19392206.2016.1208474.

Hartmann, Christof. 2010. Die ECOWAS als Regionale Ordnungsmacht Westafrikas? *Die Friedens-Warte – Journal of International Peace and Organization* 85 (1–2): 73–93.

———. 2013. *Governance Transfer by the Economic Community of West African States (ECOWAS): A B2 Case Study Report.* SFB-Governance Working Paper Series No. 47. Berlin: Collaborative Research Center (SFB) 700.

Hartmann, Christof and Kai Striebinger. 2015. Writing the Script? ECOWAS's Military Intervention Mechanism. In *Governance Transfer by Regional Organizations: Patching Together a Global Script*, eds Tanja A. Börzel and Vera van Hüllen, 68–83. Basingstoke: Palgrave Macmillan.

Healy, Sally. 2014. IGAD and Regional Security at the Horn. In *Routledge Handbook of African Security*, eds James J. Hentz and James Hentz, 217–28. London, New York: Routledge.

Herpolsheimer, Jens. 2019. Spatializing Practices of Regional Organizations During Conflict Intervention: The Politics of ECOWAS and the African Union in Guinea-Bissau. Unpublished doctoral thesis, Leipzig University.

Herpolsheimer, Jens and Skollan E. Warnck. 2020. *Mapping Intervention Practices of ECOWAS and the African Union: Methodological and Practical Challenges.* SFB 1199 Working Paper Series No. 22. Leipzig: Leipziger Universitätsverlag.

ICG. 2008. *Guinea-Bissau: In Need of a State.* Africa Report 142 (2 July). Brussels: International Crisis Group.

———. 2009. *Guinea-Bissau: Beyond Rule of the Gun.* Africa Briefing 61 (25 June). Dakar/Brussels: International Crisis Group.

———. 2011. *Implementing Peace and Security Architecture (I): Central Africa.* Africa Report 181 (7 November). Brussels: International Crisis Group.

———. 2012a. *Beyond Turf Wars: Managing the Post-Coup Transition in Guinea-Bissau.* Africa Report 190 (17 August). Brussels: International Crisis Group.

———. 2012b. *Implementing Peace and Security Architecture (II): Southern Africa.* Africa Report 191 (15 October). Brussels: International Crisis Group.

Ismail, Olawale. 2008. *The Dynamics of Post-Conflict Reconstruction and Peace Building in West Africa: Between Change and Stability.* Discussion Paper 41. Uppsala: Nordiska Afrikainstitutet.

———. 2015. *Toward a Community of Practice: ECOWAS and Peace and Security Policy Communities in West Africa.* APN Working Papers 3: African Peacebuilding Network.

Iwilade, Akin and Johnson U. Agbo. 2012. ECOWAS and the Regulation of Regional Peace and Security in West Africa. *Democracy and Security* 8 (4): 358–73. doi: 10.1080/17419166.2012.734228.

Jackson, Paul. 2012. Regional Security in Sub-Saharan Africa. In *Comparative Regional Security Governance*, eds Shaun Breslin and Stuart Croft, 113–30. London: Routledge.

Jaye, Thomas. 2016. ECOWAS Intervention in Liberia and Sierra Leone: Lessons for the Evolving APSA. In *A Comprehensive Review of African Conflicts and Regional Interventions [CRACRI]*, ed. Festus B. Aboagye, 93–108. Addis Ababa: African Union Commission; APSTA Secretariat.

Kabia, John M. 2009. *Humanitarian Intervention and Conflict Resolution in West Africa: From ECOMOG to ECOMIL.* Burlington, VT: Ashgate.

Katzenstein, Peter J. 2005. *A World of Regions: Asia and Europe in the American Imperium.* Ithaca, NY: Cornell University Press.

Keller, Edmond J. 1997. Rethinking African Regional Security. In *Regional Orders: Building Security in a New World*, eds David A. Lake and Patrick M. Morgan, 296–317. University Park, PA: Pennsylvania State University Press.

Khadiagala, Gilbert M. 2016. Eminent Peacemakers in African Conflicts: Contributions, Potential and Limits. In *Minding the Gap: African Conflict Management in a Time of Change*, eds Pamela R. Aall and Chester A. Crocker, 201–18. Waterloo: Centre for International Governance Innovation.

Kohl, Christoph. 2013. *Irrwege und Auswege: Guinea-Bissau nach dem Putsch im April 2012.* HSFK Standpunkte 1/2013. Frankfurt am Main: Hessische Stiftung Friedens- und Konfliktforschung.

———. 2014. *The Reform of the Guinea-Bissau's Security Sector: Between Demand and Practice.* PRIF report 126. Frankfurt am Main: Peace Research Institute Frankfurt (PRIF).

Lacher, Wolfram. 2013. *Challenging the Myth of the Drug-Terror Nexus in the Sahel.* WACD Background Paper. Geneva: West African Commission on Drugs, Kofi Annan Foundation.

Law, John. 2004. *After Method: Mess in Social Science Research.* London: Routledge.

Leininger, Julia. 2015. Against All Odds: Strong Democratic Norms in the African Union. In *Governance Transfer by Regional Organizations: Patching Together a Global Script*, eds Tanja A. Börzel and Vera van Hüllen, 51–67. Basingstoke: Palgrave Macmillan.

Lewis, David and Richard Valdmanis. 2013. Special Report: How U.S. Drug Sting Targeted West African Military Chiefs, Reuters, 24 July 2013. Accessed 3 May 2019. https://www.reuters.com/article/us-guinea-bissau-sting-special-report/special-report-how-u-s-drug-sting-targeted-west-african-military-chiefs-idUSBRE96N0AR20130724.

Lisakafu, Jacob. 2016. Exploring the Role and Place of the Permanent Representative Committee within the African Union. *South African Journal of International Affairs* 23 (2): 225–41. doi: 10.1080/10220461.2016.1208771.

Loewenstein, Antony. 2016. How Not to Fix an African Narco-State: Europe is Trying to Stop Guinea-Bissau's Drug Trade by Throwing Money at the Traffickers, Foreign Policy, 6 January 2016. Accessed 28 January 2016. http://foreignpolicy.com/2016/01/06/how-not-to-deal-with-an-african-narco-state-guinea-bissau/.

Maiangwa, Benjamin. 2016. Assessing the Responses of the Economic Community of West African States to the Recurring and Emerging Security Threats in West Africa. *Journal of Asian and African Studies* 52 (1): 103–20. doi: 10.1177/0021909615570951.

Makinda, Samuel M., F.W. Okumu and David Mickler. 2016. *The African Union: Addressing the Challenges of Peace, Security, and Governance.* London: Routledge.

Massey, Doreen B. 2005. *For Space.* Los Angeles, CA: SAGE.

Mays, Terry M. 2003. African Solutions for African Problems: The Changing Face of African-Mandated Peace Operations. *Journal of Conflict Studies* 23 (1): 106–25.

Mellor, Nigel. 2001. Messy Method: The Unfolding Story. *Educational Action Research* 9 (3): 465–84. doi: 10.1080/09650790100200166.

Meyer, Angela. 2011. *Peace and Security Cooperation in Central Africa: Developments, Challenges and Prospects.* Discussion Paper 56. Uppsala: Nordiska Afrikainstitutet.

Mikecz, Robert. 2012. Interviewing Elites: Addressing Methodological Issues. *Qualitative Inquiry* 18 (6): 482–93. doi: 10.1177/1077800412442818.

Murithi, Tim. 2016. The African Union as a Norm Entrepreneur: The Limits of Human Protection and Mass Atrocities Prevention. *Global Responsibility to Protect* 8 (2–3): 227–48. doi: 10.1163/1875984X-00803008.

Murithi, Tim and Charles Mwaura. 2010. The Panel of the Wise. In *Africa's New Peace and Security Architecture: Promoting Norms, Institutionalzing Solutions*, eds Ulf Engel and João G. Porto, 77–90. Farnham: Ashgate.

Nathan, Laurie. 2006. SADC's Uncommon Approach to Common Security, 1992–2003. *Journal of Southern African Studies* 32 (3): 605–22. doi: 10.1080/03057070600830755.

———. 2017. *A Survey of Mediation in African Coups.* APN Working Papers 15. New York: African Peacebuilding Network.

Nathan, Laurie, Gen R. Kibochi, Claude Mainge, Michelle Ndiaye and Yahia Zoubir. 2015. African Peace and Security Architecture (APSA): 2014 Assessment Study, 16 April 2015.

Noyes, Alexander and Janette Yarwood. 2013. The AU Continental Early Warning System: From Conceptual to Operational? *International Peacekeeping* 20 (3): 249–62. doi: 10.1080/13533312.2013.838393.

Obi, Cyril I. 2009. Economic Community of West African States on the Ground: Comparing Peacekeeping in Liberia, Sierra Leone, Guinea Bissau, and Côte D'Ivoire. *African Security* 2 (2): 119–35. doi: 10.1080/19362200903361945.

Odigie, Brown. 2017. *In Defense of Democracy: Lessons from ECOWAS' Management of The Gambia's 2016 Post-Election Impasse.* Policy & Practice Brief (PPB) 46. Pretoria: ACCORD.

OIF. 2012. "Communiqué de Presse: La Francophonie Suspend la Guinée-Bissau (CP/SG/07/JT/12)", Paris, 18 April 2012.

Onditi, Francis and Pontian G. Okoth. 2017. Politics of African Peace Support Operation Architecture: What Next Post-2015 African Standby Force? *African Studies* 76 (4): 597–620. doi: 10.1080/00020184.2017.1376851.

O'Regan, Davin and Peter Thompson. 2013. *Advancing Stability and Reconciliation in Guinea-Bissau: Lessons from Africa's First Narco State.* Washington, DC: Africa Center for Strategic Studies.

Ostheimer, Andrea E. 2001. The Structural Crisis in Guinea-Bissau's Political System. *African Security Review* 10 (4): 45–58. doi: 10.1080/10246029.2001.9627951.

Pirozzi, Nicoletta and Andréas Litsegård. 2018. The EU and Africa: Regionalism and Interregionalism Beyond Institutions. In *Interregionalism Across the Atlantic Space*, eds Frank Mattheis and Andréas Litsegård, 75–94. Cham: Springer.

Plank, Friedrich. 2017. The Effectiveness of Interregional Security Cooperation: Evaluating the Joint Engagement of the EU and the AU in Response to the 2013 Crisis in the Central African Republic. *European Security* 26 (4): 485–506. doi: 10.1080/09662839.2017.1327849.

Siewert, Markus B. 2017. Process Tracing. In *Neue Trends in den Sozialwissenschafte n: Innovative Techniken für Qualitative und Quantitative Forschung*, ed. Sebastian Jäckle, 239–71. Wiesbaden: Springer.

Söderbaum, Fredrik. 2016. *Rethinking Regionalism.* London, New York: Palgrave.

Souaré, Issaka K. 2014. The African Union as a Norm Entrepreneur on Military Coups d'État in Africa (1952–2012): An Empirical Assessment. *The Journal of Modern African Studies* 52 (1): 69–94. doi: 10.1017/s0022278x13000785.

Tadesse, Medhane. 2010. *The African Union and Security Sector Reform. A Review of the Post-Conflict Reconstruction & Development (PCRD) Policy.* Addis Ababa: Friedrich-Ebert-Stiftung.

Tardy, Thierry and Marco Wyss, eds. 2014. *Peacekeeping in Africa: The Evolving Security Architecture.* New York: Routledge.

Tavares, Rodrigo. 2011. The Participation of SADC and ECOWAS in Military Operations: The Weight of National Interests in Decision-Making. *African Studies Review* 54 (2): 145–76. doi: 10.1353/arw.2011.0037.

Tieku, Thomas K. 2011. The Evolution of the African Union Commission and Africrats: Drivers of African Regionalisms. In *The Ashgate Research Companion to Regionalisms*, eds Timothy M. Shaw, J. Andrew Grant and Scarlett Cornelissen, 193–212. Farnham: Ashgate.

———. 2016. *Governing Africa: 3D Analysis of the African Union's Performance.* Lanham, MD, Boulder, CO: Rowman & Littlefield.

———. 2019a. Ruling from the Shadows: The Nature and Functions of Informal International Rules in World Politics. *International Studies Review* 10 (1): 55. doi: 10.1093/isr/viz012.

———. 2019b. The African Union: Successes and Failures. In *Oxford Research Encyclopedia of Politics*, 1–25. Oxford: Oxford University Press.

Tieku, Thomas K., Cyril Obi and Lindsay Scorgie-Porter. 2014. The African Peace and Security Architecture: Introduction to the Special Issue. *African Conflict and Peacebuilding Review* 4 (2): 1–10. doi: 10.2979/africonfpeacrevi.4.2.1.

Ukeje, Charles and Rhuks T. Ako. 2017. *The African Union Peace and Security Council (PSC): Challenges and Policy Options.* Policy Brief 6.8. Addis Ababa: Institute for Peace and Security Studies.

UN DPA. 2018. United Nations – African Union Cooperation. Accessed 1 May 2019. https://www.un.org/undpa/ru/node/183322.

UNSC. 2012a. "Resolution 2048 (S/Res/2048 [2012])", 6774th Meeting, New York, 18 May 2012.

———. 2012b. "Statement by the President of the Security Council (S/PRST/2012/15)", New York, 21 April 2012.

UNSG. 2012. "Report of the Secretary-General on Developments in Guinea-Bissau and on the Activities of the United Nations Integrated Peacebuilding Office in that Country (S/2012/554)", New York, 17 July 2012.

Uzoechina, Okey. 2014. *Security Sector Reform and Governance Processes in West Africa: From Concepts to Reality.* Policy Paper 35. Geneva: Geneva Centre for the Democratic Control of Armed Forces (DCAF).

Vines, Alex. 2013. A Decade of African Peace and Security Architecture. *International Affairs* 89 (1): 89–109. doi: 10.1111/1468–2346.12006.

Vulliamy, Ed. 2008. How a Tiny West African Country Became the World's First Narco State, *The Guardian*, 9 March 2008. Accessed 28 January 2016. http://www.theguardian.com/world/2008/mar/09/drugstrade.

Wane, El-Ghassim, Charles Mwaura, Shewit Hailu, Simone Kopfmüller, Doug Bond, Ulf Engel and João G. Porto. 2010. The Continental Early Warning System: Methodology and Approach. In *Africa's New Peace and Security Architecture: Promoting Norms, Institutionalzing Solutions*, eds Ulf Engel and João G. Porto, 91–110. Farnham: Ashgate.

Welz, Martin. 2016. Multi-Actor Peace Operations and Inter-Organizational Relations: Insights from the Central African Republic. *International Peacekeeping* 23 (4): 568–91. doi: 10.1080/13533312.2016.1178070.

———. 2018. Cooperation and Competition: United Nations-African Union Relations. In *Inter-Organisational Relations in International Security: Cooperation and Competition*, eds Stephen Aris, Aglaya Snetkov and Andreas Wenger, 54–70. London: Routledge.

Williams, Paul D. 2007. From Non-Intervention to Non-Indifference: The Origins and Development of the African Union's Security Culture. *African Affairs* 106 (423): 253–79. doi: 10.1093/afraf/adm001.

———. 2009. The Peace and Security Council of the African Union: Evaluating an Embryonic International Institution. *The Journal of Modern African Studies* 47 (4): 603–26. doi: 10.1017/s0022278x09990048.

———. 2013. *Peace Operations in Africa: Lessons Learned Since 2000.* Africa Security Brief No. 25. Washington, DC: Africa Center for Strategic Studies.

Williams, Paul D. and Arthur Boutellis. 2014. Partnership Peacekeeping: Challenges and Opportunities in the United Nations-African Union Relationship. *African Affairs* 113 (451): 254–78. doi: 10.1093/afraf/adu021.

Williams, Paul D. and Jürgen Haacke. 2008. Security Culture, Transnational Challenges and the Economic Community of West African States. *Journal of Contemporary African Studies* 26 (2): 119–36. doi: 10.1080/02589000802124813.

Witt, Antonia. 2013. The African Union and Contested Political Order(s). In *Towards an African Peace and Security Regime: Continental Embeddedness, Transnational Linkages, Strategic Relevance*, eds Ulf Engel and João G. Porto, 11–30. Farnham: Ashgate.

Wondemagegnehu, Dawit Y. 2017. *The African Union-United Nations Inter-Organizational Cooperation for Peace: Unraveling an Emerging Partnership.* Leipzig: Leipziger Universitätsverlag.

World Bank. 2019. Guinea-Bissau. Accessed 17 April 2019. https://data.worldbank.org/country/guinea-bissau.

World Bank and African Development Bank. 2012. "Joint Statement of the African Development Bank and the World Bank on the Situation in Guinea-Bissau (2012/405/AFR)", Washington, DC, 18 April 2012.

World Food Programme. 2018. Guinea-Bissau. Accessed 17 April 2019. https://www1.wfp.org/countries/guinea-bissau.

Wulf, Herbert and Tobias Debiel. 2010. Systemic Disconnects: Why Regional Organizations Fail to Use Early Warning and Response Mechanisms. *Global Governance* 16 (4): 525–47. doi: 10.1163/19426720-01604007.

Yabi, Gilles O. 2010. *The Role of ECOWAS in Managing Political Crisis and Conflict: The Cases of Guinea and Guinea-Bissau.* Abuja: Friedrich-Ebert-Stiftung.

Yanow, Dvora and Peregrine Schwartz-Shea. 2009. Interpretive Research: Characteristics and Criteria. *Revue internationale de psychosociologie* XV (35): 29. doi: 10.3917/rips.035.0029.

Zähringer, Natalie. 2013. Norm Evolution Within and Across the African Union and the United Nations: The Responsibility to Protect (R2P) as a Contested Norm. *South African Journal of International Affairs* 20 (2): 187–205. doi: 10.1080/10220461.2013.811336.

Zartman, William I. 2016. Mediation and Political Tools in Africa. In *Minding the Gap: African Conflict Management in a Time of Change*, eds Pamela R. Aall and Chester A. Crocker, 187–200. Waterloo: Centre for International Governance Innovation.

2 A spatial approach to African Peace and Security

Introduction

Despite a vast body of academic literature on African Peace and Security,[1] dealing with responses by African regional organizations (ROs) to most violent conflicts on the African continent empirically and to a lesser extent from a theoretical perspective (see Chapter 1), the understanding of their 'internal' modes of operation is still very limited in several regards. As pointed out in the previous chapter, problems relate in particular to explaining, conceptualizing and theorizing complexity. Here, complexity refers especially to the multiple, varied and changing interrelated constellations of actors, interests, agendas and political projects, cooperating or competing around various issues that relate to African peace and security dynamics. More recently, these aspects have received increasing scholarly attention, including burgeoning efforts to conceptualize and theorize them creatively (see below). However, complexity also refers to a multiplicity of practices employed by different actors, many of which have received little or no attention so far. Finally, complexity also refers to a multiplicity of interconnected spatial dimensions of conflict situations and regional responses to them. To date, despite pervasive spatial references, literature on African Peace and Security has largely ignored 'space'[2] as an analytical category and an empirical dimension.

To be fair, the neglect of explicit attention to space is a more general one, until fairly recently extending to most of the humanities and social sciences. On the one hand, spatial terminology is often used inconsiderately, going along with unreflective imaginations of space (cf. Massey 2005, 17). Mostly, 'time' is prioritized over 'space', opposing the two, with the former being considered as dynamic, open and moving, whereas the latter is considered to be static, closed and immobile (Massey 2005, 17–19, Part Two). Consequently, space appears as given, being merely the background against which things happen, itself unchanging and without any influence (Shields 2013, 15, 97–8). Against this backdrop, critical geographers such as Doreen Massey have deplored such "unhelpful associations" as a "failure (deliberate or not) of spatial imagination" (Massey 2005, 61). Not only do they prevent us from recognizing space as being as "equally lively and challenging" as time (Massey

2005, 14), and deeply embedded in our everyday lives. They also "hinder a full recognition of the challenge posed by practical socio-political space" (Massey 2005, 61) and are, thus, inadequate to face up to these challenges (Massey 2005, 8; see also Shields 2013, 15, 18).

Therefore, in this chapter, I introduce a spatial approach to study African ROs and specifically their role and practices regarding African Peace and Security, in order to address some of the gaps in the existing literature. I argue that applying a spatial approach, first, allows giving direct attention to space as an empirical dimension of conflict interventions. What is more, as a theory-oriented approach, it also allows us to make sense of how space, on the one hand, influences perceptions and framings of conflict situations (i.e., spatial imaginations) and, on the other, guides interventions and is actively made (i.e., constructed, formatted and ordered) during interventions – by different actors, at different sites, using different spatializing practices. Second, in the process, a spatial approach is also apt to capture and make sense of complex processes of conflict interventions by African ROs (and others) more generally, involving multiple, entangled actors, practices, interests and agendas (see below).

In this, the spatial approach proposed in this chapter draws from and builds on existing innovative approaches that have emerged in the partly overlapping academic fields of International Relations (IR), International Studies and Global Studies, which I outline in the section "Rethinking actors, practices and entanglements" in this chapter. In addition, it takes its key inspiration from Critical Geography, elaborated on in the section "The concept of 'space' in Critical Geography". Finally, the section "Towards a spatial approach to study African peace and security" outlines the spatial approach in more detail and explains how it changes the perspective on African ROs and African peace and security dynamics, complementing existing research and approaches.

Rethinking actors, practices and entanglements

As pointed out in Chapter 1, although extensive and multi-faceted, the existing literature on African Peace and Security, so far, still insufficiently captures the complex processes of conflict interventions by African ROs, in particular regarding the involvement of multiple and entangled actors, their interests and agendas, different practices and, last but not least, their spatial dimensions. This section briefly outlines the main approaches recently advanced in IR, International Studies and Global Studies to work towards closing these gaps. Important to note at this point is that, with few exceptions, these contributions have not yet focused on actors at African ROs. The overview, presented in the following, necessarily constitutes a selection of approaches (and aspects thereof) that seem particularly helpful, and that have influenced or inspired the spatial approach proposed in this book, in one way or another. In particular, it highlights those aspects and approaches that, although not yet explicitly, already point to the relevance of 'space' in analysis. Consequently, the following considerations neither aim nor claim to account for all nuances and matters of ongoing debates, which would be beyond the scope of this section. Moreover, despite the following grouping of approaches, distinctions are not clear-cut, as several interlinkages and overlaps exist.

The 'local' scale

Within wider academic debates on Critical Peacebuilding as well as Peace and Conflict Studies, a 'local turn' has increasingly gained prominence since the mid-2000s, seeking to direct attention to the practices and experiences of both interveners and affected societies at the local level.[3] Prominently represented by Roger Mac Ginty and Oliver Richmond, proponents of this turn have reacted to "real-world events", such as the apparent shortcomings of the liberal peacebuilding paradigm, and actors from the so-called Global South increasingly gaining influence (Mac Ginty and Richmond 2013, 766, 771–2). Among their central objectives is to recognize power as diffuse and circulating among various actors, locally and globally. Moreover, they seek to highlight the importance of culture, history and identity, the significance of local critical agency and resistance, based on rights and everyday needs, as well as to pay attention to the unintended consequences of external blueprints (Mac Ginty and Richmond 2013, 769).[4]

However, while appreciating the change of perspective, a number of scholars have criticized that much of this literature has left 'the local' underanalyzed, lacking empirical grounding (Simons and Zanker 2014, 3; see also Randazzo 2016; Paffenholz 2015). Proponents have acknowledged the elasticity of 'the local' (both geographically and conceptually), local hierarchies and unequal power relations, as well as local actors being part of networks that reach beyond the local, nevertheless continuing to emphasize the distinctiveness of scales (Mac Ginty and Richmond 2013, 770; see also Mac Ginty 2015). However, they appear to have underestimated how complex and fragmented the local actually is.[5] Thus, their contributions fail to account adequately for the complexity of local power and their entanglement with complex relations spanning multiple scales beyond the local, as well as for the contestation of local concepts and agency among local actors, including of who or what is truly 'local' – meanwhile maintaining the assumption of the local as inherently more legitimate (Simons and Zanker 2014, 5–6). Moreover, much of the literature on the local in peacebuilding does not sufficiently capture how blurred and fluid the local may be, as actors may switch their identities (e.g., from 'local' to 'international'), or may become 'localized' (cf. Kappler 2015; see also Randazzo 2016). Some authors have also explicitly adopted a spatial perspective, which has allowed them to reflect more on some of the intricacies of space and place, studying peacebuilding efforts and their effects on local societies (e.g., Björkdahl and Buckley-Zistel 2016; Björkdahl and Kappler 2017), in some cases combining it with feminist approaches (e.g., Hudson 2016; Rigual 2018).

A few scholars have tried to re-think the 'local turn', at the same time linking it more directly to the literature on African Peace and Security, which to date has been largely disconnected. With this in mind, Antonia Witt (2013, 2018) has suggested the study of conflict interventions in Africa focusing on processes of contested ordering and meaning-making during specific conflict interventions (cf. Witt 2020), and adopting a perspective 'from below', looking at practices, knowledge and perceptions (see contributions in Witt 2018). In that regard, Witt suggests reframing the 'local turn' to take the locality of interventions as an analytical starting point, paying attention to the actual 'site' while not essentializing it and remaining aware that interventions are simultaneously "planned, negotiated, enacted, contested and transformed at multiple sites" (Witt 2018, 6).

Going in a similar direction and closely linked to the 'local turn' are anthropological approaches to peacebuilding. Key proponents of the local turn have also called for research on conflict interventions to increase attention to 'the everyday'. However, such studies appear to be mainly interested in local actors, as well as local effects of peacebuilding efforts and policies (e.g., Richmond 2012, 2018; Mac Ginty 2011; Millar 2018). In contrast to this perspective, Séverine Autesserre (2014, 2016) has prominently used an ethnographic approach to focus on those performing the interventions 'locally'. Drawing on empirical material from Africa, among other places, she has studied the 'everyday elements' characteristic of the lives and work of interveners. Adopting this perspective allows us to see how common modes of operations of a global "peaceland", actions, behaviors and discourses based on standard practices, shared habits and dominant narratives actually play out at the local scale (Autesserre 2014, 6). While often inefficient or sometimes even detrimental, these modes of operation persist. At the same time, mandates and instructions from capitals and headquarters do not translate into action in any automatic or mechanistic way. With large divides between capitals and field offices, local staff interprets and adapts instructions, often informally (Autesserre 2014, 25–6). In turn, sociological and anthropological approaches have also (re)emerged as illuminating tools to study international organizations at their headquarters (e.g., Barnett and Finnemore 2004; Sapignoli and Niezen 2017).

Overall, the turn of attention to the 'local', despite justified criticism, has introduced a new spatial scale, complementing the hitherto dominant 'national', 'regional' or 'global' ones. What is more, through the critical debate around the term local itself, and through the change to a perspective 'from below', these scholars have started to think about the constructedness and interlinkage of different spatial scales. Autesserre's work particularly points to this aspect, as it looks at how a specific mindset or operational mode of 'peaceland', produced and playing out on a global scale, affects different local settings, hinting at a multi-directional link between 'local' and 'global' scales. However, much more research in that direction is required to understand how actors and practices at different sites relate to each other. Moreover, how interventions in specific conflict situations and different intervention practices have related to larger regional and trans-regional space-making still remains under-explored.

International practices

Building on the works of post-structuralist IR scholars (e.g., Der Derian 1987; Doty 1996) and the 'practice turn' in social theory (e.g., Savigny, Knorr-Cetina and Schatzki 2001), since the early 2000s, some scholars have increasingly developed an interest in 'international practices' (among many, e.g., Neumann 2002; Adler and Pouliot 2011; Bueger and Gadinger 2015).[6] What some have referred to as international practice theory (e.g., Bueger and Gadinger 2014; Pouliot and Cornut 2015) is not one approach but actually brings together various diverse approaches, which in one way or another seek to direct more attention to everyday practices. More importantly, however, these approaches – if international practice approaches proper[7] – represent an epistemological and ontological shift, to the extent that they think and study global politics or "the international" from the perspective of practices (Bueger and Gadinger 2015, 449). This means that, instead of practices resulting from structures, ideas and so on, they precede those or are at the very least coevolving (Adler and Pouliot 2011, 23–4). According to Emanuel Adler and Vincent Pouliot, agency and agents emerge from and are continually reproduced by practices, which stabilize social structures, ideas and mindsets (Adler and Pouliot 2011, 20). At the same time, practices also enable and are at the heart of change (Adler and Pouliot 2011, 5; see also Neumann 2002, 628; Bueger and Gadinger 2015, 456). Thus, methodologically, a focus on empirical – that is, actual – everyday practices allows to reach beyond traditional levels or units of analysis, whose construction relates to academic practices themselves, and to avoid entrenched dichotomies, such as structure/agency, idea/matter and stability/change (Adler and Pouliot 2011, 4, 6; Bueger and Gadinger 2015, 456–7).

By definition, practices are "socially meaningful patterns of action, which, in being performed more or less competently, simultaneously embody, act out, and possibly reify background knowledge and discourse in and on the material world" (Adler and Pouliot 2011, 4; see also Bueger and Gadinger 2015, 453; Neumann 2002, 630–1). In this, theorists of international practices emphasize performativity and process, a distinct perspective on knowledge tied to and situated in practice, the inherently collective, social character of these processes and the interweaving of discursive and material "worlds" (Adler and Pouliot 2011, 6–7; Bueger and Gadinger 2015, 456–7).

To reflect the inherently collective aspect of practices, Adler and Pouliot have proposed the additional concept 'communities of practice' (e.g., Adler 2004; Adler and Pouliot 2011).[8] The two authors define 'communities of practice' as "intersubjective social structures that constitute the normative and epistemic ground for action", adding that they simultaneously "also are agents, made up of real people, who – working via network channels, across national borders, across organizational divides, and in the halls of government – affect political, economic and social events" (Adler and Pouliot 2011, 18–19). They are a configuration of a continuously renegotiated knowledge domain that constitutes like-mindedness, a community (sense of joint enterprise) and shared practice, which in turn embodies the knowledge shared within the community. Community members collectively develop and sustain these practice(s), drawing on communal resources, such as routines, sensibilities and discourse, and thereby establish relationships of mutual engagement (Adler and Pouliot 2011, 18).

Applying practice theory, or at least practice-oriented approaches, recent studies have analyzed 'interventions' as practice (e.g., see contributions to the special section introduced by Olsson 2015), also covering cases in Africa (e.g., Pomarède and Schjødt 2015, exploring NATO's support mission to the AU peacekeeping operation in Darfur, Sudan between 2005 and 2007). However, to date, only very few studies have applied practice approaches to study African ROs in African Peace and Security literature. Three notable exceptions are the studies by Christian Bueger (2013), dealing with emerging communities of practice around maritime security concerns in Africa, Rebecca Adler-Nissen and Vincent Pouliot (2014), analyzing the negotiation of the international intervention in Libya in 2011, as well as Olawale Ismail (2015), studying ECOWAS and peace and security policy communities in West Africa.

Overall, 'space' has been almost completely absent from the literature on 'international practices' (except to some extent in Neumann 2002). This is remarkable as the central elements of this debate draw attention to some of the fundamental aspects and dynamics of the construction of different spaces. Although apparently aware of the existence and political construction of different spatial scales, these are not the subject of actual direct attention. The focus on what people 'do' seems to eclipse any interest in 'where' people do it (e.g., cf. Adler and Pouliot 2011, 29–30), and how different places and scales are connected to each other. In other words, while focusing on the essential role of practices in the construction, stabilization and change of agency/agents, ideas and social structures, international practice theory, so far, has ignored how these practices also relate to space-making – that is, the continuous construction, formatting and ordering of social spaces – thereby simultaneously becoming *spatializing practices*.

Assemblages and fields

Since the late 2000s, assemblage thinking has found its way increasingly into International Studies research (among many others, e.g., see contributions in Acuto and Curtis 2014),[9] and into debates about IR in Africa as well as the role of 'Africa' in and for IR (short Africa/IR). Here, most prominently, Rita Abrahamsen and Michael Williams (2009, 2011) have introduced this approach to study 'global security assemblages', drawing on and applying the concept to empirical cases in Africa. They define the concept as "settings where a range of different global and local, public and private security agents and normativities interact, cooperate and compete to produce new institutions, practices, and forms of security governance" (Abrahamsen and Williams 2009, 3). Their central interest is with understanding and explaining the 'privatization' of security. In this, assemblage thinking enables them to see beyond a simple (mono-directional) transfer, and to describe a broader rearticulation (or reassembly) of public–private and global–local relations, structures of political power and authority, as well as of the actors themselves, as opposed to unchanging states just losing relevance or being overtaken by other actors (Abrahamsen and Williams 2009, 3).[10]

Extending the approach to the study of Africa/IR more generally, Abrahamsen (2017) further explains the advantages of understanding and analyzing 'social worlds' (or 'social orders') as assembled. First, it helps to discover contingent elements from the 'ground up', as opposed to an analysis in pre-given categories. Second, it directs attention to multi-scalar connections, as opposed to unhelpful dichotomies (e.g., inside–outside, local–global, domestic–international). Third, it recognizes difference and pluralism, as opposed to universalism and/or Western-centrism. Finally, fourth, it attunes researchers to the emergence, maintenance and change of 'social orders', drawing attention to multiple forms and sources of agency (Acuto and Curtis 2014), different forms of power, resources and capacities (Abrahamsen 2017, 133–4). Several studies have started to apply assemblage approaches to study African peace and security dynamics, although not yet focusing on African ROs.[11]

In addition to assemblage approaches, studies proposing an analysis based on Bourdieusian field theory have become very prominent in International Studies, since the early 2000s.[12] Here again, it have been Abrahamsen and Williams who have proposed to complement assemblage thinking with parts of the sociology of Bourdieu, in particular his 'fields of practice' (Abrahamsen and Williams 2011, 89ff.).[13] Approaching 'security' (in Africa) as a field, the two authors show how the growth of private security relates to "its increasing acquisition of forms of capital" (material, symbolic and/or cultural) and its being "part of a reconfiguration of the security field" (Abrahamsen and Williams 2011, 110). In this, according to Bourdieu, a field denotes a "structured space of positions in which the positions and their interrelations are determined by the distribution of different kinds of resources or 'capital'" (Bourdieu, quoted in Abrahamsen and Williams 2011, 102–103).[14] However, the distribution of capital, what exactly is considered 'capital' and, thus, the field as such and relations within it are not fixed, nor easy to maintain. Within these fields, different actors struggle over the "distribution of currently recognized forms of capital" and try to change social relationships "by transforming the structures of valorization within the field" (Abrahamsen and Williams 2011, 102–103). However, to date, only very few such studies have focused on Africa (besides Abrahamsen and Williams 2011; e.g., Frowd 2014).

Although not explicitly, assemblage approaches nevertheless come close to actively considering the constitution and (re)construction of space(s), as they move between and across multiple interlinked spatial scales, looking at how social relations are established and ordered by different actors, with different forms of power and resources, through different practices. This becomes even more apparent when the assemblage approach is combined and complemented with specific aspects of Bourdieu's field theory, as Abrahamsen and Williams (2011) have suggested, as it highlights even more strongly how social interrelations – the essence of space (see below) – are made, maintained and contested. However, due to the lack of active, explicit consideration of 'space', these approaches miss its central relevance, namely that space is not merely a by-product or the background, but something that different actors actively *use*, to achieve specific goals, and *make*, as an objective in its own right.

Transboundary formations and portals of globalization

A precursor to the studies mentioned above, employing an implicit assemblage ontology, has been the approach proposed by Thomas Callaghy, Ronald Kassimir and Robert Latham (2001) around the concept of 'transboundary formations'. Concerned with political analysis of Africa in particular, these authors are interested in *how* and *where* the 'local' and 'global' intersect. That means going beyond descriptions of how they shape one another (the local and the global remaining distinct), instead focusing on the "rich kernels of specific junctures joining diverse structures, actors, ideas, practices, and institutions with varying ranges in a common social and political frame" (Latham, Kassimir and Callaghy 2001, 6). These defy clear distinctions of separate scales as well as between 'internal' and 'external'. The central concern of Latham et al. is to identify how these intersections form and operate at specific sites or across territories and to analyze how cross-boundary forces and transboundary formations are involved in the constitution of forms of order and authority in different scalar contexts (Latham, Kassimir and Callaghy 2001, 7). Thus, rather than something to be discovered, they understand and look at order as continually made, i.e., pursued, produced and contested in often novel ways (Latham, Kassimir and Callaghy 2001, 9). Consequently, multiple, overlapping transboundary formations coexist (Latham, Kassimir and Callaghy 2001, 13–14). 'Interventions', understood in the broadest possible sense, can be a particular form of transboundary formation, although the line distinguishing them from "natural outgrowth of regular socio-economic and political interaction" is blurred (Latham, Kassimir and Callaghy 2001, 7).[15]

This approach has come very close to actively considering 'space'. However, despite its proclaimed interest in how the 'global' and the 'local' are linked in and through particular sites and practices, it does not talk about nor explicitly refer to 'space', instead framing its research interest around the concepts of 'authority' and 'order', and how they are produced through 'transboundary formations'. Moreover, despite the highly interesting edited volume, the concept and the related approach do not seem to have taken hold; unfortunately to date, no further studies appear to have applied it.

A similar objective has been behind the concept of 'portals of globalization', which is interested in 'space' more explicitly. The concept emerged within the field of Global Studies as one of several analytical categories to investigate the historicity and (changing) spatiality of modern globalization processes (Middell and Naumann 2010, 5–6, 14–15; see also Geyer 2010). Portals are those places or sites that serve as entrance points for cultural transfer and where specific actors contribute to developing institutions and practices for dealing with global connectedness; they examine the production and products of new spatial orders (Middell and Naumann 2010, 14). Application of the concept in research is still incipient (e.g., Baumann, Dietze and Maruschke 2017). For the study of African Peace and Security, Ulf Engel (2017) has introduced this approach, looking at how the headquarters of the AU and the UN (in Addis Ababa and New York respectively) have become sites of dense policy processes, increasingly entangled with one another, and how they have turned themselves into drivers of specific forms of knowledge production and transfer (see also Engel 2020).

However, although interested in *how* different spatial boundaries have emerged, changed and been transgressed historically (cf. Middell and Naumann 2010), as well as *how* different scales and spaces are interconnected and entangled (cf. Engel 2017, 152), contributions working on or with the concept of the 'portal of globalization' have not yet considered actively *what* spaces these processes actually produce and connect. Instead, the approach apparently assumes that the spaces linked by portals are essentially given (e.g., 'outside'/the global and 'inside'/the national, apparent especially in Geyer 2010). Moreover, the understanding of space is one of dialectical change between only two opposite extremes, i.e., complete de- and re-territorialization (cf. Middell and Naumann 2010, 4, 14). This reduces space to its territorial dimension, in contrast to a topological multiplicity of spatial dimensions and spaces that critical geographers have observed (see below).

In summary. The approaches presented so far have contributed significantly to increasing our sensitivity towards the complexity of processes relating to African peace and security dynamics, allowing us to overcome some misleading dichotomies to focus on African agency, highlighting diverse actors and to some extent places, sites and practices. Providing highly valuable insights, these studies and approaches have started to change our views, our understanding and concepts of what different actors involved in African peace and security dynamics *do*, to a limited extent also including African ROs, and looking beyond formal and/or official claims. In that endeavor, they already implicitly hint at 'space', its importance and intricacies, but do not actually, actively consider it yet (except to some extent Callaghy, Kassimir and Latham 2001; and Engel 2017). Therefore, the spatial approach suggested in this book builds on the insights and sensitivity generated by the contributions discussed above, but actively seeks to take 'space' center stage, as this will allow us to combine and integrate these aspects, while adding another. To further explain and substantiate this claim, the following sections ponder the question of why space matters and needs to be included explicitly in analysis, before outlining in more detail a spatial approach to meet that challenge in the study of African Peace and Security.

The concept of 'space' in Critical Geography

In this book, I start from the main observation of the 'spatial turn' (or spatial turns, cf. Warf and Arias 2009) in the social sciences and humanities, namely that, despite long-time neglect in favor of time, space matters in various often unexpected ways and needs to become part of scientific analysis. This does not only mean to pay direct attention to the empirical relevance of space, but also to overcome traditional conceptualizations, largely presenting space as unchanging, in an either fully territorialized or completely space-less world (Middell and Naumann 2010, 6). The US human geographer Edward W. Soja first used the term 'spatial turn' in 1989, calling for renewed attention and a re-evaluation of the work of French sociologist Henri Lefebvre (in particular Lefebvre 2000 [1974]), to overcome the ignorance or lack of attention towards space, especially by critical scholars (Döring and Thielmann 2008a, 7).

Since then, the 'spatial turn' has found its way into many academic fields of the social sciences and humanities (e.g., see contributions in Döring and Thielmann 2008b; and Warf and Arias 2009). However, its respective impact has varied greatly, triggering significant change in some (e.g., Human Geography, cf. Engel and Nugent 2009a), assuming foundational importance in others (e.g., Global History, cf. Middell and Naumann 2010, 6ff.), while in still others exerting little although slowly increasing influence (e.g., Political Science, cf. Horner and Rule 2013; Chojnacki and Engels 2013; and African Studies, cf. Engel and Nugent 2009b). Within Security Studies, for example, a call for a 'spatial turn' came only very recently (cf. Adamson 2016; Charbonneau 2017). Overall, however – and this is true in particular for the study of African Peace and Security – 'space' has received only very limited direct attention.

Therefore, arguing for the relevance and importance of space as an analytical category, I take my clue from a number of writers that have contributed to the academic field of Critical Geography. Among others, these are Doreen Massey, Gearóid Ó Tuathail (Gerard Toal), Rob Shields and John Allen. Drawing on a long history (or entire epochs; Shields 2013, 41ff.) of thinking about space (and time), these have sought to raise awareness for the importance of space and the many, often unexpected ways in which it matters (Massey 2005, 15).[16] They have justified this endeavor by pointing to the deep embeddedness of space in our everyday lives (Massey 2005, 105; Shields 2013, 7). Consequently, their works have alerted us that assumptions about space, often implicit rather than explicit, are important, as they influence how we imagine and act upon or through space (e.g., as a "surface", something that can be crossed and conquered; Massey 2005, 4).

In the following, this section outlines the main points that inform the conception of space in this book, and which are at the basis of the proposed spatial approach to the study of African Peace and Security. A cautionary note is warranted, however. In the face of the vast number of texts and authors (including philosophers, sociologists and geographers) trying to increasingly work towards new ways of thinking about space and related social phenomena, the following elaborations necessarily constitute a selection. Most likely, they also reduce and simplify and thus do not do justice to an academic debate that is very broad.[17] Nevertheless, the following considerations may serve as a helpful starting point.

Relational space

At the very core of the conceptualization of 'space' in this book is its inherently relational character. It is socially constructed, resulting from multiple, continuous, open-ended social interactions and changing sets of heterogeneous social relations among different actors. These constructions are continuously ongoing, taking place simultaneously at different levels and scales (e.g., Thrift 2009, 96; Massey 2005, 9, 99). On the one hand, this stands in stark contrast to still widespread assumptions about space as a fixed 'container', within which social relations unfold over time. Contrary to such assumptions, a relational understanding allows us to see dynamic and complex processes of change, and how space is always only provisionally "stabilized" (e.g., Thrift 2009, 96; Massey 2005, 95–6). On the other hand, it emphasizes that multiple, heterogeneous spaces coexist, at any given time. In fact, multiplicity and space need to be seen as co-constitutive, in the sense that space allows multiple contemporaneous actors, objects, identities, practices, imaginations etc. to coexist, which in turn form the basis for the possibility of multiple social interrelations, producing multiple spaces (Massey 2005, 9, 89, 99).[18]

Although this multiplicity of sets of social relations has the potential to span the entire globe, Doreen Massey alerts us that not everything and "everywhere" is always already connected to everything and "everywhere" else (Massey 2005, 11–12, 107). Instead, connections and disconnections are continuously made and remade – constructed, maintained, contested – by various actors – consciously or unconsciously, intentionally or unintentionally – through everyday practices (Massey 2005, 9, 118; Shields 2013, 12; Werlen 2009, 286). Therefore, existing sets of interrelations, connections and disconnections represent specific temporary achievements, which in order to continue to exist need constant stabilization – missing links, loose ends and openings always remain (Massey 2005, 11–12, 107).

In turn, as part of everyday practices and performances, 'space' is also a category of thought, or an imaginative structure (Massey 2005, 9), that allows people to make sense of the world around them, to give meaning to it and to act upon it (Werlen 2009, 286; see also Shields 2013, 7). These thoughts and related practices make up reality, which in turn impacts back on people's thoughts and acts (Werlen 2009, 287; DeLanda 2016, 21). Put in other words, space influences social interaction, which at the same influences space. Focusing on ideas and practices, therefore, allows us to study how people "mark out [...] what they evidently regard and act upon as meaningful places or 'regional' entities [...] in the course of which they lend a constructed reality to such 'regions' within the conduct of their daily lives" (Werlen 2009, 286). From this, according to Benno Werlen, "everyday regionalizations" emerge, based on people's imaginations of the geographies they live in, which they suffuse with (shared) meanings, and which are central to all ensuing activities, events and processes (economic, political, cultural) (Werlen 2009, 287). The regions resulting from this only possess reality as "thought-and-practiced constructs" (Werlen 2009, 286).[19]

In this regard, specific places assume an important position, as many closely associate them with 'the everyday', 'local', 'here', 'meaningful', 'lived' etc. – i.e., what really matters. However, while these places are often opposed to space, erroneously considered more 'abstract' and 'out there', we need to understand place and space as interlinked (cf. Massey 2005, 6). Here it is again Doreen Massey sensitizing us that a place is not a point or an area on a map, but rather a spatio-temporal event, an integration of space and time (Massey 2005, 130). This emphasizes an understanding of place as "open ('a global sense of place'), as woven together out of ongoing stories, as a moment within power-geometries, as a particular constellation within the wider topographies of space, and as in process, as unfinished business" (Massey 2005, 131). Similarly, Rob Shields tells us that places form part of a geography or relational networks of difference, that is, a specific spatialization of places and regions as 'places-for-this' and/or 'places-for-that', constructing 'place-images' and 'place myths' (Shields 2013, 31).

What becomes apparent from the above is that the way in which space is imagined has effects – it matters.[20] While much of this may be unconscious or unintended, often it also links to specific projects that actively seek to order global space (e.g., legitimating and structuring action), trying to "tame" the spatial, fix or stabilize what is inherently instable and creative (Massey 2005, 64–5). That is why we also need to understand space as something inherently linked to power and politics.

Political spaces, spatial politics and power

Closely linked to the intimate relationship between the social and the spatial, the spatial is always also political *and* vice versa, as it is constituted by social interrelations (Massey 2005, 9, 15; Shields 2013, 7). In the words of Massey:

> [It is] not just that the spatial is political (which, after many years and much writing thereupon, can be taken as given), but rather that thinking the spatial in a particular way can shake up the manner in which certain political questions are formulated, can contribute to political arguments already under way, and – most deeply – can be an essential element in the imaginative structure which enables in the first place an opening up to the very sphere of the political.
>
> (Massey 2005, 9)

Put differently, it is not only politics that is involved in the construction, maintenance, contestation and reconstruction of different spaces. Space also influences the ways in which politics play out. Informed by and resulting in particular spatial imaginations, space can be the site, object and means of politics (Jessop 2016, 10–12). This also points to the importance and, in fact, ubiquity of power and unequal power relations in space-making (cf. also Shields 2013, 35). Drawing on Foucault, critical geographers have highlighted the nature of space and geography as reflecting specific power-knowledge relationships (Ó Tuathail 1996, 10; Murdoch 2005, 48). As such, spaces relate to discursive formations or regimes, which specify how particular sites should be organized (Murdoch 2005, 35, 48), and who has the right and/or capacity to speak "sovereignly" about space (Ó Tuathail 1996, 11). In this, power, knowledge, practice and space are interwoven and cannot be clearly distinguished (Murdoch 2005, 48). Struggles over different imaginations, representations and implementations (e.g., issues of [forcible] inclusion and exclusion) relate to continuous efforts to construct, reconstruct or deconstruct as well as to stabilize or destabilize certain spatial relations (Shields 2013, 32; Ó Tuathail 1996, 15). The outcomes of these struggles are always precarious and underdetermined in the sense that they may involve "openings" or the emergence of new forms (Murdoch 2005, 18–20).

The entangled relationship between power, knowledge, practice and space becomes particularly apparent in the academic project of Critical Geopolitics, pursued prominently by Gearóid Ó Tuathail (e.g., 1996).[21] The project starts by questioning the very term 'geopolitics' as both a "convenient" (referring to a multiplicity of practices, efforts etc.) and an "inconvenient fiction" (overloaded with various different meanings) (Ó Tuathail 1996, 15–16). Based on this, Ó Tuathail aims at uncovering the historical and geographical particularity of geopolitics as a specific way of "envisioning and writing space-as-global from the turn of the century" (Ó Tuathail 1996, 16). It highlights modern geography as a particular power–knowledge relationship and an institutionalized way of seeing and displaying space, which "needs to be situated in the general power relations of the centralization and imperialist expansion of the modern European state system across the globe, since the sixteenth century onward" (Ó Tuathail 1996, 10). Above all, geopolitics refers to a discursive practice, the political "geo-graphing", attempting to produce international politics geographically, "spatializing" it to represent the world in a specific way (Ó Tuathail 1996, 10, 59). As such, it should lead us to ask questions whenever actors rhetorically deploy geopolitics (Ó Tuathail 1996, 16). Moreover, we need to pay attention to "spatializing practices" of both actors, as well as strategic thinkers and public intellectuals, "practical" and "formal geopolitics" respectively (Ó Tuathail 1996, 60).

Thinking space topologically

Contrary to widespread assumptions, 'space' does not only refer to territory; 'spatialization' does not only refer to territorialization. Socio-spatial relations are polymorphous, playing on one or several spatial dimensions at certain times or simultaneously. These include but are not limited to territoriality, instead stretching other spatial dimensions such as, for example, scales, networks and places – which need to become part of more fine-grained and complex analysis (Jessop, Brenner and Jones 2008; see also Jessop 2016). However, while including and differentiating between concepts such as place, scale, network and territory introduces a greater sensitivity to the variety of spatial dimensions, descriptions and analyses in these terms often remain two-dimensional (i.e., straight lines connecting different points). To overcome and move beyond such 'easy geometries', some proponents of relational approaches have argued for the need to complement topography with a topological understanding of space. Using a vocabulary that includes terms like 'fluidity', 'folding' and 'distorting', this approach seeks to draw attention to the ways in which 'proximity' and 'distance' are not absolute but produced by actors with the power to make the "far near" and the "near far" (Murdoch 2005, 94–5).[22]

More recently, this point has been brought home forcefully by John Allen, describing the "changing same" of power in topological terms (Allen 2011, 2016). Allen argues that both space and power are continuously under transformation. Therefore, while the outcome (e.g., state power) may seem to stay the same, the ways in which this outcome is reproduced may differ and may come along with subtle spatial shifts that need to be captured (Allen 2016, 1–2). In particular, Allen sensitizes us to the different aspects of distorted or folded topological "reach", which is rather about felt "presence" than about geographical distance, about intensity rather than extensity. This means that, being inherently relational, 'proximity' (making presence felt) or 'distance' (placing beyond reach) may be produced in different ways by actors with more or less power to do so (cf. Allen 2016, 46ff.). Consequently, researchers need to study "how actors use their resources, technological, financial or otherwise, to produce the tenuous effect that is power" (Allen 2016, 11).

Going in a similar direction, Rob Shields argues for a topological approach as a "rigorous method" to work with multiple spatialities (Shields 2013, 102), including "virtual", that is, real but not actual ones (Shields 2013, 34), "by focusing on connections and fluid networks of relations" (Shields 2013, 102). He alerts us that, from a topological perspective, all scales matter. As actors continually try to reconfigure power relations, topology changes. Resulting from this, relations among different scales may defy clear hierarchization or nesting – smaller scales in some cases contain larger ones (e.g., the former becoming "inflated" and/or the latter "crumbled"; Shields 2013, 138–40). The challenge thus becomes to "capture the multiple, conflicting spatialisations that intersect, usually remaining separate but at certain times and places breaking in on each other" (Shields 2013, 102) – to capture 'space' as a "field of stresses or forces" (Shields 2013, 107).

In sum, critical geographers have drawn attention to spatial phenomena, shifts and more or less subtle changes that cannot be captured with traditional understandings of space and spatiality, which are often limited to a taken-for-granted state territoriality (Agnew 1994; Brenner 1999; Allen 2016). Instead, we are confronted with multi-scalar, polycentric and intertwined processes of de- and re-territorialization (Brenner 1999, 43–4), and, as I argue in this book, of *re-spatialization*. In order to detect and account for the continuous changes, shifts and transformations of space and the complex social relations it consists of, we require new ways of imagining, seeing and talking about space and politics (Massey 2005, 13; Murdoch 2005, 99; Allen 2016, 3). Only then can we account for the spaces that do emerge (and those that do not) and ask how specific spatial arrangements are maintained as well as how some actors become powerful while others do not, using specific spatial arrangements to generate this power (Murdoch 2005, 20; Allen 2016, 1–2; Massey 2005, 11–12). Based on these considerations, the following section seeks to outline and operationalize a spatial approach towards the study of African Peace and Security.

Towards a spatial approach to study African Peace and Security

Based on the above elaborations, I argue that it is necessary to understand conflict intervention by African ROs, and African peace and security dynamics more generally, as a multiplicity of open-ended processes comprising social interrelations among a multiplicity of actors, objects, ideas, projects and so on. These do not only reach across different spaces and are not only shaped by space, but also actively – consciously or unconsciously, intentionally or unintentionally – contribute to space-making: the continuous, open-ended construction, formatting and ordering of space. This space-making centrally involves unequal power–knowledge relations that are inherently political, as connections and relations do not emerge, exist and persist just by themselves. Instead, specific more- or less-powerful actors make and maintain, remake or undo them, employing different practices and resources. The results are ever-precarious and changing spaces that are inherently relational and topological, defying easy geometries and straightforward, two-dimensional geographies.

Moving beyond analyses that take space for granted, the spatial approach proposed in this book adopts a critical, constructivist and historicizing perspective. This reflects the ever-changing, relational and political character of space (and time), and allows us to focus on and unpack specific constellations of multiple actors, practices and relations, all while being sensitive to constellations of power and knowledge. Such a spatial approach, while theoretically guided and aiming at theorization, is not about claiming a single, universal truth, but about finding a new way of engaging the world (cf. Thrift 1999, 304), and in particular African ROs and African peace and security dynamics. Especially, it seeks to unravel how places and spaces as well as specific spatializations emerge and change in relation to others, and in relation to specific political projects, pursued at African ROs in and around matters of African peace and security.

To achieve this goal, the following outlines the basic features of a spatial approach, introducing the main theoretical and analytical concepts and tools, and reflecting on how they may help to access space in practical research. Finally, taking a first glimpse through the spatial lens, I reframe the interactions between different actors at ECOWAS and the AU, as well as other regional and international actors, from a spatial perspective.

How to access 'space' in research on Peace and Security in Africa

From the considerations so far, it has become clear "how *little*, actually, space is thought about explicitly" (Massey 2005, 7, emphasis in the original). From this, the question emerges of how to access something that is mostly implicit and often unreflected. The main response and objective of the approach proposed here is through 'sensitization' of the researcher. Most importantly, this means the creation of an awareness of the different ways in which space is (made) relevant, who makes it relevant and how. Although definitely a challenge in research, the implicitness of space also offers an advantage, as it allows the assumption of a position slightly outside official or formal narratives. Therefore, it enables us to question and critically analyze these narratives and related practices, instead of following, repeating and reproducing official discourses – as is often the case in studies that rely heavily on official, publicly available documents.

To these effects, I propose a set of analytical concepts and sensitizing tools, which in addition, I argue, also help to understand and theorize complex dynamics around conflict interventions, the role of ROs therein, as well as intervention practices and their spatializing effects. In this book, I refer to three basic concepts to analyze, understand and explain the relevance of space in African peace and security dynamics: space-making, spatial formats and spatial order.[23]

Space-making refers to the continuous (re)construction, (re)formatting and (re)ordering of social spaces, being a central dimension of every social interaction (Middell 2019). Thus, it refers to the spatial (re)organization, that is, the (re)spatialization of potentially all aspects of social life (economic, political, cultural; cf. Shields 2013, 168),[24] comprising sets of processes and practices involving various individual and/or collective actors as well as negotiation, contestation and unequal power relations among them. Typical examples of spatializations (or as Shields calls them "archetypes") include 'center-periphery', 'nesting scales', 'binary' divisions and 'mosaic' patterns (Shields 2013, 168).

At the basis of space-making, and simultaneously its outcome, are particular spatial formats and spatial orders. *Spatial formats* constitute historically contingent, relatively persistent lenses or patterns that enable actors to select, name, give meaning to and communicate particular spaces relevant to their actions. Thus, they relate to specific material and/or discursive practices (e.g., strategies of signification), which allow acting through and upon space. Spatial formats are tied to specific groups of actors, as they require social recognition (i.e., they need to be shared inter-subjectively), and are based on ideas about how to imagine, name, communicate, manage and perform (i.e., how *to format*) space. More fundamentally, they contain ideas about what 'relevant' or 'appropriate' spatial formats are (cf. Engel 2018, 3–5; Middell 2019, 5–6, 10–11; Middell and Wardenga 2019, 148).

In turn, s*patial orders* both influence and result from spatial formatting. Several spatial orders coexist and increasingly overlap and interfuse, mutually influencing each other (Middell 2019, 10–11). Emerging historically, spatial orders relate different spaces and spatial formats to one another in specific ways. However, this is always achieved only temporarily, as construction, maintenance and contestation are constantly ongoing – spatial orders are continuously transforming. Therefore, it is impossible to describe any spatial order completely; even if one could freeze it or take a snapshot, its complexity would defy any effort at full description. What we can and should study instead are processes of *spatial ordering*. Here again, it takes specific constellations of ideas, more- or less-powerful actors and practices that do the ordering of space (cf. Engel 2018, 4).[25]

Spatial semantics, spatial actors, spatializing practices, sites and connections

In order to identify, analyze and describe the role of specific processes of spatialization, spatial formatting and spatial ordering with regard to African peace and security dynamics, and especially during conflict interventions by African ROs, it is necessary to look at several interrelated aspects. *Spatializing practices*, at the same time, constitute one of these aspects as well as a crucial link between the remaining ones. I introduce these briefly in the following.

(i) Take *spatial semantics* seriously. This means looking at common spatial terms and references, trying to identify what they refer to, who uses them, how, when and for what reason. Based on that analysis, it is possible to infer spatial imaginations, that is, imaginations of particular spatializations (see above).[26] These imaginations and related semantics are historically contingent, and both are influenced by existing spatial formats and spatial orders as well as impacting back on those, contributing to change or the emergence of new ones. Moreover, they are also linked to particular spatializing practices, one of them being the use of spatial semantics as such (i.e., speech acts; see below). For example, the literature on African Peace and Security as well as official documents of African ROs, on the one hand, contain various spatial references (e.g., nation/state, region, architecture, landscape). These references point to specific spatial imaginations and related spatial formats and, sometimes, spatial orders. On the other hand, we come across a number of terms that are frequently employed to describe specific dynamics in and around conflict situations and responses to them (e.g., national interest, sovereignty, hegemony and geopolitics), which, although not always in any obvious fashion, are also intimately linked to particular spatial imaginations and related spatializing practices.

(ii) Identify and follow *spatial actors*. This means trying to identify and follow different actors that contribute to space-making, seeking to implement a specific spatial format (spatial formatting) as well as a spatial order (spatial ordering). In these efforts, consciously or unconsciously, intentionally or unintentionally, spatial actors employ particular spatializing practices. For example, during the creation process of the OAU and ECOWAS, as well as during the transformation from the OAU to the AU, it was different heads of state, along with some high-level government representatives and non-state actors, that pursued partly competing agendas, aiming to construct, format and order regional spaces according to different ideas, preferences and objectives (on the OAU/AU, e.g., cf. van Walraven 1999; Tieku 2016; on ECOWAS, e.g., cf. Gambari 1991; Adebajo 2002). Identifying spatial actors also sensitizes for the multiple and entangled actors at African ROs, allowing us to complement state-centric accounts and move beyond portrayals of ECOWAS and the AU as unitary actors. Moreover, following actors leads to the different, interconnected sites at which they contribute to space-making (see below).

(iii) Identify and analyze *spatializing practices*.[27] Ensuing directly from the previous two aspects, this means looking at *how* exactly different actors construct, format and order space – how different practices relate to space-making in one way or another. It also refers to how different actors use space to argue for or against something, or to achieve certain objectives. As mentioned above, this prominently includes speech acts, and therefore directly interrelates with spatial semantics. Spatializing practices are also interrelated with spatial formats, which they help to bring about while they are also patterned by them. Likewise, the same practices are also intimately tied to spatial ordering. Put differently, the same spatializing practices may have different effects, contributing to both spatial formatting and spatial ordering. For example, the division of Africa into eight partly overlapping Regional Economic Communities (RECs) and Regional Mechanisms (RMs), recognized by the AU as pillars of its African Peace and Security Architecture (APSA,) clearly refers to spatializing practices that aim both to format and order space in relation to peace and security efforts in Africa (see below).

(iv) Identify relevant *sites* and *connections* between them. This means identifying the different places where interventions play out and space is made, and how these places relate to each other – how different actors connect these sites through different *spatializing practices*. From such a perspective, it becomes clear that interventions by African ROs have not only taken place at the actual conflict site. Instead, they have been acted out and/or performed at several sites both 'near' and 'far away' from the actual conflict. For example, this may include the organizational headquarters (e.g., in Abuja, Addis Ababa, Brussels and New York), conference or summit venues and regional capital cities.

Spatializing the study of African Peace and Security

Applying the above considerations to the study of African Peace and Security means to identify, follow and analyze: (i) spatial semantics in various forms of text produced by actors at African ROs; (ii) the concrete actors that drive or contribute to space-making during conflict interventions (i.e., spatial actors); (iii) their spatializing practices; as well as (iv) the specific sites where all of this takes place.[28] Through such an analysis, African peace and security dynamics, and in particular APSA and conflict interventions by different actors at African ROs, become visible as complex multidimensional processes, constantly 'in the making'. These involve continuous negotiation and contestation among different actors (Chapter 6) both within and across African ROs, linked to particular spatial imaginations (Chapter 5), employing different practices at different interconnected sites (Chapters 3 and 4) – all of which contributes to space-making.

Several insights emerge from this, which help us to understand, describe and theorize better how African ROs operate, internally and in relation to other actors, and how they act during conflict interventions. First, interested in how space is constructed, formatted and ordered, a spatial approach directs attention to *what* actors at ECOWAS and the AU actually *do* (practices) when they respond to conflict in their respective regions, going beyond official ambitions, claims and rhetoric. Second, it sheds more light on *who* exactly does what (actors), thereby contributing to an increasing unpacking of African ROs as unitary actors. Following spatial actors and their practices (including patterned speech acts), then, allows us to see how 'ECOWAS' and the 'AU' emerge as complex, collective actors during conflict interventions and forge specific connections 'internally', among different African ROs, as well as with other regional or international actors. It allows us to see connections and entanglements and to move between different sites and scales, which different actors deem relevant and give meaning to. It also allows us to see how multiple, simultaneous processes, agendas and projects intersect.

In the remaining chapters of this book, therefore, I describe 'ECOWAS' and the 'AU' as political and spatial projects with partly overlapping sets of multiple and entangled actors and practices. In that respect, conflict interventions constitute moments of particularly dense interaction, which allow the study of many of these aspects and dynamics while they are 'at work'.

Conclusion

This chapter has started from the observation that space as an analytical category has been largely absent from academic contributions to the study of African Peace and Security, going along with several other gaps regarding the complexity of processes and dynamics around conflicts in Africa and responses to them. To address and overcome these gaps, this chapter has proposed a spatial approach, which builds on recent innovative academic approaches in IR, International Studies and Global Studies that have sought to understand, explain and conceptualize a multiplicity of entangled actors and practices involved in matters of African peace and security. The spatial approach also draws on insights from Critical Geography, conceptualizing space as constructed, relational and topological, as well as a central dimension of all social and political interaction.

The spatial approach directs attention to space-making, applying several heuristic concepts. 'Spatial formats' pattern the way that actors make sense of processes of spatialization, and try to construct 'spatial order(s)' relating several 'spatial formats' to each other in specific ways. 'Spatial semantics' offer access to spatial imaginations, underlying spatial formats and spatial ordering by 'spatial actors', in some cases intentionally and actively driving processes of re-spatialization. These actors use different 'spatializing practices' and pursue their efforts at different, interconnected 'sites'. The spatial approach consists of sensitizing for and identifying these different aspects, thereby directing attention to space as an empirical dimension of conflict intervention by African ROs, as well as a methodological and theoretical tool to analyze and understand complex processes of conflict intervention and African peace and security dynamics.

What is important to keep in mind during the following chapters is that, in all of this, space is the result of multiple, heterogeneous interactions and interrelations between different actors. Moreover, it always involves relations of power and is constantly in the process of being made, maintained or remade. In this, a multiplicity of spaces coexists – as do imaginations, ascriptions of meaning and representations (i.e., making sense), which are based on particular power–knowledge constellations and accompanied by different practices. Thus, the spatial is always also political, and, in turn, space (in one way or another) influences politics and is mobilized for political reasons (e.g., arguments, justification, goals). Finally, this book follows a topological understanding of space, meaning that 'proximity' and 'distance' (what is 'near' and 'far') are also relative terms. Actors with the ability and capacity to do so may extend their 'reach' into 'far-off' places, making their 'presence' felt 'from afar'.

Drawing on these elaborations, the following chapters apply the spatial approach, focusing on different actors at ECOWAS and the AU and their response to conflict in West/Africa. Doing so, they seek to bring together an account of complex and entangled space-making around conflict in Africa specifically and African peace and security dynamics more generally, in which African ROs (along with other regional and international actors) have sought to construct, format and order space, in their respective regions and in relation to others.

Notes

1 By 'African Peace and Security' I mean the broad and somewhat diffuse interdisciplinary research field that has the African Peace and Security Architecture (APSA) as its central reference point and specifically studies the role of African ROs therein, along with several other state and non-state actors. Although often relating to academic literature on UN peacekeeping and/or peacebuilding in Africa, it specifically highlights African actors and African agency (see Chapter 1).

2 I use 'space' in inverted commas when I want to highlight it as a concept or analytical dimension.

3 The 'local turn' has been one of several 'turns' proclaimed since the mid-2000s, aiming to unpack liberal peacebuilding, all of which have largely focused on 'local' dynamics, including most recently a 'material turn' or 'new materialism', seeking to direct attention to the dynamic relationship between (local) agency and material objects (cf. Mac Ginty 2017).

4 For an overview of the debate around the 'local turn' in peacebuilding literature, see Leonardsson and Rudd (2015).

5 One suggestion to deal with that aspect has been to use 'complexity theory' (cf. de Coning 2016; Brusset, de Coning and Hughes 2016), and related to it "adaptive peacebuilding" (de Coning 2018). However, the existing contributions, so far, appear to be mostly interested in providing policy advice to improve the effectiveness of peacekeeping missions. Detailed studies of peacekeeping settings in Africa that employ 'complexity theory' do not exist yet.

6 These draw on the works of De Certeau, Foucault, Bourdieu, Latour (cf. Bueger and Gadinger 2015, 454).

7 Bueger and Gadinger assert that while many IR scholars discuss practice(s), not all of them share the epistemological and ontological commitment implied by practice theory. Consequently, not every IR theory is, nor should be, a practice theory (Bueger and Gadinger 2015, 450).

8 Outside IR, Étienne Wenger (1998) first proposed the concept 'community of practice'.

9 Assemblage thinking, more generally, most prominently draws on the works of Gilles Deleuze and Felix Guattari (e.g., 2013 [1987]) and Bruno Latour (e.g., 2005).

10 Another related influential approach that I have not included here has been actor-network theory (ANT). Although going into a similar direction, I am siding with

Abrahamsen and Williams, who have decided not to use ANT because of its unifying tendencies and linear, network-centric logic (cf. Abrahamsen and Williams 2014, 26). Likewise, in Critical Geography, network approaches and ANT have played and continue to play an important role. However, some have criticized especially the Latourian version for its relative neglect of 'power' and a focus on 'panoptic' networks (i.e., highly centralized) only, failing to account for more flexible, multidimensional and 'fluid' constellations (e.g., cf. Murdoch 2005, 75–6, 79).

11 Here, several former PhD students of Abrahamsen and Williams have contributed (e.g., Sandor 2016a, 2016b; Doucet 2016; Frowd and Sandor 2018) along with other scholars (e.g., Bachmann, Bell and Holmqvist 2016; Higate and Utas 2017; Bueger 2017).

12 Among the various contributions, e.g., Williams (2007); Leander (2011); Bigo and Madsen (2011); Berling (2012); Adler-Nissen (2013).

13 Here their approach partly links with studies of international practices, as discussed above.

14 They apply Bourdieu's theory selectively, for example, decidedly not using 'habitus' (Abrahamsen and Williams 2011, footnote 34, 103–104).

15 Latham identifies three forms of interactions across boundaries of social spaces: international arenas, trans-local networks and trans-territorial deployments (Latham 2001, 71).

16 Of particular importance, however, have been Western philosophers and sociologists, such as Kant, Hegel and sometimes Heidegger, as well as Durkheim, Foucault, Bourdieu, Simmel, Derrida, Serres, Deleuze, Harvey and Lefebvre, to name but a few of the most important (e.g., cf. Massey 2005; Murdoch 2005; Shields 2013).

17 For a much more detailed discussion of the emergence and intellectual basis of post-structuralist geography, see, e.g., Murdoch (2005) and, more recently, Shields (2013) and Allen (2016, 17ff.).

18 As Massey has put it: "If time unfolds as change then space unfolds as interaction. In that sense space is the social dimension [...] in the sense of engagement within a multiplicity" (Massey 2005, 60).

19 For this reason, some have argued that we should best think of space as a verb (i.e., 'to space'), rather than a noun, studying how actors 'do' space (e.g., Doel, referred to in Murdoch 2005, 18, 91).

20 Derek Gregory also makes this point powerfully in his works on 'geographical imaginations' (Gregory 1994) and 'imaginative geographies' (Gregory 1995).

21 Other scholars that have significantly contributed to this project, for example, include Dalby (2008, 2014) and Dodds, Kuus and Sharp (2013).

22 Most notably John Law, Michel Serres and Gilles Deleuze (cf. Allen 2016, 17ff.).

23 These concepts have also been at the core of the Collaborative Research Centre (SFB) 1199 'Processes of Spatialization under the Global Condition', based at Leipzig University.

24 Shields defines spatialization as "the ongoing spatial organisation of all facets and scales of life, in the context of previously created spatial organisations to create a cultural formation that includes dispositions, representations and framings of the environment as a space of action. A 'spacing' of activities and ideas into 'places for this' and 'places for that'" (Shields 2013, 168).

25 Similar to space, which some have argued is best understood as a 'verb' rather than a 'noun', i.e., *to space/spacing*, something that is 'being done' or performed (Doel, referred to in Murdoch 2005, 18, 91).

26 In this context, speaking about 'imaginations' does not involve any judgements as to whether or not something is 'real'. Instead it refers to actors' perceptions, framings or sense-making efforts.

27 The notion of practice, employed in this book, follows the understanding of Adler and Pouliot (2011, 4–7), outlined above. Just to repeat briefly, practices are "socially meaningful patterns of action, which, in being performed more or less competently, simultaneously embody, act out, and possibly reify background knowledge and discourse in and on the material world" (Adler and Pouliot 2011, 4)

28 For initial steps in that direction, see Döring and Herpolsheimer (2018); Herpolsheimer (2018); and Engel (2020).

References

Abrahamsen, Rita. 2017. Africa and International Relations: Assembling Africa, Studying the World. *African Affairs* 116 (462): 125–39. doi: 10.1093/afraf/adw071.

Abrahamsen, Rita, and Michael C. Williams. 2009. Security Beyond the State: Global Security Assemblages in International Politics. *International Political Sociology* 3 (1): 1–17. doi: 10.1111/j.1749-5687.2008.00060.x.

———. 2011. *Security Beyond the State: Private Security in International Politics.* Cambridge: Cambridge University Press.

———. 2014. Tracing Global Assemblages, Bringing Bourdieu to the Field: A Conversation with Rita Abrahamsen and Michael Williams. In *Reassembling International Theory: Assemblage Thinking and International Relations*, eds Michele Acuto and Simon Curtis, 25–31. Basingstoke: Palgrave Macmillan.

Acuto, Michele and Simon Curtis, eds. 2014. *Reassembling International Theory: Assemblage Thinking and International Relations.* Basingstoke: Palgrave Macmillan.

Adamson, Fiona B. 2016. Spaces of Global Security: Beyond Methodological Nationalism. *Journal of Global Security Studies* 1 (1): 19–35. doi: 10.1093/jogss/ogv003.

Adebajo, Adekeye. 2002. *Building Peace in West Africa: Liberia, Sierra Leone, and Guinea-Bissau.* Boulder, CO: Lynne Rienner.

Adler, Emanuel. 2004. *Communitarian International Relations: The Epistemic Foundations of International Relations.* London: Routledge.

Adler, Emanuel and Vincent Pouliot. 2011. International Practices. *International Theory* 3 (1): 1–36. doi: 10.1017/S175297191000031X.

Adler-Nissen, Rebecca, ed. 2013. *Bourdieu in International Relations: Rethinking Key Concepts in IR.* London: Routledge; Taylor and Francis.

Adler-Nissen, Rebecca and Vincent Pouliot. 2014. Power in Practice: Negotiating the International Intervention in Libya. *European Journal of International Relations* 20 (4): 889–911. doi: 10.1177/1354066113512702.

Agnew, John. 1994. The Territorial Trap: The Geographical Assumptions of International Relations Theory. *Review of International Political Economy* 1 (1): 53–80. doi: 10.1080/09692299408434268.

Allen, John. 2011. Topological Twists: Power's Shifting Geographies. *Dialogues in Human Geography* 1 (3): 283–98. doi: 10.1177/2043820611421546.

———. 2016. *Topologies of Power: Beyond Territory and Networks.* London, New York: Routledge.

Autesserre, Séverine. 2014. *Peaceland: Conflict Resolution and the Everyday Politics of International Intervention.* Cambridge: Cambridge University Press.

———. 2016. The Responsibility to Protect in Congo: The Failure of Grassroots Prevention. *International Peacekeeping* 23 (1): 29–51. doi: 10.1080/13533312.2015.1080595.

Bachmann, Jan, Colleen Bell and Caroline Holmqvist, eds. 2016. *War, Police and Assemblages of Intervention.* London: Routledge.

Barnett, Michael N. and Martha Finnemore. 2004. *Rules for the World: International Organizations in Global Politics.* Ithaca, NY: Cornell University Press.

Baumann, Claudia, Antje Dietze and Megan Maruschke, eds. 2017. *Portals of Globalization in Africa, Asia, and Latin America.* Comparativ 27 (3/4). Leipzig: Leipziger Universitätsverlag.

Berling, Trine V. 2012. Bourdieu, International Relations, and European Security. *Theory and Society* 41 (5): 451–78. doi: 10.1007/s11186-012-9175-7.

Bigo, Didier and Mikael R. Madsen. 2011. Introduction to Symposium 'A Different Reading of the International': Pierre Bourdieu and International Studies. *International Political Sociology* 5 (3): 219–24. doi: 10.1111/j.1749-5687.2011.00131.x.

Björkdahl, Annika and Susanne Buckley-Zistel, eds. 2016. *Spatializing Peace and Conflict.* London: Palgrave Macmillan.

Björkdahl, Annika and Stefanie Kappler. 2017. *Peacebuilding and Spatial Transformation: Peace, Space and Place.* London, New York: Routledge.

Brenner, Neil. 1999. Beyond State-Centrism? Space, Territoriality, and Geographical Scale in Globalization Studies. *Theory and Society* 28 (1): 39–78. doi: 10.1023/A:1006996806674.

Brusset, Emery, Cedric de Coning and Bryn Hughes. 2016. *Complexity Thinking for Peacebuilding Practice and Evaluation.* London: Palgrave Macmillan.

Bueger, Christian. 2013. Communities of Security Practice at Work? The Emerging African Maritime Security Regime. *African Security* 6 (3–4): 297–316. doi: 10.1080/19392206.2013.853579.

———. 2017. Territory, Authority, Expertise: Global Governance and the Counter-Piracy Assemblage. *European Journal of International Relations* 46 (2): 1–24. doi: 10.1177/1354066117725155.

Bueger, Christian and Frank Gadinger. 2014. *International Practice Theory: New Perspectives.* Basingstoke: Palgrave Macmillan.

———. 2015. The Play of International Practice. *International Studies Quarterly* 59 (3): 449–60. doi: 10.1111/isqu.12202.

Callaghy, Thomas M., Ronald Kassimir and Robert Latham, eds. 2001. *Intervention and Transnationalism in Africa: Global-Local Networks of Power.* Cambridge: Cambridge University Press.

Charbonneau, Bruno. 2017. Whose 'West Africa'? The Regional Dynamics of Peace and Security. *Journal of Contemporary African Studies* 17 (2): 1–8. doi: 10.1080/02589001.2017.1365117.

Chojnacki, Sven and Bettina Engels. 2013. *Material Determinism and Beyond: Spatial Categories in the Study of Violent Conflict.* SFB-Governance Working Paper Series 55. Berlin: Sonderforschungsbereich (SFB) 700.

Dalby, Simon. 2008. Imperialism, Domination, Culture: The Continued Relevance of Critical Geopolitics. *Geopolitics* 13 (3): 413–36. doi: 10.1080/14650040802203679.

———. 2014. Rethinking Geopolitics: Climate Security in the Anthropocene. *Global Policy* 5 (1): 1–9. doi: 10.1111/1758–5899.12074.

de Coning, Cedric. 2016. From Peacebuilding to Sustaining Peace: Implications of Complexity for Resilience and Sustainability. *Resilience* 4 (3): 166–81. doi: 10.1080/21693293.2016.1153773.

———. 2018. Adaptive Peacebuilding. *International Affairs* 94 (2): 301–17. doi: 10.1093/ia/iix251.

DeLanda, Manuel. 2016. *Assemblage Theory.* Edinburgh: Edinburgh University Press.

Deleuze, Gilles and Félix Guattari. 2013 [1987]. *A Thousand Plateaus: Capitalism and Schizophrenia.* Bloomsbury Revelations. London: Bloomsbury Academic.

Der Derian, James. 1987. *On Diplomacy: A Genealogy of Western Estrangement.* Oxford: Basil Blackwell.

Dodds, Klaus, Merje Kuus and Joanne P. Sharp, eds. 2013. *The Ashgate Research Companion to Critical Geopolitics.* Burlington, VA: Ashgate.

Döring, Jörg and Tristan Thielmann. 2008a. Einleitung: Was lesen wir im Raume? Der Spatial Turn und das geheime Wissen der Geographen. In *Spatial Turn: Das Raumparadigma in den Kultur- und Sozialwissenschaften*, ed. Jörg Döring and Tristan Thielmann, 7–46. Bielefeld: Transcript.

———, eds. 2008b. *Spatial Turn: Das Raumparadigma in den Kultur- und Sozialwissenschaften.* Bielefeld: Transcript.

Döring, Katharina P.W. and Jens Herpolsheimer. 2017. Bringing Space into the Study of African Peace and Security Politics: Paper Presented at the Workshop 'African Security and Unbridled Militarization? New Approaches to African Peace and Security Governance', Uppsala, 22–24 November 2017.

———. 2018. The Spaces of Intervention for Mali and Guinea-Bissau. *South African Journal of International Affairs* 25 (1): 61–82. doi: 10.1080/10220461.2018.1417898.

Doty, Roxanne L. 1996. *Imperial Encounters: The Politics of Representation in North-South Relations.* Minneapolis, MN: University of Minnesota Press.

Doucet, Marc G. 2016. Global Assemblages of Security Governance and Contemporary International Intervention. *Journal of Intervention and Statebuilding* 10 (1): 116–32. doi: 10.1080/17502977.2015.1054656.

Engel, Ulf. 2017. Headquarters of International Organizations as Portals of Globalization: The African Union Commission and its Peace and Security Policies. *Comparativ* 27 (3–4). doi: 10.26014/j.comp.2017.03/04.09.

———. 2018. *Regionalismen.* Berlin: De Gruyter.

———. 2020. Peace-Building Through Space-Making: The Spatializing Effects of the African Union's Peace and Security Policies. *Journal of Intervention and Statebuilding* 14 (2): 221–36. doi: 10.1080/17502977.2020.1717132.

Engel, Ulf and Paul Nugent. 2009a. Introduction: The Spatial Turn in African Studies. In *Respacing Africa*, eds Ulf Engel and Paul Nugent, 1–9. Leiden: Brill.

———, eds. 2009b. *Respacing Africa.* Leiden: Brill.

Frowd, Philippe M. 2014. The Field of Border Control in Mauritania. *Security Dialogue* 45 (3): 226–41. doi: 10.1177/0967010614525001.

Frowd, Philippe M. and Adam J. Sandor. 2018. Militarism and its Limits: Sociological Insights on Security Assemblages in the Sahel. *Security Dialogue* 49 (1–2): 70–82. doi: 10.1177/0967010617739534.

Gambari, Ibrahim A. 1991. *Political and Comparative Dimensions of Regional Integration: The Case of ECOWAS.* Atlantic Highlands, NJ: Humanities Press International.

Geyer, Michael. 2010. Portals of Globalisation. In *The Plurality of Europe: Identities and Spaces*, eds Winfried Eberhard and Christian Lübke, 509–20. Leipzig: Leipziger Universitätsverlag.

Gregory, Derek. 1994. *Geographical Imaginations.* Cambridge, Oxford: Blackwell.

———. 1995. Imaginative Geographies. *Progress in Human Geography* 19 (4): 447–85. doi: 10.1177/030913259501900402.

Herpolsheimer, Jens. 2018. Transregional Conflicts and the Re-spatialisation of Regions 'At Sea': The Yaoundé Process in the Gulf of Guinea. *Comparativ* 28 (6): 68–89. doi: 10.26014/j.comp.2018.06.04.

Higate, Paul and Mats Utas, eds. 2017. *Private Security in Africa: From the Global Assemblage to the Everyday.* London: Zed Books.

Horner, Jed and John Rule. 2013. The Politics of Space and the Spatialisation of Politics: New Directions for Examining the Connections between Immigration and Contagion. *New Political Science* 35 (3): 463–78. doi: 10.1080/07393148.2013.813699.

Hudson, Heidi. 2016. Decolonising Gender and Peacebuilding: Feminist Frontiers and Border Thinking in Africa. *Peacebuilding* 4 (2): 194–209. doi: 10.1080/21647259.2016.1192242.

Ismail, Olawale. 2015. *Toward a Community of Practice: ECOWAS and Peace and Security Policy Communities in West Africa.* APN Working Papers 3: African Peacebuilding Network.

Jessop, Bob. 2016. Territory, Politics, Governance and Multispatial Metagovernance. *Territory, Politics, Governance* 4 (1): 8–32. doi: 10.1080/21622671.2015.1123173.

Jessop, Bob, Neil Brenner and Martin Jones. 2008. Theorizing Sociospatial Relations. *Environment and Planning D: Society and Space* 26 (3): 389–401. doi: 10.1068/d9107.

Kappler, Stefanie. 2015. The Dynamic Local: Delocalisation and (Re-)localisation in the Search for Peacebuilding Identity. *Third World Quarterly* 36 (5): 875–89. doi: 10.1080/01436597.2015.1025740.

Latham, Robert. 2001. Identifying the Contours of Transboundary Political Life. In *Intervention and Transnationalism in Africa: Global-Local Networks of Power*, eds Thomas M. Callaghy, Ronald Kassimir and Robert Latham, 69–92. Cambridge: Cambridge University Press.

Latham, Robert, Ronald Kassimir and Thomas M. Callaghy. 2001. Introduction: Transboundary Formations, Intervention, Order, and Authority. In *Intervention and Transnationalism in Africa: Global-Local Networks of Power*, eds Thomas M. Callaghy, Ronald Kassimir and Robert Latham, 1–20. Cambridge: Cambridge University Press.

Latour, Bruno. 2005. *Reassembling the Social: An Introduction to Actor-Network-Theory.* Oxford, New York: Oxford University Press.

Leander, Anna. 2011. The Promises, Problems, and Potentials of a Bourdieu-Inspired Staging of International Relations. *International Political Sociology* 5 (3): 294–313. doi: 10.1111/j.1749-5687.2011.00135.x.

Lefebvre, Henri. 2000 [1974]. *La Production de L'espace.* Paris: Anthropos.

Leonardsson, Hanna and Gustav Rudd. 2015. The 'Local Turn' in Peacebuilding: A Literature Review of Effective and Emancipatory Local Peacebuilding. *Third World Quarterly* 36 (5): 825–39. doi: 10.1080/01436597.2015.1029905.

Mac Ginty, Roger. 2011. *International Peacebuilding and Local Resistance: Hybrid Forms of Peace.* New York: Palgrave Macmillan.

———. 2015. Where is the Local? Critical Localism and Peacebuilding. *Third World Quarterly* 36 (5): 840–56. doi: 10.1080/01436597.2015.1045482.

———. 2017. A Material Turn in International Relations: The 4x4, Intervention and Resistance. *Review of International Studies* 43 (5): 855–74. doi: 10.1017/S0260210517000146.

Mac Ginty, Roger and Oliver P. Richmond. 2013. The Local Turn in Peace Building: A Critical Agenda for Peace. *Third World Quarterly* 34 (5): 763–83. doi: 10.1080/01436597.2013.800750.

Massey, Doreen B. 2005. *For Space.* Los Angeles, CA: SAGE.

Middell, Matthias. 2019. *Raumformate – Bausteine in Prozessen der Neuverräumlichung.* Working paper series des SFB 1199 an der Universität Leipzig 14. Leipzig: Leipziger Universitätsverlag.

Middell, Matthias and Katja Naumann. 2010. Global History and the Spatial Turn: From the Impact of Area Studies to the Study of Critical Junctures of Globalisation. *Journal of Global History* 5 (1): 1–22. doi: 10.1017/S1740022809990362.

Middell, Matthias and Ute Wardenga. 2019. Part III – Spatial Formats: Introduction. In *The Routledge Handbook of Transregional Studies*, ed. Matthias Middell, 147–50. London: Routledge.

Millar, Gearoid. 2018. Engaging Ethnographic Peace Research: Exploring an Approach. *International Peacekeeping* 25 (5): 597–609. doi: 10.1080/13533312.2018.1521700.

Murdoch, Jonathan. 2005. *Post-Structuralist Geography: A Guide to Relational Space.* London: SAGE.

Neumann, Iver B. 2002. Returning Practice to the Linguistic Turn: The Case of Diplomacy. *Millennium – Journal of International Studies* 31 (3): 627–51. doi: 10.1177/03058298020310031201.

Ó Tuathail, Gearóid. 1996. *Critical Geopolitics: The Politics of Writing Global Space.* Minneapolis, MN: University of Minnesota Press.

Olsson, Christian. 2015. Interventionism as Practice: On 'Ordinary Transgressions' and their Routinization. *Journal of Intervention and Statebuilding* 9 (4): 425–41. doi: 10.1080/17502977.2015.1089664.

Paffenholz, Thania. 2015. Unpacking the Local turn in Peacebuilding: A Critical Assessment Towards an Agenda for Future Research. *Third World Quarterly* 36 (5): 857–74. doi: 10.1080/01436597.2015.1029908.

Pomarède, Julien and Théa Schjødt. 2015. Security Identities and 'No More, No Less' Operations: On Making NATO's Involvement in Darfur Possible. *Journal of Intervention and Statebuilding* 9 (4): 495–518. doi: 10.1080/17502977.2015.1089665.

Pouliot, Vincent and Jérémie Cornut. 2015. Practice Theory and the Study of Diplomacy: A Research Agenda. *Cooperation and Conflict* 50 (3): 297–315. doi: 10.1177/0010836715574913.

Randazzo, Elisa. 2016. The Paradoxes of the 'Everyday': Scrutinising the Local Turn in Peace Building. *Third World Quarterly* 37 (8): 1351–70. doi: 10.1080/01436597.2015.1120154.

Richmond, Oliver P. 2012. *A Post-Liberal Peace.* London: Routledge.

———. 2018. Rescuing Peacebuilding? Anthropology and Peace Formation. *Global Society* 32 (2): 221–39. doi: 10.1080/13600826.2018.1451828.

Rigual, Christelle. 2018. Rethinking the Ontology of Peacebuilding: Gender, Spaces and the Limits of the Local Turn. *Peacebuilding* 6 (2): 144–69. doi: 10.1080/21647259.2018.1453640.

Sandor, Adam. 2016a. Assemblages of Intervention: Politics, Security, and Drug Trafficking in West Africa. Doctoral thesis, University of Ottawa.

———. 2016b. Border Security and Drug Trafficking in Senegal: AIRCOP and Global Security Assemblages. *Journal of Intervention and Statebuilding* 10 (4): 490–512. doi: 10.1080/17502977.2016.1240425.

Sapignoli, Maria and Ronald Niezen, eds. 2017. *Palaces of Hope: The Anthropology of Global Organizations.* Cambridge: Cambridge University Press.

Savigny, Eike von, Karin Knorr-Cetina and Theodore R. Schatzki, eds. 2001. *The Practice Turn in Contemporary Theory.* London: Routledge.

Shields, Rob. 2013. *Spatial Questions: Cultural Topologies and Social Spatialisations.* London, Thousand Oaks, CA: SAGE.

Simons, Claudia and Franzisca Zanker. 2014. *Questioning the Local in Peacebuilding.* Working Papers of the Priority Programme 1448 of the German Research Foundation 10. Leipzig and Halle: Leipzig University; University of Halle.

Thrift, Nigel. 1999. Steps to an Ecology of Place. In *Human Geography Today*, eds Doreen B. Massey, John Allen and Phil Sarre, 295–322. Cambridge: Polity Press.

———. 2009. Space: The Fundamental Stuff of Geography. In *Key Concepts in Geography*, eds N.J. Clifford, Sarah L. Holloway, Stephen P. Rice and Gill Valentine, 95–107. London: SAGE.

Tieku, Thomas K. 2016. *Governing Africa: 3D Analysis of the African Union's Performance.* Lanham, MD, Boulder, CO: Rowman & Littlefield.

van Walraven, Klaas. 1999. *Dreams of Power: The role of the Organization of African Unity in the Politics of Africa, 1963–1993.* Aldershot: Ashgate.

Warf, Barney and Santa Arias, eds. 2009. *The Spatial Turn: Interdisciplinary Perspectives.* Abingdon, New York: Routledge.

Wenger, Etienne. 1998. *Communities of Practice: Learning, Meaning, and Identity.* Cambridge: Cambridge University Press.

Werlen, Benno. 2009. Regionalisations, Everyday. In *The International Encyclopedia of Human Geography*, eds Rob Kitchin and Nigel Thrift, 286–93. Oxford: Oxford University Press.

Williams, Michael C. 2007. *Culture and Security: Symbolic Power and the Politics of International Security.* London: Routledge.

Witt, Antonia. 2013. The African Union and Contested Political Order(s). In *Towards an African Peace and Security Regime: Continental Embeddedness, Transnational Linkages, Strategic Relevance*, eds Ulf Engel and João G. Porto, 11–30. Farnham: Ashgate.

———. 2018. Studying African Interventions 'From Below': Exploring Practices, Knowledges and Perceptions. *South African Journal of International Affairs* 25 (1): 1–19. doi: 10.1080/10220461.2018.1417904.

———. 2020. *Undoing Coups: The African Union and Post-Coup Intervention in Madagascar.* London: Zed Books.

3 Establishing 'reach'

ECOWAS and AU intervention practices 'from afar'

Introduction

To date, African regional organizations (ROs), and ECOWAS and the AU in particular, have received most attention for their military peacekeeping efforts, earning them both praise and criticism (see Chapter 1). However, in this and following chapters, I argue that military and police deployments have been only one intervention practice among several important, interrelated practices employed by African ROs. Moreover, I argue that the actual conflict site has been only one of several important, interrelated sites at which conflict interventions have unfolded. Both become visible through a spatial approach, which in addition points to the spatializing effects of these intervention practices – essentially making them also spatializing practices.

A survey of official ECOWAS and AU documents, covering the period from 1998 to 2018, shows that both organizations have shown remarkable continuity in their engagement with different crises in West Africa and Africa respectively (see Chapter 1, Figures 1.1 and 1.2). While actors at the AU, historically, have taken a lower profile in interventions in West Africa, mostly letting ECOWAS actors take the lead, both have remained 'actively seized' of conflict situations in the region. While this standard phrase at the end of the communiqués of the AU Peace and Security Council (PSC), as well as of some final communiqués of the ECOWAS Authority, has been subject to some ridicule among practitioners,[1] it actually refers to a set of important basic intervention practices that actors at African ROs have actively performed and consolidated over time. Specifically, both organizations have continuously (i) produced conflict knowledge, (ii) met, discussed and decided ('internal' communication); (iii) publicly pronounced themselves ('external' communication); deployed field missions of (iv) diplomatic, (v) 'technical', as well as (vi) military or police nature; and (vii) strategically engaged other regional and international actors (e.g., different UN agencies and EU actors).[2] While some of these practices have been enacted 'on the ground', others have been enacted 'from afar', at sites other than the conflict site as such, for example, including organizational headquarters and summit venues.

To begin filling this gap, and analyzing intervention practices of African ROs and their spatializing effects more systematically, this and the following chapters take a detailed look at ECOWAS and AU practices. First of all, this chapter focuses on the headquarters of ECOWAS and the AU and affiliate locations (e.g., different meeting venues) as important intervention sites. Specifically, it scrutinizes the three main sets of interrelated and partly overlapping intervention practices performed 'from afar'. The following chapters focus on intervention practices 'on the ground' (Chapter 4) and on the strategic engagement of other regional and international actors (Chapter 6). While reflecting about intervention practices more generally, all of these chapters use ECOWAS and AU interventions in Guinea-Bissau (especially but not exclusively following the coup d'état in April 2012) to offer additional detail and explanation. This has the advantage of teasing out the simultaneity and complexity of multiple and entangled intervention practices performed by different actors at African ROs and their spatializing effects.

In that regard, this chapter argues that a spatial approach allows us to see and understand the central importance of several basic practices – which so far have been largely ignored or underestimated (e.g., considered as 'weak' or 'soft'). Three reasons in particular help to explain why they demand systematic and detailed attention nonetheless. First, the resources spent on these practices (e.g., time, money, personnel) are non-negligible and reflect high-level priorities. Second, employed in extremely complex settings, characterized by a multitude of interests, actors and interrelations among them, the practices discussed in this chapter are of key importance in 'sorting things out' (e.g., assessing, discussing, negotiating and coordinating interventions). Third, as moments of particularly 'dense' inter/action, they contribute in different ways to the construction of 'community' and regional spaces. Therefore, studying these practices will enhance the analysis and understanding of the inner workings of African ROs more generally and during conflict intervention in particular. Moreover, it will also allow disaggregating 'ECOWAS' and 'AU', identifying different actors 'within' them.

Producing conflict knowledge

A key practice that has been constitutive of both the legitimacy and autonomy as well as the agency of many international organizations is the privileged access to information and the production of specialized knowledge. On the one hand, this allows them to claim objective expertise and thus relevance and responsibility. On the other hand, it enables international organizations to frame problems and subsequently propose solutions. Thus, they are able to assess, frame and constitute reality (Barnett and Finnemore 2004).

Both ECOWAS and AU actors have actively contributed to producing conflict knowledge, both for internal use (e.g., analysis, briefs) and for external representation of the conflict (e.g., final communiqués, statements and press releases). Within both organizations, different actors, sources and ways of producing knowledge exist – some complementary, others not; some openly available, others confidential or secret (cf. Engel 2018, 119–21). The argument here is that this knowledge has played an important role influencing perceptions, framings and spatial imaginations of conflict. It has also influenced discussions and decisions on possible responses, and eventually guided interventions. Therefore, the following paragraphs analyze how actors at ECOWAS and the AU have produced conflict knowledge on conflict more generally and with regard to conflict in Guinea-Bissau in particular, and how this knowledge production has related to space-making.

Sites, channels and actors

Generally, in the AU as well as in ECOWAS, conflict-related knowledge is constructed at "multiple sites and institutions" (Engel 2018, 119), largely but not exclusively based on legal agreements among member states, using different sources and kinds of information as well as different procedures for their coordination and reconciliation (for the AU, cf. Engel 2018, 120–1).[3] Within the commissions of the two organizations, conflict knowledge is produced primarily by the AU Peace and Security Department (PSD) and the ECOWAS Department of Political Affairs, Peace and Security (DPAPS), and more recently the Office of the Vice President of the ECOWAS Commission. Both have early warning systems, the AU's Continental Early Warning System (CEWS) and the ECOWAS Warning and Response Network (ECOWARN), managed by the AU Conflict Prevention and Early Warning Division (CPEWD) and the ECOWAS Early Warning Directorate (EWD), respectively.[4] Established through the Protocol Relating to the Establishment of the PSC (the PSC Protocol, 2002), the operationalization of CEWS started in 2007. Since 2009/10 it has been fully operational (cf. Wane et al. 2010). ECOWARN, established through the ECOWAS Protocol Relating to the Mechanism for Conflict Prevention, Management, Resolution, Peace-Keeping and Security (the 1999 Mechanism), started implementation in 2003, in collaboration with the West African Network for Peacebuilding, a civil society organization (cf. WANEP 2019), and with support from the US Agency for International Development (cf. Lewis and Shinoda 2012, 8–9). Using specialized software, both systems largely draw on open-source information, such as, for example, online media and news agencies. In addition, ECOWARN also draws on more than 70 field monitors, spread across West Africa (on CEWS, e.g., cf. Wane et al. 2010; on ECOWARN, e.g., cf. Lewis and Shinoda 2012).

However, other departments (e.g., Social, Political or Gender Affairs) may and sometimes do engage in collecting information that is directly or indirectly linked to conflict (e.g., democratic governance, health and migration; cf. Engel 2018, 121). In addition, at the AU, a Committee of Intelligence and Security Services of Africa (CISSA), established in 2004 and formally endorsed by the AU Assembly in 2005, provides intelligence-based information to the AUC, through the Intelligence and Security Committee (ISC), located in the Office of the AUC Chairperson (cf. CISSA 2019). The ISC has the task to reconcile information coming from different sources and channels. All these mechanisms (as well as additional and planned ones) are continuously evolving (Engel 2018, 121). Similarly at ECOWAS, several additional mechanisms and organs exist, which in principle may also produce specialized conflict knowledge (e.g., Committee of Chiefs of Security Services, West African Police Chiefs Committee).

In addition to institutional structures, conflict knowledge is generated through assessment missions at different levels (e.g., 'technical' and 'political', commission staff and members of different organs) as well as through the dispatch of special envoys or special representatives, and the establishment of liaison offices (see Chapter 4). Structurally, these envoys and representatives are attached to the offices of the ECOWAS Commission President and the AUC Chairperson respectively. In the case of the AU, the liaison offices also link to the AU Commission through the respective desk officers of the Conflict Management and Post-Conflict Reconstruction and Development Division (CMPCRD). Therefore, while information (e.g., reports and memos) coming through these channels may also flow to early warning staff, it is not necessarily automatically shared among all AU PSD and ECOWAS DPAPS staff working on a specific conflict situation.[5]

Through these contacts, the AUC Chairperson and the AU Commissioner for Peace and Security as well as the President of the ECOWAS Commission and the ECOWAS PAPS Commissioner (CPAPS) formally and informally access privileged information, adding to their personal networks. These multiple sites and channels are further complemented (or competing) with intelligence gathered by and sometimes shared among member states, as well as information and knowledge provided by other international and regional actors (for the AU, cf. Engel 2018, 120–1). Here, EU and UN actors play particularly important roles. However, others also significantly influence these processes, including Africa-based think tanks (cf. Engel 2020).

The conflict-related information so gathered is communicated in the form of field or mission reports, inter-office memoranda or simply in personal calls and conversations. If not directly consumed by top-level officials or member states' representatives, it is analyzed and processed by desk officers, synthesizing information coming from different sources, again producing reports, memos and briefings. These feed into the head offices of the commissions, and eventually, directly or indirectly, through the head offices, into the main decision making bodies and structures of ECOWAS and the AU. Included in these reports and briefs are usually a summary of main events, an overview of the acts and positions of the main conflict actors (local and international), followed by some analysis, as well as scenario building and recommendations. Overall, actors at ECOWAS and the AU, assisted by development partners, have devoted considerable effort and resources into practices of information gathering and knowledge production.[6]

Ultimately, these 'internal' stages of knowledge production turn 'public' or 'external' in the form of press releases, communiqués, statements and declarations (i.e., public pronouncements) or annual reports. In the public pronouncements following the meetings of the decision making bodies, a selection of the available information usually translates into short references to key events, specific positions adopted by those bodies (e.g., support or rejection) and calls for specific actions by different stakeholders (see below). However, it is very difficult to assess exactly how and to what extent these inputs actually influence decision making, as well as which of the other channels of information have played a role.[7] While these pronouncements have other functions as well (see below), they produce an official version of conflict knowledge that is communicated to stakeholders in the conflicts and a more general 'outside' or public (e.g., including international media, researchers, donors and policy makers).

ECOWAS and AU knowledge production on conflict in Guinea-Bissau

To illustrate these points, reacting to the conflict in Guinea-Bissau, in 2012, actors at ECOWAS and the AU used established sources and channels of information. Drawing on information from their early warning systems, several field missions, as well as their respective special representatives and liaison offices in Guinea-Bissau (see Chapter 4), AU and ECOWAS analysts and desk officers produced numerous reports (e.g., early warning, mission and update) and policy briefs. Here, it is important to note that a considerable overlap exists, as AU staff (at CEWS and in CMPCRD) rely heavily on information they get from ECOWAS staff, whom they frequently email, call, or, less frequently but regularly, meet. ECOWAS actors are commonly considered to be 'closer', holding more intimate and direct knowledge (e.g., due to their field monitors and cultural similarities). This perception is held by AU staff, but also actively promoted by ECOWAS staff, claiming expertise for West Africa.[8] The briefings and reports, subsequently, fed into briefings by top-level officials of both organizations (e.g., the ECOWAS Commission President, AUC Chairperson, commissioners and directors) at every meeting of the AU and ECOWAS decision making bodies, in particular the ECOWAS Authority and the AU Assembly (both summits of the respective heads of state and government) as well as the ECOWAS Mediation and Security Council (MSC) and the AU Peace and Security Council (PSC). These briefings, along with written reports, form the basis of discussions among member states (see below). In addition, representatives of specific member states have also briefed. For example, this has included the rotating chairs of different organs, such as the ECOWAS Committee of Chiefs of Defense Staff (CCDS), or the chairs of international contact groups.[9]

Due to confidentiality procedures – sessions of the MSC and PSC are usually closed and many reports classified[10] – it is very difficult to account for the full content, detail and complexity of knowledge being produced, flowing and circulating among the different actors and organs within ECOWAS and the AU. Even more difficult is any assessment of how this knowledge may have linked to decisions and eventually action taken by the two organizations. Nevertheless, judging from publicly available communiqués and reports (e.g., AUC Chairperson reports, Annual Reports of the ECOWAS Commission), combined with staff interviews, at least final declarations and press releases on Guinea-Bissau in 2012 have generally reflected the knowledge produced in reports and briefs by analysts and staff of field offices. For the AU, this is evident when comparing reports on Guinea-Bissau by the AUC Chairperson to the PSC Communiqués (e.g., cf. AUC Chairperson 2012; AU PSC 2012a; AUC Chairperson 2013; AU PSC 2013). For ECOWAS, no such reports are publicly accessible; nevertheless, interviews suggest a similar conclusion.[11]

However, drawing on publicly available and published documents comes with the complication that it fuses knowledge production with its dissemination – two stages and sets of practices that I would like to keep apart analytically, although they are empirically intertwined. Therefore, and to avoid repetition, I will discuss the knowledge and messages contained therein not here, but below, in the section "Making public pronouncements". Similarly, I will not go into detail on the grand themes of knowledge on conflict in Guinea-Bissau – namely 'political instability' and to a lesser extent the 'narco-state' – as these are the subject of Chapter 5 in the context of spatial imaginations and narrative framings of conflict in West Africa. In very general terms, knowledge produced on conflict in Guinea-Bissau has focused mostly on 'internal' political dynamics in Guinea-Bissau, referring to key events and constellations of actors and interests, including particular attention to the role of the military, stressing the need to return to 'constitutional order' and for defense and security sector reform (DSSR).[12] In addition, action taken by other regional and international actors (especially ECOWAS, the AU, the CPLP and the UN) has played an important role in particular with regard to how these actions have related to efforts by ECOWAS and the AU (e.g., AUC Chairperson 2012, 2–5, 2013, 1–3, 2014; ECOWAS Commission President 2012, 2015; AU 2013).

Interestingly, a certain tension exists between knowledge held by staff (i.e., circulating 'internally') and knowledge produced and communicated in official texts. In interviews and personal communication, many staffers put stronger emphasis on Guinea-Bissau as a 'failed state' and the role and significance of drug trafficking – something that finds almost no reference in ECOWAS documents (especially 2012 and following years), and only short and rather general mention in AU documents, including internal briefs and reports (in the same period). This observation points to at least two important aspects of the complex dynamics around the production of conflict knowledge within these organizations. First, a certain degree of self-censorship on behalf of analysts and desk officers (or their superiors), as their analyses have to take into account member states' sensitivities. Of course, this is even more relevant in publicly available documents.[13] Second, lines between different sources and actors of knowledge production blur during the process, among other things, making it hard to distinguish between knowledge produced within and between ECOWAS and the AU, as well as 'external' actors, most importantly EU and UN actors, providing information and exerting influence through formal (e.g., regular meetings) and informal channels (e.g., personal relationships).

More recently, since the deadlock between the president and the parliament, as well as the PAIGC leadership, that emerged in August 2015, analyses have also identified Guinea-Bissau's constitution and linked institutions as problematic, and in need of reform, especially its semi-presidential system and the dominant role of the PAIGC. Whereas earlier references to a 'constitutional crisis' in Guinea-Bissau referred to the coup and military transition as 'unconstitutional', now it is the constitution as such, and different interpretations about what exactly is 'constitutional' that actors at ECOWAS, the AU, as well as at the EU and UN have framed as a problem.[14] Consequently and because of the seeming restraint shown by Guinea-Bissau's military actors more recently, ECOWAS and AU staff, as well as member states, have increasingly reframed the crisis in Guinea-Bissau as a 'political problem', as opposed to the previous 'military' one. Especially within ECOWAS, this shift went along with calls to withdraw ECOMIB growing louder, as a military mission was no longer required to solve what now was only a 'political problem' (see also Chapter 4).[15] That change clearly points to the importance of conflict-related knowledge in framing and co-constituting reality, as it presents conflict situations in a specific way and offers specific guidance and options on how to act upon it.

The production of conflict knowledge and space-making

The knowledge that ECOWAS and AU actors produce about different conflict situations enables them to grasp what is going on,[16] making them accessible, assessable, knowable and communicable and actionable (see below). In other words, based on this knowledge, different actors at the AU and ECOWAS discuss these situations during various meetings (see "Meeting, debating, deciding action" below) and make pronouncements (see "Making public pronouncements" below). Therefore, although not in any definite nor mechanical manner, it forms the backdrop against which AU and ECOWAS actors respond to conflicts in their respective regions.

Closely related to these observations, I argue that the conflict-related knowledge and its different functions also directly link and contribute to space-making in West/Africa. First of all, as pointed out in more detail in Chapter 5, AU and ECOWAS conflict knowledge has fed into the co-production of particular spatial imaginations, for example, the general framings of conflict in Guinea-Bissau (and elsewhere) as a transnational, regional and trans-regional threat, due to its 'political instability' and its links to 'transnational organized crime', in particular illicit drug trafficking. At the basis of both framings and conflict knowledge produced on Guinea-Bissau, more generally, stand two specific spatial formats, namely the 'nation state' and the 'region'. Whereas the former is considered 'out of order' or 'threatened', the latter claims to be committed to assisting in restablishing a 'functioning' member of the West African state community. Thus, the production of knowledge on conflict in Guinea-Bissau has contributed to understanding its spatial dimensions and to spatially framing the conflict – most importantly as a threat for 'regional stability' (see Chapter 5).

Second, and equally important, collecting and processing information from various sources and through different channels means bringing 'local' knowledge or at least knowledge about 'local' conflict to the regional scale. Thereby, it contributes to raising awareness among member states and other regional actors, sensitizing them about both conflict in one of their fellow member states as well as their mutual regional belonging. At the same time, by categorizing that knowledge and linking it to established legal texts and procedures, it also creates legitimacy and responsibility for the region to act or at least 'care'. Thereby, the production of conflict-related knowledge by AU and ECOWAS actors makes an important contribution to constructing the respective 'regions', by creating awareness (or even 'identity', cf. Neumann 2003).

While this knowledge production starts out 'technical' and 'objective', with subsequent stages of processing, culminating in public pronouncements, it becomes increasingly involved in ECOWAS and AU politics towards regional conflicts. Therefore, the following sections take closer looks at these stages.

Meeting, debating, deciding action

A well-known criticism sometimes advanced against international or regional organizations is their tendency to meet and discuss, while often nothing much tangible seems to come out of it (i.e., calling these organizations mere talk shops; e.g., cf. Allison 2014). Moreover, some observers have criticized African regional organizations as clubs of heads of state (or, even worse, autocrats and dictators; e.g., Fritzon 2015; Mhaka 2018), whose only goal was to mutually bolster their regimes or personal power.[17] Although some of this criticism is certainly warranted, the argument advanced in the following runs partly counter to such perspectives. While neither replacing nor precluding other actions, meetings are in themselves an important practice that needs analytic scholarly attention.[18]

First of all, especially when involving top-level politicians or representatives of international or regional organizations, planning, organizing and convening meetings consumes a lot of resources, with respect to time, money and personnel.[19] This fact alone indicates relevance and importance of this common practice, and consequently warrants closer attention to actors and processes involved in them (cf. Mace et al. 2016, 3–4; Melissen 2003, 16–17). However, second, some scholars have argued for the importance of meetings at an even more fundamental level, as they constitute the "social action through which institutions produce and reproduce themselves" (Boden 1994, 81), generate appearance of reason and logical process, but really "facilitate relationship negotiations, struggle, and commentary" (Schwartzman 1989, 42) and present the organization as an entity to its members, negotiating who they are, both as individuals and as a group (Schwartzman 1989).[20]

Therefore, this section takes a closer look at meeting practices at ECOWAS and the AU. My primary concern here is to identify meetings, in particular but not only at higher levels (i.e., ambassadors, ministers and heads of state) as a key practice of African ROs, with regard to African peace and security dynamics and specifically conflict interventions. To this end, following a more general description of ECOWAS and AU meeting practices, this section reflects upon the frequency, types and contents of meetings that have dealt with conflict in Guinea-Bissau after the coup of April 2012. Finally, the section analyzes how these meeting practices have related to space-making.

As already pointed out in Chapter 1, access to information about meetings of different ECOWAS and AU organs is greatly unequal. Therefore, the following concentrates on meetings of the AU PSC and Assembly, as well as the ECOWAS MSC and Authority, for which relatively consistent information has been available, despite some remaining gaps. Meetings of specialized and/or 'technical' organs as well as at different sub-levels of the commissions, both formal and informal, are covered only in a general fashion.

Meeting practices at ECOWAS and the AU

Within the AU, the Constitutive Act (2000) and the PSC Protocol (2002) provide the main textual basis for meeting practices when it comes to dealing with African peace and security concerns.[21] In addition, guiding instruments, such as the African Charter on Democracy, Elections and Governance (of 2007), have clarified underlying norms and principles. The PSC Protocol identifies the main responsible organs, but only to a limited extent how exactly they relate to one another. While some scholarly attention has focused on their set-up, on paper, and assessed their implementation (e.g., Williams 2009; Engel 2016), the following paragraphs begin analyzing how these meetings and relations among them have played out in practice.

In general, actors at the AU deal with political issues at three levels with increasing authority. The AU's Permanent Representatives Committee (PRC, ambassadors accredited to Addis Ababa), and various sub-committees thereof, have come to take care of day-to-day political decisions at the AU, representing the member states (cf. Tieku 2019). The PRC meets at least once a month in ordinary and extraordinary sessions, acting on behalf of and reporting to the AU Executive Council (foreign affairs ministers). Some have interpreted the strong role of the PRC in everyday AU business as a relative loss of power for the AU Assembly (heads of state and government) (cf. Tieku 2019). However, it might also indicate a relative neglect or disinterest of African heads of state in the AU, especially when compared to the high degree of direct engagement by West African heads of state and government in ECOWAS day-to-day business (see below).

Meetings of the Executive Council precede and prepare the AU Assembly, which usually convenes immediately after the Council in ordinary sessions. Extraordinary sessions are much less frequent (e.g., recently on the African Continental Free Trade Area). To date, 11 such extraordinary sessions have taken place, complementing 31 ordinary ones.[22] For issues relating to African peace and security dynamics, however, the AU has a specialized mechanism, which is the AU PSC, which, depending on the situation at hand, holds sessions at the levels of ambassadors, foreign affairs ministers and, less often, heads of state and government (presidential). Among other issues, the PSC deals with active conflict situations (see Figure 3.1), and reports to the Assembly on its activities once or twice a year. On security issues, a Specialized Technical Committee on Defense, Safety and Security (STCDSS) also supports the Executive Council. The STCDSS comprises experts and sectoral ministers, supposedly meeting once a year. However, the STCDSS only deals with thematic issues (e.g., implementation of the African Standby Force), and does not meet and discuss on active conflicts. The following paragraphs, therefore, focus on the PSC.

The AU PSC began its work in May 2004. However, it took several years, until about 2010, to develop adequate procedures and a more consistent approach reacting to crises and conflicts on the continent (e.g., Dersso 2013; Engel 2012). The PSC constitutes an institutionalized meeting, with a rotating chair, supported by the PSC Secretariat, which is located at the AU Commission within the AU PSD. The 15 seats on the PSC rotate among AU member states according to regional quota (i.e., two from the 'North', three each from 'East', 'South' and 'Central Africa', and four from 'West Africa'). In principle, the AU Executive Council elects and the Assembly endorses five PSC members for a three-year term and ten for a term of two years, all of them renewable infinitely (cf. AU 2002, Art. 5). However, in practice, who takes a seat on the PSC is subject to negotiations within the regional groupings. While open in principle, some states are set based on informal agreements. In particular, Nigeria and South Africa have always had a seat on the PSC – the latter with the sole exception of 2012–14, when it left its seat to Angola, most tellingly during the crisis in Guinea-Bissau, which involved the Angolan government as a stakeholder.[23]

Algeria has been a member of the PSC most of the time – with the exception of between April 2010 and April 2013, when it left its seat to Mauritania. More recently, in April 2018, Morocco for the first time took a seat on the PSC, serving together with Egypt, finishing a three-year term (cf. AU Commission and New Zealand Crown 2019, 72–3). In Northern Africa, Egypt and Libya have taken turns serving on the PSC. In Central Africa, Cameroon and Congo Republic, until 2016, have taken turns, with Chad and Burundi, Gabon (2005–10) and Equatorial Guinea (2010–16) filling the third spot. Since 2016, Burundi and Chad have served together with Congo

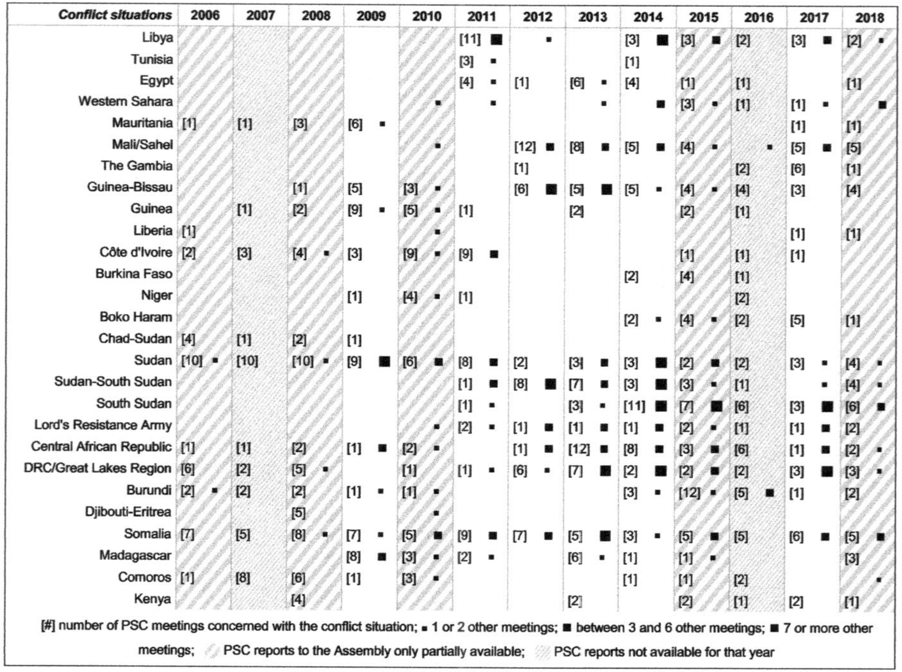

Figure 3.1 AU PSC Meetings and other meetings of AU actors on conflict situations, 2006–18

Notes: This is an exploratory mapping. Counting has been based on available documents and information provided therein only (see Chapter 1); actual numbers may therefore be higher than indicated in this figure. For a detailed discussion of the challenges and limitations of quantifying ECOWAS and AU intervention practices, see Herpolsheimer and Warnck (2020).

Source: *(cc) BY-NC-ND Jens Herpolsheimer, Skollan Elisabeth Warnck*

Republic. Since 2018, Congo Republic has served together with Gabon and Equatorial Guinea. The Democratic Republic of Congo has never served on the PSC. In Eastern Africa, Ethiopia held a seat on the PSC for the first six years (2004–10). Since then, the rotation among members of the East African grouping has been completely open.[24]

Most of the time, the AU PSC convenes at the level of ambassadors, less frequently at the level of foreign ministers. Only if special circumstances call for it, the PSC meets at the level of heads of state and government.[25] It does not hold 'extraordinary' sessions (contrary to the ECOWAS MSC; see below), but convenes "continuously" (AU 2002, Art. 8.1) – ambassadors meet at least twice a month, often much more frequently. Effectively supported by the PSC Commissioner and PSD staff, the AUC Chairperson and PSC member states may bring up issues and put them on the agenda whenever they arise (cf. AU 2002, Art. 8.7). A particular role belongs to the PSC Chair of the time, who is supposed to guide and facilitate discussions. In practice, the extent to which this role is played varies depending on interest and capacity of the respective chair (cf. Dersso 2013, 14). In principle, no one can oppose the inclusion of a particular issue on the agenda (AU 2002, Art. 8.7). In reality, however, some situations never make it onto the PSC agenda (e.g., critical events in Nigeria and South Africa). The Assembly endorses decisions taken by the PSC, unless controversies persist and are put on the agenda of the summits (cf. Dersso 2013).

Normally, the PSC considers active conflicts in closed-door sessions and informal consultations. It takes decisions by consensus, although theoretically it may resolve controversial issues by adopting a decision with a majority of two-thirds. PSC member states or other AU member states that are party to a conflict situation under consideration may present their case, if invited to do so, but otherwise may not participate in discussion and decision making (AU 2002, para. 8.9). In the decision making of the PSC, state representatives from the region where conflict occurs usually take the lead, supposedly representing a regional position.[26] However, very little is known about how exactly the PSC reaches its decisions. Depending on the situation, dynamics within the PSC may be anything but straightforward. For example, Dersso (2016) provides an interesting example. Analyzing the dynamics around the crisis in Burundi in 2015/16, he describes how the PSC took a groundbreaking decision at ministerial level – for the very first time invoking Article 4(h) of the AU Constitutive Act, authorizing the organization to intervene in member states in cases of 'grave circumstances'. However, revisiting the issue at the level of heads of state, the PSC subsequently overturned the decision previously taken at the ministerial level. Nevertheless, testifying to the agency of the AU Commission, the Commissioner for Peace and Security, Smaïl Chergui, brought the issue back on the agenda during the session of the AU Assembly, where it was eventually voted down (Dersso 2016). The PSC dynamics around the crisis in Guinea-Bissau in 2012/13 present another interesting example, showing that national and regional controversies may unfold during sessions, influencing the decision making in sometimes unexpected or untransparent ways (see below).

Within ECOWAS, meeting practices with respect to regional conflicts, as we can observe them today, emerged in the late 1990s and early 2000s, and have consolidated since then. Those practices, and the relevant organs, are based on the Revised ECOWAS Treaty (1993), the 1999 Mechanism, the Supplementary Protocol on Democracy and Good Governance (short 2001 Supplementary Protocol), as well as the ECOWAS Conflict Prevention Framework (ECPF, 2008). These documents lay down the tasks, principles and procedures of the different organs and mechanisms that are responsible for dealing with matters of peace and security within the ECOWAS region. As these documents have been subject to some academic scrutiny (e.g., cf. Hartmann 2013; Aggad and Miyandazi 2017), I will not go into detail about what they say. Instead, I will focus on actual practice, as it has emerged in relation to ECOWAS conflict intervention since the 1990s.

In very general terms, meetings of the Council of Ministers usually precede meetings of the Authority (immediately, or by a month or two), which on average take place twice a year, unless extraordinary circumstances require otherwise. Issues that require decisions move from lower levels of authority (issuing recommendations) to higher ones, starting from the commission or some of the 'technical' organs (e.g., CCDS), and subsequently moving to the different levels of the ECOWAS MSC and to the Authority. During that procedure, political issues are cleared on their way up, to the extent that this is possible, to facilitate summits that run as smoothly as possible. In practice, however, the different hierarchical levels are somewhat overlapping, and in some cases ECOWAS member state representatives decide to jump a step or go directly to the highest level, the heads of state and government. For example, issues frequently jump the MSC at ambassadorial level, going directly to the ministerial level, and in some cases straight to the presidential level.[27] In fact, unless explicitly identified as 'ambassadorial', 'MSC' normally refers to meetings at the ministerial level, sometimes coinciding with meetings of the Council of Ministers. Meetings at the presidential level take place during summits, the 'MSC' being only a different session (or time slot) on the same occasion, at the same location and featuring the same participants (see Figure 3.2). Therefore, the documents of the Council of Ministers rarely touch upon security issues, as ministerial MSC sessions cover those; on the other hand, documents of the Authority do, as it doubles as the MSC at presidential level.[28]

During political and/or military crises, ECOWAS has developed a practice of frequent extraordinary meetings, whenever a situation requires it, especially by the Authority (posing as the MSC at presidential level), sometimes called 'emergency' or convened as 'mini' summits, if not all ECOWAS member states can or want to participate. Often such emergency meetings take place at the Abuja airport, where member states' representatives fly in, meet and discuss, and fly off again. Sometimes they occur at the margins of other events that

Conflict situations	2000	2001	2002	2003	2004	2005	2006	2007	2008	2009	2010	2011	2012	2013	2014	2015	2016	2017	2018
Cabo Verde																	[2]		
Senegal	[1]												[2]	[1]					[1]
The Gambia																	[2]	[2]	[3]
Guinea-Bissau	[2]	[1]					[1]	[1]	[2]	[1]	[3]	[1]	[5]	[4]	[3]	[4]	[2]	[3]	[4]
Guinea								[1]	[2]	[1]	[2]	[1]		[2]	[3]	[4]			
Sierra Leone	[3]	[1]		[1]			[1]	[1]	[1]					[1]				[1]	
Liberia		[1]	[1]	[2]			[1]	[1]				[1]					[1]	[2]	[1]
Côte d'Ivoire	[2]	[1]	[1]	[3]	[1]	[1]	[2]	[1]	[2]	[1]	[4]	[2]			[3]	[4]			
Mano River Region	[2]	[1]		[1]									[1]						
Burkina Faso														[1]	[3]	[4]	[2]	[1]	
Ghana									[1]					[1]			[2]	[1]	
Togo						[1]	[1]	[1]		[1]	[2]			[2]	[3]	[1]		[1]	[2]
Benin							[1]												
Nigeria									[1]						[3]	[1]			[1]
Boko Haram													[1]		[2]	[2]	[2]	[1]	[2]
Niger										[1]	[2]	[1]					[1]		
Mali/Sahel									[2]	[1]			[6]	[4]	[3]	[2]	[2]	[2]	[2]

[#] number of Authority meetings concerned with the conflict situation

Figure 3.2 Meetings of the ECOWAS Authority on conflict situations, 2000–18

Notes: This is an exploratory mapping. Counting has been based on available documents and information provided therein only (see Chapter 1); actual numbers may therefore be higher than indicated in this figure. For a detailed discussion of the challenges and limitations of quantifying ECOWAS and AU intervention practices, see Herpolsheimer and Warnck (2020).

Source: *(cc) BY-NC-ND Jens Herpolsheimer, Skollan Elisabeth Warnck*

bring together a sufficient number of ECOWAS members' representatives.[29] During those 'extraordinary' periods, the Council of Ministers takes care of 'ordinary' business (i.e., 'non-security-related'), as heads of state sometimes meet more often in extraordinary sessions than in ordinary ones (e.g., in 2010, 2012 and 2013). Likewise, the MSC at ministerial level and the CCDS have also held extraordinary sessions, whenever they were deemed necessary.[30]

Originally, according to the 1999 Protocol, the MSC was supposed to comprise only nine out of the 15 ECOWAS member states, with a rotating membership. In practice, however, member state governments decided to include everyone, since important decisions, sometimes infringing on their sovereignty, should be taken by the entire community and by consensus, as opposed to the two-thirds majority stipulated in the 1999 Protocol.[31] Consequently, contrary to AU practice, even representatives of states that are the target of ECOWAS action, host to conflict situations and sometimes a party to the conflict participate during debates.

These meetings of different actors and organs within ECOWAS and the AU normally follow a clear and very similar procedure. They usually start with opening statements, then consider reports, briefs and statements, before exchanging views, and if possible find common ground on which to base authoritative decisions. Actual controversial discussion, however, does not necessarily take place during these sessions. Often, contentious issues come up already before the meeting. Commission staff, the respective chair and other member states may then work to resolve them beforehand. If controversial aspects emerge during sessions, participants leave them open, discussing and negotiating them afterwards. Sometimes, this may take weeks and a lot of effort to facilitate a common position, reflected in the final documents.[32]

These meetings of political decision making organs are prepared and complemented by various formal 'technical' meetings at the commissions of ECOWAS and the AU. This includes regular staff meetings at the levels of directorates, divisions and units. However, it also includes several inter-office (or inter-agency) meetings, platforms or taskforces, which aim to enhance communication and coordination among different actors within ECOWAS and the AU.[33] Commission staff prepare all documents for sessions of both 'technical' and 'political' organs – drafting, circulating and if necessary re-drafting them – including the agenda, briefs, memos and reports, as well as final reports, communiqués or declarations, and sometimes resolutions or regulations. While member states' representatives are continuously consulted throughout the entire process, commission staff hold significant agency and may work with the respective rotating chairs to achieve specific objectives (e.g., to include a certain formulation in a communiqué or to lend weight to a specific agenda item).[34]

Moreover, in addition to the various formal and institutionalized meetings and settings discussed so far, informal meetings and *ad hoc* meetings also play a role. While dependent on personal relationships, it is common for staff at the headquarters to share information, discuss and coordinate informally at all levels. This may involve calling a colleague at another sub-division by phone, or simply stopping by her or his office; however, it may also happen during lunch time at the cafeteria, or during meetings on completely different subjects (e.g., workshops), at organizational headquarters or other places.[35] By their nature, these kinds of exchanges are hard to assess, for example, regarding their frequency, contents and relative importance. More easy to assess are *ad hoc* meetings, at least when focusing on specific instances. Among the most important, in this regard, have been meetings of international contact groups (ICGs), among many other participants, including several ECOWAS and AU representatives, and, in the case of ECOWAS, regional contact groups (RCGs), which have been formed in response to specific conflict situations. Both ICGs and RCGs have been means to intervene 'on the ground' (see Chapters 4 and 6) and 'from afar' (see below, and Chapter 6).

Meetings that discussed conflict in Guinea-Bissau in 2012

In ECOWAS and AU responses to the crisis ensuing from the coup d'état of April 2012 in Guinea-Bissau, meetings have played a key role. This has been with regard to (i) 'internal' debate and organization, to (ii) the interaction between the political actors of Guinea-Bissau and the two regional organizations, as well as to (iii) the interactions between ECOWAS, the AU and other regional and international actors (dealt with in more detail in Chapter 6).

In particular, ECOWAS actors have shown a remarkable intensity and frequency of meetings on Guinea-Bissau throughout 2012 and early 2013 – mostly as a double issue together with the developing situation in Mali – which stands out both against previous and subsequent periods. Between March 2012 and March 2013 alone, member state representatives held six extraordinary sessions of the MSC at ministerial level, and five extraordinary summits that discussed the developing situation in Guinea-Bissau, some of them in a 'mini' constellation, all simultaneously passing off as the MSC at the presidential level.[36] This way of reacting to an active crisis has not been new for ECOWAS. For example, the conflict in Côte d'Ivoire in 2010–11 triggered a similar engagement.

In addition, during the same period, the situation in Guinea-Bissau was discussed during two ordinary summits, and at least two extraordinary sessions of the ECOWAS CCDS (cf. ECOWAS Commission 2012a, para. 280).[37] Moreover, several meetings took place in the formats of a Regional Contact Group for Guinea-Bissau (RCG-GB), an International Contact Group for Guinea-Bissau (ICG-GB), as well as in the context of an *ad hoc* consultation framework involving actors from ECOWAS, the AU, UN and CPLP (see Chapter 6). 'Guinea-Bissau' has also been a persistent item on the agenda of almost every staff meeting, as well as the topic of many informal contacts and conversations.[38] After March 2013, ECOWAS organs went back to treating Guinea-Bissau mostly during ordinary sessions, as they had done before the coup in April 2012. Since the war of 1998/9, the intensity of debates on Guinea-Bissau has closely related to the conjuncture of political crises, violence and coups in Guinea-Bissau. However, neither the coup d'état in September 2003, removing then-President Kumba Yalá from office, nor the double assassination of then-President João Bernardo ("Nino") Vieira and the Chief of the Armed Forces General Batista Tagme Na Waie in March 2009, triggered a similar rise in attention to Guinea-Bissau during ECOWAS meetings, especially during extraordinary sessions.[39]

During these meetings – mostly taking place in Côte d'Ivoire (Abidjan and Yamoussoukro), due to the country's chairmanship at the time, as well as in Abuja[40] – ECOWAS heads of state, foreign affairs ministers, ministers of defense and chiefs of defense staff discussed the situation in Bissau, as well as possible steps towards its resolution.[41] Discussions by the Authority and the MSC at ministerial level were based on briefings provided by the President of the ECOWAS Commission, Kadré Désiré Ouédraogo, later on complemented by reports by the ECOWAS Mediator, Alpha Condé (President of Guinea-Conakry), the Chair of the RCG-GB, Goodluck Jonathan (President of Nigeria, or some representative of his), as well as the Chair of the CCDS, Lieutenant-General Soumaila Bakayoko (from Côte d'Ivoire). As the main elements of the discussions, as well as decisions taken are presented below (see also Chapter 4), suffice it to highlight that during these meetings the different ECOWAS actors and organs sought to consolidate a strong 'regional' position and a fast, resolute response to the coup d'état. To that end, they decided to set up the RCG-GB, chaired by Nigerian president Goodluck Jonathan, to engage stakeholders in Guinea-Bissau directly and on the 'highest level' (i.e., heads of state and foreign ministers) (see Chapter 4). However, ECOWAS heads of state (acting as the MSC at presidential level) also addressed representatives of the transitional authorities of Guinea-Bissau directly during their summits, telling them bluntly what ECOWAS would or would not accept. Moreover, they also unified their position with regard to the inappropriate role of other regional actors involved in Guinea-Bissau, especially CPLP actors (see Chapter 6).[42]

AU actors have dealt with the 2012 crisis in Guinea-Bissau mostly during meetings of the PSC at ambassadorial level. Between March 2012 and March 2013, five such meetings took place (sessions 318, 324, 340, 351 and 361), three of them exclusively on Guinea-Bissau (sessions 318, 351 and 361). In addition, two high-level meetings of the PSC dealt with the conflict in Guinea-Bissau, among other issues, one at ministerial (session 319) and one at presidential level (session 327). Moreover, the two ordinary sessions of the AU Assembly (sessions 19 and 20) also considered the situation, during the same period. Since then, attention to Guinea-Bissau during AU meetings has slightly decreased, but maintained by the persistent political crisis remained stable, averaging three mostly ambassadorial PSC meetings per year, and figuring among the issues brought up during the ordinary sessions of the Assembly. Prior to 2012, actors at the AU had persistently engaged crises in Guinea-Bissau during their meetings. However, it appears that in particular between 2006 and 2008 attention had dropped, before re-emerging in December 2008, following an attack on the residence of the President of Guinea-Bissau in November that year. Following this, the year 2009 saw a spike of five PSC meetings on Guinea-Bissau, particularly after the double assassination. Both the PSC and the AUC Chairperson extensively reported to the Executive Council and the Assembly on several occasions (cf. AUC Chairperson 2009, 37, 144ff., 220ff.; AU Assembly 2009, 12, 18, 69–71). Interestingly, 2009 is also the only year that the available documentation shows activity of the Panel of the Wise on Guinea-Bissau, during two sessions (numbers five and six) in March and June respectively. Subsequently, attention faded somewhat throughout 2010 (three PSC meetings) and 2011 (one PSC meeting), before picking up again in 2012.

During 2012, and early 2013, briefed by the Chairperson of the AU Commission, Jean Ping (until October 2012) and Nkosazana Dlamini-Zuma (thereafter), the Peace and Security Commissioner, Ramtane Lamamra, as well as hearing statements by ECOWAS and CPLP representatives (their chairs and commission/secretariat staff), the AU PSC continuously discussed the situation in Guinea-Bissau. While the main themes and decisions of these meetings are covered below (see also Chapter 4), a few words on general dynamics are warranted. In general, the AU PSC has stood back somewhat behind ECOWAS efforts, assuming a supporting or complementary role. However, with regard to Guinea-Bissau, tensions have emerged over different interpretations regarding the principled position on unconstitutional changes of government (UCGs) and how to respond to them (see Chapters 5 and 6). Interestingly, due to the overlap of membership between ECOWAS and the AU PSC, these tensions also played out at PSC meetings.

Normally, in the AU PSC, debates and decisions on a conflict in a specific sub-region are usually driven by member states that hail from that sub-region (see above). Therefore, West African PSC members would decide what should happen with regard to Guinea-Bissau. However, in late 2012 and early 2013, the Nigerian ambassador to the AU, supported by his colleagues from Côte d'Ivoire and Gambia, was not successful in asserting the Nigerian (read ECOWAS) position, when it came to the question of whether or not to lift Guinea-Bissau's suspension from the AU. In line with the ECOWAS position, which considered 'constitutional order' as restored via the transition agreement and government, brokered by ECOWAS, the Nigerian government wanted the sanctions lifted (see also Chapters 5 and 6). This was opposed especially by the Angolan representative (apparently supported by South Africa, which had left its seat on the PSC to Angola), as well as staff of the AU Commission. In the end, they requested an assessment by the AU Legal Counsel to overcome the deadlock, and Guinea-Bissau remained suspended from the AU.[43]

At this point, the differences in meeting practices of ECOWAS and the AU also came to bear. West African states, and ECOWAS representatives and staff, were upset that, in effect, the AU PSC opposed at the ambassadorial level what the ECOWAS MSC had decided at the level of heads of state. It was also due to these different hierarchical levels that actors at the AU, in particular at the AU Commission, sought to tread carefully in order not to oppose and alienate ECOWAS too much, as a powerful group also within the AU, and to avoid lasting damage to the relationship.[44]

Meetings and space-making

From the above considerations, it becomes clear that different actors both at ECOWAS and at the AU have paid regular, frequent attention to conflict in Guinea-Bissau and elsewhere during various meetings at different levels (see Figures 3.1 and 3.2). Doing so, they have spent considerable resources. Although taken only by themselves these meetings might not have made much of a difference, I argue that they have performed several important functions, enabling, framing and complementing other practices. As mentioned above, first, especially meetings of top-level state and non-state officials signal interest, importance, commitment and readiness to act. Second, debates and decisions of these meetings form the basis for identifying and enabling possible courses of action. They allow for debates among 'peers' and to exert 'peer pressure', for example, by pointing out consequences of 'deviant' behavior (cf. Mace et al. 2016, 6; Melissen 2003, 3). Third, they bring together different actors (e.g., member states, organization staff and 'outsiders'), allowing them to get to know each other, consult, discuss, negotiate and coordinate (including shared principles and norms).

Closely related to these functions, meetings are also of essential importance for and intimately linked to space-making. First, closely related to the production of conflict knowledge, the deliberations among members and staff of the regional organizations contribute to the creation of regional awareness (and potentially identity), linking them as part of the region to a specific local conflict that they otherwise might have no interest in. In that regard, they play an important role in mediating different interests and organizing buy-in of different member states. The driving force behind this process may be one or several interested member states, or the commissions, or a combination of both. Both sets of actors may also be influenced by 'external' actors and interests, which also try to bring their agenda directly to these meetings, if invited. Therefore, constituting moments of 'dense' regional interaction, those meetings work as 'magnifying glasses' or arenas through and in which different actors construct and format the respective regions 'internally' (see Chapter 5), but also order their relations towards other regional and international actors and spaces (see Chapter 6).

Second, once such spatial, regional awareness is created, these meetings allow organizing regional scales 'internally', in two steps. First, they help finding the relevant constellation of most-interested or most-affected actors, which usually are the ones willing to take action or contribute in one way or another (sometimes called 'coalitions of the willing', e.g., Stanley and Malcomson

2019). This process may be characterized as 'focusing down'. Subsequently, second, driven by those actors, participants construct a common position that is supported by all or at least most members (e.g., all AU and ECOWAS member states), and which justifies labelling the action, in practice taken by a few, as 'regional'. This process may be characterized as 'scaling up' to the regional scale (cf. Döring and Herpolsheimer 2018, 69–70). To show how this 'internal' construction process translates into 'external' presentation and further 'internal' construction and formatting of the region, the following section focuses on the public pronouncements following these meetings.

Making public pronouncements

Drawing on conflict-related knowledge produced by different AU and ECOWAS actors, discussions during meetings usually result in some form of public pronouncement, most commonly a final communiqué, a statement or a press release. In these, the participants of the meetings send out messages of different kinds to different recipients or audiences, such as, for example, local populations, national and international political actors (cf. Ecker-Ehrhardt 2018). Going 'public' or turning from the 'inside' to the 'outside', those messages carry multiple contents and perform several important functions. Therefore, this common, patterned and routinized speech act, or in fact several acts produced by specific actors with specific intentions (cf. Searle 2013 [1964]), constitutes a practice in itself.[45] Consequently, this practice employed by African ROs needs to be taken seriously and to be given detailed analytical attention.[46]

Similar to the practice of meeting, and even more visibly so, public pronouncements are a way of signaling interest, importance, commitment and readiness to act. Moreover, in and through them, ROs convey shared principles, norms and ideas. Engaging different actors at different scales, they point out possible and probable courses of action (e.g., in cases of deviant behavior), seeking to influence their actions, as well as their perceptions of the intervening ROs. As will become clear in the following, and in later chapters, there are several additional functions of public pronouncements and their messages to different audiences. Such messages are as much about the conflict as they are about the issuing organization and its relations to other actors (see also Chapter 6). Therefore, to illustrate some of the multiple contents and functions of such public or 'external' communication, this section takes a detailed look at ECOWAS and AU practices, as well as at the information and messages they have conveyed through public pronouncements in response to the crisis in Guinea-Bissau in 2012. Finally, it relates communication practices to space-making by African ROs, in particular during conflict intervention in West/Africa.

ECOWAS and AU 'external' communication practices

Since the late 1990s and early 2000s, actors at ECOWAS and the AU have increasingly sought to communicate their interpretation and framing of, as well as their responses to, conflict situations to a wider public. They have done this in different forms, depending on the issuing actor and the intended weight and reach of the message.

The commissions of ECOWAS and the AU inform the public about scheduled and/or past meetings, missions or other initiatives and events, using press releases that they circulate to national and international media outlets, and which they publish on their respective websites. Such press releases contain information about who is going to meet on which issues, including some context information, putting the respective meetings into perspective, relating them to previous or ongoing efforts. The information thus provided creates a certain degree of transparency, allowing commission staff to show, as well as interested groups and individuals to follow, activities of these organizations regarding developing conflict situations (among other issues, e.g., thematic issues and/or policy fields; see Chapter 5). In addition, the President of the ECOWAS Commission and the AUC Chairperson, respectively, can and often do issue press statements, pronouncing themselves on conflicts within their respective regions. Such statements draw on their mandate and authority as chief representatives of the two regional organizations. However, they also require great political sensitivity, and often require prior consultation with member states' representatives, especially the current chairs of the political decision making organs. As mentioned above, commission staff, in particular from the security departments (DPAPS and PSD, for ECOWAS and the AU respectively), support and actively influence the drafting of these statements.[47]

Much less immediately, but containing a lot of information regarding the commissions' activities, both organizations publish different reports of their activities online or in print (e.g., AUC Chairperson Reports, AU PSC Reports and Annual Reports of the ECOWAS Commission). However, publication practices in this regard are still inconsistent. Reports are available for some periods or issues, while not for others. A similar limitation applies to press releases that appear (or not) on the websites of ECOWAS and the AU. Nevertheless, overall, an emerging practice of communicating and making more transparent what ECOWAS and the AU are doing in order to deal with various crises in their respective regions is increasingly observable.

As the prime bearers of regional authority, the different political decision making organs of ECOWAS and the AU, above all the ECOWAS MSC and the AU PSC, pronounce themselves on active conflicts, although in slightly different ways. On the side of ECOWAS, the MSC at ambassadorial and ministerial level does not issue final communiqués on its sessions (the same applies to the CCDS). It produces final reports, which, however, circulate only internally, or may be shared with other 'partner' organizations (e.g., the AU, EU and UN). Based on these reports, the commission issues press releases, informing about these sessions (see above). At the summit level (i.e., presidential MSC), ECOWAS heads of state pronounce themselves in final communiqués. If they want to put more weight behind their position, they make a political declaration.[48] On the side of the AU, the PSC (at all levels) in most cases issues either a press statement or a final communiqué, depending on the importance and extent of considerations (cf. Dersso 2013). However, as part of its conflict monitoring, the PSC also holds briefing sessions, and may decide not to make any pronouncements, if members do not deem it necessary. The AU Assembly and the Executive Council normally do not produce a final communiqué, but may decide to issue a declaration (e.g., on Mali in 2012). The decisions taken at this level are subsequently available at the AU's website. The respective chairs of different political ECOWAS and AU organs, as well as heads of field missions, may also decide to make a statement in that capacity.

Again, as already mentioned above, commission staff play an important role in providing expertise and knowledge, as well as crafting these pronouncements. The latter constitutes an additional important process of 'internal' communication, during which commission staff and individual member state representatives try to resolve outstanding issues that were not resolved during meetings. To this end, outcome documents that did not receive unanimous approval during a meeting enter a 'silencing procedure', during which no 'external' communication is allowed. Meanwhile, the documents circulate back and forth between different stakeholders, especially diplomatic missions of member states, in rare cases for weeks (e.g., on Libya in 2011, in response to UNSC Resolution 1973; cf. Apuuli 2013, 129–30), until a compromise is reached, and a public pronouncement can follow.[49]

Of course, complementing 'public' pronouncements, both organizations also communicate their action or meeting outcomes to other organizations and actors strategically, through formal and informal channels – for example, by inviting representatives, making statements during their meetings or circulating outcome documents of their own. This can be considered a key intervention practice in itself, which Chapter 6 deals with in more detail.

ECOWAS and AU pronouncements on Guinea-Bissau in 2012

Ever since the war of 1998/9, ECOWAS actors have been following developments in the country closely. Public communication practices have been consistent and have largely reflected the ones described in the following. The same applies to AU actors, in particular since 2006/7, when the PSC began increasingly consolidating its working procedures (see "Meeting, debating, deciding action").

In direct response to the coup of April 2012 in Guinea-Bissau, the *ECOWAS Commission* issued press releases in high frequency throughout April and May 2012 – six, not counting another seven announcing or summarizing ECOWAS meetings that also dealt with Guinea-Bissau. On 13 April, Commission President Kadré Désiré Ouédraogo (former Prime Minister and Ambassador of Burkina Faso) pronounced his "unresolved condemnation" of the "ongoing coup attempt", just shortly after a joint mission by ECOWAS, the AU and the UN had visited Bissau on 31 March to calm down tensions after the first round of the elections. Emphasizing ECOWAS' principle of "zero tolerance" for unconstitutional changes of government, Ouédraogo said that the military had "outlawed Guinea-Bissau from the ECOWAS community", and demanded the completion of the ongoing electoral process (ECOWAS Commission 2012j).

Only days before the coup, on 9 April, Ouédraogo had voiced his "increasing concern" (ECOWAS Commission 2012l), which also fed into a press release (11 April) announcing a ministerial MSC meeting, among other things to consider the post-electoral crisis in Guinea-Bissau, following the first round of the presidential election, and Ouédraogo's proposals on how to resolve it (ECOWAS Commission 2012g).[50] On 16 April, a press release by the ECOWAS Commission announced that an ECOWAS delegation was to deliver a "special message" from the ECOWAS Chair to the "military command", referring to ECOWAS' principled position (i.e., "zero tolerance") and calling for the restoration of "constitutional order" (ECOWAS Commission 2012e). At this point, already, the press release did not clarify anymore what "restoration of constitutional order" would mean (ECOWAS Commission 2012e). Three days later, in another press statement on 19 April, Commission President Ouédraogo strongly condemned the establishment of a national transition council including members of the military, which apparently stood in contradiction to an agreement reached between the ECOWAS delegation and the 'military command' in Guinea-Bissau. The statement also left the "modalities for the restoration of constitutional order" to ongoing consultations with stakeholders in Guinea-Bissau and up to discussion during an emergency summit announced for 26 April (ECOWAS Commission 2012q).

Between 29 April and 2 May 2012, a series of four press releases informed of a meeting of foreign ministers of a seven-member Regional Contact Group for Guinea-Bissau (RCG-GB) with political stakeholders from Guinea-Bissau, hosted by President Jammeh of Gambia in Banjul on 29 April (see also Chapter 4). According to these press releases, after 12 hours of ultimately failed talks, the RCG-GB left Banjul for Abuja, briefing the ECOWAS Chair of the time, Nigerian president Jonathan (ECOWAS Commission 2012d, 2012f), and decided to impose sanctions on Guinea-Bissau's military-political actors (ECOWAS Commission 2012k), in line with an ultimatum set by the ECOWAS Authority during the summit of 26 April (see below). To review the failed negotiations, another meeting of the RCG-GB, this time at presidential level, was announced for 3 May, preceding another extraordinary summit to take place on the same day in Dakar (ECOWAS Commission 2012m).

After this initial engagement, press releases and statements by the ECOWAS Commission and its president specifically on Guinea-Bissau became less frequent. However, press releases on various meetings that discussed Guinea-Bissau among other conflicts, most importantly the one in Mali, have continuously appeared throughout the remainder of 2012. In November, four press releases (1, 6, 7 and 8 November) provided information on progress achieved in Guinea-Bissau, in particular regarding negotiations on the transition, and the formalization of the deployment of ECOMIB and the DSSR mission in the country – respective agreements were signed on 7 November in Bissau (ECOWAS Commission 2012o, 2012h, 2012p, 2012c). In late 2012 (26 November and 13 December), two press releases informed the public about visits by a Spanish delegation and the US AFRICOM Commander, General Carter Ham, to the ECOWAS headquarters in Abuja, during which the ECOWAS Commission President and the CPAPS respectively also briefed on developments and ECOWAS efforts in Guinea-Bissau (cf. ECOWAS Commission 2012i, 2012b).

Since late April 2012, final communiqués of three extraordinary and one ordinary ECOWAS summits (presidential MSC sessions) carried the key messages of ECOWAS member states in that year. Coming together for the first time after the coup in Guinea-Bissau, during an extraordinary summit on 26 April (Abidjan, Côte d'Ivoire), *ECOWAS heads of state and government* reiterated the condemnation of the coup, as well as the disruption of the electoral process and the detention of the prime minister (Carlos Gomes Junior) and the interim president (Raimundo Pereira). Referring to the principle of "zero tolerance" for unconstitutional changes of government (as stated in the 2001 Supplementary Protocol; see Chapter 5), they stressed that they would "never recognize any unconstitutional transitional arrangement", demanding the release of the detained and the completion of the electoral process (ECOWAS Authority 2012c, para. 27). The latter, as the communiqué further explained, however, referred to a "consensual transition through the holding of [fresh] elections within twelve months", based on modalities negotiated by ECOWAS (ECOWAS Authority 2012c, para. 29). Furthermore, ECOWAS heads of state announced three measures: (i) the deployment of the ECOWAS Standby Force (ESF), above all to facilitate the withdrawal of the Angolan military mission (MISSANG); (ii) a 72-hour ultimatum to the "military command", threatening sanctions and explicitly not excluding the possibility of prosecution through the International Criminal Court; and (iii) the establishment of the RCG-GB to coordinate the implementation of decisions (ECOWAS Authority 2012c, para. 30–2). The communiqué also stressed "subsidiarity", as the "cardinal principle" to organize and intensify close cooperation between ECOWAS, the AU, the UN and "other partners" in their collective efforts to maintain peace and security in West Africa (ECOWAS Authority 2012c, para. 33). Seemingly somewhat unrelated, ECOWAS heads of state also urged the ECOWAS Commission to "expedite action" regarding the implementation of the ECOWAS action plan on drug trafficking through the mobilization of financial resources, with explicit reference to Guinea-Bissau (ECOWAS Authority 2012c, para. 34).[51] Some additional information transpired in a subsequent press release, summarizing the summit results, including the strength and composition of the mandated ESF force (ECOWAS Commission 2012n; see also Chapter 4).

In 2012, final communiqués of three additional summits (two extraordinary and one ordinary) subsequently reiterated the calls made on 26 April 2012. On 3 May, ECOWAS heads of state repeated their firm condemnation of the coup ("zero tolerance") and demanded the immediate "return to constitutional order" (ECOWAS Authority 2012d, para. 19–20). While they welcomed the release (on 27 April) of Prime Minister Gomes Junior and Interim President Pereira, at this point still calling them by their titles, they also insisted that the "military command" released unnamed others that were still detained. They also reaffirmed their decisions to deploy the ESF and to hold fresh elections after a transition period of 12 months and a respective agreement negotiated by ECOWAS. For the time being, sanctions should remain in place, so that "all the protagonists accept the modalities for a return to constitutional order" (ECOWAS Authority 2012d, para. 29). The ECOWAS Authority furthermore mandated the RCG-GB to take all required action, on its behalf, in line with these decisions (ECOWAS Authority 2012d, para. 30).

In the final communiqué of the ordinary ECOWAS summit on 29 June 2012, ECOWAS heads of state endorsed transitional authorities, established with ECOWAS support, suspended sanctions and called on the international community to do the same, and to provide financial support. They welcomed the deployment of the ESF and congratulated the Angolan government for the "successful withdrawal" of MISSANG (ECOWAS Authority 2012a, para. 36). The ECOWAS Commission was tasked to "take urgent steps" towards pressing reforms (e.g., constitutional, electoral, economic and DSSR), and to "intensify" consultations with international "partners" to forge a consensus on the transition (ECOWAS Authority 2012a, para. 38–9). Pointing in the same direction, the final communiqué of the extraordinary ECOWAS summit on 11 November "instructs" the ECOWAS Commission to "expedite action" on a joint assessment mission (JAM), seen as an important process in international consensus-building (ECOWAS Authority 2012b, para. 20). In response to recent events, heads of state condemned the "destabilization attempts" of 21 October (i.e., an armed attack on the Bissalanca airbase), and welcomed the signing of the Status of Mission Agreement for ECOMIB and the Memorandum of Understanding on DSSR. They expressed their appreciation to ECOMIB troops, and extended their mandate by six months.[52] Referring to the "suffering of the population" (ECOWAS Authority 2012b, para. 26), the summit called again on the international community, and specifically on the AU, appealing to its current chair, President Boni Yayi of Benin, to suspend its sanctions and recognize the transitional authorities, established through ECOWAS' facilitation (ECOWAS Authority 2012b, para. 24).

On their part, AU actors also responded to the crisis, ensuing from the coup in April 2012 in Guinea-Bissau, through a number of public pronouncements. Similar to ECOWAS, it was the *AUC Chairperson*, Jean Ping (former Minister and State Minister of Gabon), who was the first to pronounce himself in two press statements, on 13 April. He expressed the AU's strong condemnation, stressing its principled position on unconstitutional changes of government, and called for the release of the Prime Minister Gomes Junior and Interim President Pereira (AU Commission 2012a, 2012c). The following day, on 14 April, Ping firmly rejected any efforts of "window dressing" the coup as constitutional. Instead, he called for the restoration of actual "constitutional order", that is, the *continuation of the interrupted electoral process* (AU Commission 2012b). Ping repeated these demands in another statement, on 19 April, renewing his condemnation and rejecting the transition agreement reached between the military actors responsible for the coup and several political actors of Guinea-Bissau. After that, press releases by the AU Commission became less frequent.

On 8 May, Ping announced his appointment of Ovídio Pequeno (former Foreign Minister of Sao Tomé and Principe) as his Special Representative (SRCC) to Guinea-Bissau, and new Head of the AU liaison office (AULO) in that country. A renewed call for the "restoration of constitutional order" remained vague as to what exactly that would mean (AU Commission 2012d). Three days later, on 11 May, another press statement by the AUC Chairperson signaled the AU's continued attention to developments in Guinea-Bissau, which it "monitor[ed] closely", in contact with international partners. Moreover, the statement recalled decisions taken by the PSC (on 24 April), on the one hand, highlighting the principle of "subsidiarity", expressing the AU's support of ECOWAS and, on the other hand, stressing the need for coordination. Therefore, Ping announced AU efforts to create a Multilateral Consultation and Coordination Framework on the Stabilization of Guinea-Bissau (i.e., meetings of international stakeholders), to develop a "comprehensive strategy" (AU Commission 2012f). Following this, the AUC issued only one additional press release, on 1 December – by then under the new leadership of Nkosazana Dlamini-Zuma (former Minister of South Africa) – informing about the AUC-initiated consultative meeting between representatives of the CPLP, ECOWAS, the EU and the UN in Addis Ababa (AU Commission 2012e).

Different from the ECOWAS MSC, the *AU PSC* issued its first communiqué already on 17 April 2012, after its 318th session, convened at ambassadorial level, exclusively on Guinea-Bissau. The ambassadors endorsed the statements by the AUC Chairperson (as well as those made by ECOWAS and CPLP representatives), themselves strongly condemning the coup, demanding the unconditional release of the detained and the immediate "restoration of constitutional order" through the *continuation of the electoral process* (AU PSC 2012c, para. 4 and 9).[53] The statement identified the continuous interference of the Bissau-Guinean army leadership in the country's political affairs as contributing to persistent instability, among other things obstructing the fight against the "scourge of drug trafficking", with serious consequences for the region and "Africa as a whole" (AU PSC 2012c, para. 3). In line with the AU's policy script on how to respond to UCGs, the PSC members suspended Guinea-Bissau's participation in the AU, and asked the AUC to submit proposals for further sanctions, in consultation with ECOWAS and AU partners (AU PSC 2012c, para. 6). Interestingly, they also expressed their gratitude for the "valuable contribution" of the Angolan government to the "stabilization of Guinea-Bissau" and DSSR (AU PSC 2012c, para. 8) – remarkable, considering that MISSANG at the same time had to withdraw from Guinea-Bissau because it caused too much tension and some saw it as one of the reasons behind the coup (see Chapter 6). Coincidentally, Angola had just started its first ever term on the PSC (see above). The PSC, finally, requested the AUC Chairperson to consult with actors at ECOWAS, the CPLP, the UN and "other partners" in order to return constitutional order to Guinea-Bissau, and continue DSSR efforts, initiated within the framework of the ECOWAS-CPLP Roadmap (AU PSC 2012c, para. 8 and 9) (see Chapter 4).

The PSC met again on 24 April 2012, this time at ministerial level, also covering developing situations in Mali and Sudan/South Sudan. With regard to the situation in Guinea-Bissau, the PSC rejected the 'military command's' transition agreement of 18 April as a "vain and unacceptable attempt to legitimize the coup d'état", demanding again the completion of the electoral process, as well as the release of Gomes Junior, Pereira and others (AU PSC 2012a, para. 5 and 7).[54] It called it a "duty of Africa, through the AU and ECOWAS, with the support of the UN, the CPLP and other members of the international community, to ensure that the coup d'état of 12 April 2012 fails and put an end to the destabilizing actions of the army in Guinea-Bissau" (AU PSC 2012a, para. 6). The PSC tasked the AU Commission to compile and disseminate a list of persons as possible targets for sanctions, and to facilitate a Multilateral Consultation and Coordination Framework on the Stabilization of Guinea-Bissau (i.e., a stakeholder meeting) (AU PSC 2012a, para. 8 and 10). Moreover, it praised the contributions by different actors involved in the management of conflict in the country. With respect to ECOWAS, the ministers reaffirmed the principle of subsidiarity, endorsing ECOWAS' decisions, especially on the deployment of the ESF, and welcomed its "commitment and dynamism" (AU PSC 2012a, para. 4). The PSC also expressed its appreciation to the CPLP, "for its principled position", to the mediation efforts by Guinean president Alpha Condé, as well as to the UN Secretary General and the UN Security Council, the EU and the International Organization of the Francophonie, which had also suspended Guinea-Bissau (AU PSC 2012a, para. 4).

Subsequently, another PSC communiqué (14 July) and a press statement (2 November 2012) mostly recalled what previous ones had said, above all others commending ECOWAS for its efforts and encouraging close coordination with other international actors (AU PSC 2012b, para. 2, 2012d, 1). Another meeting of the PSC on 21 June had considered the situation, among other issues, but did not issue a press statement or communiqué on Guinea-Bissau (cf. AU Assembly 2012, Annex I, p. 3). The communiqué from July also "welcomed" ongoing consultations towards convening another session of the ICG-GB, which had collapsed due to the tensions between representatives of ECOWAS and the CPLP (AU PSC 2012b, para. 5) (for more, see Chapter 6). Besides that, PSC members decided to "remain actively seized" (AU PSC

2012b, para. 6; see also PSC communiqués referred to above). The statement from November strongly condemned the attacks of 21 October 2012 on the Bissalanca airbase, near Bissau. After referring to the September 2012 consultative meeting in New York, the November 2012 statement also encouraged the AU Commission to continue its efforts, especially aiming at facilitating close collaboration among the international stakeholders. It also endorsed the joint assessment mission decided at the consultative meeting in New York, and requested a "comprehensive report" by the AUC Chairperson within 60 days (AU PSC 2012d, 1).

Less clear in the latter pronouncements of the PSC (at presidential level in July, and ambassadorial level in November 2012) has been its position on how to proceed regarding the 'restoration of constitutional order' in Guinea-Bissau. While repeating that phrase, contrary to the statements of April 2012, these no longer call for the completion of the electoral process. Instead of clarifying what the phrase should mean, they refer only to the "implementation of decisions relating to the return to constitutional order" (AU PSC 2012b, para. 3), or do not mention it at all (cf. also AU PSC 2012d).

The struggle and ultimately the change of heart behind this becomes much more visible in the PSC reports to the Assembly, in July 2012, as well as in the report of the AUC Chairperson to the PSC, in January 2013. The PSC report, while summarizing AU activities in response to the conflict in Guinea-Bissau, does not refer to the completion of the electoral process at any point (cf. AU Assembly 2012, para. 8ff, 121ff.). However, the same PSC report has annexed to it joint public statements ensuing from joint consultative meetings between the AU PSC and the EU Political and Security Council on the one hand (May 2012), and the UN Security Council (UNSC) on the other (June 2012). Whereas the former explicitly demands the reinstatement of the "legitimate democratic government" and the "resumption of the interrupted electoral process (AU PSC and EU PSC 2012, 3), the latter does not clarify what "restoration of constitutional order" should mean (UNSC and AU PSC 2012, para. 13–16). Implicit in the report by the AUC Chairperson is that throughout the second half of 2012, AU actors changed their position from demanding the completion of the electoral process, thereby effectively supporting the position of the PAIGC, to perceiving the PAIGC's refusal to join the transition arrangements brokered by ECOWAS as an obstacle, creating an "impasse" (AUC Chairperson 2013, 2). The 'victim' thus became the 'problem', until the PAIGC finally decided to join the agreement in late 2012/early 2013.

This change of heart once more reflected the ongoing competition and tensions between representatives of ECOWAS as well as the CPLP and EU, but also between ECOWAS and AU actors, which also played out in different AU meetings (see "Meeting, debating, deciding action"). It also reflected different positions of different actors within the AU, and even tensions between different objectives within the AU Commission, opposing a pragmatic perspective of actors closely involved in actual conflict management (e.g., the Special Representative of the AUC Chairperson for Guinea-Bissau and the CMPCRD desk officers; see Chapter 4) to a policy perspective, trying to enact and consolidate a coherent practice (see Chapter 5).

'External' communication and space-making

From the above, some of the most important functions performed in public pronouncements by ECOWAS and the AU become discernible. Among others, they include, first, creating a certain degree of transparency for their actions. They inform interested populations, media, as well as other regional and international actors about key events, including the meetings themselves, positions adopted and actions taken or intended. Second, at the same time, they also frame, categorize and order this information in specific ways (i.e., produce and communicate knowledge), thereby simultaneously linking it to established norms and ideas, practices and procedures, as well as developing them and in some cases introducing new ones. In this way, these pronouncements contribute to framing and creating social reality (cf. Barnett and Finnemore 2004, 6–7). Third, in their public statements, both organizations position themselves vis-à-vis the conflict, different local conflict actors, as well as other regional or international actors (see Chapter 6), signaling regional unity (consensus) while claiming authority and responsibility. This kind of message is sent both towards the 'region' (or actors 'therein') as well as to the 'outside', and contributes to framing and constructing relations. Fourth, through these pronouncements, ECOWAS and AU actors issue directives for action, to actors 'on the ground' (e.g., calling on them to do this or refrain from that), at the commissions (e.g., tasking them to implement decisions) or international 'partners' (e.g., urging them to support the process). Fifth, and closely linked, especially through final decisions, resolutions, final declarations and communiqués, ECOWAS and AU actors have established a body of interlinking texts and cross-references, which contributes to producing a certain degree of legitimacy and a growing legal basis (i.e., a 'mandate') for justified action, simultaneously drawing on, interpreting and complementing existing legal frameworks (cf. also Melissen 2003).[55]

All of these functions closely link to space-making in one or several ways. First, by emanating selected knowledge about conflict situations, public communication contributes to creating regional awareness among the different audiences, which either identify as part *of* the region or look *at* the region. In both cases, specific spatial imaginations are at play (see Chapter 5). Once more, knowledge about 'local' conflict is distributed at the regional scale (and beyond it); events at the local level are identified as linked to and part of the regional, as well as to specific regional norms and policies. Thereby, different actors at ECOWAS and the AU establish their 'reach' over conflict situations discursively. In addition, they try to format regional spaces according to different spatial imaginations, norms and policies (see Chapter 5). Second, constituting the next step after the 'internal' organization of scales, ECOWAS and AU actors send out common messages, which at that point on paper and per definition become the 'regional position', on the face of it supported by all of their member states ('internal' differences notwithstanding). These messages position the organizations towards the conflict and communicate claims to legitimacy and responsibility to take action, to different 'outsides', such as, for example, international media as well as other regional and international actors (see Chapter 6).

Third, and closely related, the messages also convey particular spatial formats and an imagined spatial order among them, establishing the 'region' as the adequate and responsible actor to 'secure', 're-establish' or construct 'nation states' as 'functioning' elements of the West African state system. What is more, at the same time, the two African ROs have also engaged in constructing spatial order among different regional actors (i.e., inter- and trans-regionally) in Africa, but also beyond it. In their public pronouncements, they have frequently referred to other actors, and how these and their efforts should relate to the efforts of ECOWAS and the AU, most importantly stressing particular interpretations of the contested concept of 'subsidiarity'. Chapter 6 discusses these aspects in more detail.

Conclusion

In this chapter, I have started to outline and analyze the range and complexity of intervention practices that different actors 'within' ECOWAS and the AU have brought forward in response to conflict situations and how these have linked to space-making. Specifically, this chapter has analyzed three main interrelated sets of practices employed 'from afar', that is, especially from organizational headquarters or meeting venues. While some of them may seem obvious, so far, they have received insufficient appreciation as important basic practices and sites of interventions. As a consequence, the different actors 'within' African ROs involved in these practices and their spatializing effects have been obscured. This chapter has shed light on all of these aspects.

In particular, I argue that in topological terms (see Chapter 2) these practices have allowed the two African ROs to establish and defend their 'reach' over conflict situations. By producing conflict-related knowledge, meeting and discussing on the subject and making public pronouncements, actors at ECOWAS and the AU have sought to establish their expertise, responsibility, legitimacy and readiness to conduct and lead conflict interventions – making it part of their respective spaces, and bringing to bear regional policies, norms and principles on it. All of this has essentially contributed to space-making, that is, the ongoing construction and formatting of regional spaces (see also Chapter 5), as well as spatial ordering (i.e., *by* and *of* space) among the different self-identified 'African' and 'non-African' actors (see Chapter 6).

To briefly sum up the three sets of practices, first, ECOWAS and the AU have followed the developing conflict situations closely, constantly producing memos, briefs and reports, thereby contributing to the production of conflict-related knowledge – by different actors, at different sites, coming from different sources and through different channels. This information, the knowledge thus produced and circulated, has played a central role in understanding and framing conflict situations, providing the basis for debate within both organizations, filtering into public pronouncements and eventually guiding action 'on the ground' (analyzed in Chapter 4), which ultimately feeds back into the production of conflict knowledge. These processes have generated awareness, creating connections among regional actors, and have been essential in formulating regional responses, leading to increased social interaction and thereby playing a key role in regional space-making.

Second, ECOWAS and AU actors have continually convened meetings, at different levels and comprising different participants, in particular including different high- and top-level representatives of member states, commission staff and 'external' observers or representatives (e.g., of other organizations, African and Western states; see Chapter 6). These meetings have played a central role in familiarizing representatives of regional member states with conflict situations – bringing the 'conflict' to the 'region'. Subsequently they have allowed them to find common understandings and common ground on which to base a common response that, at least in principle or on paper, all member states support and legitimize – bringing the 'region' to bear on the 'conflict'. Thus, a process of 'internal' communication and organization becomes observable, in which the two commissions, their chief executives and specifically the peace and security departments of ECOWAS and the AU have played critical roles – creating and consolidating connections and increasing social interaction.

Third, different actors at ECOWAS and the AU have regularly and frequently used public pronouncements to provide information on both conflict situations and their responses to them, and to communicate their respective positions and approaches to a wider public, interested groups and individuals at national, regional and international levels. Thereby, the two African ROs have selectively turned parts of the preceding 'internal' process 'public', providing a certain degree of transparency and more importantly legitimacy to their action, establishing their 'reach' over conflict situations discursively. However, simultaneously they have used these pronouncements to negotiate, contest and reorder spatial relations among different intervening regional and international actors (see Chapter 6).

Although empirical examples in this chapter have primarily focused on interventions in response to the coup of April 2012 in Guinea-Bissau, it is important to mention that ECOWAS and the AU have consistently developed the intervention practices highlighted and systematized in this chapter, at least since the early 2000s. Therefore, a remarkable continuity becomes observable with regard to forms and actors involved in these practices, and to some extent regarding the content of concrete actions taken. While what I have described in this chapter reflects general approaches of actors at ECOWAS and the AU, it will nevertheless require more in-depth analysis of different conflict interventions to identify subtle or more substantial differences in the exact application of individual sets of practices as well as interlinkages and interactions among them.

In the following, Chapter 4 directly continues the analysis of ECOWAS and AU practices of conflict intervention and their spatializing effects, turning towards the actual 'conflict site', taking a closer look at how the two ROs have acted 'on the ground'.

Notes

1 Cf. Field Notes, Abuja, 29 October 2018; Field Notes, Addis Ababa, 26 September 2016. The ECOWAS Authority uses a similar phrase, but without the 'actively' (i.e., "Authority remains seized with [...]"; e.g., ECOWAS Authority 2012c, para. 38, 2012d, para. 30).

2 I use single quotation marks to raise awareness that these terms are markers that different actors, including me as a researcher, use for different reasons and towards specific objectives, often to distinguish binary opposites (e.g., 'internal' versus 'external'; 'technical' versus 'political'). As such they are part of different discourses, knowledge–power relations and subject to socio-political contestation.

3 For ECOWAS, such an analysis does not exist yet; merely the Early Warning System (ECOWARN) has received some limited attention (see below).

4 In 2017, the ECOWAS Early Warning Directorate has moved from DPAPS to the Office of the Vice President of the ECOWAS Commission, to cover a broader range of issues related to a much broader understanding of 'security' (cf. Interview 158, Senior ECOWAS Officer, Office of the Vice President, Abuja, 25 October 2018).

5 Cf. Interview 158, Senior ECOWAS Officer, Office of the Vice President of the ECOWAS Commission, Abuja, 25 October 2018; Interview 165, Senior ECOWAS Officer, Department of Political Affairs, Peace and Security, Abuja, 31 October 2018.

6 Cf. Interview 49, Senior ECOWAS Officer, Department for Political Affairs, Peace and Security, Abuja, 2 March 2017; Interview 155, Senior ECOWAS Officer, Department for Political Affairs, Peace and Security, Abuja, 24 October 2018; Interview 134, AU Officer, Peace and Security Department, Addis Ababa, 24 September 2018; Interview 130, AU Officer, Peace and Security Department, Addis Ababa, 21 September 2018.

7 Interview 49, Senior ECOWAS Officer, Department for Political Affairs, Peace and Security, Abuja, 2 March 2017; Interview 16, AU Officer, Peace and Security Department, Addis Ababa, 22 September 2016; Interview 134, AU Officer, Peace and Security Department, Addis Ababa, 24 September 2018.

8 E.g., cf. Interview 13, Senior AU Officer, Peace and Security Department, Addis Ababa, 21 September 2016; Interview 8, Senior AU Officer, Department of Political Affairs, Addis Ababa, 14 September 2016; Interview 22, Senior ECOWAS Official, Addis Ababa, 26 September 2016.

9 Cf. Interview 49, Senior ECOWAS Officer, Department for Political Affairs, Peace and Security, Abuja, 2 March 2017; Interview 7, AU Officer, Peace and Security Department, Addis Ababa, 14 September 2016; Interview 16, AU Officer, Peace and Security Department, Addis Ababa, 22 September 2016; Interview 130, AU Officer, Peace and Security Department, Addis Ababa, 21 September 2018.

10 Cf. Interview 20, AU Officer, Peace and Security Department, Addis Ababa, 23 September 2016; see also Engel 2018, 119).

11 Cf. Interview 49, Senior ECOWAS Officer, Department for Political Affairs, Peace and Security, Abuja, 2 March 2017. I have also had access to some of the confidential reports and briefs, produced by ECOWAS and AU staff, but confidentiality does not allow discussing those in detail.

12 Both organizations have also produced (more) detailed knowledge on specific issues, as the result of thematic assessment missions (e.g., pre/post-electoral, SSR; cf. AU Commission 2014; AU et al. 2015; for more details, see Chapter 4).

13 Cf. Interview 134, AU Officer, Peace and Security Department, Addis Ababa, 24 September 2018; Interview 20, AU Officer, Peace and Security Department, Addis Ababa, 23 September 2016.

14 Cf. Interview 133, Senior AU Officer, Peace and Security Department, Addis Ababa, 24 September 2018; Interview 145, Senior AU Officer, Peace and Security Department, Addis Ababa, 28 September 2018; Interview 43, Senior ECOWAS Officer, Department for Political Affairs, Peace and Security, Abuja, 28 February 2017; Interview 157, ECOWAS Officer, Office of the Vice President, Abuja, 24 October 2018.

15 E.g., cf. Interview 28, Senior ECOWAS Officer, Department for Political Affairs, Peace and Security, Abuja, 16 February 2017; Interview 43, Senior ECOWAS Officer, Department for Political Affairs, Peace and Security, Abuja, 28 February 2017; Interview 164, Senior ECOWAS Officer, Department for Political Affairs, Peace and Security, Abuja, 30 October 2018.

16 This is not to say that all information gathered and analyses produced on that basis necessarily is 'correct'. In fact, a criticism repeatedly advanced by 'local' actors in Guinea-Bissau has been that ECOWAS and AU actors would not understand the situation and dynamics in that country (e.g., cf. Interview 72, Senior Representative of the Instituto Nacional de Estudos e Pesquisa (INEP) of Guinea-Bissau, Bissau, 8 April 2017; Interview 76, Local NGO Representative, Bissau, 11 April 2017).

17 Söderbaum (2004) has called this 'sovereignty boosting'.

18 Other research fields have already acknowledged this (e.g., cf. Schwartzman 1989; Boden 1994; Alvesson 1996; van Vree 2011; Sandler and Thedvall 2017).

19 As a special type of meeting, summits or the related international practice of "summitry" have received considerable scientific attention at least since the 1960s (e.g., Galtung 1964; Eubank 1966). However, the phenomenon has not only continuously grown in importance, but also continuously evolved and changed (among the various contributions, e.g., cf. Adelman 1986; Dunn 1996; Reynolds 2007). Consequently, it has been hard to "keep up with the phenomenon", which until today remains understudied (Mace et al. 2016, 3).

20 Van Vree has reflected upon the "meetingization of society", describing meetings as the "frontline of civilization" (van Vree 2011).

21 The PSC Protocol became the successor of the OAU Mechanism of 1993, reflecting the normative turn that accompanied the transition from the OAU to the AU (e.g., cf. Tieku 2004; see also Chapter 5).

22 By 2005, four extraordinary sessions had taken place; five occurred between 2006 and 2017, two in 2018. It would require additional research to clarify the underlying logics, actors and practices of such extraordinary summits.

23 In April 2018, Angola started another two-year term, replacing South Africa on the PSC.

24 I have compiled this overview based on information provided in the African Union Handbook (cf. AU Commission and New Zealand Crown 2019, 72–73)

25 Cf. Interview 20, AU Officer, Peace and Security Department, Addis Ababa, 23 September 2016; Interview 22, Senior ECOWAS Official, Addis Ababa, 26 September 2016.

26 Cf. Interview 140, ISS Researcher, PSC Report Program, Addis Ababa, 25 September 2018.

27 Cf. Interview 22, Senior ECOWAS Official, Addis Ababa, 26 September 2016. By May 2016, only 24 ambassadorial MSC sessions had taken place, as opposed to 37 sessions of the ministerial MSC by December 2016. As presidential MSC sessions coincide with the summits, these are not counted and do not necessarily produce separate reports.

28 Cf. Interview 163, Senior ECOWAS Officer, Department for Gender and Social Affairs, Abuja, 29 October 2018; Interview 165, Senior ECOWAS Officer, Department for Political Affairs, Peace and Security, Abuja, 31 October 2018.

29 Cf. Interview 163, Senior ECOWAS Officer, Department for Gender and Social Affairs, Abuja, 29 October 2018.

30 Cf. Interview 154, Senior ECOWAS Officer, Department for Political Affairs, Peace and Security, Abuja, 23 October 2018.

31 Cf. Interview 163, Senior ECOWAS Officer, Department for Gender and Social Affairs, Abuja, 29 October 2018.

32 Cf. Interview 20, AU Officer, Peace and Security Department, Addis Ababa, 23 September 2016; cf. Interview 165, Senior ECOWAS Officer, Department for Political Affairs, Peace and Security, Abuja, 31 October 2018.

33 Cf. Interview 20, AU Officer, Peace and Security Department, Addis Ababa, 23 September 2016; cf. Interview 165, Senior ECOWAS Officer, Department for Political Affairs, Peace and Security, Abuja, 31 October 2018.

34 Cf. Interview 20, AU Officer, Peace and Security Department, Addis Ababa, 23 September 2016; cf. Interview 165, Senior ECOWAS Officer, Department for Political Affairs, Peace and Security, Abuja, 31 October 2018.

35 E.g., cf. Interview 41, Senior ECOWAS Officer, Department for Gender and Social Affairs, Abuja, 27 February 2017; Interview 146, AU Officer, Peace and Security Department, Addis Ababa, 28 September 2018; Interview 16, AU Officer, Peace and Security Department, Addis Ababa, 22 September 2016; Interview 139, EU Officer, EU to AU Delegation, Addis Ababa, 25 September 2018.

36 Cf. Interview 163, Senior ECOWAS Officer, Department for Social Affairs and Gender, Abuja, 29 October 2018.

37 The ECOWAS CCDS had become more involved in Guinea-Bissau, especially since 2008/9, when ECOWAS engaged in the SSR process in the country (together with the EU, CPLP and later also the AU).

38 Cf. Interview 49, Senior ECOWAS Officer, Department for Political Affairs, Peace and Security, Abuja, 2 March 2017.

39 Of course, the high priority given to the situation in Mali developing since March 2012 partly explains this conjuncture. Nevertheless, Guinea-Bissau also continuously received high-level attention.

40 In addition to these places, the situation in Guinea-Bissau was the subject of an extraordinary summit in Dakar (in May 2012), two meetings of the RCG-GB, once in Banjul (in April 2012) and once in Dakar (May 2012), and consultations in New York (in September 2012) and Addis Ababa (December 2012).
41 All information here and in the following is based on press releases, final reports and final communiqués of the ECOWAS Commission, the MSC and the Authority respectively.
42 Cf. Field notes, Addis Ababa, 13 September 2016.
43 Cf. Personal Conversation, Senior AU Officer, Peace and Security Department, Addis Ababa, 28 September 2018; Personal Conversation, AU Officer, Peace and Security Department, Addis Ababa, 27 September 2018.
44 Cf. Interview 6, Senior AU Officer, Peace and Security Department, Addis Ababa, 14 September 2016.
45 On 'speech act' theory, see also Austin (1962) and Skinner (1970). On the importance of such 'speech acts' in the context of security dynamics, see the conceptual elaborations on 'securitization theory' by Ole Wæver and his colleagues (in particular Buzan, Wæver and Wilde 1998).
46 On the relevance of public communication of international organizations, see Ecker-Ehrhardt (2018).
47 Cf. Interview 20, AU Officer, Peace and Security Department, Addis Ababa, 23 September 2016; Interview 165, Senior ECOWAS Officer, Abuja, 31 October 2018; Interview 140, ISS Researcher, PSC Report Program, Addis Ababa, 25 September 2018.
48 Decisions and resolutions find mention in communiqués or declarations, but usually appear publicly only later on, in the *Official Community Journal*. However, access to these specific documents remains incomplete (see Chapter 1).
49 Interview 20, AU Officer, Peace and Security Department, Addis Ababa, 23 September 2016.
50 Already since late 2011, alerted by what appeared to be an attempted coup in December 2011 and especially after the death of then-President Malam Bacai Sanhá in early January 2012, President of the ECOWAS Commission Victor Gbeho and ECOWAS Chair, President Jonathan of Nigeria, issued several press releases. In March 2012, ECOWAS deployed an election observation mission (EOM) to Guinea-Bissau, which went along with continuous press releases, mostly from Bissau, made by former Nigerian interim president Salou Bjibo, head of the EOM.
51 The ECOWAS heads of state first adopted the action plan on drug trafficking in 2008. Four years later, however, implementation had not yet taken off.
52 Since then, they have continuously renewed the mandate by periods of six months or one year (see Chapter 4).
53 As legal basis and normative framework, the communiqué refers to the AU Constitutive Act, the PSC Protocol, and Chapter VIII of the African Charter on Democracy, Elections and Governance (on UCGs) (AU PSC 2012c, para. 2).
54 This time, in addition to the AU Constitutive Act, the PSC Protocol and Chapter VIII of the African Charter on Democracy, Elections and Governance, the communiqué also refers to the ECOWAS 1999 Mechanism and the 2001 Supplementary Protocol (AU PSC 2012a, para. 2).
55 Several different research strands have touched upon related issues (e.g., cf. Snow and Taylor 2009; O'Neil 2015; Ecker-Ehrhardt 2018), but not explicitly focused on the public communication of regional organizations, and not in relation to conflict management.

References

Adelman, Kenneth L. 1986. Summitry: The Historical Perspective. *Presidential Studies Quarterly* 16 (3): 435–41.

Aggad, Faten and Luckystar Miyandazi. 2017. *Understanding ECOWAS Efforts in Promoting a Governance Agenda: Adapting Regional Norms to Lessons from National Crises.* Maastricht: ECDPM.

Allison, Simon. 2014. Think Again: In Defence of the African Union. Accessed 23 May 2019. https://issafrica.org/iss-today/think-again-in-defence-of-the-african-union.

Alvesson, Mats. 1996. *Communication, Power and Organization.* Berlin: De Gruyter.

Apuuli, Kasaija P. 2013. The African Union (AU), the Libya Crisis and the Notion of 'African Solutions to African Problems'. *Journal of Contemporary African Studies* 31 (1): 117–38. doi: 10.1080/02589001.2012.761463.

AU. 2002. "Protocol Relating to the Establishment of the Peace and Security Council of the African Union", 1st Ordinary Session of the Assembly of the African Union, Durban, 9 July 2002.

———. 2013. "Report of the Joint ECOWAS/AU/CPLP/EU/UN Assessment Mission to Guinea-Bissau", 23 March 2013. Accessed 15 June 2019. www.peaceau.org/en/article/report-of-the-joint-ecowas-au-cplp-eu-un-assessment-mission-to-guinea-bissau.

AU, ECOWAS, EU, African Security Sector Network and the UN. 2015. "Report of the Joint Security Sector Reform (SSR) Assessment Mission to Guinea-Bissau", 2–12 March 2015.

AU Assembly. 2009. "Report of the Peace and Security Council of the African Union on its Activities and the State of Peace and Security in Africa (Assembly/AU/6[XIII])", 13th Ordinary Session, Sirte, 1–3 July 2009.

———. 2012. "Report of the PSC on its Activities and the State of Peace and Security in Africa (Assembly/AU/6[XIX])", 19th Ordinary Session of the AU Assembly, Addis Ababa, 15–16 July 2012.

AU Commission. 2012a. "Press Release: The African Union Demands the Immediate Release of the Bissau-Guinean Leaders and Reiterates the Imperative of Respect of Constitutional Order in the Country", Addis Ababa, 13 April 2012.

———. 2012b. "Press Release: The African Union Rejects the Ongoing Unconstitutional Manoeuvers in Guinea-Bissau", Addis Ababa, 14 April 2012.

———. 2012c. "Press Release: The African Union Warns Against any Attempt to Interrupt the Electoral Process in Guinea-Bissau and to Seize Power by Force", Addis Ababa, 13 April 2012.

———. 2012d. "Press Release: The AU Appoints a New Special Representative in Guinea-Bissau, Head of the AU Liaison Office in that Country", Addis Ababa, 8 May 2012.

———. 2012e. "Press Release: The AU Convenes Consultations on the Situation in Guinea-Bissau", Addis Ababa, 1 December 2012.

———. 2012f. "Press Release: The AU Reaffirms its Support to the Efforts Aimed at Ensuring an Early Return to Constitutional Order", Addis Ababa, 11 May 2012.

———. 2014. "Rapport Final: Mission d'Obsérvation Électorale de l'Union Africaine pour les Élections Générales du 13 avril 2014 et le Second tour de l'Élection Présidentielle du 18 mai 2014 en République de Guinée-Bissau", June 2014.

AU Commission and New Zealand Crown. 2019. *African Union Handbook 2019: A Guide for Those Working with and within the African Union.* Addis Ababa, Wellington: AU Commission and New Zealand MFAT.

AU PSC. 2012a. "Communiqué (PSC/MIN/COMM/1. (CCCXIX))", 319th Meeting, Addis Ababa, 24 April 2012.

———. 2012b. "Communiqué (PSC/AHG/COMM.3[CCCXXVII])", 327th Meeting at the level of Heads of State and Government, Addis Ababa, 14 July 2012.

———. 2012c. "Communiqué (PSC/PR/COMM[CCCXVIII])", 318th Meeting, Addis Ababa, 17 April 2012.

———. 2012d. "Press Statement (PSC/PR/BR.2[CCCXL])", 340th Meeting, Addis Ababa, 2 November 2012.

———. 2013. "Communiqué (PSC/PR/COMM[CCCLI])", 351st Meeting, Addis Ababa, 16 January 2013.

AU PSC and EU PSC. 2012. "Press Statement", 5th Joint Consultative Meeting between the EU PSC and the AU PSC, Brussels, 29 May 2012.

AUC Chairperson. 2009. "Report of the Chairperson on the Activities of the Commission Covering the Period January to June 2009 [EX.CL/520(XV])", Executive Council, 15th Ordinary Session, Sirte, 24–30 June 2009.

———. 2012. "Report of the Chairperson of the Commission on the Situations in Guinea Bissau, Mali and Between the Sudan and South Sudan (PSC/Min/3 [CCXIX])", PSC, 319th Meeting at Ministerial Level, Addis Ababa, 24 April 2012.

———. 2013. "Progress Report of the Chairperson of the Commission on the Situation in Guinea-Bissau (PSC/PR/2[CCCLI])", 351st Meeting, Addis Ababa, 16 January 2013.

———. 2014. "Report of the Chairperson of the Commission on the Situation in Guinea Bissau (PSC/PR/2 [CDXLII])", 442nd Meeting, Addis Ababa, 17 June 2014.

Austin, John L. 1962. *How to do Things with Words.* Cambridge, MA: Harvard University Press; Clarendon Press.

Barnett, Michael N. and Martha Finnemore. 2004. *Rules for the World: International Organizations in Global Politics.* Ithaca, NY: Cornell University Press.

Boden, Deirdre. 1994. *The Business of Talk: Organizations in Action.* Cambridge: Polity Press.

Buzan, Barry, Ole Wæver and Jaap d. Wilde. 1998. *Security: A New Framework for Analysis.* Boulder, CO: Lynne Rienner.

CISSA. 2019. Committee of Intelligence & Security Service of Africa. Accessed 23 May 2019. https://cissaau.org/about-cissa/.

Dersso, Solomon A. 2013. *Annual Review of the Peace and Security Council 2012/2013.* Pretoria: Institute for Security Studies (ISS).

———. 2016. *To Intervene or Not to Intervene? An Inside View of the AU's Decision-Making on Article 4(h) and Burundi.* Occasional Paper. Somerville, MA: World Peace Foundation.

Döring, Katharina P.W. and Jens Herpolsheimer. 2018. The Spaces of Intervention for Mali and Guinea-Bissau. *South African Journal of International Affairs* 25 (1): 61–82. doi: 10.1080/10220461.2018.1417898.

Dunn, David H., ed. 1996. *Diplomacy at the Highest Level: The Evolution of International Summitry.* London: Palgrave Macmillan.

Ecker-Ehrhardt, Matthias. 2018. International Organizations "Going Public"? An Event History Analysis of Public Communication Reforms 1950–2015. *International Studies Quarterly* 62 (4): 723–36. doi: 10.1093/isq/sqy025.

ECOWAS Authority. 2012a. "Final Communiqué", 41st Ordinary Session of the Authority of Heads of State and Government, Yamoussoukro, 28–29 June 2012.

———. 2012b. "Final Communiqué", Extraordinary Session of the Authority of ECOWAS Heads of State and Government, Abuja, 11 November 2012.

———. 2012c. "Final Communiqué", Extraordinary Summit of ECOWAS Heads of State and Government, Abuja, 26 April 2012.

———. 2012d. "Final Communiqué", Extraordinary Summit of ECOWAS Heads of State and Government, Dakar, 3 May 2012.

ECOWAS Commission. 2012a. "Annual Report (December 2012): Integration and Political Stability in West Africa", Abuja.

———. 2012b. "Press Release: ECOWAS Cautions Against Protracted Dialogue on Mali", 13 December 2012. Accessed May 16, 2019. https://reliefweb.int/report/mali/ecowas-cautions-against-protracted-dialogue-mali.

———. 2012c. "Press Release: ECOWAS Commission President visits Bissau (N°: 308/2012)", Bissau, 8 November 2012.

———. 2012d. "Press Release: ECOWAS Contact Group Ministers on Guinea Bissau meet in Banjul (N°:122/2012)", Banjul, 29 April 2012.

———. 2012e. "Press Release: ECOWAS Delegation due in Bissau to Impress Immediate Return to Constitutional rule", Abuja, 16 April 2012. Accessed 1 February 2016. http://news.ecowas.int/presseshow.php?nb=106&lang=en&annee=2012.

———. 2012f. "Press Release: ECOWAS Losing Patience over Perennial Crisis in Guinea-Bissau, says Jammeh (123/2012)", Banjul, 30 April 2012.

———. 2012g. "Press Release: ECOWAS Mediation, Security Council to meet in Abidjan on Mali, Guinea Bissau (N°: 102/2012)", Abidjan, 11 April 2012.

———. 2012h. "Press Release: ECOWAS Mission in Guinea-Bissau to be Formalized", Bissau, 6 November 2012. Accessed 15 August 2014. http://news.ecowas.int/presseshow.php?nb=298&lang=en&annee=2012.

———. 2012i. "Press Release: ECOWAS Rallies International Support on Mali (N°: 325/2012)", Report from ECOWAS, Abuja, 26 November 2012. Accessed 16 May 2019. https://reliefweb.int/report/mali/ecowas-rallies-international-support-mali.

———. 2012j. "Press Release: ECOWAS Reaction to Ongoing Coup Attempt in Guinea-Bissau (104/2012)", Abuja, 13 April 2012.

———. 2012k. "Press Release: ECOWAS Sanctions Guinea-Bissau after Failed Talks (124/2012)", Abuja, 1 May 2012.

———. 2012l. "Press Release: ECOWAS Statement on Guinea Bissau (N°: 100/2012)", Abuja, 9 April 2012.

———. 2012m. "Press Release: ECOWAS to Hold Second Extra-Ordinary Summit on Guinea Bissau, Mali (N°:126/2012)", Dakar, 2 May 2012.

———. 2012n. "Press Release: ECOWAS to send Troops to Guinea Bissau, Mali (N°:121/2012)", Abidjan, 27 April 2012.

———. 2012o. "Press Release: La Situation de la Guinee-Bissau Exposee aux Partenaires de la CEDEAO (N°: 296/2012)", Abuja, 1 November 2012.

———. 2012p. "Press Release: Signing of the Memorandum of Understanding of the Defence and Security Sector in Guinea-Bissau (305/2012)", Bissau, 7 November 2012.

———. 2012q. "Presse Release: ECOWAS Statement on Guinea Bissau (N°:109/2012)", Sogakope, 19 April 2012.

ECOWAS Commission President. 2012. "Memorandum on the Situation in Guinea Bissau", Extraordinary Meeting of the Mediation and Security Council, Abuja, 9 November 2012.

———. 2015. "Memorandum on the Situation of the ECOWAS Mission in Guinea Bissau (ECOMIB)", 34th Ordinary Session of the Mediation and Security Council, Accra, May 2015.

Engel, Ulf. 2012. The African Union and Mediation in Cases of Unconstitutional Changes of Government, 2008–2011. In *New Mediation Practices in African Conflicts*, ed. Ulf Engel, 55–82. Leipzig: Leipziger Universitätsverlag.

———. 2016. The 2007 African Charter on Democracy, Elections and Governance: Explaining Late Ratification and Non-Implementation of Compliance Mechanisms. Paper Presented at the 59th Meeting of the African Studies Association, Marriott Wardman Park Hotel, Washington, DC, 1–3 December.

———. 2018. Knowledge Production on Conflict Early Warning at the African Union. *South African Journal of International Affairs* 25 (1): 117–32. doi: 10.1080/10220461.2018.1417902.

———. 2020. *Knowledge Production by African Peace and Security Think Tanks (APSTTs)*. ReCentGlobe Working Paper 43. Leipzig: Leipzig University.

Eubank, Keith. 1966. *The Summit Conferences, 1919–1960*. Norman, OK: University of Oklahoma Press.

Fritzon, Vilhelm. 2015. The African Union: Real Power or Just a Dictators' Club? The Perspective, 20 November 2015. Accessed 23 May 2019. www.theperspective.se/?p=1491.

Galtung, Johan. 1964. Summit Meetings and International Relations. *Journal of Peace Research* 1 (1): 36–54. doi: 10.1177/002234336400100104.

Hartmann, Christof. 2013. *Governance Transfer by the Economic Community of West African States (ECOWAS): A B2 Case Study Report*. SFB-Governance Working Paper Series No. 47. Berlin: Collaborative Research Center (SFB) 700.

Herpolsheimer, Jens and Skollan E. Warnck. 2020. *Mapping Intervention Practices of ECOWAS and the African Union: Methodological and Practical Challenges*. SFB 1199 Working Paper Series No. 22. Leipzig: Leipziger Universitätsverlag.

Lewis, Reuben and Hideaki Shinoda. 2012. Operationalizing Early Warning for Conflict Prevention and Peacebuilding in West Africa: A Case Study of ECOWAS Early Warning System. *Hiroshima Peace Science* 34: 1–32.

Mace, Gordon, Jean-Philippe Thérien, Diana Tussie and Olivier Dabène. 2016. Introduction: Summitry and Governance in Comparative Perspective. In *Summits and Regional Governance: The Americas in Comparative Perspective*, eds Gordon Mace, Jean-Philippe Thérien, Diana Tussie and Olivier Dabène, 1–10. New York: Routledge.

Melissen, Jan. 2003. *Summit Diplomacy Coming of Age.* Discussion Papers in Diplomacy. The Hague: Netherlands Institute of International Relations 'Clingendael'.

Mhaka, Tafi. 2018. The African Union: An Exclusive Club for Brutish Despots, Al Jazeera, 9 June 2018. Accessed 23 2019. www.aljazeera.com/indepth/opinion/africa n-union-exclusive-club-brutish-despots-180607100707234.html.

Neumann, Iver B. 2003. A Region-Building Approach. In *Theories of New Regionalism: A Palgrave Reader*, eds Fredrik Söderbaum and Timothy M. Shaw, 160–78. Houndmills, New York: Palgrave Macmillan.

O'Neil, Glenn. 2015. Communication Evaluation in International Organisations: Methodology, Influence and Use. Doctoral thesis, the London School of Economics.

Reynolds, David. 2007. *Summits: Six Meetings That Shaped the Twentieth Century.* New York: Basic Books.

Sandler, Jen and Renita Thedvall, eds. 2017. *Meeting Ethnography: Meetings as key Technologies of Contemporary Governance, Development, and Resistance.* New York, London: Routledge.

Schwartzman, Helen B. 1989. *The Meeting: Gatherings in Organizations and Communities.* Boston, MA: Springer.

Searle, John. 2013 [1964]. What is a Speech Act? In *Philosophy in America*, ed. Max Black, 221–39. New York: Routledge.

Skinner, Quentin. 1970. Conventions and the Understanding of Speech Acts. *The Philosophical Quarterly* 20 (79): 118–38. doi: 10.2307/2218084.

Snow, Nancy and Philip M. Taylor, eds. 2009. *Routledge Handbook of Public Diplomacy.* New York: Routledge.

Söderbaum, Fredrik. 2004. Modes of Regional Governance in Africa: Neoliberalism, Sovereignty Boosting, and Shadow Networks. *Global Governance* 10 (4): 419–36. doi: 10.1163/19426720-01004004.

Stanley, Aaron and Scott Malcomson. 2019. African Union Shifting to 'Coalitions of the Willing', *The East African*, 23 May 2019. Accessed 23 May 2019. https://www.theeastafrican.co.ke/oped/comment/African-Union-shifting-to-Coalitions-of-the-Willing/434750-4576422-118x6l9/index.html.

Tieku, Thomas K. 2004. Explaining the Clash and Accommodation of Interests of Major Actors in the Creation of the African Union. *African Affairs* 103 (411): 249–67. doi: 10.1093/afraf/adh041.

———. 2019. Ruling from the Shadows: The Nature and Functions of Informal International Rules in World Politics. *International Studies Review* 10 (1): 55. doi: 10.1093/isr/viz012.

UNSC and AU PSC. 2012. "Communiqué of the Consultative Meeting between Members of the Security Council of the United Nations and the Peace and Security Council of the African Union", New York, 13 June 2012.

van Vree, Wilbert. 2011. Meetings: The Frontline of Civilization. *The Sociological Review* 59 (1 suppl.): 241–62. doi: 10.1111/j.1467-954X.2011.01987.x.

Wane, El-Ghassim, Charles Mwaura, Shewit Hailu, Simone Kopfmüller, Doug Bond, Ulf Engel and João G. Porto. 2010. The Continental Early Warning System: Methodology and Approach. In *Africa's New Peace and Security Architecture: Promoting Norms, Institutionalzing Solutions*, eds Ulf Engel and João G. Porto, 91–110. Farnham: Ashgate.

WANEP. 2019. The West Africa Network for Peacebuilding (WANEP): About Us. Accessed 23 May 2019. www.wanep.org/wanep/index.php?option=com_content&view=section&layout=blog&id=1&Itemid=4.

Williams, Paul D. 2009. The Peace and Security Council of the African Union: Evaluating an Embryonic International Institution. *The Journal of Modern African Studies* 47 (4): 603–26. doi: 10.1017/s0022278x09990048.

4 Establishing 'presence'

ECOWAS and AU intervention practices 'on the ground'

Introduction

Recent military and police deployments to conflict situations in West Africa, such as the ESF missions to Guinea-Bissau (ECOMIB) and Gambia (ECOMIG) as well as the 3000 AU troops announced in February 2020 to deploy to the Sahel, seem to suggest a (re)militarization of conflict interventions by African regional organizations (ROs) in that area.[1] A similar trend has been observed at the continental level more generally (e.g., cf. Gelot 2016; Abrahamsen 2018). However, military and police deployments have neither been the only nor the primary practice that actors at ECOWAS and the AU have employed to intervene 'on the ground'. Rather, I argue, these need to be understood as complementary measures adopted selectively in order to make use of all available tools. From this perspective, military and police deployments have aimed to enhance ongoing non-military practices 'on the ground', not to replace them, and have complemented intervention practices employed 'from afar' (see Chapter 3).[2]

As pointed out in previous chapters (see Chapters 1 and 3), at least three sets of interrelated practices have characterized their efforts 'on the ground'. These have been, first, dispatching diplomatic field missions and establishing liaison offices, second, deploying 'technical' support missions and, third, deploying military and police missions. In addition, as has been the case 'from afar', ECOWAS and AU actors have also engaged other regional or international actors 'on the ground' (dealt with separately in Chapter 6). From a spatial perspective, it becomes clear that ECOWAS and AU actors have pursued all of these practices aiming to create direct connections between the conflict site and their headquarters, and to establish their 'presence' *in* conflict situations, aiming to integrate them into their respective regional spaces. Therefore, this chapter subsequently takes closer looks at each of these sets of practices, the specific actors behind them and their spatializing effects.

Dispatching diplomatic field missions and establishing liaison offices

As discussed in Chapter 3, ECOWAS and the AU have collected information and produced conflict-related knowledge from different sources, through different channels and at different sites. In this regard, field missions, special envoys and representatives, as well as liaison offices, have played a key role. A common practice for many international and regional organizations, these have allowed 'connecting' to the situation 'on the ground', visiting relevant places and meeting relevant actors. However, even though gathering and channeling information is of central importance, such missions also fulfill several additional functions. To date, neither diplomatic missions dispatched to conflict sites nor special representatives and liaison offices have received sufficient analytical attention in the existing literature. Therefore, this section takes a closer look at this set of intervention practices of ECOWAS and AU actors more generally, and specifically with regard to diplomatic missions dispatched to Guinea-Bissau in the aftermath of the coup of April 2012. Finally, the section also analyzes how this prominent set of practices has related to space-making during conflict interventions.

ECOWAS and AU field missions

At least since the 1990s, dispatching different kinds of field missions to conflict situations in West Africa and Africa respectively has become a regular response by ECOWAS and AU actors (see Figures 4.1 and 4.2). Most common have been 'fact-finding' missions. However, these missions have often gone beyond finding 'mere facts', instead also assuming important roles in the direct, 'face-to-face' messaging of African ROs towards actors in conflict situations (e.g., in the form of 'sensitization' missions). While such messages may include general information, covered also in public communication, they also allow speaking more bluntly and the use of information not meant for the wider public.[3] Second, these missions often involve diplomatic and mediation efforts, facilitating dialogue among 'local' stakeholders, either through some sort of 'shuttle diplomacy' or by bringing them together physically for joint meetings and discussion. Here, it is often the seniority of mission participants, often current or former heads of state and ministers, that lends them authority and some influence (cf. Khadiagala 2016). Finally, these missions provide opportunities to engage other international or regional actors involved at the ground level (see Chapter 6).[4] While most of these missions are short- or medium-term, ECOWAS and AU actors have also used liaison offices and special representatives as a way of long-term engagement in conflict situations (see below).

In the ECOWAS context, fact-finding became an increasing concern during the ECOMOG interventions of the 1990s in Liberia, Sierra Leone and Guinea-Bissau (see Chapter 5). These experiences also led to the formal inclusion of fact-finding and mediation missions in the 1999 Protocol Relating to the Mechanism for Conflict Prevention, Management, Resolution, Peace-Keeping and Security (the 1999 Mechanism), as one of the actions available to the ECOWAS Executive Secretary (since 2007 the President of the ECOWAS Commission) to prevent or manage conflicts (ECOWAS 1999 , Art.

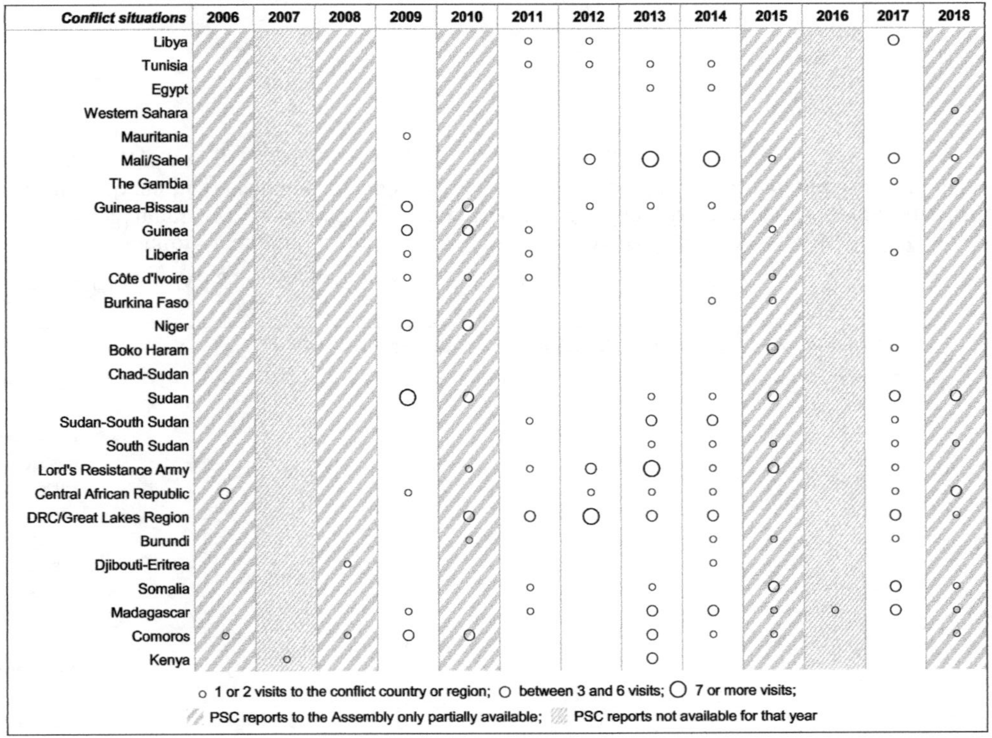

Figure 4.1 Visits of AU actors to conflict sites, 2006–18

Notes: This is an exploratory mapping. Counting has been based on available documents and information provided therein only (see Chapter 1); actual numbers may therefore be higher than indicated in this figure. For a detailed discussion of the challenges and limitations of quantifying ECOWAS and AU intervention practices, see Herpolsheimer and Warnck (2020)

Source: *(cc) BY-NC-ND Jens Herpolsheimer, Skollan Elisabeth Warnck*

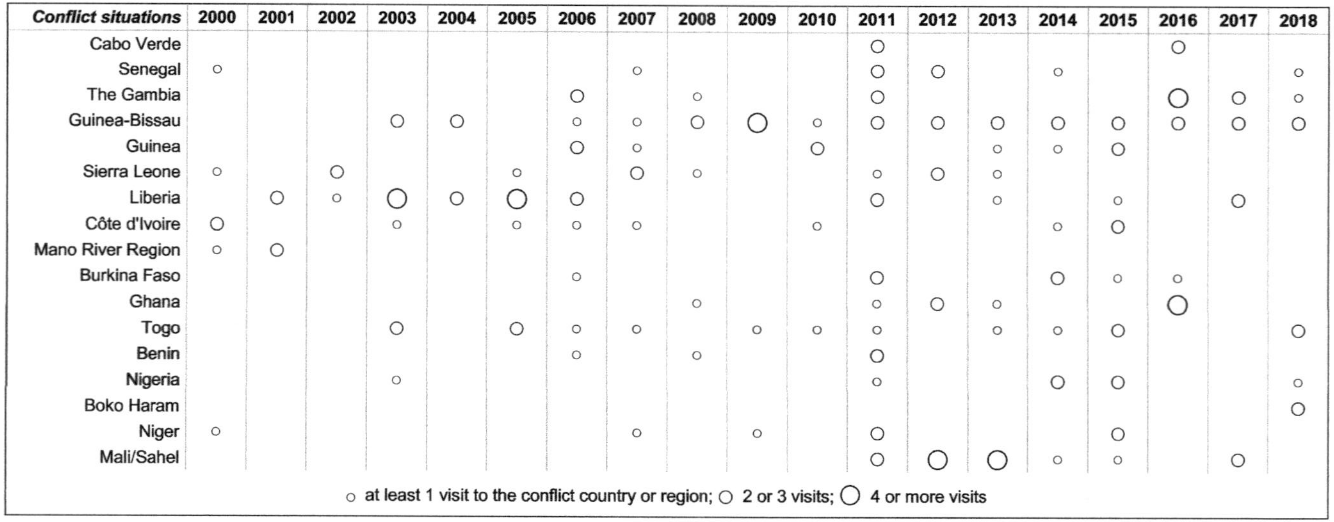

Figure 4.2 Visits of ECOWAS actors to conflict sites, 2000–18

Notes: This is an exploratory mapping. Counting has been based on available documents and information provided therein only (see Chapter 1); actual numbers may therefore be higher than indicated in this figure. For a detailed discussion of the challenges and limitations of quantifying ECOWAS and AU intervention practices, see Herpolsheimer and Warnck (2020)

Source: *(cc) BY-NC-ND Jens Herpolsheimer, Skollan Elisabeth Warnck*

15). With regard to election observation, the 2001 Supplementary Protocol on Democracy and Good Governance specifically tasks the Executive Secretary/Commission President to dispatch fact-finding and "exploratory missions" (ECOWAS 2001, Art. 13). Since then, field missions of different constellations of ECOWAS actors (e.g., high-level delegations, contact groups) have become a cornerstone of ECOWAS conflict prevention and intervention in West Africa, as the example of Guinea-Bissau demonstrates below.

At the continental scale, fact-finding was formally established as a means for conflict management as early as 1964, in the Protocol of the OAU Commission of Mediation, Conciliation and Arbitration (OAU 1964, Art. XVIII). Subsequently, OAU fact-finding missions have been a tool to gather information at least since the 1970s. For example, in 1974, an OAU fact-finding mission visited South Africa to assess whether the OAU should recognize the Unity Movement of South Africa as another liberation movement (cf. OAU 1974). However, since the 1990s, they have become a common element of OAU (e.g., cf. OAU Central Organ 1998) and subsequently AU conflict interventions. The 1993 OAU Mechanism for Conflict Prevention, Management and Resolution reaffirmed fact-finding missions as one of the tools available to the OAU Secretary General in order to "prevent, manage and resolve conflicts" (OAU Assembly 1993, Art. 22). While the AU PSC Protocol does not explicitly refer to fact-finding missions, it includes this kind of action in the 'functions' (e.g., good offices and mediation, AU 2002, Art. 6) and 'powers' of the AU PSC (e.g., "undertake peace-making and peace-building functions", AU 2002, Art. 7). Likewise, the Chairperson of the AU Commission may "deploy efforts and take all initiatives deemed appropriate to prevent, manage and resolve conflicts" (e.g., using his/her good offices, AU 2002, Art. 10).

ECOWAS and AU field missions to Guinea-Bissau in 2012

Following the coup on 12 April 2012, the first ECOWAS field mission arrived in Bissau on 16 April for a one-day visit. It was led by the ECOWAS Commission President, Kadré Désiré Ouédraogo (appointed in February 2012), and comprised, among others, the Minister of Foreign Affairs of Côte d'Ivoire, the Nigerian Minister of State for Foreign Affairs, as well as the Chiefs of Defense Staff of Côte d'Ivoire, Guinea and Nigeria. Their main directive was to deliver a "special message" from the Chairman of the ECOWAS Authority, President Ouattara of Côte d'Ivoire at the time (cf. ECOWAS Commission 2012e; ECOWAS MSC 2012b). Stressing ECOWAS' principled position, rejecting the coup, the delegation negotiated a written agreement with the 'military command', accepting the restoration of 'constitutional order' based on "modalities to be worked out with the help of ECOWAS" (ECOWAS MSC 2012c, 2). However, just the next day, on 17 April, the 'military command' nevertheless signed an agreement with several political parties creating a 'national transition council', which the ECOWAS Commission President rejected in a press statement on 19 April (see Chapter 3).

Following that, at an extraordinary summit on 26 April 2012, ECOWAS heads of state created the Regional Contact Group for Guinea-Bissau (RCG-GB), composed of representatives from seven member states (Burkina Faso, Cabo Verde, Gambia, Guinea, Nigeria, Senegal and Togo), chaired by Nigeria (cf. ECOWAS MSC 2012c, 2–3). Initial negotiations between the RCG-GB (at ministerial level) and the principal political stakeholders of Guinea-Bissau, in Banjul on 29 April, failed, triggering ECOWAS sanctions. Subsequently, the RCG-GB Chairman met with Guinea-Bissau's political actors on 4 May, and an RCG-GB mission comprising political and military officials from Nigeria and Côte d'Ivoire (RCG-GB and ECOWAS Chairs respectively) visited Bissau from 10 to 11 May. As it turned out impossible to foster agreement among all political parties, on these occasions, the delegation decided to recognize the Speaker of Guinea-Bissau's National Assembly, Manuel Serifo Nhamadjo, as interim president, in accordance with the country's constitution, and tasked him with "wide-ranging consultations" regarding the appointment of a "consensual" prime minister (ECOWAS MSC 2012c, 3). This helped to trigger a negotiation process among political actors in Bissau, eventually on 16 May confirming Nhamadjo as interim president and appointing Rui Duarte de Barros (then UEMOA Commissioner of Administration and Finance) as new 'consensual' prime minister. However, the PAIGC refused to participate in the consultation process and logically rejected its outcome, instead insisting on the reinstatement of the overthrown government and the completion of the electoral process that the coup had interrupted (see Chapters 1 and 3).

On 17 May 2012, one day after the new, ECOWAS-brokered transition deal was reached, the ESF started to deploy to Bissau. ECOWAS Chiefs of Defense Staff had worked their contacts with the military in Bissau, and obtained a formal request from the new ECOWAS-facilitated authorities (cf. ECOWAS MSC 2012c, 4). The deployment process of ECOMIB continued throughout the following months (see "Deploying military and police peacekeeping forces" below).

After the initial engagement 'on the ground', another ECOWAS field mission followed only in November 2012. Following negotiations since September, on 7 November, ECOWAS Commission President Ouédraogo and Guinea-Bissau's Minister of Foreign Affairs, Faustino Fudut Imbali, signed the Status of Mission Agreement, formalizing ECOMIB, and a Memorandum of Understanding (MoU) on the Defense and Security Sector Reform Program in Bissau. The ECOWAS delegation also comprised the Commissioner for Political Affairs, Peace and Security, Salamatu Husseini Suleiman (from Nigeria), and the Chair of the Committee of Chiefs of Defense Staff (CCDS), General Soumaila Bakayoko (of Côte d'Ivoire), as well as the Chiefs of Defense Staff of Burkina Faso, Nigeria and Senegal, representing the three main troop and police contributors to ECOMIB (cf.

ECOWAS Commission 2012h). In addition, since September 2012, ECOWAS actors had been working towards realizing the joint assessment mission that the representatives of the AU, CPLP, EU, UN and ECOWAS had agreed upon during consultations in New York (see Chapter 3). For ECOWAS, this mission meant a possible way to overcome its differences with the other organizations (cf. ECOWAS MSC 2012a, para. 23). Originally proposed for late November, the mission eventually took place in late December 2012 (see Chapter 6).

ECOWAS field missions to Guinea-Bissau in 2012 largely reflected similar engagements 'on the ground' during previous crises, and even more so in more recent years. ECOWAS has dispatched various delegations, envoys and mediators since the war of 1998/9. More recently, in particular in response to the political deadlock that emerged in August 2015 and lasted until February 2018, we have seen persistent, frequent and intense high-level engagement – even more so than in 2012. In these efforts, interestingly, tensions and competition have repeatedly emerged between different ECOWAS representatives (e.g., chairs, mediators and special envoys). For example, when President Jonathan of Nigeria, in 2012, made himself Chairman of the RCG-GB, this meant also sidelining President Condé of Guinea, the appointed ECOWAS Mediator for Guinea-Bissau.[5] In a similar way, Presidents Sall and Condé (of Senegal and Guinea, respectively) started competing diplomatic initiatives throughout 2016 and 2017, a situation that was further complicated with the appointment of former Nigerian president Obasanjo as ECOWAS Special Envoy for Guinea-Bissau in 2016.[6]

Contrary to ECOWAS, and contrary to more general patterns of engagement with conflict in Guinea-Bissau and elsewhere, AU actors did not field a single mission to engage the crisis 'on the ground' in 2012. However, the AUC Chairperson, Jean Ping, on 8 May 2012 announced the appointment of Ovídio Manuel Barbosa Pequeno (former Foreign Minister and Ambassador of Sao Tomé and Principe) as his Special Representative (SRCC) and Head of the AU liaison office in Guinea-Bissau (AULO-GB) (cf. AU Commission 2012b), to take action *in* Bissau on behalf of the AU (AUC Chairperson 2013, para. 14). During previous crises in Guinea-Bissau, AU actors had authorized and dispatched various diplomatic missions. For example, already during the conflict in 1998/9, then-OAU Secretary General Salim Ahmed Salim (former Prime Minister of Tanzania) appointed Alexandre Zandamela (then Ambassador of Mozambique to Ethiopia and Permanent Representative to the OAU) as his Special Envoy to Guinea-Bissau, who traveled to Bissau and neighboring countries, together with OAU Secretariat officials, for consultations and to brief back in Addis (cf. OAU Central Organ 1998, para. 12). Likewise, more recently, since the political stalemate, beginning in late 2015, the AU PSC has dispatched several field missions to Guinea-Bissau. For example, this included a PSC delegation visiting Bissau in March 2016 (cf. AU Commission 2016b).

In addition to the fact-finding, assessment or mediation initiatives, 'on the ground', actors at ECOWAS and the AU also have continuously deployed election-observation missions (EOMs), short- and long-term, to Guinea-Bissau. These have played a double role. On the one hand, ECOWAS and AU EOMs have contributed to live, first-hand information gathering and reporting, as well as mediating or managing tensions before, during and following elections. Like envoys and representatives, these EOMs have often profited from high-level leadership. For example, President Joaquim Chissano of Mozambique headed the AU EOM in Guinea-Bissau during the 2014 electoral process. There, he played an important role, constantly engaging political parties and opponents, using his stature to get access, bring people together and if necessary apply pressure, all to ensure a smooth running of the elections.[7] On the other hand, the teams deployed in the EOM frameworks have provided technical expertise, which I will come back to in the section "Providing 'technical' support".

ECOWAS and AU special representatives and liaison offices

The legal basis for the Special Representatives of the President of the ECOWAS Commission (SRPC) is provided by the 1999 Mechanism. Article 32, in particular, states that the ECOWAS Mediation and Security Council (MSC) appoints special representatives on the recommendation of the Executive Secretary (now the Commission President). The principal role and functions of these representatives mainly include providing political orientation for the mission, initiating negotiations with different stakeholders, briefing on the situation, coordinating activities with other regional and international actors and maintaining constant contact with and regularly reporting to the Commission President (ECOWAS 1999, Art. 32). Article 34 of the 1999 Mechanism makes additional provisions regarding the "chain of command". In this way, the SRPCs and their offices help the Commission President to maintain direct and regular contact with authorities of member states that experience crises or conflicts, helping to address key issues on peace, security, elections and post-conflict reconstruction (e.g., ECOWAS Commission 2006, para. 371). For the ECOWAS Commission, its special representatives and liaison offices are the "principal actors on the ground", "in the field", their "presence" being "essential" to supporting peacemaking efforts and ending violence and conflict (ECOWAS Commission 2007, para. 232, 2008a, para. 299).

The first offices of ECOWAS special representatives opened in the early 2000s – in Côte d'Ivoire (2002/3), Liberia (2004) and Guinea-Bissau (2004/5) (cf. ECOWAS Commission 2003, para. 384, 2004, 253, 2005, 251). The experience with these offices and special representatives contributed to the emergence and consolidation of the more general practice of creating long-term local representations in conflict areas (cf. ECOWAS Commission 2007, 231, 2008a, 298). Since then, the number of ECOWAS liaison offices and SRPCs in member states has increased to ten, adding offices in Burkina Faso, Cabo Verde, Gambia, Guinea-Conakry, Mali, Niger and Togo to the list. Whereas, initially, the status of these offices distinguished between 'special' and 'permanent representations' and representatives, more recently they have subsequently been transformed into 'resident representations' (cf. ECOWAS 2020), to increase the presence and visibility of ECOWAS across all member states (cf. ECOWAS Commission and CMI 2018, 29). In addition, ECOWAS maintains liaison offices at the AU in Addis Ababa and the EU in Brussels, as well as a permanent representation at the UN in New York (ECOWAS 2020).

Within the AU, the PSC Protocol (2002) provides the legal basis for the Special Representatives of the Chairperson of the AU Commission (SRCC). Article 10.c stipulates that the AUC Chairperson may at her own initiative or upon request by the PSC make use of special representatives, among other actors, to prevent or resolve conflicts and promote peacebuilding and post-conflict reconstruction (AU 2002, Art. 10.c).[8] Moreover, apparently influenced by the provisions in the 1999 Mechanism of ECOWAS (Article 34), the PSC Protocol further clarifies the "chain of command", the SRCC reporting "through the appropriate channels to the AUC Chairperson" (AU 2002, Art. 13.7). The only reference to liaison offices is with respect to strengthening coordination and cooperation with regional mechanisms (AU 2002, Art. 16.8). Nevertheless, liaison offices in countries experiencing conflict or crises have assumed a "fundamental role in the implementation of APSA" (AU Commission 2015, 57).

Currently, the AU has 13 liaison offices in (former) conflict countries, most of them headed by special representatives, working with the AU PSD as part of APSA. In addition, the AU sustains seven permanent representational and specialized offices, mostly at international organizations (cf. AU Commission and New Zealand Crown 2020, 112–15).[9] Despite doubts about their relevance and efficiency, creating such liaison offices has become one of the AU's standard practices to respond to conflict in Africa 'on the ground' (Butedi 2018, 100).[10] The first such liaison office opened already in 1994 in Western Sahara (and was maintained until 2019), then still operated by the OAU, supporting the process that was supposed to lead towards the independence referendum (Global Peace Operations Review 2011). Subsequently, the OAU Central Organ (the forerunner of the AU PSC, created by the 1993 OAU Mechanism) established liaison offices in the Comoros (1997–2018), the Democratic Republic of the Congo (1999) and Côte d'Ivoire (2002/3). During the early years of the AU, the PSC established liaison offices in Liberia (2004), Burundi (2004), Chad and Somalia (both 2005)[11] and Sudan and South Sudan (both 2007/8). Later followed offices in the Central African Republic and Guinea-Bissau (both 2010), Libya and Madagascar (both 2011) and Mali (2013).

Liaison offices of both ECOWAS and the AU have exercised a certain degree of autonomy, using the room for maneuver provided in their respective mandates, which are not always clearly defined, and making pragmatic decisions in the face of 'realities on the ground'. While this has allowed them to develop their own agency, they have also been left somewhat on their own by their respective headquarters. In any case, the effectiveness of their work has very much depended on individual actors (personalities). In the case of the AU, the work of AULOs has been perceived overall as a positive contribution to the maintenance of peace and security. However, assessments commissioned by the AU PSD reported 'morale and motivation issues', AULO staff felt overburdened with responsibilities, pointing to flaws in the recruitment process, and isolated from the 'mainstream AU structures' (Nathan et al. 2015, para. 15.9–15.10; see also AU Commission 2015, 57). Despite some improvement in recent years, these challenges largely persist (cf. Nathan et al. 2015, para. 15.15ff. and 15.25ff.). For ECOWAS, such information is less available, but interview partners pointed out very similar challenges for ECOWAS liaison offices.[12]

Nevertheless, in some cases, these offices have played important roles, as Butedi (2018) explains for the AULO in Madagascar, and the following considerations show with respect to ECOWAS and AU liaison offices in Guinea-Bissau.

ECOWAS and AU liaison offices in Guinea-Bissau

The *ECOWAS Commission* first decided to create a local representation in Bissau in response to military uprisings in October 2004, resulting in the killing of Army Chief of Staff General Veríssimo Correia Seabra (cf. UNSG 2004, para. 11). The office took up its work in January 2005 (cf. ECOWAS 2005, 157–8).[13] During the following months, the UN Office in Guinea-Bissau provided logistical support for the setup of the ECOWAS office (cf. UNSG 2005, para. 15). In July 2005, the ECOWAS Executive Secretary appointed Colonel Hamed Sidibé (a Malian national) as his Special Representative to Guinea-Bissau.[14] Sidibé and his office played an important role supporting the presidential elections in that year, and mediating in the post-electoral crisis, overcoming Malam Bacai Sanhá's refusal to accept that he had lost the presidential run-off to João Bernardo ("Nino") Vieira (Mendy and Lobban 2013, 130). ECOWAS actors subsequently decided to maintain the office due to continuing political instability in Guinea-Bissau, after President Vieira had dissolved the government and dismissed the prime minister in late October 2005. Therefore, they tasked the special representative to report regularly on the situation in the country (cf. ECOWAS Commission 2005, para. 251), to work with national stakeholders, as well as the AU, EU and other partners to stabilize Guinea-Bissau through post-conflict reconstruction and security sector reform (SSR) (ECOWAS Commission 2006, 346–7, 2007, 262–3).

Although very little information is available on the period between 2006 and 2010, the Office of the Special Representative of the ECOWAS Executive Secretary (since 2007 President of the ECOWAS Commission) seems to have discretely continued its work in Guinea-Bissau under the leadership of Sidibé (e.g., cf. ECOWAS Commission 2006, 346–7, 2007, 262–3, 2008a, 298, 2008b; ECOWAS CCDS 2010; UNIOGBIS 2009).[15] In March 2011, ECOWAS heads of state approved a reinforcement of the Office of the SRPC, in anticipation of the deployment of a "security assistance team", which the liaison office should coordinate, in collaboration with the CPLP (cf. ECOWAS Commission 2011).[16] In early 2012, ECOWAS Commission President Ouédraogo appointed Ambassador Ansoumane Ceesay (from Gambia, previously SRPC to Liberia) as new SRPC to Guinea-Bissau. Since then, references to the SRPC and his office have increased, although still providing only very limited information about the activities of the ECOWAS liaison office and its top official in Guinea-Bissau (e.g., ECOWAS Commission 2013, 2014b, 2014d, 2016a, 2016b). This is also true for its response to the coup of April 2012. In August 2016, Blaise Diplo-Djomand assumed the position of SRPC (national of Côte d'Ivoire, former executive of the Central Bank of West African States).

During 2012 and following years, the SRPC and his staff largely played a supporting role, in particular reporting on developments 'on the ground' to the ECOWAS Commission, and providing logistical support for the different high-level field missions that visited Bissau in 2012. However, especially when compared with the AU's engagement 'on the ground', the role of the ECOWAS liaison office and the SRPC has been secondary to efforts of regional chiefs of defense staff, foreign ministers and heads of state, as well as the ECOWAS Commission President. Their initiatives and missions feature in MSC final reports and memos on the situation and ECOWAS efforts in Guinea-Bissau. Contrary to that, the available material does not show any reference to ECOWAS' local representation in the country (e.g., cf. ECOWAS MSC 2012c; ECOWAS Commission President 2012).[17] Since early 2013, different ECOWAS organs have agreed and called on the Commission to strengthen the ECOWAS liaison office in Bissau, because of "additional responsibilities", linked to the reinforcement of ECOMIB (ECOWAS MSC 2013a, para. 56; see also ECOWAS Authority 2014, para. 48).[18]

Differences in relative status have also affected what the SRPC has been able to achieve in Guinea-Bissau. For example, during the political crisis emerging in August 2015, when President Vaz sacked Prime Minister Domingos Simões Pereira, having been 'on the ground', Ceesay knew the political environment but could not access the President of Guinea-Bissau in the same way that Special Envoy Obasanjo could. On the one hand, Obasanjo carried more weight due to his status as former President of Nigeria, widely respected throughout Africa. On the other hand, he had been appointed by the ECOWAS Authority (i.e., heads of state), as opposed to Ceesay, who had been appointed by the Commission President (although via the MSC). Therefore, Obasanjo was able to broker a deal in September 2015, getting Vaz to accept a consensual prime minister, Carlos Correia. However, eight months later, in May 2016, Vaz reversed that decision, reappointing Baciro Djá, who had held that position before Correia (cf. Perdigao 2016).

In late 2016, the ECOWAS Special Representative drew serious criticism from civil society in Bissau and the EU for publicly siding with President Vaz on his controversial interpretation of the Conakry Agreement, in particular regarding the appointment of Umaro Sissoko Embalo as 'consensual' prime minister. The SRPC claimed that the international community supported this appointment, which was not the case.[19] This came amid increasing disappointment of regional and international actors with the behavior of President Vaz of Guinea-Bissau and subsequent public aggressions by Sissoko against ECOWAS Commission President Marcel Alain de Souza (from Benin).[20] The perception that the ECOWAS SRPC may at times have been too close to the President of Guinea-Bissau also applied to the previous SRPC.[21]

The idea to open an *AU liaison office in Guinea-Bissau* (AULO-GB) first arose in June 2005, when AUC Chairperson Alpha Oumar Konaré (from Mali) suggested to the PSC to follow the example of ECOWAS (AUC Chairperson 2005).[22] However, more seriously, the idea re-emerged in the aftermath of the double assassinations of President Vieira and Army Chief of Staff NaWaie in March 2009. During a special session of the AU Assembly in Tripoli, on 30–31 August 2009, African heads of state adopted a plan of action, including several decisions on Guinea-Bissau, in line with the AU's emerging approach towards post-conflict reconstruction and development (PCRD; see Chapter 5).[23] Among other provisions, the plan envisioned the 'rapid' deployment of a joint AU–ECOWAS stabilization mission with support from the UN, EU and other partners. This mission should support the consolidation of peace and security in the country, supporting SSR, PCRD and the fight against drug trafficking (AU Assembly 2009, para. 9). In line with these provisions, and following another request by the AU Assembly in February 2010 (cf. AU Assembly 2010, para. 26), the AU Commission suggested setting up a liaison office in Guinea-Bissau, to prepare the ground for the stabilization mission. In March 2010, the PSC requested that the AU Commission "accelerate the process of establishing" the AULO-GB, in anticipation of an "AU/ECOWAS Joint Civilian Mission" (AU PSC 2010, para. 9).

On 7 October 2010, AUC Chairperson Ping publicly announced the appointment of Sebastião da Silva Isata (former Angolan Vice Minister of Foreign Affairs) as SRCC and Head of the newly established AULO-GB, who had taken office on 4 October, tasked to "spearhead and coordinate the implementation of AU decisions" (cf. AU Commission 2010).[24] Additional staff joined the office in January 2011. However, in March 2011, Isata was reappointed as SRCC to Burundi, leaving the position vacant until the appointment of Ovídio Pequeno in April 2012, which was announced in May, and who joined the office in July 2012.[25] In the meantime, the office continued working, led by Matthieu Kinouani as Acting Head of the AULO-GB, until then and thereafter working as analyst at the AU PSD.[26]

After the coup of April 2012, staff of the AU liaison office assumed a central role in the AU's approach towards Guinea-Bissau, especially with the appointment of SRCC Pequeno. Different from ECOWAS, the AULO-GB constituted the AU's only direct engagement 'on the ground'.[27] The conference room of the AULO-GB became the site of many meetings, and staff of the AU office played a key role in bringing different actors and conflict parties together, facilitating dialogue among them. In this, they sought and succeeded to act and be perceived as a neutral body, accessible for all actors. From that position, they tried building confidence and moving forward through persuasion and continuous dialogue.[28] Adopting a pragmatic approach, very similar to ECOWAS, the AU office worked from 'realities' in Bissau, pursuing the main objective of establishing a viable government, and thereby hopefully lasting peace.[29] Interestingly, although not shared among AU staff in Bissau, a perception of 'the AU' as 'far away' by local actors, but consequently also with less vested interests, may have helped.[30] In addition, SRPC Pequeno was widely respected among national and international stakeholders in Bissau for his diplomatic qualities.[31]

Throughout the second half of 2012, Pequeno also helped to mediate tensions between actors at ECOWAS and the CPLP, shuttling between their different representatives and trying to bring them together (see Chapter 6). He frequently travelled to meet with high-level government officials in and outside the region with a stake in Guinea-Bissau.[32] For example, this included a trip to Abuja, together with the Special Representative of the UN Secretary General for Guinea-Bissau, at the time Joseph Mutaboba (former Rwandan Secretary General in the Ministries of Foreign Affairs and Internal Affairs and Permanent Representative to the UN), in August 2012, where the two special representatives tried to overcome opposing positions of ECOWAS and CPLP actors. Despite reaching some common ground, as it turned out by November 2012, little actual progress in that direction had been achieved. At this point, the planned joint assessment mission appeared as the only way out of the persisting opposition of the two organizations, and especially key member states (cf. ECOWAS Commission President 2012, para. 10). More so than the ECOWAS liaison office, the AULO-GB has been involved also with technical support provided to government agencies of Guinea-Bissau (see "Providing 'technical' support" below).[33]

Both liaison offices, of ECOWAS and the AU, have maintained close connections with their respective headquarters, constantly communicating by phone or email, exchanging memos and meetings.[34] As mentioned in Chapter 3, the information coming from 'the field' (e.g., calls, emails, reports) has crucially fed into the production of conflict-related knowledge at the headquarters of ECOWAS and the AU. However, some differences exist. At the AU, regular reporting and personal communication with AULO-GB staff has formed a key ingredient for analysis that PSD staff compiles. While SRCCs and AULOs report to the AUC Chairperson, they do so through the 'appropriate channels', and in practice are managed through the PSD. Somewhat different, at ECOWAS, SRPCs and ECOWAS liaison offices *directly* report to the President of the ECOWAS Commission. Therefore, reports and exchanges do not automatically run through nor are necessarily always by officers working in the Department of Political Affairs, Peace and Security.

Consequently, they often have to use their own networks, and cannot always rely on information from the SRPC or the liaison office.[35]

Field missions, liaison offices and space-making

Summing up the above, it becomes clear that different diplomatic missions and the establishment of local liaison offices have played a key role in the approaches of ECOWAS and the AU towards conflict in their respective regions. They have continuously dispatched missions to get a feeling for the situation 'on the ground', to get to know local actors and to have 'first-hand' information about conflicts. However, especially in moments of crisis, these missions have allowed the two organizations to get a 'handle' on the situations: enabling them to convey messages from headquarters and member states directly, and at the highest levels, to negotiate with or mediate among stakeholders (local, regional and international), and if necessary apply pressure, in order to work towards conflict management.

All of these aspects also relate directly to space-making, especially through the creation of connections and the establishment of 'physical' presence *in* specific conflict situations. Even more directly than public communication, the communication running through missions, delegations, envoys or special representatives and liaison offices brings the 'region' to the 'local' scale – that is, working in the opposite direction than the production of conflict knowledge at headquarters. For example, representatives of ECOWAS and the AU go to Guinea-Bissau, communicating and seeking to implement regional positions and decisions.

The physical presence of individuals or groups, representing their respective regions, signals interest in and importance of 'local' affairs. It also creates popular visibility and attention for the region at the local level, for example, through local media and blogs reporting on the missions, logos on cars and flags moving through Bissau. At the same time, it sensitizes 'local' actors, especially but not exclusively elites, about their 'belonging' not only to the national but also to different regional scales. While that may constrain their actions, it may also allow them to use these scales actively in order to enlarge or diversify their 'playing field'.

All of this contributes to the construction of regional spaces. Specific spatial formats (i.e., 'nation state' and 'region') guide action taken by ECOWAS and AU actors, and simultaneously are the objectives of that action. Actors within both organizations to some extent share imaginations of what states in the region should be and how they should relate to other states and the region (see the following section and Chapter 5). Once more, the nation state is linked to the region in a way that legitimizes intervention by the latter in the former. However, what becomes apparent 'on the ground', much less visible in actions taken 'from afar', is that in the example of interventions in Guinea-Bissau, while formally addressing or targeting the 'nation state', ECOWAS and AU interventions have largely focused on Bissau, the capital, almost entirely leaving aside the rest of the country. Thus, interventions commonly engage actors and institutions associated with the central state in the capital, which is a part of the spatial format 'nation state' that is supposed to stand in for the whole national territory. ECOWAS and AU interventions in Mali during 2012 are another example of this logic. Although ECOWAS efforts also included an intense planning process for military deployment to Mali, immediate action 'on the ground' targeted Bamako, preventing the insurgents from capturing the capital and focusing on a quick 'return to constitutional order' through diplomatic and mediation efforts among political actors in the capital (cf. Döring 2019, 5–6, 66).

A similar tendency to focus on central state institutions, mostly located in the capital, can be observed in the technical and material support that ECOWAS and AU actors have provided to Guinea-Bissau in the pursuit of finding lasting solutions. These are the subject of the next section.

Providing 'technical' support

A practice rather common for big international or regional organizations, such as the EU or the UN, has been the provision of technical and material support to countries or institutions in crisis. Often aiming to build state capacities, this has included among other things sending expert teams either to assist in specific exercises (e.g., elections, training of military, police or civil society) or to integrate into existing government structures, providing long-term support. It has also included budget support or the provision of specific goods or equipment. With regard to the latter, different NGOs have also played a role. Although much of this support commonly counts as 'development aid', in a more general sense, it has also been a key practice by different actors aiming to 'stabilize' conflict situations, build peace and engage in post-conflict reconstruction. Most importantly, these efforts have sought to (re-)construct 'functioning' states, assumed to be the only viable basis for sustainable peace and security. Therefore, the preparation and holding of democratic elections, and reforms targeting the economic, justice and security sectors, have been at the top of most intervention agendas – along with more general humanitarian support (e.g., cf. Grävingholt, Gänzle and Ziaja 2009; Kohnert 2010; Anten, Briscoe and Mezzera 2012).

While this is well documented for UN and EU agencies, it is often overlooked that, although to differing degrees, ECOWAS and AU actors have also provided 'technical' and/or material support, aiming to manage crises in their respective regions (cf. Hartmann 2013, 44). Of course, the scope of this kind of support has been limited, especially when compared to better-resourced organizations. However, this section argues that it is nevertheless worthwhile to take a closer look, for two reasons. First, to get a full picture of the intervention practices of ECOWAS and the AU, it is necessary to include as much as possible without prejudice. Second, analyzing the scope and content of this support is important to understand how it has related to space-making in West/Africa. It is important to note that ECOWAS and AU 'technical' support has mostly developed along specific policy areas, such as, for example, 'security sector reform', 'post-conflict reconstruction and development' and 'election observation'. Whereas the following sub-sections focus on specific 'technical' efforts employed 'on the ground', to intervene and manage conflict in Guinea-Bissau, Chapter 5 reflects upon how actors at ECOWAS and the AU have developed, consolidated and enacted some of these policies more generally.

ECOWAS and AU electoral assistance to Guinea-Bissau

As mentioned above, electoral observation missions of ECOWAS and the AU, in addition to observing elections, have simultaneously performed several tasks. First, they have gathered information and assessed situations prior to elections (i.e., fact-finding), reporting to organizational headquarters. Second, they have engaged in political mediation and diplomatic efforts, aimed to ensure smooth electoral processes. Third and last, they have provided active technical support, expertise and material, including financial assistance.

OAU and AU observers have accompanied elections in member states since the late 1980s (cf. Aniekwe and Atuobi 2016). However, a more coherent approach only began to emerge after the early 2000s, following the Durban Declaration on Principles Governing Democratic Elections in Africa (OAU Assembly 2002), adopting the AU Guidelines for Election Observation and Monitoring Missions (OAU 2002). Around the same time, ECOWAS started to deploy election observers, based on provisions in the 2001 Supplementary Protocol (ECOWAS 2001, Art. 12–18). However, these documents mostly refer to fact-finding and observation (as have been early EOMs); electoral assistance in the sense of technical and material support became a stronger concern only in subsequent frameworks and missions developed by ECOWAS and AU actors. For ECOWAS, the Conflict Prevention Framework (ECPF, 2008) provided additional guidance. For the AU, the African Charter on Democracy, Elections and Governance (ACDEG, 2007) sought to make certain norms and principles binding on member states.[36] In all this, the main objectives behind ECOWAS and AU observer missions and electoral assistance were to manage tensions during the process, enhancing transparency and credibility as well as acceptance of results (cf. AU Commission 2013, 6–7).[37] Today, providing electoral assistance constitutes a key practice in the two organizations' efforts to restore 'peace and stability' and/or 'constitutional order' in post-conflict countries (cf. Hartmann 2013, 42–4; Aniekwe and Atuobi 2016).

Representatives of ECOWAS and the O/AU have observed elections in Guinea-Bissau since the first round of presidential elections in 1999 (cf. UNSG 1999, para. 19). Other examples include the parliamentary elections in 2004, presidential elections in 2005, parliamentary elections in 2008 and presidential elections in 2009. In 2012, both ECOWAS and the AU had EOMs 'on the ground' for the first round of the presidential elections in Guinea-Bissau (on 18 March). The AU Commission dispatched 40 observers, led by Leonardo Simão, former Minister of Foreign Affairs of Mozambique; the AUC had also decided to provide financial support to the National Electoral Commission (NEC) of Guinea-Bissau. The AU EOM arrived in Guinea-Bissau on 10 March and stayed until one week after the first round of elections (cf. AU Commission 2012a). The ECOWAS Commission, for its part, sent a team of 80 election observers, headed by former Nigerian Interim President General Salou Djibo. Deployed several days ahead of the election, the mission followed in the footsteps of an earlier assessment mission (cf. ECOWAS Commission 2012g). Following the first, successful though inconclusive, round of voting, both organizations described the election as "free", "fair" and "transparent", despite some concerns over minor obstacles or incidents (ECOWAS Commission 2012b; see also Walker 2012). However, five presidential candidates contested the results, claiming fraud. Amid these controversies, ECOWAS and the AU initiated preparations towards the second round (scheduled for 29 April). On 31 March 2012, a joint ECOWAS–AU–UN fact-finding mission visited Bissau to assess the security situation in the country and lower tensions (see above). In the session on the day of the coup, on 12 April, the ECOWAS MSC (meeting at ministerial level) agreed to send another, mixed civilian-military delegation to Bissau to calm down opponents (cf. ECOWAS MSC 2012b, para. 19.vi) (see also Chapter 3). Almost simultaneously, the coup in Bissau prevented the presidential run-off between Gomes Junior and Kumba Yalá from ever taking place (see Chapter 1).

While the EOMs and electoral assistance efforts of ECOWAS and the AU were unable to prevent tensions from rising during the electoral process in 2012, ultimately culminating in the coup d'état, the EOMs of both ECOWAS and the AU played important roles during the process leading to the general elections on 13 April 2014. The AUC Chairperson, on 31 March 2014, authorized an AU EOM for the general election in Guinea-Bissau on 13 April 2014. Led by former Mozambican president Joaquim A. Chissano, the mission reached Bissau on 3 April, comprising 56 observers, who stayed in the country until after the publication of definitive results (AU Commission 2014a). Already in December 2013, the AU Commission had organized a training for officials of Guinea-Bissau's NEC, and seconded a consultant to assist the NEC with its information and communication strategy. Since 9 February 2014, nine long-term observers of the AUC closely monitored the situation in the country (AUC Chairperson 2014, para. 10). For the electoral run-off, on 18 May, the AUC deployed 38 observers (cf. also AU Commission 2014b, para. 2–4).

The ECOWAS Commission put together an EOM comprising 200 election observers under the leadership of former Liberian interim president Amos Sawyer, and former Guinean prime minister Kabiné Komara as his deputy. The mission stayed in Bissau from 16 February to 15 April 2014, until two days after the first round of voting. In addition, a long-term technical assistance team, the first of its kind, comprising nine electoral experts had been 'on the ground' already before the EOM's arrival, since October 2013, and stayed on until after the run-off on 18 May.[38] During this time, the technical assistance team supported national election management bodies and facilitated political dialogue (cf. ECOWAS Commission President 2014a, para. 18). Among other things, the ECOWAS team sought to address shortcomings of the first round, such as the delayed and insufficient delivery of materials, unclear directives to the electorate regarding their respective polling stations, and the delayed deployment of polling officials to their stations. Moreover, it remained 'in the field' after the first round, thereby easing the deployment of another ECOWAS EOM for the run-off, 120 observers arriving on 11 May, again led by Amos Sawyer (ECOWAS Commission 2014a, para. 2ff.). In addition, ECOWAS and its member states provided financial and material support: about 25 million US dollars from different sources, computers and vehicles (cf. AU PSC 2014, 37–8; AUC Chairperson 2014, 3; see also ECOWAS MSC 2014a, para. 21; ECOWAS Commission President 2014a, Part E).

During the process leading up to the elections, the observation missions of ECOWAS, the AU and other international observers cooperated, holding joint briefings and info sessions, jointly calling on or appealing to political and military actors in Bissau and issuing a joint concluding statement (cf. ECOWAS Commission 2014e, 2014c, 2014a; AUC Chairperson 2014; AU Commission 2014b). In that, the Special Representative of the UN Secretary General José Ramos Horta (former President of Timor-Leste) also played a critical role as another Lusophone, political 'heavyweight', able to access all political stakeholders and exert pressure where necessary.[39]

Likewise, in the run-up to the most recent parliamentary elections in Guinea-Bissau, originally scheduled for late 2018, ECOWAS and to a lesser extent the AU were important actors. Together with EU and UN actors, they supported and, if necessary, pushed political actors in Bissau towards organizing and eventually holding elections. ECOWAS actors in particular were instrumental in putting and keeping pressure on President Vaz and others, which sought to delay the process. In addition, ECOWAS member states and in particular the Nigerian government provided material support, on short notice buying voter registration kits from China to speed up and facilitate the electoral process. After several postponements, the election took place on 10 March 2019.[40]

ECOWAS and AU SSR efforts in Guinea-Bissau

The SSR efforts of actors at ECOWAS find their legal basis in the already-mentioned foundational and normative frameworks, such as the 2001 Supplementary Protocol and the 2008 ECPF.[41] In addition, ECOWAS has a Code of Conduct of the Armed Forces and Security Services, adopted in 2011, and since 2008/9 both ECOWAS and AU actors have worked towards their own dedicated policy frameworks, which were adopted by the ECOWAS Authority in 2016 and by the AU Assembly in 2013. In practice, however,

ECOWAS actors have been involved in SSR in different member states since the early 2000s. These experiences – in particular, however, the ECOWAS efforts in Guinea-Bissau since 2010 (cf. Uzoechina 2014, 20ff.) – have influenced respective policy processes at ECOWAS and the AU (see Chapter 5).

Efforts to reform the security sector in Guinea-Bissau reach back at least to the mid-2000s. In 2005, driven by an initiative of the government of the United Kingdom, EU actors began preparations for an SSR mission, which eventually deployed in early 2008 in the framework of the EU's Common Security and Defense Policy (CSDP). However, the mission faced serious challenges in the country, and withdrew already two years later, in September 2010, in response to a mutiny within the armed forces of Guinea-Bissau in April 2010 (cf. Bahnson 2011; Kohl 2014). Around 2009, following the double assassination of President Vieira and Army Chief of Staff NaWaie, actors at ECOWAS and the CPLP had started to work on a joint road map for the reform of Guinea-Bissau's security sector. After the EU mission had withdrawn, they took over the lead of the SSR process, adopting a joint road map, in March and July 2011 respectively, supported by a range of international actors and donors (cf. Herpolsheimer 2014, 53).[42] As mentioned above, the AU later also got involved in that process.

However, the coup d'état of April 2012 disrupted this process, and led most of the actors involved to stop their support. ECOWAS actors, however, not only continued their engagement, but increased their efforts, deploying both ECOMIB in May 2012 (see "Deploying military and police peacekeeping forces" below) and subsequently an ECOWAS Defense and Security Sector Reform (DSSR) Team in June 2013. Therefore, the coup of April 2012 not only propelled the lead role of ECOWAS on SSR in Guinea-Bissau, but it also triggered a renewed and intensified engagement by the West African regional organization, reflected in the DSSR MoU that Commission President Ouédraogo signed together with then-Foreign Affairs Minister of Guinea-Bissau Faustino Fudut Imbali, on 7 November 2012. On the one hand, the MoU allowed formalizing ongoing efforts, at the same time enabling ECOWAS to cement its leadership, further pushing aside the CPLP – after revisions, the 'ECOWAS-CPLP Road Map' became the 'ECOWAS Roadmap'. On the other hand, concomitantly, it set the stage for the deployment of the ECOWAS DSSR Team.[43] The ECOWAS DSSR Team started out with three experts, who arrived in Bissau in June 2013. Later on, in December 2013, the team increased in size to seven technical experts. These were supposed to work in a 'joint cell' at the Ministry of Defense of Guinea-Bissau (cf. ECOWAS Commission President 2014a, para. 10).

Of the priority areas mentioned in the ECOWAS Roadmap, the DSSR Team initially focused primarily on the rehabilitation of barracks as well as negotiations with regard to demobilization or retirement and a respective pension fund. The latter has been subject to controversial debate among the different regional and international intervening actors, in particular with respect to the issue of 'gratuities' (e.g., cars and houses), which might complement the pension fund to persuade redundant and overaged military personnel to retire. Most international actors outright reject any additional one-off payments.[44] Contrary to this, ECOWAS actors have been more open to at least discuss 'gratuities'. Nevertheless, the ECOWAS DSSR Team appears to have given an inaccurate impression of what might fly with the international community, thereby complicating negotiations with Bissau-Guinean military stakeholders.[45] In principle, the ECOWAS DSSR Team is supposed to work together with ECOMIB, especially regarding the 'down-' or 'right-sizing' of Guinea-Bissau's armed forces (cf. ECOWAS MSC 2013b, para. 49), and ECOMIB was supposed to provide logistics support (cf. ECOWAS MSC 2013c, para. 22). However, the two components of ECOWAS intervention efforts *in* Bissau have not very actively cooperated, or even coordinated their efforts. More recently, with the urge to withdraw ECOMIB rising among ECOWAS member states, the DSSR Team began to develop ideas regarding the recruitment and training of Bissau-Guinean military personnel that eventually could take over the functions of ECOMIB. However, by early 2019, little had been achieved in that regard.[46]

For the AU, the main avenue for engaging in the reform of the security sector in Guinea-Bissau has been through the AULO-GB, which among its staff has a dedicated Security Sector Reform Officer (although also performing other tasks). However, apart from continuously gathering information and reporting on the subject, this engagement has been less frequent and less formalized, ranging from occasionally organizing workshops and training of military and police to the provision of equipment and the renovation of barracks. For example, between 2011 and 2018, through the AULO-GB, the AU has provided furniture, desktop computers and printers to the Institute of National Defense (at the Ministry of Defense). It conducted a training workshop on SSR and 'disarmament, demobilization, and reintegration' (DDR) for 63 participants drawn from the Bissau-Guinean military, police, members of the Parliamentary Committee on Defense, journalists and representatives of civil society organizations – inviting SSR experts and representatives from other African countries to share experience of their SSR processes. Another training, for 40 military and police members, focused on the acquisition of skills and provided initial basic working tools for military staff, allowing them to take up civilian occupation after their retirement from active service. The office also organized the renovation and expansion of a prison in Bandim (central Bissau) and provided a car and three motorcycles, as well as 'border security equipment', for three posts along the international land border of Guinea-Bissau. Costs for individual activities have ranged between 15,000 and 70,000 US dollars. However, as AU officers have emphasized, not everything submits to easy quantification. Less visible but more frequent political efforts of the AULO-GB and interactions with national stakeholders (see above) have also played an important role with respect to the SSR process in Guinea-Bissau.[47]

Overall, however, the resources of the AULO-GB have been limited, and AU actors have consequently left the lead to ECOWAS and other international actors, in particular the UN, working through its Integrated Office in Guinea-Bissau (UNIOGBIS). With them, AU actors have occasionally engaged in joint assessments, for example, hosting the comprehensive joint SSR assessment mission at the AULO-GB, from 2 to 12 March 2015 (cf. AU et al. 2015) (see also Chapter 6).[48] As a follow-up to this mission and once more facilitated by the AULO-GB, in November 2016, the AU Defense and Security Division organized a three-day planning workshop on DDR and SSR in Bissau (cf. AU Commission 2016a). Among other objectives, this workshop tried to link SSR experience in Guinea-Bissau to experiences elsewhere (e.g., Madagascar and Liberia), and all of those to the larger process of establishing and consolidating a coherent approach, policy and practice towards SSR in AU member states (see Chapter 5).

'Technical' support and space-making

Although limited in scope and with mixed results, the above considerations show that actors at ECOWAS and the AU have sought to follow up on their public pronouncements and implement decisions regarding 'technical' and material support 'on the ground'. Most importantly, they have sought to contribute to capacity building aiming to (re-)construct institutions essentially associated with 'functioning' states. Thereby, ECOWAS and AU actors have sought to maintain and reintegrate 'conflict states' as 'functioning' members of the West African state community.

It becomes immediately clear that this set of practices intimately links to space-making. First, spending resources, deploying personnel 'on the ground' and contributing materially, ECOWAS and AU actors signal importance of and regional interest in a conflict situation. Thereby, they further add to the 'sensitization' of local actors about their regional belonging and all that implies regarding regional norms and practices. As described in the previous section (and in Chapter 3), this contributes to the construction of regional spaces. Second, and even more importantly, the resources spent are supposed to address key elements associated with the spatial format 'nation state' – that is, above all, a legitimate, democratically elected central government and professional security forces that are subject to civil oversight. In that way, 'technical' assistance has reflected efforts to format space in a specific way, linked to specific regional norms and policies (see Chapter 5). Therefore, it has complemented and sought to enhance the effects of diplomatic interventions, both 'from afar' and 'on the ground'. In some cases, it has also accompanied the deployment of military and police peacekeeping forces, which are the subject of the following section.

Deploying military and police peacekeeping forces

The set of intervention practices that, so far, has received the most attention in academic and policy debates on African Peace and Security has been the deployment of regional and/or international peacekeeping forces, both military and police. Consequently, their various aspects and functions are well covered in the existing literature and do not require repetition at this point (among many, e.g., Adebajo 2011; Tardy and Wyss 2014; Cocodia 2017). Suffice it to highlight that in addition to UN peacekeeping missions, different EU missions have played important roles in international efforts to deal with conflicts in Africa (e.g., Whitman and Wolff 2012; Gibert and Nivet 2013; Whitman and Haastrup 2015), as have military and police deployments by different African ROs.[49] In that regard, especially AU and ECOWAS peacekeeping missions have stood out.

African peacekeeping missions have received extensive scholarly attention (see Chapter 1). However, surprisingly against this backdrop, the deployment of the ECOWAS Standby Force (ESF) in Guinea-Bissau (ECOMIB) has received almost no scholarly attention so far.[50] As explained in Chapter 1, this neglect is remarkable since ECOMIB stands out from other African peacekeeping missions in several regards – that the mission has been self-mandated and self-funded for three full years is particularly worth highlighting – and points to interesting dynamics around the deployment and maintenance of such missions, which so far have received only scant scholarly attention. This refers, for example, to the intersecting objectives, interests and policies of different regional and international intervening actors (see also Chapters 5 and 6). Therefore, this section describes the process leading up to deployment of ECOMIB. Moreover, it analyzes the mission's changing mandate, strength and composition, as well as its funding and its spatializing effects 'on the ground'.

Mandating and deploying ECOMIB

The deployment of the ESF (previously the ECOWAS Cease-fire Monitoring Group, ECOMOG) follows the legal provisions laid out in the Revised ECOWAS Treaty (1993), the 1999 Mechanism and the 2001 Supplementary Protocol.[51] Based on these frameworks, on 26 April 2012, at an extraordinary summit, the ECOWAS Authority of Heads of State and Government, acting as the MSC, authorized the deployment of ECOMIB (ECOWAS Authority 2012, 7–8). However, it is worth mentioning that such a mission had been under consideration at different levels already since early April 2012.[52] On 12 April, just before the coup, the MSC (meeting at ministerial level) had already agreed to dispatch troops to Guinea-Bissau in order to secure the second round of elections scheduled for 29 April, to ensure the implementation of the regional road map for DSSR and most importantly to replace the Angolan military-technical SSR mission (MISSANG) (cf. ECOWAS MSC 2012b, 4; ECOWAS Commission 2012f). MISSANG had been deployed by the Angolan government in early 2011, based on bilateral agreements, but was eyed with suspicion by Bissau-Guinean military actors (see Chapter 6).

After a few adjustments, the status-of-mission agreement, eventually signed in November 2017 between ECOWAS and the Republic of Guinea-Bissau, defined the ECOMIB mandate in more detail (ECOWAS Commission 2012h, 5–6), as follows:

a) provision of security for the transitional process;
b) support the electoral process through the provision of security for all stakeholders and institutions involved therein;
c) provision of security for all other institutions, VIPs and vulnerable persons in the country;
d) ensure security of witnesses and institutions involved in criminal investigation and prosecution of assassination and other acts of impunity;
e) establish and protect humanitarian corridors for humanitarian assistance;
f) provision of security for the populace and creation of conducive environment to guarantee personal freedoms and normal operations of businesses;
g) assist in the effective implementation of DSSR;
h) perform any other security duty that the situation may require.

Initially, ECOMIB deployed without any mandate, neither from the UN Security Council (UNSC) nor from the AU PSC, other than the one issued by the ECOWAS Authority. Until November 2012, there was also no agreement with the national authorities. Thus, the military and police intervention by ECOWAS was solely based on the authority of the organization's own legal texts. It was only after the fact that the AU PSC endorsed ECOWAS' efforts, and specifically the deployment of the ESF (cf. AU PSC 2012, para. 4; see also Chapter 3), and the UNSC "welcomed" (UNSC 2013, 2) and "commended" (UNSC 2014, 2) the efforts by ECOWAS and ECOMIB, before "recognizing" its important role and "supporting" the continuation of the mission (UNSC 2015, 5). However, despite vocally supporting the ECOWAS efforts early on (AU Commission 2012c), the AU Commission and some AU member states were not fully behind ECOWAS' approach. This would become clear when the AU PSC did not give in to repeated calls by ECOWAS actors to lift sanctions against the transition authorities in Guinea-Bissau (see Chapter 6).

Within the ECOWAS Department of Political Affairs, Peace and Security, staff at the Directorate for Peacekeeping and Regional Security began working on logistical planning and preparations.[53] Simultaneously, the ECOWAS Committee of Chiefs of Defense Staff (CCDS) worked on the concept of operations (cf. ECOWAS Commission 2012c, 2012d, 2013). Meanwhile, ECOWAS Chiefs of Defense Staff used their contacts in the Bissau-Guinean military to prepare the ground for the mission to deploy, resulting in a formal request by the new authorities in the country, the moment they took office (cf. ECOWAS MSC 2012c, 4). Subsequently, the CCDS continued to accompany the operations of ECOMIB, continually briefing and making recommendations to the MSC (e.g., cf. ECOWAS MSC 2013a, para. 48, 2013b, para. 49).

Following the decision by the ECOWAS Authority, four member states pledged troops: Nigeria, Senegal, Burkina-Faso and Togo. Deployment started on 17 May 2012, with the arrival of a first contingent of about 70 police officers from Burkina Faso (UNSG 2012a, 7). By early July, a little over 500 troops had deployed (UNSG 2012b, 7). By late November, deployment was completed, totaling some 640 military and police forces (about 670 including logistical personnel, UNSG 2013): 140 police and 160 military from Nigeria; 140 police from Burkina Faso; and about 200 soldiers, mostly engineers and a medical unit from Senegal (ICG 2012, 4).[54] Since July 2012, and throughout 2013, ECOMIB forces patrolled, mostly in Bissau and its outskirts, provided protection to central state institutions and VIPs and tried to improve living conditions in the barracks of Guinea-Bissau's military (e.g., cf. UNSG 2012b, 7; ECOWAS Commission President 2012, para. 14; ECOWAS MSC 2013b, para. 49; ECOWAS Commission President 2014a, para. 9).

According to ECOWAS sources, in 2014, ECOMIB comprised of 797 military and police, 36 staffers at the mission headquarters, the force commander and his deputy, as well as 10 civilian personnel – a total strength of 833.[55] This was at the height of the mission, also regarding its national and international visibility, securing the 2014 elections in Guinea-Bissau. To this end, ECOMIB staff and the CCDS developed contingency plans ahead of the elections, to secure the transport of electoral materials, escorting VIPs to voting centers, dispatching mobile teams to prevent disorder and protecting election observers (cf. ECOWAS Commission President 2014a, para. 9, 11 and 19). Following the elections, the MSC again reviewed the mission mandate and strength to reflect developments on the ground (cf. ECOWAS Commission President 2014b, para. 14 and 23.h). At this point, ECOWAS Commission President Ouédraogo suggested the maintenance of a credible force, a 'robust' deployment of ECOMIB in order to support a comprehensive post-transitional reform strategy, developed by the ECOWAS Commission together with the RCG-GB, aiming to maintain stability and rebuild the state in Guinea-Bissau in the immediate, mid- and long term (cf. ECOWAS Commission President 2014b, para. 22).[56] The CCDS also recommended extension but revision of the mandate retaining the existing force strength, and the MSC (subsequently meeting at ministerial and presidential level) followed that recommendation in December 2014. At the same time, it also strongly appealed to international partners to reduce the financial burden on ECOWAS member states (ECOWAS MSC 2014b, para. 30).[57]

However, the mood changed within ECOWAS in early 2015, in the face of high mission costs, financial constraints of the ECOWAS Commission and rising arrears to troop- and police-contributing countries (T/PCCs), as well as a continued absence of support by international partners (cf. ECOWAS Commission President 2015, para. 5ff.). In addition, the Guinea-Bissau government, despite requesting that ECOMIB stay in Bissau, did not indicate clearly what precisely it required from the mission (cf. ECOWAS MSC 2014b, para. 21). Despite the EU's commitment to take over operational costs, excluding troop salaries (cf. ECOWAS Commission President 2015, para. 8 and 13), the ECOWAS Authority requested that the Commission develop an exit strategy, based on a gradual withdrawal of the remaining troops, starting at the end of June 2016. ECOWAS Chairman Macky Sall (President of Senegal) subsequently authorized the withdrawal to commence (cf. ECOWAS MSC 2016a, para. 26). Although the financial burden of the mission has played a major role, some observers have also argued that the threat of withdrawing ECOMIB had been a move by ECOWAS heads of state in order to increase the pressure on President Vaz to implement the Conakry Agreement.[58]

In 2015, ECOMIB comprised 666 military and police, 16 headquarters staffers, the force commander and his deputy, as well as 5 civilian personnel – a total strength of 689 (cf. ECOWAS Commission President 2015). Despite continuously renewing ECOMIB's mandate for short periods between three and six months, since late 2016, the ECOWAS MSC has constantly decreased the mission strength. By the end of 2017, 476 military and police, as well as a few civilians, remained in Bissau (cf. EU Commission 2016b, 2017, 2018). In November 2016, citing financial and logistical constraints ever since the initial deployment in 2012, as well as the now rather political nature of the crisis in Bissau, the CCDS came to the conclusion that ECOMIB was no longer adequate to the issues at hand (ECOWAS MSC 2016b, para. 21). The ECOWAS MSC (meeting at ministerial level) therefore recommended that the Authority withdraw ECOMIB by 30 June 2017, gradually starting during the first quarter of 2017, to avoid potential destabilization of unpaid troops, or to transform ECOMIB into a mere police mission (ECOWAS MSC 2016b, para. 27 and 36). Despite that decision, it further extended the mission's mandate several times (cf. ECOWAS MSC 2017, para. 23, 2018, para. 23.iii), and well into 2020 (cf. ECOWAS Authority 2019, para. 38).

Consequently, ECOMIB forces have been less visible in everyday life in Bissau, with fewer patrols, limiting their activities almost exclusively to guarding key buildings (e.g., government institutions and VIP residences).[59] Since then, the actual role and effect of ECOMIB's presence in Guinea-Bissau have formed the core of debates about the envisioned final withdrawal of the mission. On that matter, opinions have differed widely on what the consequences might really be. Nevertheless, especially many representatives of international organizations in Guinea-Bissau have been concerned about a further deterioration of the political conflict in Bissau and a possible more open reengagement of the army.[60]

It is important to note, however, that while ECOMIB has received a lot of praise for its stabilizing role in Guinea-Bissau, deterring army factions from violent interference in the country's political affairs, its strength always has been rather symbolical. Depending on the source, the size of Guinea-Bissau's army lies somewhere between 4,000 and 5,000. Thus, despite more or less obvious structural problems,[61] in relative terms, Guinea-Bissau's army is one of the biggest in West Africa (UN PBC 2008, 2).[62] Interviewees repeatedly argued that ECOMIB forces had only very limited ability to physically prevent the army of Guinea-Bissau from doing anything. In the same line of reasoning, some interviewees pointed out that in April 2012 some 200–300 heavily armed Angolan forces did not dissuade the 'military command' from staging a coup.[63]

What is more, despite positive indirect effects on the general security situation in Bissau, ECOMIB's protection has not extended directly to non-VIPs. In its everyday practice, ECOMIB has primarily focused on item c) of its mandate (i.e., protecting institutions and VIPs). Despite some positive indirect effects for other items, citizens in Guinea-Bissau have occasionally criticized ECOMIB for failing to protect them during protests against the government.[64] Nevertheless, at least Bissau-Guinean elites, including civil society representatives, have largely perceived the mission overall as a positive factor in the complex political and military environment in the country's capital. In addition, ECOMIB's level II hospital in Bissau has also treated the local population, thereby making a critical (although temporary) contribution to the country's desolate health system.[65]

Paying for ECOMIB

When it comes to the financing of military missions, similar to the UN or other organizations, it is the regular ECOWAS procedure to hold a pledging conference following the decision by the Authority. At this point, some member states offer to contribute to the mission, and to self-supply their contingents for three months. Later on, the ECOWAS Commission reimburses them for their expenses. At the same time, the organization tries to mobilize support from other sources, most importantly trying to tap resources from the EU or the UN and, to some extent, from the African Union.[66]

In the example of ECOMIB, the governments of Nigeria, Senegal, Burkina-Faso and Togo pledged troops and initially covered the costs of deployment for their respective contingents. Subsequently, the ECOWAS Commission started to reimburse the T/PCCs, in this effort actively lobbying for international support. It is the last part of this procedure, however, that went sideways. Shortly after the decision of the ECOWAS Authority, on 26 April 2012, the Commission put in a request with the African Union to endorse its application for financial support from the EU's African Peace Facility (APF, under the European Development Fund).[67] However, it was only in November 2015 that the EU Commission decided to allocate APF funds to ECOMIB (EU Commission 2015b). Before that moment, the ECOWAS Commission and T/PCCs had been paying the entire bill for three years (from May 2012 to July 2015).

So, how much did ECOMIB actually cost? In that regard, the available data once more comes with gaps and incoherences. Starting in 2012, different sources refer to significantly differing numbers. For example, a "sum of 135,266,568 US dollars for six months military deployment in

Guinea-Bissau", mentioned in the 2012 Annual Report of the ECOWAS Commission (ECOWAS Commission 2012a, 61), contrasts with 181,869,827 US dollars stated by the EU Commission as the total budget of the mission in July 2015 since deployment in May 2012 (EU Commission 2015a, 3). The latter, in turn, seems to stand in some tension also to a grand total of 304 million US dollars, as of June 2016, according to ECOWAS sources.[68] Taken together, this indicates problems relating to issues of transparency and accountability, but also to possible incompatibilities between different systems of accounting. To give another example, in 2014, at the height of deployment, mission costs stood at a grand total of about 20 million units of account (roughly 30 million US dollars, or 23 million euros).[69] When the EU eventually decided to support ECOMIB, it first granted about 5 million euros for seven months (July 2015 to February 2016), and subsequently about 10 million euros for 12 months (July 2015 to June 2016) (EU Commission 2015b, 2016a). Thus, the EU apparently contributed to the costs of ECOMIB and did not take over its financing entirely.[70] However, how these figures add up to the grand total(s) mentioned above remains unclear.

Nevertheless, what these numbers show, despite the limitations of the available data, is, first, that ECOWAS actors actually spent significant resources on ECOMIB.[71] On the one hand, this indicates a considerable commitment to deal with the situation in Guinea-Bissau. On the other, it also represents a strong statement demonstrating its will to take responsibility in matters of peace and security in the region more generally. Moreover, it also sends a strong signal to other, 'extra-regional' actors asserting its lead in its 'own' regional space. Second, the above considerations show that although refusing support at first, when ECOWAS actors lost motivation to pay, EU actors began contributing to the mission. This shift, I would argue, points to a change in relative positions and interests of actors at ECOWAS and the EU vis-à-vis ECOMIB and the conflict in Guinea-Bissau (see also Chapter 6). Therefore, the question of who pays does not always automatically translate into a clear relationship of dependency or any obvious power relation, even in the face of unequal financial resources.

Military and police deployments and space-making

In general, deploying the ESF to Guinea-Bissau – as well as other African peacekeeping missions to other conflict situations – has clearly complemented other intervention practices by ECOWAS and the AU, signaling regional interest, getting a direct handle on the situation 'on the ground' and establishing regional 'presence' at the local level – making connections and translating the 'region' to the local scale. At the same time, deploying ECOMIB has also been a signal to other actors in the region, demonstrating ECOWAS' capability and willingness to take charge of conflicts in the region, and asserting the West African ROs 'primacy' vis-à-vis other regional and international actors (see Chapter 6).

In addition, three things in particular are worth highlighting with regard to ECOMIB's underlying spatial logics. First, military and police intervention in Guinea-Bissau has clearly been guided by the spatial format 'nation state'. This has been most visible in the concentration of ECOMIB activity around the protection of key individuals and institutions associated with the state (e.g., party leaders and headquarters, top-level government officials and buildings). The focus on the state is further reflected in the ECOMIB mandate, tasking it among other things to assist in DSSR and to support the electoral process.

Second, while focusing on 'the state', establishing control over its territory has been largely symbolic. ECOMIB established effective control only over its bases, as well as certain places considered of strategic importance. Between and around those places ECOWAS troops only occasionally exerted a limited degree of control (e.g., through patrols or during certain events). What is more, ECOMIB activity has almost exclusively focused on the capital, Bissau. With few exceptions, its presence rarely covered the rest of the country. To some extent this particular troop distribution has reflected the conflict situation 'on the ground' in Guinea-Bissau, largely centered in the capital, and remarkably disconnected from much of the rest of the country (see Chapter 1). To some extent, it has also reflected limitations of resources and/or political will on behalf of ECOWAS and AU member states. However, the argument here is that it also reflects a specific spatial logic, which assumes the state capital to stand in for the country as a whole – deployment to the capital is thus highly symbolic. The example of international interventions in Mali, triggered by the immediate capture of the capital, Bamako, also testify to this (cf. Döring 2019, 5–6, 66).

Finally, the deployment of ECOMIB spurred tensions regarding the organization and hierarchization of the different scales that constitute the global and regional security 'architectures'. This is commonly assumed as straightforward, with the UN at the top, followed by the AU, and ECOWAS at the bottom. The principle of 'subsidiarity' supposedly identifies the most appropriate actor for intervention, starting with the 'lowest' scale (i.e., the 'closest' to the 'ground'). However, neither that hierarchy nor the principle of subsidiarity, and what exactly it should mean in practice, are a given. Instead, they are subject to continuous contestation and negotiation. From that perspective deploying the ESF, without any mandate from the UN or the AU, also represented a strategy of ECOWAS actors to position themselves towards and strategically engage other international and regional actors involved in conflict intervention in Guinea-Bissau, most importantly the AU, CPLP, EU and UN (see Chapter 6). From this perspective, the deployment of ECOMIB constituted a way for ECOWAS actors to claim and assert what they consider their 'own' regional space.

Conclusion

This chapter has identified and analyzed three main sets of practices that actors at ECOWAS and the AU have employed in order to establish their presence 'physically' *in* conflict situations, and which have complemented practices employed 'from afar'. Diplomatic missions, 'technical' (and material) support, as well as military and police deployments have allowed ECOWAS and AU actors to construct direct connections to the conflict site. This has enabled them to access information, but also to convey messages and knowledge from the regional to the local scale, and to embed specific conflict situations in a wider regional space. Thus, these practices have worked at least in two ways, signaling regional interest and readiness to act in support of a member state (and to some extent also its population), first, to local actors and, second, to other actors within the region.

The practices discussed in this chapter have also allowed the two organizations to establish a certain degree of influence and physical control over the situation 'on the ground', although with limitations, and to position themselves vis-à-vis other regional and international actors, both *in* a specific conflict situation, but also more generally (see Chapter 6). Especially the various diplomatic missions and special representatives have been able to influence conflict 'on the ground' more or less directly, for example, by facilitating dialogue, bringing actors together or exerting pressure. In the example of interventions in Guinea-Bissau, the physical presence of ECOWAS and AU actors (both temporarily and long-term) constantly reminded local actors of the continuous international attention to the situation in the country and, conversely, create that international attention using their respective platforms (see Chapter 3).

Like interventions 'from afar', ECOWAS and AU practices 'on the ground' have privileged the spatial formats of the 'nation state' and the 'region'. Consequently, most efforts have targeted actors, institutions and spaces that are directly associated with central state authority. Interventions by the two regional organizations have been justified or framed in terms of 'fixing' a member state that is not 'functioning properly' and, thus, presents a threat both to its citizens and 'regional stability', peace and security (see Chapter 5). Interestingly, in the example of Guinea-Bissau, this focus on the state has resulted in interventions that address only specific parts of that state, that is, central state institutions situated in the capital, which are assumed to relate to others in a specific way.

Another important spatial dimension becomes apparent in the differences in the interaction of actors at ECOWAS and the AU with other regional and international actors 'on the ground', when compared to their interaction at the level of headquarters, and other intervention sites 'afar'. Although certain differences, imbalances and hierarchies persist, working relations and cooperation among representatives of the different regional organizations involved in Guinea-Bissau have been relatively close, with frequent day-to-day interactions. This has resulted in understandings of the conflict and possible solutions that are largely shared, although not identical in every respect, and thus to some extent blurs the distinctions between different regional actors and their positions (see also Chapter 6). Therefore, common distinctions between ECOWAS as 'close' to conflicts in West Africa, with an implied better understanding of these conflicts and relevant actors (etc.) and the AU as 'far' (or at least further) 'away' are partly put into question.

Notes

1 This is even more so when taking into account the failed efforts to deploy the ESF to Mali during the same time (i.e., 2012) – what was supposed to become MICEMA then turned into AFISMA and ended up as MINUSMA (cf. Théroux-Bénoni 2014). In 2012, ECOWAS actors in particular seem to have reverted to considering military (and police) action more seriously, after almost ten years of prioritizing non-military means, following the short stint of the ESF in Liberia in 2003.

2 I use single quotation marks to raise awareness that these terms are markers that different actors, including me as a researcher, use for different reasons and towards specific objectives, often to distinguish binary opposites (e.g., 'internal' versus 'external'; 'technical' versus 'political'). As such they are part of different discourses, knowledge–power relations and subject to socio-political contestation.

3 Cf. Interview 8, Senior AU Officer, Department of Political Affairs, Addis Ababa, 14 September 2016.

4 While not covering the entire spectrum of diplomatic field missions, and not referring to liaison offices, several publications have started to analyze mediation efforts of Africa ROs (e.g., Yabi 2010; Engel 2012; Zartman 2016; Nathan 2017).

5 Cf. Interview 79, Senior UN Officer, UNIOGBIS, Bissau, 12 April 2017; Interview 169, Senior UN Officer, Department of Political Affairs, New York, 6 December 2018.

6 Cf. Interview 43, ECOWAS Officer, Department of Political Affairs, Peace and Security, Abuja, 28 February 2017; Interview 64, Senior ECOWAS Official, Bissau, 6 April 2017.

7 Cf. Interview 8, Senior AU Officer, Department of Political Affairs, Addis Ababa, 14 September 2016.

8 This provision goes back to the Declaration by the OAU Assembly on the Establishment of a Mechanism for Conflict Prevention, Management and Resolution (AHG/DECL.2 (XXIX)), adopted at its 29th Ordinary Session, on 28–30 June 1993 in Cairo (cf. OAU Assembly 1993, para. 22).

9 The AU Handbook also lists several special representatives, special envoys and high representatives without designated offices (cf. AU Commission and New Zealand Crown 2020, 116–17).

10 AU liaison offices are largely funded by the EU through a joint financing arrangement under the EDF (cf. European Court of Auditors 2018, para. 41–2).

11 The liaison office for Somalia was later integrated into the AU Mission in Somalia (AMISOM), and relocated to its rear headquarters in Nairobi, Kenya (cf. AU Commission and New Zealand Crown 2020, 115).

12 Cf. Interview 23, Senior ECOWAS Official, Ouagadougou, 29 January 2017.

13 This refers to the final communiqué of the 28th session of the ECOWAS Authority, as printed in the *ECOWAS Community Journal* Vol. 46 (of January 2005). However, a digitalized version, available on the internet, incorrectly refers to the opening of the "Office of the Special Representative of the UN Secretary General in Guinea-Bissau", which in reality already opened in 1999/2000.

14 Already before that, apparently in March 2005, Sidibé had been an "envoy" of the ECOWAS Executive Secretary (cf. RTP 2005).

15 This work was apparently appreciated by local actors in Bissau (cf. Yabi 2010, 31).

16 The security assistance team was supposed to assist with the creation of formed police units, to protect VIPs, national institutions, as well as the National Commission of Inquiry (into the double assassination) and its witnesses (cf. ECOWAS Commission 2011).

17 Continuously mentioned in Annual Reports of the Commission until 2008, following reports do not refer to the ECOWAS liaison offices anymore.

18 Among other things, the coordination of the military component (ECOMIB) and DSSR efforts (etc.) was supposed to work through the SRPC's office, but did not work well, as these efforts developed relatively independently of each other (cf. Interview 43, ECOWAS Officer, Department of Political Affairs, Peace and Security, Abuja, 28 February 2017; Interview 154, Senior ECOWAS Officer, Department for Political Affairs, Peace and Security, Abuja 23 October 2018).

19 Cf. Interview 60, Senior UN Officer, UNIOGBIS, Bissau, 4 April 2017; Interview 59, Senior EU Officer, Bissau, 4 April 2017.

20 Cf. Interview 59, Senior EU Officer, Bissau, 4 April 2017; Interview 55, Senior UN Officer, UNIOGBIS, Bissau, 30 March 2017.

21 Cf. Personal conversation 71, NGO Representative, Bissau, 8 April 2017.

22 The PSC, then, supported the idea "in principle" and requested the AU Commission to submit a more detailed proposal, and to elaborate mandate and modalities for the interaction with other institutions "on the ground" (AU PSC 2005, para. 8).

23 On invitation by Libyan president Gaddafi, the AU Assembly convened a Special Session on the Consideration and Resolution of Conflicts in Africa, at the margins of the celebrations of the 40th anniversary of the "Libyan Revolution" (cf. AUC Chairperson 2009, para. 1).

24 Apparently, AU actors initially wanted to have a joint liaison office, but ECOWAS decided to maintain its own office (cf. Interview 63, Senior AU Officer, Bissau, 5 April 2017).

25 Previously, Ambassador Pequeno had also mediated in Guinea-Bissau for the CPLP (while Foreign Minister of Sao Tomé and Principe, 2004–6).

26 Cf. Interview 63, Senior AU Officer, Bissau, 5 April 2017; Field Notes, Addis Ababa, 13 September 2016.

27 The relevance and importance of local representation is obvious in Guinea-Bissau, especially for organizations that have not been as frequently and directly involved 'on the ground' through field missions as ECOWAS. In the case of the CPLP, a relative loss of influence is discernible since the discontinuation of its local liaison office (cf. Döring and Herpolsheimer 2018, 74).

28 Cf. Interview 62, AU Officer, Bissau, 5 April 2017; Interview 68, Senior AU Official, Bissau, 7 April 2017; see also AUC Chairperson (2013, para. 14).

29 Cf. Interview 2, Senior AU Official, Addis Ababa, 7 September 2016.

30 E.g., cf. Interview 85, Senior Analyst, Lecturer and Former Politician of Guinea-Bissau, Bissau, 14 April 2017; Interview 82, Senior Researcher and Former

Politician of Guinea-Bissau, Bissau, 13 April 2017; Interview 76, Local NGO Representative, Bissau, 11 April 2017; Interview 81, Businessman and Former Politician of Guinea-Bissau, Bissau, 13 April 2017; Interview 62, AU Officer, Bissau, 5 April 2017; Interview 68, Senior AU Official, Bissau, 7 April 2017.

31 E.g., cf. Interview 83, Diplomatic Source, Bissau, 13 April 2017; Interview 65, EU Officer, Bissau, 6 April 2017; Interview 81, Businessman and Former Politician of Guinea-Bissau, Bissau, 13 April 2017.

32 Cf. Field Notes, Addis Ababa, 15 September 2016.

33 An interesting aspect that I cannot expand on here has been the access to their organizations that ECOWAS and AU liaison offices have provided to civil society in Guinea-Bissau (e.g., cf. DW 2018).

34 Cf. Interview 2, Senior AU Official, Addis Ababa, 7 September 2016; Interview 7, AU Officer, Peace and Security Department, Addis Ababa, 14 September 2016.

35 Cf. Interview 158, Senior ECOWAS Officer, Office of the Vice President of the ECOWAS Commission, Abuja, 25 October 2018; Interview 165, Senior ECOWAS Officer, Department of Political Affairs, Peace and Security, Abuja, 31 October 2018.

36 On the lack of implementation of the ACDEG, see Engel (2016).

37 More specifically, the AU Election Observation Manual identifies eight main purposes. For more details, see AU Commission (2013, 7).

38 Cf. Interview 53, Senior ECOWAS Officer, Department for Political Affairs, Peace and Security, Abuja, 3 March 2017.

39 Cf. Interview 8, Senior AU Officer, Department of Political Affairs, Addis Ababa, 14 September 2016; Interview 126, EU Officer, EU External Action Service, Brussels, 6 June 2018.

40 Cf. Interview 132, AU Officer, Addis Ababa, 22 September 2018; see also UNIOGBIS (2018).

41 In the ECOWAS context, the term 'DSSR' is more commonly used than 'SSR'. Both at ECOWAS and the AU, D/SSR efforts have often closely related to 'disarmament, demobilization, and reintegration' (DDR), which I do not address separately in this book.

42 The adoption of the joint road map, at the time, signified an important step towards overcoming tensions between ECOWAS and the CPLP, harmonizing their approaches towards Guinea-Bissau. Since their clash during the war of 1998/9 in Guinea-Bissau, when both tried to lead the intervention process, the two organizations have wavered between outright competition and some degree of cooperation (see Chapter 6).

43 As mentioned above (in "Dispatching diplomatic field missions and establishing liaison offices"), something similar was previously envisioned as a CPLP–ECOWAS–AU stabilization mission.

44 Cf. Interview 65, EU Officer, Bissau, 6 April 2017; Interview 80, Portuguese Source, Bissau, 12 April 2017; Interview 29, Senior ECOWAS Officer, Department for Political Affairs, Peace and Security, Abuja, 16 February 2017; Interview 36, ECOWAS Officer, Department for Political Affairs, Peace and Security, Abuja, 23 February 2017.

45 Cf. Interview 154, Senior ECOWAS Officer, Department for Political Affairs, Peace and Security, Abuja, 23 October 2018; Interview 65, EU Officer, Bissau, 6 April 2017.

46 Cf. Interview 58, UN Officer, UNIOGBIS, Bissau, 3 April 2017; Interview 164, Senior ECOWAS Officer, Department for Political Affairs, Peace and Security, Abuja, 30 October 2018; Interview 64, Senior ECOWAS Official, Bissau, 6 April 2017; Interview 68, Senior AU Official, Bissau, 7 April 2017.

47 Cf. Interview 132, AU Officer, Addis Ababa, 22 September 2018; Personal Communication, AU Officer, 19 October 2018.

48 A similar although less extensive mission had taken place in October/November 2009, comprising representatives of the AU, ECOWAS and the CPLP.

49 For an overview of current (and previous) 'multilateral peace operations', see www.sipri.org/databases/pko (accessed 15 May 2019).

50 For a rare though limited exception, see Okyere (2016).

51 For an analysis of these texts as a basis of ECOWAS' military intervention, see, for example, Hartmann and Striebinger (2015).

52 In fact, ECOWAS' engagement with Guinea-Bissau and the process leading to the deployment had already begun around 2009/10 in the context of efforts to coordinate a joint DSSR approach between ECOWAS and CPLP actors (see above).

53 Cf. Interview 26, ECOWAS Officer, Department for Political Affairs, Peace and Security, Abuja, 15 February 2017; Interview 28, Senior ECOWAS Officer, Department for Political Affairs, Peace and Security, Abuja, 16 February 2017.

54 Across different sources, numbers vary slightly and thus need to be treated with caution; the exact composition of ECOMIB and changes therein are not fully transparent.

55 Cf. Field Notes, Abuja, 28 February 2017.

56 This might have included constitutional and electoral reforms, justice administration and rule of law reforms, DSSR, public sector and institutional, economic and infrastructure reforms, and support for small and medium-scale enterprises, all as an "intervention support package" for Guinea Bissau to target the "root causes" of conflict in the country (cf. ECOWAS Commission President 2014b, para. 16–17).

57 Specifically, the new mandate included the following tasks: (i) support the Government of Guinea Bissau in asserting its authority to address security challenges; (ii) support in the provision of security for the institutions and citizens; (iii) support in the delivery of humanitarian assistance when needed; (iv) provide support to the Defense and Security Sector Reform Program in the area of security, training and restructuring of designated security agencies; (v) provide support for the post-election reform program of Guinea Bissau; (vi) perform any other security duties that the situation may require (cf. ECOWAS Commission President 2015, para. 3).

58 E.g., cf. Interview 59, Senior EU Officer, Bissau, 4 April 2017; Interview 112, Senior ECOWAS Official, New York, 8 November 2017; see also ECOWAS MSC (2016a, para. 29) and ECOWAS Commission (2017).

59 Personal conversations with representatives of civil society organizations, Bissau, 1, 7 and 8 April 2017.

60 E.g., cf. Interview 59, Senior EU Officer, Bissau, 4 April 2017; Interview 55, Senior UN Officer, UNIOGBIS, Bissau, 30 March; Interview 62, AU Officer, Bissau, 5 April 2017.

61 Most importantly, this refers to an aged and badly educated "inverted pyramid", with generals and commissioned officers outnumbering rank-and-file soldiers (Kohl 2014, 5–6).

62 In Guinea-Bissau, a ratio of 2.73 military personnel per 1,000 inhabitants is well above the average of 1.23 for West Africa (according to a 2008 census; cf. Center on International Cooperation 2011, 51, footnote 5).

63 Interview 5, Senior Government Official of Guinea-Bissau, Addis Ababa, 8 September 2016; Interview 75, Senior Government Official of Guinea-Bissau, Bissau, 11 April 2017; Cf. also Interview 65, EU Officer, Bissau, 6 April 2017.

64 Cf. Interview 55, Senior UN Officer, UNIOGBIS, Bissau, 30 March; Interview 83, Diplomatic Source, Bissau, 13 April.

65 E.g., cf. Interview 72, Senior Representative of the Instituto Nacional de Estudos e Pesquisa of Guinea-Bissau, Bissau, 8 April 2017; Interview 76, Local NGO Representative, Bissau, 11 April 2017; Interview 81, Businessman and Former Politician of Guinea-Bissau; Interview 83, Diplomatic Source, Bissau, 13 April 2017; Interview 60, Senior UN Officer, UNIOGBIS, 4 April 2017.

66 Interview 54, Senior ECOWAS Officer, Department of Political Affairs, Peace and Security, Abuja, 3 March 2017.

67 Field Notes, Addis Ababa, 22 September 2016.

68 Cf. also Interview 54, Senior ECOWAS Officer, Department of Political Affairs, Peace and Security, Abuja, 3 March 2017.

69 Cf. Field Notes, Abuja, 28 February 2017.

70 Cf. also Interview 54, Senior ECOWAS Officer, Department of Political Affairs, Peace and Security, Abuja, 3 March 2017.

71 Much of the costs actually came out of the ECOWAS budget. In early 2017, arrears that ECOWAS owed to TCCs amounted to roughly 24 million units of account (about 33 million US dollars, or 29 million euros) (cf. Interview 54, Senior ECOWAS Officer, Department of Political Affairs, Peace and Security, Abuja, 3 March 2017).

References

Abrahamsen, Rita. 2018. Return of the Generals? Global Militarism in Africa from the Cold War to the Present. *Security Dialogue* 49 (1–2): 19–31. doi: 10.1177/0967010617742243.

Adebajo, Adekeye. 2011. *UN Peacekeeping in Africa: From the Suez Crisis to the Sudan Conflicts.* Boulder, CO: Lynne Rienner.

Aniekwe, Chika C. and Samuel Atuobi. 2016. Two Decades of Election Observation by the African Union: A Review. *Journal of African Elections* 15 (1): 25–44. doi: 10.20940/jae/2016/v15i1a2.

Anten, Louise, Ivan Briscoe and Marco Mezzera. 2012. *The Political Economy of State-building in Situations of Fragility and Conflict: from Analysis to Strategy.* The Hague: Netherlands Institute of International Relations 'Clingendael'.

AU. 2002. "Protocol Relating to the Establishment of the Peace and Security Council of the African Union", 1st Ordinary Session of the Assembly of the African Union, Durban, 9 July 2002.

AU, ECOWAS, EU, African Security Sector Network and UN. 2015. "Report of the Joint Security Sectory Reform (SSR) Assessment Mission to Guinea-Bissau", 2–12 March 2015.

AU Assembly. 2009. "Plan d'Action (SP/Assembly/PS/PLAN[I])", Session Speciale de la Conference l'Union sur l'Exement et le Reglement des Conflits en Afrique, Tripoli, 31 August 2009.

———. 2010. "Decision on the Report of the Peace and Security Council on its Activities and the State of Peace and Security in Africa (Doc.Assembly/AU/3(XVI))", 14th Ordinary Session of the AU Assembly, Addis Ababa, 31 January–2 Febuary 2010.

AU Commission. 2010. "Press Release: AU: The Chairperson of the Commission appoints a Special Representative for Guinea Bissau", Addis Ababa, 7 October 2010. Accessed 23 May 2019. https://reliefweb.int/report/guinea/au-chairperson-commission-appoints-special-representative-guinea-bissau.

———. 2012a. "Press Release: The Africa Union Provides Support for the Holding of the Early Presidential Elections in Guinea-Bissau", Addis Ababa, 13 March 2012.

———. 2012b. "Press Release: The AU Appoints a New Special Representative in Guinea-Bissau, Head of the AU Liaison Office in that Country", Addis Ababa, 8 May 2012.

———. 2012c. "Press Release: The AU Reaffirms its Support to the Efforts Aimed at Ensuring an Early Return to Constitutional Order", Addis Ababa, 11 May 2012.

———. 2013. *African Union Election Observation Manual.* Addis Ababa: AU Commission.

———. 2014a. "Press Release: La Présidente de la Commission de l'Union Africaine Autorise le Déploiement d'une Mission d'Observation Electorale de l'Union Africaine en Guinée Bissau dans le Cadre des Élections Législatives et Présidentielle du 13 avril 2014", 31 March 2014.

———. 2014b. "Rapport Final: Mission d'Obsérvation Électorale de l'Union Africaine pour les Élections Générales du 13 avril 2014 et le Second tour de l'Élection Présidentielle du 18 mai 2014 en République de Guinée-Bissau", June 2014.

———. 2015. "African Peace and Security Architecture. APSA Roadmap 2016–2020", Addis Ababa: AU Commsion, Peace and Security Department.

———. 2016a. "Press Release: AU and Government of Guinea Bissau Conclude a Security Sector Reform (SSR) and Disarmament, Demobilization and Reintegration (DDR) Planning Workshop", Bissau, 24 November 2016. Accessed 16 September 2020. www.peaceau.org/en/article/au-and-government-of-guinea-bissau-conclude- a-security-sector-reform-ssr- and-disarmament-demobilization-and-reintegration-ddr- planning-workshop-in-bissau-22-24-november-2016.

———. 2016b. "Press Release: AU Peace and Security Council Concludes its Field Mission to Guinea-Bissau", Addis Ababa, 21 March 2016.

AU Commission and New Zealand Crown. 2020. *African Union Handbook 2020: A Guide for Those Working with and within the African Union.* Addis Ababa, Wellington: AU Commission and New Zealand MFAT.

AU PSC. 2005. "Communiqué (PSC/PR/Comm. [XXXI])", 31st Meeting, Addis Ababa, 8 June 2005.

———. 2010. "Communiqué (PSC/PR/COMM. [CCXXII])", 222nd Meeting, Addis Ababa, 29 March 2010.

———. 2012. "Communiqué (PSC/MIN/COMM/1. (CCCXIX))", 319th Meeting, Addis Ababa, 24 April 2012.

———. 2014. "Report of the Peace and Security Council on its Activities and the State of Peace and Security in Africa (Assembly/AU/4[XXII]a)", AU Assembly, Addis Ababa, 30–31 January 2014.

AUC Chairperson. 2005. "Report of the Chairperson of the Commission on the Situation in Guinea-Bissau (PSC/PR/2[XXXI])", PSC, 31st Meeting, Addis Ababa, 8 June 2005.

———. 2009. "Report of the Chairperson of the Commission, Enhancing Africa's Resolve and Effectiveness in Ending Conflict and Sustaining Peace (SP/ASSEMBLY/PS/RPT[I])", Special Session of the Assembly of the Union on the Consideration and Resolution of Conflicts in Africa, Tripoli, 30–31 August 2009.

———. 2013. "Progress Report of the Chairperson of the Commission on the Situation in Guinea-Bissau (PSC/PR/2[CCCLI])", 351st Meeting, Addis Ababa, 16 January 2013.

———. 2014. "Report of the Chairperson of the Commission on the Situation in Guinea Bissau (PSC/PR/2 [CDXLII])", 442nd Meeting, Addis Ababa, 17 June 2014.

Bahnson, Caroline. 2011. The European Union and SSR in Guinea-Bissau. In *The Politics of Security Sector Reform: Challenges and Opportunities for the European Union's Global Role*, eds Magnus Ekengren and Greg Simons, 259–72. London: Ashgate.

Butedi, Nzolani F. 2018. The Work of the African Union Liaison Office in Building Peace on the Ground: A Case Study of Madagascar. *South African Journal of International Affairs* 25 (1): 99–116. doi: 10.1080/10220461.2018.1417900.

Center on International Cooperation. 2011. *Review of Political Missions* 2011. New York: Center on International Cooperation.

Cocodia, Jude. 2017. *Peacekeeping and the African Union: Building Negative Peace.* London: Routledge.

Döring, Katharina P.W. 2019. Making Room for War: The Spatialization of African Security Politics in the Quest for African-led Military Deployment. Unpublished doctoral thesis, Leipzig University.

Döring, Katharina P.W. and Jens Herpolsheimer. 2018. The Spaces of Intervention for Mali and Guinea-Bissau. *South African Journal of International Affairs* 25 (1): 61–82. doi: 10.1080/10220461.2018.1417898.

DW. 2018. Jovens Guineenses Pedem Sanções Políticas Contra José Mário Vaz, DW and Agência Lusa, tms, 4 March 2018. Accessed 22 March 2019. https://p.dw.com/p/2tfh2.

ECOWAS. 1993. "Revised Ecowas Treaty". Abuja, 24 July 1993.

———. 1999. "Protocol Relating to the Mechanism for Conflict Prevention, Management, Resolution, Peacekeeping and Security (A/P.1/12/99)", Lomé, 10 December 1999.

———. 2001. "Protocol A/SP1/12/01 on Democracy and Good Governance Supplementary to the Protocol relating to the Mechanism For Conflict Prevention, Management, Resolution, Peacekeeping and Security", Dakar. Accessed 24 February 2011. www.comm.ecowas.int/sec/en/protocoles/Protocol%20on%20good-governance-and-democracy-rev-5EN.pdf.

———. 2005. *Official Journal of the Economic Community of West African States*, Vol. 46, January 2005.

———. 2020. "List of ECOWAS Representations", n.p., May 2020. Accessed 12 August 2020. www.ecowas.int/wp-content/uploads/2020/05/Mai-2020-ECOWAS-Permanent-and-Special-Representatives.pdf.

ECOWAS Authority. 2012. "Final Communiqué", Extraordinary Summit of ECOWAS Heads of State and Government, Abuja, 26 April 2012.

———. 2014. "Final Communiqué", 45th Ordinary Session of the Authority of Heads of State and Government, Accra, 10 July 2014.

———. 2019. "Final Communiqué", 55th Ordinary Session of the Authority of Heads of State and Government, Abuja, 29 June 2019.

ECOWAS CCDS. 2010. "Final Report", Extraordinary Meeting of the ECOWAS Committee of Chiefs of Defense Staff (CCDS), Bissau, Guinea Bissau, 11–12 August 2010.

ECOWAS Commission. 2003. "Rapport Annuel: Les Defis Immediats du Development et de l'Integratioin de l'Afrique de l'Ouest".

———. 2004. "Rapport Annuel 2004: Perspectives d'Integration de l'Afrique de l'Ouest – A la Recherche d'un Nouveau Modele de Developement".

———. 2005. "Rapport Annuel 2005".

———. 2006. "Annual Report 2006: Transformation of Community Institutions: Re-positioning ECOWAS for Effective Regional Development".

———. 2007. "Rapport Annuel 2007: La Consolidation des Institutions Restructurées de la Communaute en vue d'une Intégration et d'un Développement Régional Acceleré et Efficace", Abuja, December 2007.

———. 2008a. "Annual Report 2008: Forging Regional Response to Global Economic and Financial Crises".

———. 2008b. "Press Release: ECOWAS observers in Guinea Bissau for Legislative Elections (N°:113/2008)", Bissau, 15 November 2008.

———. 2011. "Press Release: ECOWAS Leaders Approve 63 Million US Dollars to Support Security Sector Reforms in Guinea Bissau (N°: 044/2011)", Abuja, 25 March 2011.

———. 2012a. "Annual Report (December 2012): Integration and Political Stability in West Africa", Abuja.

———. 2012b. "ECOWAS Observation Mission says Guinea Bissau Presidential Election was Transparent", Report from ECOWAS, 20 March 2012. Accessed 16 May 2019. https://reliefweb.int/report/guinea-bissau/ecowas-observation-mission-says-guinea-bissau-presidential-election-was.

———. 2012c. "Press Release: ECOWAS Chiefs of Defence Staff to Meet in Abuja on Regional Security (N°:134/2012)", Abuja, 11 May 2012.

———. 2012d. "Press Release: ECOWAS Defence Chiefs Urged to Intensify Efforts toward Enduring Regional Peace and Security (N°: 204/2012)", Abidjan, 25 July 2012.

———. 2012e. "Press Release: ECOWAS Delegation Due in Bissau to Impress Immediate Return to Constitutional rule", Abuja, 16 April 2012. Accessed 1 February 2016. http://news.ecowas.int/presseshow.php?nb=106&lang=en&annee=2012.

———. 2012f. "Press Release: ECOWAS Reaction to Ongoing Coup Attempt in Guinea-Bissau (104/2012)", Abuja, 13 April 2012.

———. 2012g. "Press Release: Niger's Former Interim President to Head ECOWAS Election Observation Mission to Guinea-Bissau (N°: 049/2012)", Abuja, 12 March 2012.

———. 2012h. "Press Release: Signing of the Memorandum of Understanding of the Defence and Security Sector in Guinea-Bissau (305/2012)", Bissau, 7 November 2012.

———. 2013. "Press Release: Regional Security Chiefs urge Strengthening of ECOWAS Mission in Guinea Bissau (N°: 159/2013)", Bissau, 6 June 2013.

———. 2014a. "Preliminary Declaration: Guinea Bissau 2014 Run-Off Presidential Election (N°: 091/2014)", Abuja, 19 May 2014.

———. 2014b. "Press Release: Amos Sawyer et Kadré Désiré Ouédraogo Visitent Plusiers Bureaux de vote a Bissau (N°: 075/2014)", Bissau, 14 April 2014.

———. 2014c. "Press Release: Heads of Election Observation Missions Appeal for Peaceful Run-Off Polls in Guinea-Bissau (N°: 089/2014)", Bissau, 17 May 2014.

———. 2014d. "Press Release: Les élections en Guinée-Bissau Revetent une Importance Particulière (N°: 088/2014)", Bissau. 16 May 2014.

———. 2014e. "Press Release: President Mahama Optimistic about Successful Elections in Guinea Bissau (N°: 073/2014)", Bissau, 11 April 2014.

———. 2016a. "Press Release: ECOWAS Defense Chiefs Review Guinea-Bissau Mission", Abuja, 23 March 2016. Accessed 15 June 2017. www.ecowas.int/ecowas-defense-chiefs-review-guinea-bissau-mission/.

———. 2016b. "Press Release: President of the ECOWAS Commission Urges Guinea-Bissau to Embrace Dialogue as the Means to Resolve the Crisis in the Country", 16 August 2016.

———. 2017. "Press Release: ECOWAS Mission to Guinea Bissau to Assess the Implementation of Conakry and Bissau Agreements", Bissau, 3 December 2017.

ECOWAS Commission and CMI. 2018. *Guide de la CEDEAO pour la Médiation.* Abuja: ECOWAS.

ECOWAS Commission President. 2012. "Memorandum on the Situation in Guinea Bissau", Extraordinary Meeting of the Mediation and Security Council, Abuja, 9 November 2012.

———. 2014a. "Memorandum on the situation in Guinea Bissau (ECW/MSC/XXXI/3)", 31st Ordinary Meeting of the ECOWAS Mediation and Security Council, Yamoussoukro, 25 March 2014.

———. 2014b. "Memorandum on the Situation in Guinea Bissau", 32nd Ordinary Meeting of the ECOWAS Mediation and Security Council, Accra, 8 July 2014.

———. 2015. "Memorandum on the Situation of the ECOWAS Mission in Guinea Bissau (ECOMIB)", 34th Ordinary Session of the Mediation and Security Council, Accra, May 2015.

ECOWAS MSC. 2012a. "Final Report", Extraordinary Session of the ECOWAS Mediation and Security Council, Abuja, 9 November 2012.

———. 2012b. "Final Report", Extraordinary Session of the Mediation and Security Council, Abidjan, 12 April 2012.

———. 2012c. "Report on the political and security situations in Guinea Bissau and Mali", Extraordinary Session of Mediation and Security Council, Abidjan, 19 May 2012.

———. 2013a. "Final Report", Extraordinary Session of the Mediation and Security Council, Abidjan, 18 January 2013.

———. 2013b. "Final Report", Extraordinary Session of the Mediation and Security Council, Abidjan, 25 February 2013.

———. 2013c. "Report", 30th Meeting of the Mediation and Security Council, Abuja, 15 July 2013.

———. 2014a. "Final Report", 31st Meeting of the Mediation and Security Council, Yamoussoukro, 25 March 2014.

———. 2014b. "Report", 33rd Meeting of the Mediation and Security Council, Abuja, 12 December 2014.

———. 2016a. "Final Report", 36th Ordinary Meeting of the Mediation and Security Council", Dakar, 12th May 2016.

———. 2016b. "Final Report", 37th Ordinary Meeting of the Mediation and Security Council at the Ministerial Level", Abuja, 14 December 2016.

———. 2017. "Final Report", 39th Ordinary Meeting of the Mediation and Security Council at the Ministerial level, Abuja, 12 December 2017.

———. 2018. "Final Report", 40th Ordinary Meeting of the ECOWAS Mediation and Security Council at the Ministerial Level, Lomé, 7 July 2018.

Engel, Ulf, ed. 2012. *New Mediation Practices in African Conflicts.* Leipzig: Leipziger Universitätsverlag.

———. 2016. The 2007 African Charter on Democracy, Elections and Governance: Explaining late Ratification and non-Implementation of Compliance Mechanisms. Paper Presented at the 59th Meeting of the African Studies Association, Marriott Wardman Park Hotel, Washington, DC, 1–3 December.

EU Commission. 2015a. "Action Document for 'Support to the Economic Community of West African States (ECOWAS) Mission in Guinea Bissau (ECOMIB)".

———. 2015b. "Commission Decision on the Allocation of Funds Under the African Peace Facility from the 11th European Development Fund in Favour of the Economic Community of West African States (ECOWAS) Mission in Guinea Bissau (ECOMIB) (C[2015] 7696 final)", Brussels, 10 November 2015.

———. 2016a. "Action Document for 'Support to the Economic Community of West African States (ECOWAS) Mission in Guinea Bissau II (ECOMIB)", Brussels, 15 September 2016.

———. 2016b. "African Peace Facility: Annual Report 2015", Luxembourg: Publications Office of the European Union.

———. 2017. "African Peace Facility: Annual Report 2016", Luxembourg: Publications Office of the European Union.

———. 2018. "African Peace Facility: Annual Report 2017", Luxembourg: Publications Office of the European Union.

European Court of Auditors. 2018. *The African Peace and Security Architecture: Need to Refocus EU Support.* Special Report 20. Luxembourg: European Court of Auditors.

Gelot, Linnéa. 2016. Prevention and Militarization in Africa's Security Governance, Mats Utas Blog, 27 July 2016. Accessed 12 October 2018. https://matsutas.wordpress.com/2016/07/27/prevention-and-militarization-in-africas-security-governance-by-linnea-gelot/.

Gibert, Marie V. and Bastien Nivet. 2013. Dissonant Paths to Partnership and Convergence: EU-Africa Relations Between Experimentation and Resistance. *African Security* 6 (3–4): 191–210. doi: 10.1080/19392206.2013.853584.

Global Peace Operations Review. 2011. The African Union Liaison Office in Western Sahara. Accessed 12 August 2020. https://peaceoperationsreview.org/wp-content/uploads/2015/06/2011_west_sahara_notes_box.pdf.

Grävingholt, Jörn, Stefan Gänzle and Sebastian Ziaja. 2009. The Convergence of Peacebuilding and State Building: Addressing a Common Purpose from Different Perspectives. Briefing Paper 4/2009. Bonn: Deutsches Institut für Entwicklungspolitik.

Hartmann, Christof. 2013. Governance Transfer by the Economic Community of West African States (ECOWAS): A B2 Case Study Report. SFB-Governance Working Paper Series No. 47. Berlin: Collaborative Research Center (SFB) 700.

Hartmann, Christof and Kai Striebinger. 2015. Writing the Script? ECOWAS's Military Intervention Mechanism. In *Governance Transfer by Regional Organizations: Patching Together a Global Script*, eds Tanja A. Börzel and Vera van Hüllen, 68–83. Basingstoke: Palgrave Macmillan.

Herpolsheimer, Jens. 2014. Security Cooperation in the Community of Portuguese-Speaking Countries (CPLP). Unpublished master's thesis, Leipzig University.

Herpolsheimer, Jens and Skollan E. Warnck. 2020. *Mapping Intervention Practices of ECOWAS and the African Union: Methodological and Practical Challenges.* SFB 1199 Working Paper Series No. 22. Leipzig: Leipziger Universitätsverlag.

ICG. 2012. *Beyond Turf Wars: Managing the Post-Coup Transition in Guinea-Bissau.* Africa Report 190 (17 August). Brussels: International Crisis Group.

Khadiagala, Gilbert M. 2016. Eminent Peacemakers in African Conflicts: Contributions, Potential and Limits. In *Minding the Gap: African Conflict Management in a Time of Change*, eds Pamela R. Aall and Chester A. Crocker, 201–18. Waterloo: Centre for International Governance Innovation.

Kohl, Christoph. 2014. *The Reform of the Guinea-Bissau's Security Sector: Between Demand and Practice.* PRIF report 126. Frankfurt am Main: Peace Research Institute Frankfurt (PRIF).

Kohnert, Dirk. 2010. *Democratization Via Elections in an African 'Narco-State'? The Case of Guinea-Bissau.* GIGA Working Paper 123. Hamburg: German Institute of Global and Area Studies.

Mendy, Peter K. and Richard A. Lobban. 2013. *Historical Dictionary of the Republic of Guinea-Bissau.* Lanham, MD: Scarecrow Press.

Nathan, Laurie. 2017. *A Survey of Mediation in African Coups.* APN Working Papers 15. New York: African Peacebuilding Network.

Nathan, Laurie, Gen R. Kibochi, Claude Mainge, Michelle Ndiaye and Yahia Zoubir. 2015. African Peace and Security Architecture (APSA): 2014 Assessment Study, 16 April 2015.

OAU. 1964. "Protocol of the Commission of Mediation, Conciliation and Arbitration", Cairo, 21 July 1964.

———. 1974. "Report of the OAU Fact-Finding Mission on the Unity Movement of South Africa", n.p., 1 November 1974.

———. 2002. "Guidelines for African Union Electoral Observation and Monitoring Missions (EX. CL/91 [V] Annex II)", 38th Ordinary Session of the Heads of State and Governments, Durban, 8 July 2002.

OAU Assembly. 1993. "Declaration of Heads of State and Government on the Establishment within the OAU of a Mechanism for Conflict Prevention, Management and Resolution (AHG/DECL.3 [XXIX])", Assembly, 29th Ordinary Session, Cairo, 28–29 June, 1993.

———. 2002. "OAU/AU Declaration on the Principles Governing Democratic Elections in Africa (AHG/Decl. 1 [XXXVIII])", 38th Ordinary Session of the Assembly, Durban, 8 July 2002.

OAU Central Organ. 1998. "Report of the Secretary General on the Conflict in Guinea Bissau (Central Organ/MEC/AHG/4c(IV))", 4th Ordinary Session of the Central Organ of the OAU Mechanism for Conflict Prevention, Management and Resolution. Ouagadougou, 17–18 December 1998.

Okyere, Frank. 2016. Guinea-Bissau: Ending the Perennial Political Imbroglio. In *Annual Review of Peace Support Operations in Africa 2016*, eds Emma Birikorang, Thomas Jaye and Frank Okyere, 179–96. Accra: Kofi Annan International Peacekeeping Training Centre (KAIPTC).

Perdigao, Yovanka P. 2016. How did Guinea-Bissau Come to Have 5 Prime Ministers in 15 Months? Africa Research Institute, 13 December 2016. Accessed 23 May 2019. www.africaresearchinstitute.org/newsite/blog/guinea-bissau-come-5-prime-ministers-15-months/.

RTP. 2005. Organização Sub-Regional Preocupada com Evolução na Guiné-Bissau, RTP Agência LUSA, 23 March 2005. Accessed 13 March 2019. www.rtp.pt/noticias/mundo/organizacao-sub-regional-preocupada-com-evolucao-na-guine-bissau_n107928.

Tardy, Thierry and Marco Wyss, eds. 2014. *Peacekeeping in Africa: The Evolving Security Architecture*. New York: Routledge.

Théroux-Bénoni, Lori-Anne. 2014. The Long Path to MINUSMA: Assessing the International Response to the Crisis in Mali. In *Peacekeeping in Africa: The Evolving Security Architecture*, eds Thierry Tardy and Marco Wyss, 171–89. New York: Routledge.

UN PBC. 2008. "Background Paper on Security Sector Reform in Guinea-Bissau", Thematic Discussion on Security Sector Reform and the Rule of Law, n.p., 18 June 2008.

UNIOGBIS. 2009. "Press Release: Joint UN, EU, AU and ECOWAS Delegation Discussed SSR with Guinea-Bissau Prime Minister", Bissau, 18 November 2009.

———. 2018. "Press Release: Voter Registration Under Way in Guinea-Bissau", Bissau, 5 October 2018.

UNSC. 2013. "Resolution 2103 (S/RES/2103 [2013])", 6869th Meeting, New York, 22 May 2013.

———. 2014. "Resolution 2157 (S/RES/2157 [2014])", 7187th Meeting, New York, 29 May 2014.

———. 2015. "Resolution 2203 (S/RES/2203 [2015])", 7385th Meeting, New York, 18 February 2015.

UNSG. 1999. "Report of the Secretary-General on Developments in Guinea-Bissau and on the Activities of the United Nations Peace-Building Support Office in that Country (S/1999/1276)", New York, 23 December 1999.

———. 2004. "Report of the Secretary-General on Developments in Guinea-Bissau and on the Activities of the United Nations Peacebuilding Support Office in that Country (S/2004/969)", New York, 15 December 2004.

———. 2005. "Report of the Secretary-General on Developments in Guinea-Bissau and on the Activities of the United Nations Peacebuilding Support Office in that Country (S/2005/380)", New York, 10 June 2005.

———. 2012a. "Report of the Secretary-General on Developments in Guinea-Bissau and on the Activities of the United Nations Integrated Peacebuilding Office in that Country (S/2012/554)", New York, 17 July 2012.

———. 2012b. "Report of the Secretary-General on the Restoration of Constitutional Order in Guinea-Bissau (S/2012/704)", New York, 12 September 2012.

———. 2013. "Report of the Secretary-General on Developments in Guinea-Bissau and on the Activities of the United Nations Integrated Peacebuilding Office in that Country (S/2013/26)", New York, 16 January 2013.

Uzoechina, Okey. 2014. Security Sector Reform and Governance Processes in West Africa: From Concepts to Reality. Policy Paper 35. Geneva: Geneva Centre for the Democratic Control of Armed Forces (DCAF).

Walker, Stephen. 2012. Vote Was Fair Say NI Election Observers, BBC News, 29 March 2012. Accessed 19 March 2019. www.bbc.com/news/uk-northern-ireland-17544518.

Whitman, Richard and Stefan Wolff, eds. 2012. *The European Union as a Global Conflict Manager*. London: Routledge.

Whitman, Richard G. and Toni Haastrup. 2015. Locating the EU's Strategic Behaviour in Sub-Saharan Africa. In *The European Union in Africa: Incoherent Policies,*

Asymmetrical Partnership, Declining Relevance?, ed. Maurizio Carbone, 57–76. Manchester: Manchester University Press.

Yabi, Gilles O. 2010. *The Role of ECOWAS in Managing Political Crisis and Conflict: The Cases of Guinea and Guinea-Bissau.* Abuja: Friedrich-Ebert-Stiftung.

Zartman, William I. 2016. Mediation and Political Tools in Africa. In *Minding the Gap: African Conflict Management in a Time of Change*, eds Pamela R. Aall and Chester A. Crocker, 187–200. Waterloo: Centre for International Governance Innovation.

5 Regional security policies

Spatial imaginations and spatial formatting

Introduction

Chapters 3 and 4 have described, analyzed and historicized different sets of intervention practices that actors at ECOWAS and the AU have developed and applied relatively consistently and coherently in response to conflict in their respective regions. These chapters have also highlighted how these practices, aiming to manage conflict, have simultaneously been spatializing practices, contributing to the construction of regional spaces. However, managing active conflicts has not been the only objective of actors at African ROs during conflict interventions. In addition to getting a grip on these conflicts, they have also pursued more general objectives, agendas and political projects. These point beyond individual conflict situations and, once more, are intimately linked to space-making.

Therefore, this chapter takes a closer look at such other objectives. In particular, it highlights the connection between specific security policies and the formatting of space (from 'within' and 'without') based on particular spatial imaginations. To this end, interventions in Guinea-Bissau once more provide a prism to reflect upon these dynamics more generally. Doing so holds several advantages. First, it allows zooming into a high level of detail while not losing the larger context out of sight. Second, selecting a seemingly 'marginal' example most convincingly allows demonstration of the link between interventions in a specific conflict situation and larger, more general objectives – every piece of the puzzle counts. Moreover, third, staying with the example of interventions in Guinea-Bissau in this chapter, as in previous ones, helps stressing the simultaneity and spatial intersection of multiple and entangled actors, practices, political projects and so on in one specific conflict situation.

To this end, the chapter, first, reflects upon two main spatial imaginations that have influenced and framed interventions by different actors in West Africa more generally and Guinea-Bissau in particular. Following that, it traces the emergence of different policy fields at ECOWAS and the AU as well as the EU, and describes how actors at these organizations have sought to implement and consolidate specific policies, filling them with content, adopting 'cases' to their agendas, one of which has been Guinea-Bissau. Finally, it analyzes the interlocking of regional security policies with the 'internal' and 'external' formatting of regional spaces.[1] Doing so, this chapter contributes to a better appreciation of the under-researched spatial dimensions of conflict interventions by African ROs, at the same time enhancing the understanding of the role, objectives and modes of operation of those organizations with respect to African peace and security dynamics more generally.

Spatial imaginations of conflict in West Africa

In the following, I analyze the two main spatial imaginations and framings that have been particularly influential among actors intervening in West Africa, driving conflict interventions *and* regional policy processes. The first, linked to concerns about 'regional in/stability', has been of key importance for actors at ECOWAS and the AU; the second, linked to concerns about 'narco-states' and 'narco-terrorism', has been particularly influential among Western state and regional actors, such as the US and the EU. Both spatial imaginations have essentially connected events in one place to security dynamics in wider regional and trans-regional spaces (e.g., through the notion of 'spill-over'). Against that backdrop, I argue that only when taking them seriously is it possible to fully understand why certain actors engage in conflict interventions, and how specific conflict sites, far from being isolated points or areas on a map, form part of highly integrated spaces – ideational or material, but always very real.

'Regional in/stability' as driver of ECOWAS and AU security cooperation

For AU actors, but even more so for ECOWAS actors, experiences of violent conflicts in West Africa during the 1990s, in Liberia, Sierra Leone and Guinea-Bissau, as well as in the early 2000s, in Côte d'Ivoire and Liberia, have been the main triggers for increased security cooperation at regional scales. This has been motivated by a double concern over potential "state implosion" and the spread of negative effects across the borders of individual nation states, with "serious regional implications" regarding both security and stability as well as "collective developmental efforts" (ECOWAS 2008, para. 23; see also OAU Assembly 1993, para. 9ff.). In other words, "[t]he ripples of [...] so-called internal conflicts were instantly felt far beyond national borders in the form of refugee flows, severe deterioration of livelihoods, health and nutrition standards, disrupted infrastructure, and the proliferation of weapons, violence and trans-national crime" (ECOWAS 2008, para. 23). Scholars of African Peace and Security have largely shared and contributed to this general assessment by politicians and practitioners (e.g., cf. Adebajo 2002, 15; Kabia 2009, 33, 48–50, 67–8). Consequently, since the early 1990s, it has been a widely shared view that "regional problems" require "regional solutions" – even more so at a time of critical revision of UN peacekeeping practices and policies (cf. Adebajo 2002, 15–16).[2]

In 1975, West African heads of state founded ECOWAS primarily as an organization for economic cooperation, as its name still suggests. Subsequently, the emergence of different security issues (e.g., mercenary attacks, military coups) during the 1970s and 1980s led to the incremental inclusion of security issues into regional cooperation (cf. Kabia 2009, 66–7). Nevertheless, actual cooperation in this domain remained very limited (e.g., cf. Aning 1999, 27), emerging more strongly only in response to conflicts during the 1990s (cf. Kabia 2009, 68). It is important to note that the creation of ECOWAS as such was driven by security interests of the Nigerian government, especially following the experience of the war in Biafra. Most importantly, Nigerian state actors have aimed to counter French meddling in neighboring states, and to loosen ties between France and its former colonies, especially Côte d'Ivoire and Senegal, which were competing with Nigerian hegemonic ambitions in the West African region (Adebajo 2002, 29).

Initially built around the concern of 'regime security' and the principle of non-interference in 'internal affairs' (e.g., cf. ECOWAS 1981), a more interventionist approach emerged in the course of the 1990s.[3] This was mostly driven by the Nigerian government, investing considerable financial and human resources in the first two interventions of the ECOWAS Cease-fire Monitoring Group (ECOMOG), in Liberia and Sierra Leone. Although some have argued that this has been merely for self-serving reasons, it is nevertheless worth stressing that such an interest prominently included 'regional stability' in West Africa (cf. Adebajo 2002, 29). After initial reluctance and persistent tensions, other ECOWAS states, including francophone ones such as Senegal and Côte d'Ivoire, also invested troops and material resources, and supported the institutionalization of an ECOWAS security mechanism (cf. Adebajo 2004, 301–302).

Out of the ECOMOG experiences grew efforts to systematize and institutionalize ECOWAS interventions in conflict in West Africa. The Revised ECOWAS Treaty of 1993 now included the "maintenance of regional peace, stability and security" among its "fundamental principles" (ECOWAS 1993, Art. 4.e). It also included Article 58 on "regional security", seeking to stimulate cross-border cooperation and allowing for a regional observation system as well as mediation and military peacekeeping in intra- and inter-state conflicts (ECOWAS 1993, Art. 58.2). Building on that, the 1999 Protocol relating to the Mechanism for Conflict Prevention, Management, Resolution, Peace-Keeping and Security (1999 Mechanism) more specifically expressed regional states' concern about a "proliferation of conflicts which constitute a threat to the peace and security in the African continent" (ECOWAS 1999, Preamble). Moreover, it referred to the negative effect of insecurity and instability on economic and social development (e.g., cross-border crimes, proliferation of small arms, illicit trafficking), emphasizing that this could only be tackled through "increased and well-coordinated multilateral cooperation" (ECOWAS 1999, Preamble).

At the continental level, the OAU had experimented with *ad hoc* initiatives aiming to manage conflict threatening regional stability during the first decades of its existence, mostly focusing on multilateral diplomacy (cf. de Coning 1996, 1; Muyangwa and Vogt 2000, 5–7). Following mediation efforts during the late 1970s, between 1980 and 1982, African heads of state and government authorized and deployed its first peacekeeping force to deal with the persistent war in Chad – once more with the Nigerian government taking a lead, sending unilateral peacekeeping forces 'on the ground' prior to the OAU deployment (cf. Amoo 1992; Mays 2002).[4] However, it was only after the end of the Cold War, faced with a proliferation of conflicts, which negatively affected collective development efforts, that African heads of state decided to work towards a more coherent, collective and institutionalized framework (cf. OAU Assembly 1990, 1992). In Addis Ababa, the OAU Assembly had tasked Salim Ahmed Salim, OAU Secretary-General at the time (former Foreign Affairs Minister and Prime Minister of Tanzania), to prepare a report on conflicts in Africa and proposals for an OAU mechanism to deal with them, which he presented in 1992 at the OAU Assembly in Dakar (cf. Muyangwa and Vogt 2000, 8). Salim subsequently became a driving force behind these efforts (cf. de Coning 1996, 1–2). Another important influence came from the African Leadership Forum, founded in the late 1980s by Olusegun Obasanjo, former and future Nigerian president but at that time acting as "private citizen", although an influential one (Iliffe 2011, 99ff.).[5] Out of these initiatives resulted the OAU Mechanism for Conflict Prevention, Management and Resolution – concerned with 'continental' peace and stability (OAU Assembly 1993, para. 11). The agenda expressed in the 1993 Mechanism, primarily focusing on 'prevention', further evolved in the following years, driven by the OAU General Secretariat, towards also including peacekeeping (cf. de Coning 1996, 1–2). Again, African leaders cautiously wanted to take charge and responsibility for regional and continental peace, stability and security, at a time of fundamental criticism and revision of the UN system (cf. de Coning 1996, 2).[6]

During the period of the transformation of the OAU into the AU (1999–2002), it was once more the Nigerian government under newly elected President Olusegun Obasanjo that drove an agenda focusing on security and stability, essentially linking it to socio-economic development. Obasanjo, continuing his work initiated in the context of the African Leadership Forum, created the Conference on Security, Stability, Development and Cooperation in Africa (Tieku 2004, 257–8). This time, however, on the continental scale, Nigerian government interests competed with other influential African states and their heads, in particular President Thabo Mbeki of South Africa, also elected in 1999, pushing NEPAD, and President Muhammar Ghaddafi of Libya (cf. Tieku 2004). In addition, the Algerian government, under President Abdelaziz Bouteflika, newly elected in 1999, became another key player, seeking to influence the security agenda of the (O)AU, specifically focusing on transnational 'terrorism' (cf. Zoubir 2013, 45ff.).[7]

With increasing formalization and institutionalization of regional peacekeeping within ECOWAS and the AU, many scholars have observed a shift in the underpinning norms and principles – most notably from 'regime security' to 'human security' and from 'non-interference' to a 'responsibility to protect' (cf. Engel 2012; Witt 2013; Hartmann and Striebinger 2015). That process was reflected in new legal frameworks and policy initiatives, such as the 2002 Protocol Relating to the Establishment of the AU Peace and Security Council (PSC) and the 2001 ECOWAS Supplementary Protocol on Democracy and Good Governance, and went along with further increasing agency on the part of the ECOWAS and AU secretariats, later transformed into commissions (cf. Engel 2013; Tieku 2011). Since then, ECOWAS and AU member states and commission staffs have employed persistent efforts, with international support, to develop and consolidate conflict intervention practices (see Chapters 3 and 4) and policies, thereby contributing to the construction and formatting (see below) as well as the ordering of regional spaces (see Chapter 6).

'Narco-state' and 'narco-terrorism' as trans-regional threats

Another closely related spatial imagination that has strongly influenced the perception and framing of conflict in West Africa centers on discourses about 'transnational organized crime' (TOC), especially 'drug trafficking', and its assumed links with 'transnational terrorism'. Since the mid-2000s, alarming voices have described regional peace and security in West/Africa as "under attack" (UNODC 2007, 1), facing a "drug problem" (Traub 2010; see also, e.g., Cockayne and Williams 2009; Holmgren 2013). These voices went along with increased international attention and concerns about West Africa's allegedly central role in the trafficking of cocaine coming from Latin America on its way to Europe. In this account, despite acknowledging more general trends in West Africa and in fact also across Southern Africa and East Africa, the example of Guinea-Bissau has stood out like no other, labeled as 'Africa's' or even 'the world's first narco-state' by journalists, policy practitioners and some scholars (e.g., Vulliamy 2008; O'Regan and Thompson 2013; Loewenstein 2016).

In 2005, the UN Office on Drugs and Crime (UNODC) stated in its annual World Drug Report that Africa, until then considered largely irrelevant, had attained a more important role in the international drug trade directed at the European market (UNODC 2005, 71).[8] In the same year, the UNODC started to publish several reports on the situation of TOC in West Africa in general (in 2005, 2009 and 2013), and cocaine trafficking in particular (in 2007 and 2008). Reporting a stark increase in cocaine seizures, the UN Office described what it saw as a strategic shift in the trade routes from Latin America to Africa, which it explained by the saturation of the cocaine market in the US, a growing demand in Europe as well as the pressure created by effective interdiction efforts in the Americas. Consequently, West Africa in particular is believed to have become a new major transit hub (UNODC 2007, 2008).

In its 2007 report, the UNODC made special reference to Guinea-Bissau, identifying the country as the 'epicenter' of the phenomenon (UNODC 2007). This report has since become the standard reference in most publications on the issue. According to the report and the media reports drawing on it, Guinea-Bissau stands out for the attractions it appears to offer to Latin American drug cartels, rerouting their operations: (i) a good logistic position 'half-way' to Europe; (ii) an advantageous geography, in particular archipelagos and long, rugged coastlines that are difficult to police; (iii) weak, inefficient and corruptible government institutions, especially regarding security, justice and territorial control; and (iv) a socio-economic-cultural context that tolerates certain "illicit" activities (i.e., poverty and a long history in informal trading) (UNODC 2007, 2008).

According to the dominant account, the 'narco-state' allows traffickers from Latin America to hide behind Guinea-Bissau's state façade, negatively impacting on local politics, economics and society. What is more, as a consequence of potential 'spill-over effects' the situation in Guinea-Bissau might further add to insecurity and instability in the region, especially since different types of TOCs are considered to be interlinked (e.g., money laundering and the trafficking of people, arms and drugs). Most importantly in this regard, Western think tanks and politicians have asserted that the narcotics trade, as a financing mechanism, directly connects to transnational terrorism. This assumed nexus has been framed as "narco-terrorism", above all by US government authorities (e.g., US DOJ 2009; The White House 2011), some media outlets (e.g., Freeman 2013; Akinyemi 2014) and EU actors (e.g., Europol 2011). Therefore, dynamics related to cocaine trafficking in Guinea-Bissau and West Africa are imagined to reach far beyond the region.

The account offered so far constitutes the widely received wisdom that is to some extent also reproduced in academic literature (e.g., Mazzitelli 2007; Aning and Pokoo 2014; Kemp, Shaw and Boutellis 2013). However, since the late 2000s, there is also a growing body of literature by academics and some investigative journalists that is at odds with this dominant account, for example, questioning its historicity, empirical substance, as well as the actual extent and significance of the phenomenon (e.g., Ellis 2009; Carrier and Klantschnig 2012; Csete and Sánchez 2013; Shaw 2015).[9] Likewise, some scholars have put the discursive framing of 'narco-terrorism', that is, the 'drug–terror nexus', into question (e.g., Lacher 2013; Thompson 2015).

In addition to this criticism, dominant accounts are closely linked to the problematic notion of 'ungoverned spaces', often associated with ideas about 'weak', 'failing' or 'failed' states. Policy advisors and some scholars consider those to pose a threat to international security because both the 'instability' in these states may spread (i.e., 'spill-over' or 'contagion') and they might harbor transnational criminal actors (i.e., 'safe havens') (Figueroa Helland and Borg 2014). Although terms such as 'weak' or 'criminal' are relational and meaningful only against their point of reference – by themselves explaining very little or even obscuring actual empirical dynamics – discourses about 'failed states' have built on and contributed to powerful spatial imaginations. For example, these comprise notions of *where* 'failed states' are (or are not), how they fail to properly organize and control space and how they connect to others (among many, e.g., cf. Patrick 2007; Piazza 2008; Coggins 2015). Interestingly, many of the proposed 'solutions' have focused on 'fixing' or establishing the spatial format 'nation state'. However, as shown in previous chapters, interventions have rarely focused on establishing territorial control, instead rather producing some sort of networked state space, centered in the capital, Bissau (see Chapter 4).

Regional security policies and the 'internal' formatting of space

Against the backdrop of the spatial imaginations discussed above, in particular, however, in response to 'regional in/stability', actors at ECOWAS and the AU have tried to develop, enact and consolidate specific regional security policies. To that end, two related logics have been of particular importance. First, staff at these organizations have adopted certain ongoing 'cases' to their agenda, making them staging grounds for their activities. Second, where policy processes have been more advanced, actors at these organizations have sought to 'globalize' their efforts, increasingly seeking to systematize implementation and encompass the entirety of their respective regional spaces. This section provides examples for both logics and demonstrates, with regard to interventions in Guinea-Bissau, how from this perspective every conflict situation becomes as important as any other, being intimately connected to the construction and 'internal' formatting of regional spaces.[10] In the following, this section draws on the empirical examples of (i) policies to confront unconstitutional changes of government (UCGs); (ii) policies on post-conflict reconstruction and development (PCRD); and (iii) policies on security sector reform (SSR). As will become clear, although all three policy areas play important roles in both organizations, AU policies have been more formalized, in the form of policy scripts and frameworks, than ECOWAS policies. Some central ECOWAS policies, instead of being based on a detailed written 'script', have taken shape primarily in practice, directly linked to actual conflict management.

Policies on unconstitutional changes of government

Probably the most important policy process that both ECOWAS and AU actors have linked to different conflict interventions are their respective efforts to act out, develop and consolidate policies on responses to so-called UCGs, building on the principle of 'zero tolerance' (Sturman 2011; Engel 2012; Witt 2013). Although both share the objective in principal, approaches towards implementation have differed. Actors at both organizations, however, have tried establishing coherence, consolidating specific norms, principles and policies.

Drawing on a process that began already during OAU times,[11] actors at the AU over the years have developed relatively clear notions of what constitutes a UCG and how to respond to them. This process reflected a more general shift regarding the international norm of 'non-interference' in internal affairs of states (i.e., 'regime security') towards 'non-indifference' (i.e., human security), which ultimately also became enshrined in the AU Constitutive Act (2000), Article 4.h. The Lomé Declaration, still made by the OAU Assembly, defined four forms of UCGs and laid down a basic policy script on how to respond to them (AU Assembly 2000, 30 and 3ff.)[12] In summarized form, these provisions subsequently found their way into the AU Constitutive Act (cf. AU 2000, Art. 4.p and 30) as well as into the PSC Protocol (cf. AU 2002, Art. 7.g).

However, these principles and policies did not automatically translate into action. Responses became only more coherent and systematic with increasing agency on the part of the AU Commission since the late 2000s, significantly contributing to the adoption of the African Charter on Democracy, Elections and Governance (ACDEG) by the AU Assembly in January 2007. The ACDEG adapted the policy script to the new institutions (i.e., the PSC, the AU Commission and its Chairperson), refined and expanded the definition of UCGs, now also including constitutional revisions or amendments to stay in power, and detailed the sanctions regime (cf. Engel 2012, 65–7).[13] Nevertheless, it took until February 2012 for the ACDEG to enter into force, following the deposit of the required 15 ratifications in January 2012 (cf. Engel 2012, 67). Since then, the AU Commission and some AU member states have sought to increase consistency in the AU's response to UCGs in Africa, but of course have depended on decisions by the PSC, and in the case of sanctions on the Assembly.[14]

For ECOWAS, the 2001 Supplementary Protocol states the principle of 'zero tolerance' for "power obtained or maintained by unconstitutional means" (ECOWAS 2001, Art. 1.c). The 2001 Supplementary Protocol further states that if democracy is brought to an end abruptly by any means (i.e., a UCG), or in case of massive violation of human rights, ECOWAS may impose sanctions, refusing participation of the concerned member state in ECOWAS activities, partly or completely, and shall monitor and support efforts to return sanctioned members to "normalcy and constitutional order" (ECOWAS 2001, Art. 45). Beyond that, definition and interpretation of what exactly constitutes a UCG and how ECOWAS organs should respond to it have remained relatively open.[15] The ECOWAS 'script' (Hartmann and Striebinger 2015), therefore, has been much more reflected in practice, which has been relatively consistent – without making any judgement in terms of 'success' or 'failure, 'good' or 'bad'.

In response to the coup of April 2012 in Guinea-Bissau, both ECOWAS and AU actors condemned it, referring to their principled position that rejects any form of UCG, and demanding the immediate 'return to constitutional order' (see also Chapter 3). However, tensions emerged towards the end of 2012, when different ECOWAS organs repeatedly called upon the AU PSC to lift the suspension of Guinea-Bissau from the AU. At the core of these tensions, persisting throughout 2013 and early 2014, were different interpretations of what 'return to constitutional' order should mean, a debate that AU actors repeatedly had with different RECs as well as other regional and international actors (cf. Witt 2020). Although AU actors dropped their insistence on the completion of the interrupted electoral process, they nevertheless continued to insist on the completion of some electoral process, sufficiently free, fair and transparent, signaling Guinea-Bissau's full 'return to constitutional order' (see Chapter 3). ECOWAS actors, on the other hand, held that 'constitutional order' had been restored by virtue of the signed transition agreement and the resulting transition authorities, negotiated by the ECOWAS field missions (see Chapters 1, 3 and 4).

For the AU Commission, closely 'following protocol' on Guinea-Bissau has been very important in its effort to systematize and consolidate its approach towards UCGs, avoiding setting another 'bad' precedent, something that in the past had proven difficult. In particular, the situations in Mauretania (2008/9) and Madagascar (2009) have been key reference points, against which actors at the AU Commission have sought to improve. In both cases the RECs, ECOWAS and SADC respectively,[16] took the lead, intervening after a coup d'état and interpreted principled positions on UCGs in a way that critics and staff at the AU Commission saw as effectively condoning coups and undermining the AU's UCG policy. ECOWAS actors, on their part, have referred precisely to these cases as precedence to justify their approach in the case of Guinea-Bissau.[17] That approach has been primarily a pragmatic one, but nevertheless in line with established ECOWAS practice – applied elsewhere in much the same way, as ECOWAS representatives have stressed in response to criticism by other regional and international actors (cf. ECOWAS Commission President 2012; ECOWAS Commission 2012).

Policies on post-conflict reconstruction and development

More recently, two other policy fields developed by two different AU PSD divisions subsequently took up the case of Guinea-Bissau to develop activities and/or consolidate a more coherent regional approach. The first example is the AU Policy Framework for Post-Conflict Reconstruction and Development (PCRD), created much earlier, but gaining new momentum in 2015/16, located at the AU PSD's Division of Conflict Management and PCRD (CMPCRD). The second example is the AU Policy Framework on Security Sector Reform (SSR), resulting from a process located at the AU PSD's Division of Defense and Security (DSD), starting in the mid-2000s, but getting more traction only around 2013. Thus, both policy fields have been 'in the making' for more than ten years, but activities in those fields increased only more recently, resulting in increasing formalization and structuring.

The process leading to the adoption of the AU's Policy Framework for PCRD started in the early 2000s, drawing on provisions in the PSC Protocol

(AU 2002, Art. 3.c and 6.e).[18] In line with similar developments at the UN around the same time (cf. Carvalho, de Coning and Ahere 2016, 2–6), in July 2005, the AU Executive Council meeting in Sirte "urged" the AU Commission to develop a policy on PCRD (AU Executive Council 2005, para. 6). Drafting started in September 2005, and after several stages of 'brainstorming' and revisions by the AU PSD, technical experts (February 2006), civil society representatives (April 2006) and governmental experts (June 2006), the AU Executive Council endorsed a draft PCRD framework in June/July 2006 in Banjul (AU Executive Council 2006, para. 3; see also AU 2006, vii–viii). In the following year, two consultative meetings with civil society organizations (Addis Ababa, March 2007) and other 'critical' stakeholders (Lusaka, July 2007) sought to discuss how best to implement the PCRD framework (cf. AU 2007a, 2007b). The first activities 'on the ground' were 'multidisciplinary' missions that assessed PCRD needs in the Central African Republic (CAR, 2006), Liberia and Sierra Leone (2009), Burundi (2010) and Sudan (2011) (cf. AU PSD 2015).[19]

The policy process and institutionalization, however, only gained new momentum after the APSA assessment studies of 2010 and 2014, which subsequently translated into the APSA Roadmap 2016–20, launched by the AU Commission in December 2015. In 2011, a PCRD unit was created at the PSD, within the Conflict Management Division (CMD), and later became a constitutive part of that division (renamed CMPCRD). Nevertheless, until 2016, ten years after the adoption of the PCRD framework, nothing much had happened, leaving PCRD the "least developed and used component of APSA" (IPSS 2017, 45). The 2014 APSA assessment study identified the following challenges in that regard: a lack of coordination and complementarity between AU PSD divisions, and between the AUC and other PCRD actors, lacking financial and human resources at the AUC, and insufficient implementation of the PCRD mechanisms proposed in the 2006 policy framework (cf. Nathan et al. 2015, 140–1).

Therefore, in 2014/15 a revision process began that was further pushed by the launch of the APSA Roadmap 2016–20, asking different actors at the AU Commission to increase their coordination and cooperation.[20] The Institute for Security Studies (ISS) in Addis Ababa, as part of the Training for Peace program,[21] provided technical and financial support to developing guiding documents, such as the recent five-year Results-Based Framework.[22] Moreover, led by CMPCRD staff, several AU departments formally established the Interdepartmental Task Force on PCRD (ITF-PCRD) in May 2016, which was already proposed in the 2006 policy framework, but had started to come together only on an *ad hoc* basis since 2014 (cf. Nathan et al. 2015, 141).[23] One of the key activities undertaken by the ITF-PCRD to fill the initiative with life has been joint assessment missions. The first such mission visited CAR in August 2016 (cf. AU Commission 2016). After that, staff of different AU departments (divisions and units) adopted Guinea-Bissau as the destination of the next mission, starting necessary preparations in the second half of 2016.[24] However, due to the persistent political deadlock in Guinea-Bissau throughout 2016 and 2017, the ITF-PCRD mission was postponed several times and eventually abandoned, for the time being.[25] Instead, Gambia became the next site of deployment (cf. AU PSC 2017), and subsequently host to the first long-term AU Technical Support Team mission, accompanying national institutional reforms (cf. AU PSC 2020).

At ECOWAS, 'PCRD' does not exist as a separate policy area and the term as such is not widely used. ECOWAS does not have a dedicated framework, nor any institutional process similar to the AU (cf. Lucey and Arewa 2016). Instead, drawing its mandate from the 1999 Mechanism and the 2001 Supplementary Protocol – both of which do not explicitly mention the term 'post-conflict' – the 2008 ECOWAS Conflict Prevention Framework (ECPF) establishes a cross-cutting concern with 'post-conflict environments', 'countries' or 'settings', as well as 'post-conflict reconstruction' (e.g., cf. ECOWAS 2008, paras. 5, 7.b, 19.b, 28.h, 53.e, 74.g, 78.f). This concern, among others, informs the work of different organizational units at ECOWAS, for example, aiming to provide humanitarian assistance, implement DDR, SSR and "small arms and light weapons" programs, support disadvantaged media and promote human rights and rule of law, as well as democratic governance. The example of ECOWAS interventions in Guinea-Bissau (see Chapters 3 and 4) indicates that, despite persistent challenges and shortcomings (cf. Ismail 2008), post-conflict reconstruction has been an objective not only pursued in principle, but also in practice. In particular, ECOWAS long-term election observation missions and SSR programs (see also Chapter 4) need to be understood as examples in that regard.

Policies on security sector reform

Slightly different from the examples above, SSR has been a policy field developed more formally at ECOWAS; however, it has drawn a lot on earlier hands-on experience, for example, supporting SSR efforts in Liberia and Côte d'Ivoire since the mid-2000s. However, early SSR efforts led by ECOWAS and CPLP actors in Guinea-Bissau since 2010 have played a particularly important role in the development of a more general policy (cf. Uzoechina 2014, 20ff.). Since 2008, drawing their mandate from the ECPF (ECOWAS 2008, Arts. 72–6), staff of the Regional Security Division started working on a policy document, assisted by staff of the International Security Sector Advisory Team (ISSAT).[26] Following an internal sensitization workshop in January 2009 in Abuja, in November 2010, nine regional experts met to produce a first draft, which was subsequently revised during a consultative meeting in September 2010, and based on input from ISSAT/DCAF (cf. Uzoechina 2014, 11).[27] In 2011, this process resulted in the adoption of the ECOWAS Code of Conduct of the Armed Forces and Security Services. Subsequently, in interaction with actors at the AU and UN (see below), RSD staff finalized the Policy Framework for Security Sector Reform and Governance, which the

ECOWAS Authority adopted in June 2016, at its 49th ordinary session (cf. ECOWAS 2016).

This process at ECOWAS co-evolved with similar developments at the AU. In direct relation to the AU Policy Framework on PCRD, which provided the larger context, the AU Policy Framework on SSR resulted out of a process that emerged at the AU Commission during the mid-2000s (cf. AU 2013, 1). Again following the emergence of a more global concern with SSR within the UN system,[28] in February 2008, the AU Assembly decided to task the AU Commission with drafting a "comprehensive" continental framework (AU Assembly 2008, para. 19). That document should aim to provide guidelines for the AU, RECs, member states and "other stakeholders" on how to implement SSR programs (AU 2013, para. 13). As in the case of ECOWAS, and happening at the same time, ISSAT/DCAF staff also assisted in the drafting of the AU document.[29] In January 2013, at the 20th ordinary session of the AU Assembly in Addis Ababa, African heads of state and government in January adopted the Policy Framework on SSR (AU Assembly 2013, para. 21).

While political approval for the SSR Framework had been achieved, implementation turned out to be more difficult, especially facing various political sensitivities of member states when it comes to their security forces. Therefore, the tool of choice again became joint assessment missions (JAM), as well as stakeholder workshops and the creation of the Africa Forum on SSR (meeting in November 2014 and October 2018), to get the process started, sensitize different stakeholders and to build some confidence among them. The first SSR JAM went to CAR in May 2014, concluded by a stakeholder workshop. Following that, a second mission visited Madagascar in October 2014 and, in March 2015, Guinea-Bissau became the third member state to receive such a mission. Subsequently, similar missions visited Mali and Gambia, in November 2015 and May 2017 respectively.[30]

These are examples taken only from the security departments of ECOWAS and the AU, where I did most of my research. However, other departments (directorates, units etc.) have also adopted specific 'cases' to their agendas (cf. Tieku 2016, 127ff.). One example, in this regard, has been the AU Department of Political Affairs, and in particular its Democracy and Electoral Assistance Unit (DEAU), which has striven to 'continentalize' its efforts as much as possible. The DEAU has increasingly covered elections in almost every African country, sending election observation missions, short- and long-term, as has been the case for Guinea-Bissau (see Chapter 4). Where respective requests by host governments were missing, AU officers have initiated the process nevertheless, using persuasion to check that formality. Here again, the aspiration has been to cover all of Africa, thereby making every country equally important for the development and consolidation of coherent regional policies and approaches.[31] At the same time, however, different units, divisions and their staff have also sought to gain or enhance their respective profiles (vis-à-vis each other, was well as towards international donors), looking out for activities that increase their visibility and testify to their abilities and value. Be that as it may, integrating as many 'cases' as possible into these different agendas has significantly contributed to the construction and formatting of regional spaces.

Regional security policies and the 'external' formatting of space

As the preceding section shows, actors at ECOWAS and the AU have turned specific conflict situations into cases of more general policy agendas; intervention in those situations has also been about consolidating specific regional policies, and has thus contributed to the construction and 'internal' formatting of regional spaces. However, it has also been important for policy development of 'external' regional actors, meaning regional organizations that do not formally comprise the conflict site as part of their region. Most importantly, this has been the case for actors at the EU, who have also sought to develop and consolidate specific security policies in African conflict situations, thereby turning them into 'cases' and trying to integrate them into larger, more general policy processes and political agendas. While these efforts 'outside' the EU's own regional space have nevertheless played an important part in constructing that very space (cf. Rayroux 2013), they have also aimed at the 'external' formatting of other regional spaces according to EU interests or imaginations, relating them to one another and the EU in specific ways (i.e., ordering space; see Chapter 6).

To illustrate this point, this section draws on two specific examples: (i) the EU's SSR missions under the Common Security and Defense Policy (CSDP); and (ii) the consultation procedure und Article 96 of the Cotonou Agreement to enforce certain governance standards. Both have been enacted in Guinea-Bissau and, in turn, these experiences have influenced EU policies more generally.

EU SSR missions and policy under the CSDP

Building on a long historical trajectory, which EU actors themselves trace back to the creation of the Western European Union in 1948 (Brussels Treaty), the European heads of state and government created the European Security and Defense Policy in 1999 (Amsterdam Treaty), which in 2007 (Lisbon Treaty) became the Common Security and Defense Policy (CSDP), as an integral part of the EU's Common Foreign and Security Policy (cf. EU External Action Service 2016). Since the 1990s, governments of EU member states increasingly identified international crises – beyond the borders of EU member states, and beyond the European continent – as threats to their national and 'European' regional security, and worked towards developing a European capability to respond to them, including through military force. The European Security Strategy (2003) expressed this most clearly, among terrorism, mentioning the proliferation of weapons of mass destruction and organized crime, "regional conflicts" and "state failure" as "key threats" to European security interests (EU 2003, 3–4). Ever since, the CSDP has become the main reference point for a developing field of policy and practice, continuously adapting (cf. Faleg 2017). In line with these imaginations and ambitions, since 2003, the EU Council has deployed many CSDP missions outside the EU space, both military and civilian (e.g., cf. Tardy 2015). For those, Africa became an important staging ground and a 'laboratory' for emerging policies and practices (cf. Gibert and Nivet 2013, 198). In that context, EU SSR missions assumed particular importance, a large portion of which targeted African countries (e.g., Ekengren, Simons and Ekengren 2011; Dursun-Özkanca 2014).[32]

Starting in 2005 – with some sense of relative stability in the country – the UK government led the first European efforts to reform the security sector in Guinea-Bissau. In 2006, it sent a security sector development team to assist national authorities in drafting a strategy document. Following this, and with no other lead actor in sight, EU actors decided to increase their support to SSR in the country, through the European Development Fund (EDF), setting up a support program (worth about 7.7 million euros), the Instrument for Stability, funding three advisers to provide technical assistance to national authorities and deploying a CSDP mission (cf. Bahnson 2011, 262–4). Apparently again driven by the UK government, the EU Council's General Secretariat started to explore modalities for such a mission in early 2007. Together with the EU Commission it dispatched two assessment missions to Bissau, in May and October 2007 (cf. EU Council 2008a, para. 4 and 9). Based on these, and now strongly supported by the Portuguese government (holding the EU presidency at the time), the Council approved CSDP action in support of SSR in Guinea-Bissau in December 2007, and the concept of operations of EU SSR-GB in February 2008 (cf. EU Council 2008a, para. 9 and 11). It argued that "SSR in partner countries constitute[d] one of the core areas for EU action as identified in the European Security Strategy" (EU Council 2008a, para. 12).

The EU SSR-GB started deployment in May 2008, officially starting its work in June 2008. It comprised eight international staff (military and civilian) from France, Portugal, Italy and Spain, assisted by 16 "local staff" (cf. EU Council Secretariat 2010). Initially set out for 12 months, the EU Council extended the mission's mandate on 18 May and 17 November 2009, as well as on 25 May 2010, until 30 September 2010 (cf. EU Council 2010a), before it decided to discontinue the EU SSR-GB in August 2010, in response to a mutiny within the armed forces of Guinea-Bissau (cf. EU Council 2010b). The main objectives of the mission were to provide advice and assistance in order to implement the national SSR strategy, with a special focus on downsizing and restructuring, as well as identifying capacity building needs (e.g., training and equipment) (cf. EU Council 2008a, Art. 2). The operating budget of the EU SSR-GB, authorized by the EU Council, totaled 7,810,000 euros for the entire 28 months of deployment (cf. EU Council 2010a, Art. 2), making it a comparatively small CSDP mission (cf. Dari et al. 2012, 85).

From a policy perspective, for actors at the EU, Guinea-Bissau became the site of the second SSR mission deployed to Africa under the CSDP, trying to work towards a more coherent policy on EU SSR missions (Gibert 2009; Gibert and Nivet 2013; Kohl 2014).[33] More specifically, it was the first integrated CSDP mission simultaneously targeting the sectors of defense, justice and police (cf. EU Council 2008b; Dari et al. 2012, 85), causing some tensions between the EU Council and the Commission, which saw the Council as encroaching into its own competences (Bahnson 2011, 264). Moreover, it was the first mission entirely planned by the Civilian Planning and Conduct Capability, the newly established headquarters for EU civilian crisis management operations (EU Council Secretariat 2010). Finally, the EU's experience with SSR in Guinea-Bissau has also coincided with an increasing effort to identify and implement 'lessons learned' at the EU Council's Secretariat. To this, the EU SSR-GB contributed with respect to (i) future integrated missions, (ii) the EU SSR concept and (iii) planning relatively small missions (cf. Dari et al. 2012, 85).

From a spatial perspective, two things are worth noting. First, in the decision authorizing the mission to Guinea-Bissau, the EU Council explicitly refers to the threat posed by, as well as the need to combat, drug trafficking (EU Council 2008a), thereby directly relating to the spatial imagination of Guinea-Bissau as a 'narco-state' linked to 'narco-terrorism' (see above). Second, the EU SSR-GB aimed to fix Guinea-Bissau according to the spatial format 'nation state', in order to play its 'proper' role with regard to the security of larger regional and trans-regional spaces. However, when it became clear that the EU SSR-GB had failed to achieve these objectives, and in anticipation of the mission's withdrawal, the EU Commission and the EU Council tried something else, putting pressure on Guinea-Bissau by suspending its development cooperation based on Article 96 of the Cotonou Agreement – following a similar logic as the EU SSR-GB, but through a different approach.

EU conditionality, good governance and Article 96 of the Cotonou Agreement

Another policy objective of actors at the EU, which they pursued prominently also in Guinea-Bissau, has been the consultation procedure according to Article 96 of the Cotonou Agreement, signed in June 2000. The Cotonou Agreement provides the basic legal framework for a virtual space that besides the EU and its member states comprises African, Caribbean and Pacific (ACP) states. Thus, the agreement aims to structure the EU's relations with a group of states (former European colonies) in the Global South, most of which fall under one or several of the categories "least-developed" (40 out of 77 ACP states), "landlocked" (15 out of 77) and "island" (33 out of 77) (cf. EU Commission 2014, 171–2). In that regard, poverty reduction is stated as the core objective (cf. EU Commission 2014, Art. 1).[34] The Cotonou Agreement represents an effort to improve coordination among European donors, with respect to development cooperation, economic and trade cooperation, but also political cooperation directly linked to specific Western norms and principles, such as ‘human rights’, ‘democratic’ governance and the ‘rule of law’ (e.g., cf. Laakso 2007).

In practice, it has been in particular Article 96 of the Cotonou Agreement that EU actors have used to enforce these norms and principles, or at least to punish states that violate them. Article 96 establishes a consultation procedure in order to identify “appropriate measures” and a roadmap towards compliance with the normative requirements (EU Commission 2014, Art. 96; for a discussion, e.g., cf. Mackie and Zinke 2005; Laakso 2007; Zimelis 2011). Since 2000, the EU has applied the consultation procedure about 17 times, in response to violent government overthrows, escalating violence or human rights violations (cf. Saltnes 2012, 10).[35] Examples include Fiji (in 2000 and again in 2007), Zimbabwe (in 2002), the Central African Republic (CAR, in 2003), Guinea-Bissau (in 2004 and 2011), Togo (in 2004), Madagascar (in 2010) and Burundi (in 2015).

However, it is only the case of Guinea-Bissau in 2011 that the EU Council highlights on its website as a successful example of Article 96 ‘in practice’ (cf. EU Council 2018). It describes the process as follows. After the army mutiny of 1 April 2010, when the former Deputy Chief of Army Staff, Antonio Indjai, took control of the Bissau-Guinean armed forces (first *de facto*, then officially), the EU Council started an “enhanced political dialogue” with national authorities, through the heads of mission of the EU country delegation in Bissau (EU Council 2018).[36] Subsequently, the EU Commission, the EU Council and the Africa Working Party (COAFR) presidency, responsible for EU external policy towards ‘Sub-Saharan Africa’, undertook a mission to Bissau to assess the situation ‘on the ground’. The mission concluded that EU requests had not been met and that the requirements for a return to constitutional order were not in place. At that point, the EU Council also decided to discontinue the EU SSR-GB (see above). Following a recommendation by the EU Commission, in a decision on 31 January 2011, the EU Council suspended most of its development cooperation and began consultations in March 2011, with representatives of the AU, ECOWAS and the CPLP as invited observers.[37] Consultations continued until July 2011, negotiating necessary conditions (measures to be taken by the Bissau-Guinean authorities) for a gradual resumption of EU development assistance to the government of Guinea-Bissau.[38] The Council subsequently reviewed the progress several times, extending the sanctions in July 2012 and July 2013, due to the coup d’état in April 2012 and the ensuing crisis (EU Council 2018). It was only in response to the “free and credible elections” in 2014 that the EU resumed its support, although still insisting on efforts regarding SSR, a “renewal of the military hierarchy” and the “fight against impunity” (EU Council 2014). However, the decision of January 2011 was repealed completely only in March 2015, after General Indjai had been dismissed as Chief of the Armed Forces. Since late 2015, the EU has once more suspended its cooperation with the government of Guinea-Bissau, in response to the political crisis following the dismissal of Prime Minister Domingos Simões Pereira (see Chapter 1), this time, however, not referring to the consultation procedure under Article 96.[39]

As becomes clear, applying Article 96 of the Cotonou Agreement has been a strategic tool and practice of the EU (i.e., commission staff, political organs and member states) to order the EU–ACP space, promoting the 'nation state' as a spatial format according to Western ideas, norms and principles.[40] After all, 'political dialogue', whether 'regular' or 'enhanced', is initiated by the EU (or its member states) and targets ACP states – not the other way around. EU actors have provided or withheld development assistance based on the terms of the Cotonou Agreement, although these leave ample room for interpretation (e.g., cf. Mackie and Zinke 2005, 5). However, at the same time, this practice has also contributed to the formatting of the EU's 'own' space. As EU actors emphasize these norms, they simultaneously make a statement about themselves, communicating a particular spatial imagination – around the spatial format 'nation state' and the 'international state system' as the spatial order constituted by their interrelation – and 'externally' performing the EU's space accordingly.

Conclusion

In this chapter, I have introduced two dominant spatial imaginations of conflict in West Africa, which have been important drivers behind regional security policies as well as legitimating narratives of conflict interventions. These have been spatial imaginations, on the one hand, linked to concerns about 'regional in/stability' and, on the other, linked to concerns about a 'narco-state' and/or 'narco-terrorism'. Both imaginations have connected 'local' conflict to wider regional and trans-regional spaces and security concerns. Consequently, developing, enacting and consolidating corresponding regional security policies has been a key concern of actors at African ROs during conflict interventions, which this chapter has demonstrated looking through the prism of ECOWAS and AU interventions in Guinea-Bissau.

In this way, first, regional responses to conflicts by different actors at ECOWAS and the AU have significantly contributed to the construction and 'internal' formatting of regional spaces. Most importantly, these policies have aimed to foster a coherent approach towards UCGs, an objective that ECOWAS and the AU share in principle, but have repeatedly clashed over with regard to its interpretation and implementation in practice. Moreover, in particular at the AU Commission, staff working in different departments and divisions have adopted different instances of conflict ('cases') to develop activities in order to advance AU policy processes, as exemplified in this chapter with respect to PCRD and SSR policies. Whereas ECOWAS actors have taken the lead in actual conflict intervention, in a pragmatic way based on established practice (see Chapters 3 and 4), for AU actors, policy development and consolidation has been a key concern with regard to conflict in

Guinea-Bissau, connected to efforts trying to systematize and 'globalize' specific policies and approaches.

Second, at the same time, EU actors in particular have connected conflict interventions in West/Africa to what I have framed as 'external' formatting of regional spaces. This has been the case in a double sense, as these efforts have simultaneously contributed to the 'external' formatting of space in West/Africa, according to the imaginations of EU actors, *and* to the formatting of the EU's 'own' regional space – both from a perspective of 'securitization' (e.g., where and how boundaries and a 'neighborhood' of the EU space are imagined) and with regard to projecting European norms, principles and procedures to other regional spaces. With regard to interventions in Guinea-Bissau and elsewhere, this has been discernible in particular in the EU's SSR missions deployed in the framework of the EU's CSDP, as well as the application of the consultation procedure according to Article 96 of the Cotonou Agreement in order to foster 'good governance' through conditionality.

As these different efforts of 'internal' and 'external' spatial formatting by different actors have coincided, they have often gone along with tensions among those actors. Therefore, the following chapter analyzes how actors at African ROs, in particular at ECOWAS and the AU, have engaged other regional and international actors strategically, to enlist them in their conflict management efforts, to (re)position themselves towards them, and in the process order space at different scales.

Notes

1 I use single quotation marks to raise awareness that these terms are markers that different actors, including me as a researcher, use for different reasons and towards specific objectives, often to distinguish binary opposites (e.g., 'internal' versus 'external'; 'technical' versus 'political'). As such they are part of different discourses, knowledge–power relations and subject to socio-political contestation.

2 This, however, did not mean that any consensus existed about how to respond to these dynamics. Mutual suspicion among some ECOWAS heads of state was pervasive, as regional cross-border entanglements did also include messy geopolitics, in the form of state-sponsored conflicts (e.g., supporting rebels in neighboring states) (Kabia 2009, 48–9). Alliances and oppositions have formed and changed according to highly entangled networks and personal relationships (cf. Adebajo 2004, 292ff.).

3 A central concern of the 1981 Protocol on Mutual Assistance on Defense was to prevent or counter 'external aggression', in particular by former colonial powers, which might trigger or sustain 'internal conflict' (e.g., cf. ECOWAS 1981, Art. 4.b and 18.1).

4 Since 1977/8, resolutions by the OAU Assembly have called upon the Presidents of Libya and Chad to cooperate in order to achieve peace and stability in the region (e.g., cf. OAU Assembly 1978). In its resolution on Chad, from July 1980, the OAU heads of state and government explicitly refer to a "massive flow of refugees into neighboring countries" as one of the reasons for their decision to try (for a second time) to deploy an "OAU Neutral Force" (OAU Assembly 1980).

5 Also influential in the process was the New York-based International Peace Academy (cf. Muyangwa and Vogt 2000, 8).
6 African leaders wanted to take charge of conflict interventions also in response to 'external' interventions (especially by France, and in the context of Cold War superpower competition) (cf. Muyangwa and Vogt 2000, 7).
7 Although not necessarily linked to Algerian national state interests, at least not in any obvious way, since the 1990s, Algerian diplomats have served in high-level positions of the (O)AU, with decisive influence over the design, setup and practice of the organization's peace and security agenda and policies. After having been influential in designing and setting up the (O)AU's African Peace and Security Architecture, Said Djinnit became the first AU Commissioner for Peace and Security in 2002 (e.g., cf. Nickels 2014). In 2008, Ramtane Lamamra took over the position, before handing it over to Smail Chergui in 2013 – all of them Algerian diplomats (former ambassadors, etc.) (cf. Abderrahim and Aggad 2018, 14–15).
8 The UNODC presents itself as "a global leader in the fight against illicit drugs and international crime" (UNODC 2019). Up to 90 percent of its funding comes from voluntary contributions from other international organizations (including other specialized UN agencies) or UN member states. The ten biggest contributors in 2017 were Colombia, the US, the EU (these three leading by far), Japan, Canada, Germany, Sweden, Norway, Italy and Australia (cf. UNODC 2017, 131). UNODC prepares projects and related funding proposals, according to its mandate and strategic plan, but also in an attempt to anticipate donors' interests (cf. Interview 44, Senior UN Officer, Abuja, 28 February 2017; Interview 92, UN Officer, Dakar, 25 April 2017). In West Africa, it managed to attach itself to an ECOWAS process, becoming the implementing partner for an EU project to support ECOWAS' anti-drug policies (cf. Interview 44, Senior UN Officer, Abuja, 28 February 2017; see also below).
9 The label 'narco-state' itself has remained ill-defined and has been used at least since the 1980s to describe various more or less similar phenomena and to label states as diverse as Afghanistan, Colombia, Mexico (cf. Chouvy 2016) and even the Netherlands (cf. Kleine-Brockhoff 1996). Some have also referred to Great Britain in the eighteenth/nineteenth century as a "narco-empire" (Frankopan 2018). For an effort to clarify the definition(s) of 'narco-state', while also testifying to its wide and imprecise usage, see Kan (2016, 48ff.).
10 E.g., cf. Interview 130, AU Officer, Peace and Security Department, Addis Ababa, 21 September 2018; Interview 137, Senior AU Officer, Department of Political Affairs, Addis Ababa, 25 September 2018.
11 For example, these concerns increasingly found expression in the OAU Mechanism for Conflict Prevention, Management and Resolution (of 1993), the OAU Council of Ministers Decision on Un-Constitutional Changes in Member States (of 1999) and the OAU Declaration on the Framework for an OAU Response to Unconstitutional Changes of Government (i.e., the Lomé Declaration, of 2000). However, those were agreements in principle; they did not yet result in much practical action (cf. Engel 2012, 61–2).
12 The four forms of UCGs defined in the Lomé Declaration are: (i) military coups; interventions by (ii) mercenaries; or (iii) armed dissidents/rebels; and (iv) incumbents' refusal to hand over power to the winners of free and fair elections. According to that policy script the response should subsequently involve public condemnation, meetings and discussions, suspension until transition, fact-finding

and engagement, including some pressure if necessary (cf. AU Assembly 2000, 3ff.; see also Engel 2012, 63–4).

13 Later, in 2009, the Ezulwini Framework further outlined measures to enhance the effectiveness and implementation of the AU's UCG policy (AU Commission 2009).

14 Cf. Interview 6, Senior AU Officer, Peace and Security Department, Addis Ababa, 14 September 2016.

15 The 2008 ECOWAS Conflict Prevention Framework (ECPF) only mentions UCGs once, referring back to the 1999 Mechanism and the 2001 Supplementary Protocol, without further refining definitions, nor any standard procedure on how to respond to them (cf. ECOWAS 2008).

16 In 2000, Mauritania ceased to be a member of ECOWAS, refocusing its regional cooperation towards the Arab Maghreb Union. Nevertheless, the country has remained connected to political and economic dynamics in the West African region, and more recently has increasingly sought to intensify its formal relations with ECOWAS (cf. Melly 2019, 6–8).

17 Cf. Interview 6, Senior AU Officer, Peace and Security Department, Addis Ababa, 14 September 2016; Interview 22, Senior ECOWAS Official, Addis Ababa, 26 September 2016.

18 For example, already in 2003, the AU Executive Council established a Ministerial Committee on PCRD for Sudan (cf. AU PSD 2015).

19 On PCRD in Africa more generally, e.g., see Kotzé and Solomon (2008); and Hudson and Neethling (2013).

20 Cf. Interview 13, Senior AU Officer, Peace and Security Department, Addis Ababa, 21 September 2016; Interview 147, AU Officer, Peace and Security Department, Addis Ababa, 28 September 2018.

21 Funded and coordinated by the Norwegian Ministry of Foreign Affairs, the Training for Peace program is implemented jointly by the ISS, the African Centre for the Constructive Resolution of Disputes (ACCORD) and the Norwegian Institute of International Affairs (NUPI).

22 Cf. Interview 147, AU Officer, Peace and Security Department, Addis Ababa, 28 September 2018; see also ISS (2017).

23 That process also profited from the appointment of a new Head of the CMPCRD, Sarjoh Bah, in January 2016 (cf. Interview 13, Senior AU Officer, Peace and Security Department, Addis Ababa, 21 September 2016.).

24 Cf. Interview 13, Senior AU Officer, Peace and Security Department, Addis Ababa, 21 September 2016.

25 Cf. Interview 130, AU Officer, Peace and Security Department, Addis Ababa, 21 September 2018.

26 Interview 162, ECOWAS Officer, Department for Political Affairs, Peace and Security, Abuja, 29 October 2018.

27 ISSAT is the 'service provider' of the Geneva Center for Security Sector Reform (formerly the Geneva Center for the Democratic Control of the Armed Forces (DCAF)), one of the leading international think tanks on 'security sector governance'. At an early stage, additional support and input were provided by the Friedrich-Ebert-Stiftung Regional Office, the African Security Sector Network and the West African Network for Security and Democratic Governance (cf. Uzoechina 2014, 11).

28 In a presidential statement on 20 February 2007, the UN Security Council had identified SSR as a critical element in consolidating peace. Subsequently, the UN

Secretary General presented a report in January 2008 outlining a UN approach towards SSR (cf. AU 2013, 1–2).

29 Cf. Interview 146, AU Officer, Peace and Security Department, Addis Ababa, 28 September 2018.

30 Cf. Interview 146, AU Officer, Peace and Security Department, Addis Ababa, 28 September 2018.

31 Cf. Interview 137, Senior AU Officer, Department of Political Affairs, Addis Ababa, 25 September 2019.

32 However, the EU no longer deploys 'SSR' missions, instead doing SSR in the framework of EU Training Missions or EU Capacity-Building Missions.

33 Operation Artemis was the first EU mission deployed under the ESDP/CSDP, in 2003, and was followed by an EU SSR mission (EUSEC-RD Congo), launched in 2005 (Gibert and Nivet 2013, 198–9).

34 The ACP Group today includes 79 countries (since 2003). However, Cuba has not signed the Cotonou Agreement and South Africa has a special budget line. The group emerged in 1975, then bringing together 46 states (cf. ECDPM 2003, 11).

35 Previous to the Cotonou Agreement, the 'consultation procedure' was stipulated under Article 366a of the Lomé Conventions, applied since 1996 in six cases, including Guinea-Bissau in 1999 (cf. Saltnes 2012, 10). The website of the EU Council refers to 15 times that Article 96 of the Cotonou Agreement has been applied. However, it mentions only nine specific cases (cf. EU Council 2018).

36 They demanded the release of the detained, above all the deposed Chief of Army Staff Zamoa Induta, threatening sanctions, and reminding the perpetrators of the coup about their due submission to legitimate democratic authorities (cf. EU Council 2018).

37 The only exception being ongoing contracts or measures in direct support of the population (e.g., humanitarian or emergency operations), as well as projects combatting trans-national crime and consolidating democracy (cf. EU Council 2011, 3).

38 These measures and/conditions in particular centered on effective implementation of SSR, an independent judicial investigation into the 2009 double assassination, the renewal of the military hierarchy and the combatting of drug trafficking and money laundering (for details, see EU Council 2011, Annex).

39 Cf. Interview 59, Senior EU Officer, Bissau, 4 April 2017; Interview 65, EU Officer, Bissau, 6 April 2017.

40 Whether this has been interest-driven or out of a more general concern with Western norms has been subject to debate (e.g., cf. Saltnes 2012). In any case, certain inconsistencies exist in that practice (cf. del Biondo 2011, 2015).

References

Abderrahim, Tasnim and Faten Aggad. 2018. *Starting Afresh: The Maghreb's Relations with Sub-Saharan Africa.* Discussion Paper 225. Brussels: ECDPM.

Adebajo, Adekeye. 2002. *Building Peace in West Africa: Liberia, Sierra Leone, and Guinea-Bissau.* Boulder, CO: Lynne Rienner.

———. 2004. Pax West Africana? Regional Security Mechanisms. In *West Africa's Security Challenges: Building Peace in a Troubled Region*, eds Adekeye Adebajo and Ismail Rashid, 291–318. Boulder, CO: Lynne Rienner.

Akinyemi, Aaron. 2014. "UK and US Target al-Qaida 'Narco-Terrorism' Drug Routes in West Africa", *International Business Times*, 6 July 2014. Accessed 24 November 2016. www.ibtimes.co.uk/uk-us-target-al-qaida-narco-terrorism-drug-routes-west-africa-1455514.

Amoo, Samuel G. 1992. *Frustrations of Regional Peacekeeping: The OAU in Chad, 1977–1982*. Conflict Resolution Program's Working Paper Series. Atlanta, GA: Carter Center of Emory University.

Aning, Emmanuel K. 1999. From 'Eco-Pessimism' to 'Eco-Optimism': ECOMOG and the West African Integration Process. *African Journal of Political Science* 4 (1): 21–39. doi: 10.4314/ajps.v4i1.27344.

Aning, Emmanuel K. and John Pokoo. 2014. Understanding the Nature and Threats of Drug Trafficking to National and Regional Security in West Africa. *Stability* 3 (1): 1–13. doi: 10.5334/sta.df.

AU. 2000. "Constitutive Act of the African Union", Lomé, 11 July 2000.

———. 2002. "Protocol Relating to the Establishment of the Peace and Security Council of the African Union", 1st Ordinary Session of the Assembly of the African Union, Durban, 9 July 2002.

———. 2006. *Policy on Post-Conflict Reconstruction and Development (PCRD)*. Addis Ababa: AU Commission.

———. 2007a. "Report of the Stakeholders Workshop on Implementation of the African Union's Post-Conflict Reconstruction and Development (PCRD) Policy (PCRD/Workshop/1[II])", Lusaka, 17–19 July 2007.

———. 2007b. "Summary Report of the Consultative Meeting with Civil Society Organisations on the African Union's Decision and Policy on Post Conflict Reconstruction and Development (PCRD)", Addis Ababa, 12–13 March 2007.

———. 2013. "African Union Policy Framework on Security Sector Reform (SSR) (Assembly/AU/Dec.472[XXX]. Para 21.)", 20th Ordinary Session, Addis Ababa, 27–28 January 2013.

AU Assembly. 2000. "Declaration on the Framework for an OAU Response to Unconstitutional Changes of Government (AHG/Decl.5 [XXXVI])", Lomé, 10–12 July 2000.

———. 2008. "Decision on the Activities of the Peace and Security Council of the African Union and the State of Peace and Security in Africa (Assembly/AU/Dec.177 [X])", 10th Ordinary Session, Addis Ababa, 31 January–2 February 2008.

———. 2013. "Decision on the Report of the Peace and Security Council on its Activities and the State of Peace and Security in Africa (Assembly/AU/Dec.472[XX])", 20th Ordinary Session, Addis Ababa, 27–28 January 2013.

AU Commission. 2009. "Ezulwini Framework for the Enhancement of the Implementation of Measures of the African Union in Situations of Unconstitutional Changes of Government in Africa", Ezulwini, 17–19 December 2009.

———. 2016. "Press Release: The African Union Commission Inter-Departmental Task Force on Post-Conflict Reconstruction and Development Reviews Progress Since its Inauguration in May 2016", Addis Ababa, 20 September 2016.

AU Executive Council. 2005. "Decision on the report of the Chairperson of the Commission on Conflict Situations in Africa - DOC. EX.CL/191 (VII) (EX.CL/Dec.225 [VII])", 7th Ordinary Session, Sirte, 28 June–2 July 2005.

———. 2006. "Decision on the AU Policy Framework on Post-Conflict Reconstruction and Development DOC.EX.CL/274 (IX) (EX.CL/Dec.302 [IX])", 9th Ordinary Session, Banjul, 25 June 2006.

AU PSC. 2017. "Mission Report 13–19 May 2017 High Level Technical and Multi-Disciplinary Needs Assessment to the Republic of the Gambia (PSC/PR/RPT.[DCXCIV])", 694th Meeting, Addis Ababa, 15 June 2017.

———. 2020. "Communiqué (PSC/PR/COMM.[CMXLII])", 942nd Meeting, Addis Ababa, 28 August 2020.

AU PSD. 2015. "African Union Post-Conflict Reconstruction and Development (AU PCRD)", 23 November 2015. Accessed 23 May 2019. www.peaceau.org/en/page/70-post-conflict-reconstruction.

Bahnson, Caroline. 2011. The European Union and SSR in Guinea-Bissau. In *The Politics of Security Sector Reform: Challenges and Opportunities for the European Union's Global Role*, eds Magnus Ekengren and Greg Simons, 259–72. London: Ashgate.

Carrier, Neil C.M. and Gernot Klantschnig. 2012. *Africa and the War on Drugs.* London: Zed Books.

Carvalho, Gustavo de, Cedric de Coning and John Ahere. 2016. *The African Union (AU) Post-Conflict Reconstruction and Development (PCRD) Framework: The First Ten Years.* Background Paper.

Chouvy, Pierre-Arnaud. 2016. The Myth of the Narco-State. *Space and Polity* 20 (1): 26–38. doi: 10.1080/13562576.2015.1052348.

Cockayne, James and Phil Williams. 2009. *The Invisible Tide: Towards an International Strategy to Deal with Drug Trafficking Through West Africa.* New York: International Peace Institute.

Coggins, Bridget L. 2015. Does State Failure Cause Terrorism? An Empirical Analysis (1999–2008). *Journal of Conflict Resolution* 59 (3): 455–83. doi: 10.1177/0022002713515403.

Csete, Joanne and Constanza Sánchez. 2013. *Telling the Story of Drugs in West Africa: The Newest Front in a Losing war?* Policy Brief. Swansea: Global Drug Policy Observatory, Swansea University.

Dari, Elisa, Megan Price, Jense Vand der Wal, Marlene Gottwald and Nicole Koenig. 2012. "CSDP Missions and Operations: Lessons Learned Process (EXPO/B/SEDE/FWC/2009-01/Lot6/16)", European Parliament, Directorate-General for External Policies, Policy Department, April 2012.

de Coning, Cedric. 1996. *The OAU and Peacekeeping.* International Update 14/96. Johannesburg, Cape Town: The South African Institute of International Affairs.

del Biondo, Karen. 2011. EU Aid Conditionality in ACP Countries: Explaining Inconsistency in EU Sanctions Practice. *Journal of Contemporary European Research* 7 (3): 380–95.

———. 2015. Donor Interests or Developmental Performance? Explaining Sanctions in EU Democracy Promotion in Sub-Saharan Africa. *World Development* 75: 74–84. doi: 10.1016/j.worlddev.2014.11.002.

Dursun-Özkanca, Oya, ed. 2014. *The European Union as an Actor in Security Sector Reform: Current Practices and Challenges of Implementation.* London: Routledge.

ECDPM. 2003. *The Cotonou Agreement: A User's Guide for Non-State-Actors.* Brussels: ACP Secretariat.

ECOWAS. 1981. "Protocol Relating to Mutual Assistance on Defence (A/SP.3/5/81)", Freetown, 29 May 1981.

———. 1993. "Revised Ecowas Treaty". Abuja, 24 July 1993.

———. 1999. "Protocol Relating to the Mechanism for Conflict Prevention, Management, Resolution, Peacekeeping and Security (A/P.1/12/99)", Lomé, 10 December 1999.

———. 2001. "Protocol A/SP1/12/01 on Democracy and Good Governance Supplementary to the Protocol relating to the Mechanism For Conflict Prevention, Management, Resolution, Peacekeeping and Security", Dakar, 2001. Accessed 24 February 2011. www.comm.ecowas.int/sec/en/protocoles/Protocol%20on%20 good-governance-and-democracy-rev-5EN.pdf.

———. 2008. "The ECOWAS Conflict Prevention Framework (Regulation MSC/ REG.1/01/08)", Abuja, January 2008.

———. 2016. "ECOWAS Policy Framework for Security Sector Reform and Governance", Dakar, 4 June 2016.

ECOWAS Commission. 2012. "Statement on Guinea-Bissau", 340th Meeting of the AU Peace and Security Council at the Ministerial Level, Addis Ababa, 2 November 2012.

ECOWAS Commission President. 2012. "Memorandum on the Situation in Guinea Bissau", Extraordinary Meeting of the Mediation and Security Council, Abuja, 9 November 2012.

Ekengren, Magnus, Greg Simons and Magnus Ekengren, eds. 2011. *The Politics of Security Sector Reform: Challenges and Opportunities for the European Union's Global Role.* London: Ashgate.

Ellis, Stephen. 2009. West Africa's International Drug Trade. *African Affairs* 108 (431): 171–96. doi: 10.1093/afraf/adp017.

Engel, Ulf. 2012. The African Union and Mediation in Cases of Unconstitutional Changes of Government, 2008–2011. In *New Mediation Practices in African Conflicts*, ed. Ulf Engel, 55–82. Leipzig: Leipziger Universitätsverlag.

———. 2013. The Changing Role of the AU Commission in Inter-African Relations: The Case of APSA and AGA. In Africa in World Politics: Engaging a Changing Global Order, eds John W. Harbeson and Donald Rothchild, 186–206. New York: Westview Press.

EU. 2003. "European Security Strategy: A Secure Europe in a Better World", Brussels, 12 December 2003.

EU Commission. 2014. "The Cotonou Agreement and Multiannual Financial Framework 2014–20", Signed in Cotonou on 23 June 2000, Revised in Luxembourg on 25 June 2005, revised in Ouagadougou on 22 June 2010.

EU Council. 2008a. "Council Joint Action 2008/112/CFSP on the European Union Mission in Support of Security Sector Reform in the Republic of Guinea-Bissau (EU SSR GUINEA-BISSAU)", Brussels, 12 February.

———. 2008b. "Javier SOLANA, EU High Representative for the CFSP, Welcomes the Appointment of General ESTEBAN VERÁSTEGUI as the Head of the EU Mission in Support of Security Sector Reform in Guinea-Bissau (S095/08)", Brussels, 4 March 2008.

———. 2010a. "Council Decision 2010/298/CFSP of 25 May 2010 Amending and Extending Joint Action 2008/112/CFSP on the European Union Mission in Support of Security Sector Reform in the Republic of Guinea-Bissau (EU SSR Guinea-Bissau)", Official Journal of the European Union (L 127/17), Brussels, 26 May 2010.

———. 2010b. "The EU SSR Guinea-Bissau Mission Completes its Mandate (12740/ 10 PRESSE 223)", Brussels, 2 August 2010.

———. 2011. "Council Decision Concerning the Conclusion of Consultations with the Republic of Guinea-Bissau under Article 96 of the Partnership Agreement between the Members of the African, Caribbean and Pacific Group of States of the one part, and the European Community and its Member States, of the Other part (12515/11)", Brussels, 13 July 2011.

———. 2014. "Press Release: EU to Resume Cooperation with Guinea-Bissau (ST 11664/14, PRESSE 389)", Brussels, 14 July 2014.

———. 2018. Cotonou Agreement: Consultation Procedure (Article 96). Accessed 29 March, 2019. www.consilium.europa.eu/en/policies/cotonou-agreement/article-96-cotonou-agreement/.

EU Council Secretariat. 2010. "EU Mission in Support of Security Sector Reform in the Republic of Guinea-Bissau (EU SSR Guinea-Bissau)", September 2010.

EU External Action Service. 2016. Shaping of a Common Security and Defence Policy, 8 July 2016. Accessed 29 March 2019. https://eeas.europa.eu/topics/common-security-and-defence-policy-csdp/5388/shaping-common-security-and-defence-policy_en.

Europol. 2011. *EU Organised Crime Threat Assessment.* The Hague: Europol.

Faleg, Giovanni. 2017. *The EU's Common Security and Defence Policy: Learning Communities in International Organizations.* Cham: Springer.

Figueroa Helland, Leonardo and Stefan Borg. 2014. The Lure of State Failure. *Interventions* 16 (6): 877–97. doi: 10.1080/1369801X.2013.798140.

Frankopan, Peter. 2018. Global Britain was Built as a Narco-Empire, *The Spectator*, 4 August 2018. Accessed 9 May 2019. www.spectator.co.uk/2018/08/global-britain-was-built-as-a-narco-empire/amp/.

Freeman, Colin. 2013. Revealed: How Saharan Caravans of Cocaine Help to fund Al-Qaeda in Terrorists' North African Domain, *The Telegraph*, January 26. Accessed 24 September 2020. www.telegraph.co.uk/news/worldnews/africaandindianocean/mali/9829099/Revealed-how-Saharan-caravans-of-cocaine-help-to-fund-al-Qaeda-in-terrorists-North-African-domain.html.

Gibert, Marie V. 2009. The Securitisation of the EU's Development Agenda in Africa: Insights from Guinea-Bissau. *Perspectives on European Politics and Society* 10 (4): 621–37. doi: 10.1080/15705850903314882.

Gibert, Marie V. and Bastien Nivet. 2013. Dissonant Paths to Partnership and Convergence: EU-Africa Relations Between Experimentation and Resistance. *African Security* 6 (3–4): 191–210. doi: 10.1080/19392206.2013.853584.

Hartmann, Christof and Kai Striebinger. 2015. Writing the Script? ECOWAS's Military Intervention Mechanism. In *Governance Transfer by Regional Organizations: Patching Together a Global Script*, eds Tanja A. Börzel and Vera van Hüllen, 68–83. Basingstoke: Palgrave Macmillan.

Holmgren, Alexander. 2013. Drug Trafficking in West Africa: Threatening Regional Peace, Stability and Security. www.wacommissionondrugs.org/drug-trafficking-in-west-africa-threatening-regional-peace-stability-and-security/.

Hudson, Heidi and Theo Neethling, eds. 2013. *Post-Conflict Reconstruction and Development in Africa: Concepts, Role-Players, Policy and Practice.* Cape Town: UCT Press.

Iliffe, John. 2011. *Obasanjo, Nigeria and the World.* Woodbridge: Boydell & Brewer.

IPSS. 2017. *APSA Impact Report 2016: Assessment of the Impacts of Intervention by the African Union and Regional Economic Communities in 2016 in the frame of the African Peace and Security Architecture (APSA).* Addis Ababa: IPSS, Addis Ababa University.

Ismail, Olawale. 2008. *The Dynamics of Post-Conflict Reconstruction and Peace Building in West Africa: Between Change and Stability.* Discussion Paper 41. Uppsala: Nordiska Afrikainstitutet.

ISS. 2017. Together, ISS and the African Union are Developing AU Policy and Capacity to Prevent Conflicts, 11 May 2017. Accessed 23 May 2019. https://issafrica.org/impact/spotlight-supporting-au-efforts-to-manage-crises-and-build-peace.

Kabia, John M. 2009. *Humanitarian Intervention and Conflict Resolution in West Africa: From ECOMOG to ECOMIL.* Burlington, VA: Ashgate.

Kan, Paul R. 2016. *Drug Trafficking and International Security.* Lanham, MD: Rowman & Littlefield Education.

Kemp, Walter, Mark Shaw and Arthur Boutellis. 2013. *The Elephant in the Room: How Can Peace Operations Deal with Organized Crime?* New York: International Peace Institute.

Kleine-Brockhoff, Thomas. 1996. Der "Narco-Staat" und Seine Nachbarn, *Zeit*, 5 April 1996. Accessed 18 April 2019. https://www.zeit.de/1996/15/Der_Narco-Staat_und_seine_Nachbarn.

Kohl, Christoph. 2014. *The Reform of the Guinea-Bissau's Security Sector: Between Demand and Practice.* PRIF report 126. Frankfurt am Main: Peace Research Institute Frankfurt (PRIF).

Kotzé, Dirk and Hussein Solomon, eds. 2008. *The State of Africa: Post-Conflict Reconstruction and Development.* Pretoria: Africa Institute of South Africa.

Laakso, Liisa. 2007. *Difficult Political Dimension of the Cotonou Agreement.* Paper Presented at the 6th Pan-European Conference on International Relations, Turin, 12–15 September 2007.

Lacher, Wolfram. 2013. *Challenging the Myth of the Drug-Terror Nexus in the Sahel.* WACD Background Paper. Geneva: West African Commission on Drugs, Kofi Annan Foundation.

Loewenstein, Antony. 2016. How Not to Fix an African Narco-State: Europe is Trying to Stop Guinea-Bissau's Drug Trade by Throwing Money at the Traffickers, *Foreign Policy*, 6 January 2016. Accessed 28 January 2016. http://foreignpolicy.com/2016/01/06/how-not-to-deal-with-an-african-narco-state-guinea-bissau/.

Lucey, Amanda and Moyosore Arewa. 2016. *Sustainable Peace: Driving the African Peace and Security Architecture Through ECOWAS.* ISS Paper 301. Pretoria: Institute for Security Studies.

Mackie, James and Julia Zinke. 2005. *When Agreement Breaks Down, what Next? The Cotonou Agreement's Article 96 Consultation Procedure.* ECDPM discussion paper 64A. Maastricht: ECDPM.

Mays, Terry M. 2002. *Africa's First Peacekeeping Operation: The OAU in Chad, 1981–1982.* Westport, CT: Praeger.

Mazzitelli, Antonio L. 2007. Transnational Organized Crime in West Africa: The Additional Challenge. *International Affairs* 83 (6): 1071–90. doi: 10.1111/j.1468-2346.2007.00674.x.

Melly, Paul. 2019. *Mauritania's Unfolding Landscape: Elections, Hydrocarbons and Socio-Economic Change.* Research Paper. London: Chatham House.

Muyangwa, Monde and Magaret A. Vogt. 2000. *An Assessment of the OAU Mechanism for Conflict Prevention, Management and Resolution, 1993–2000.* New York: International Peace Institute.

Nathan, Laurie, Gen R. Kibochi, Claude Mainge, Michelle Ndiaye and Yahia Zoubir. 2015. African Peace and Security Architecture (APSA): 2014 Assessment Study, 16 April 2015.

Nickels, Benjamin. 2014. Algeria's Role in African Security, 3 April 2014. Accessed 18 May 2019. https://carnegieendowment.org/sada/55239.

OAU Assembly. 1978. "Resolution sur le Differend Libye/Tchad (AHG/Res.94 [XV])", 15th Ordinary Session of the Authority of Heads of State and Government, Khartoum, 18–22 July 1978.

———. 1980. "Resolution sur le Tchad (AHG/Res.101 [XVII])", 10th Session of the Member States of OAU, Freetown, 4 July 1980.

———. 1990. "Declaration of the Assembly of Heads of State and Government of the Organization of African Unity on the Political and Socio-Economic Situation in Africa and the Fundamental Changes Taking Place in the World (AHG/Decl.1 [XXVI])", 26th Ordinary Session, Addis Ababa, 9–11 July 1990.

———. 1992. "Decision on a Mechanism for Conflict Prevention, Management and Resolution (AHG/Decl. 1 [XXVIII])", 28th Ordinary Session of the Assembly of Heads of State and Government, Dakar, 29 June–1 July 1992.

———. 1993. "Declaration of Heads of State and Government on the Establishment within the OAU of a Mechanism for Conflict Prevention, Management and Resolution (AHG/DECL.3 [XXIX])", Assembly, Twenty-ninth Ordinary Session, Cairo, 28–29 June 1993.

O'Regan, Davin and Peter Thompson. 2013. *Advancing Stability and Reconciliation in Guinea-Bissau: Lessons from Africa's First Narco State.* Washington, DC: Africa Center for Strategic Studies.

Patrick, Stewart. 2007. 'Failed' States and Global Security: Empirical Questions and Policy Dilemmas. *International Studies Review* 9 (4): 644–62. doi: 10.1111/j.1468-2486.2007.00728.x.

Piazza, James A. 2008. Incubators of Terror: Do Failed and Failing States Promote Transnational Terrorism? *International Studies Quarterly* 52 (3): 469–88. doi: 10.1111/j.1468-2478.2008.00511.x.

Rayroux, Antoine. 2013. Beyond Actorness in EU Crisis Management: Internal Functions of External Peacekeeping. *Journal of European Integration* 35 (7): 731–48. doi: 10.1080/07036337.2012.728212.

Saltnes, Johanne D. 2012. The EU's Implementation of the Human Rights and Democracy Clause in the Cotonou-Agreement: Questioning the Status quo. Paper Presented at the ECPR Graduate Conference, Bremen, 4–6 July 2012.

Shaw, Mark. 2015. Drug Trafficking in Guinea-Bissau, 1998–2014: The Evolution of an Elite Protection Network. *Journal of Modern African Studies* 53 (3): 339–64. doi: 10.1017/S0022278X15000361.

Sturman, Kathryn. 2011. *Unconstitutional Changes of Government: The Democrat's Dilemma in Africa.* Policy Briefing 30. Johannesburg: SAIIA.

Tardy, Thierry. 2015. *CSDP in Action: What Contribution to International Security?* Chaillot Papers, May 2015. EU Institute for Security Studies (ISS): Paris.

The White House. 2011. "Strategy to Combat Transnational Organized Crime: Addressing Converging Threats to National Security", Washington, DC, 9 July 2011.

Thompson, Ginger. 2015. The Narco-Terror Trap, ProPublica, 7 December. Accessed 31 January 2016. www.propublica.org/article/the-dea-narco-terror-trap.

Tieku, Thomas K. 2004. Explaining the Clash and Accommodation of Interests of Major Actors in the Creation of the African Union. *African Affairs* 103 (411): 249–67. doi: 10.1093/afraf/adh041.

———. 2011. The Evolution of the African Union Commission and Africrats: Drivers of African Regionalisms. In The Ashgate Research Companion to Regionalisms, eds Timothy M. Shaw, J. Andrew Grant and Scarlett Cornelissen, 193–212. Farnham: Ashgate.

———. 2016. *Governing Africa: 3D Analysis of the African Union's Performance.* Lanham, MD, Boulder, CO: Rowman & Littlefield.

Traub, James. 2010. Africa's Drug Problem, *The New York Times Magazine*, 9 April 2010. Accessed 24 November 2016. www.nytimes.com/2010/04/11/magazine/11Trade-t.html.

UNODC. 2005. *World Drug Report: Volume 1: Analysis.* Vienna: United Nations Office on Drugs and Crime.

———. 2007. *Cocaine Trafficking in West Africa: The Threat to Stability and Development (with Special Reference to Guinea-Bissau).* Vienna: UNODC.

———. 2008. *Drug Trafficking as a Security Threat in West Africa.* Vienna: United Nations Office on Drugs and Crime.

———. 2017. *Annual Report: Covering Activities During 2017.* Vienna: UNODC.

———. 2019. About UNODC. Accessed 18 May 2019. www.unodc.org/unodc/en/about-unodc/index.html?ref=menutop.

US DOJ. 2009. "Statement of Thomas M. Harrigan, Assistant Administrator and Chief of Operations, Operations Division, Drug Enforcement Administration, United States Department of Justice, Before the United States Senate Committee on Foreign Relations, Subcommittee on African Affairs", Hearing entitled "Confronting Drug Trafficking in West Africa", 23 June 2009.

Uzoechina, Okey. 2014. *Security Sector Reform and Governance Processes in West Africa: From Concepts to Reality.* Policy Paper 35. Geneva: Geneva Centre for the Democratic Control of Armed Forces (DCAF).

Vulliamy, Ed. 2008. How a Tiny West African Country Became the World's First Narco State, *The Guardian*, 9 March 2008. Accessed 28 January 2016. www.theguardian.com/world/2008/mar/09/drugstrade.

Witt, Antonia. 2013. The African Union and Contested Political Order(s). In *Towards an African Peace and Security Regime: Continental Embeddedness, Transnational Linkages, Strategic Relevance*, eds Ulf Engel and João G. Porto, 11–30. Farnham: Ashgate.

———. 2020. *Undoing Coups: The African Union and Post-Coup Intervention in Madagascar.* London: Zed Books.

Zimelis, Andris. 2011. Conditionality and the EU–ACP Partnership: A Misguided Approach to Development? *Australian Journal of Political Science* 46 (3): 389–406. doi: 10.1080/10361146.2011.595698.

Zoubir, Yahia H. 2013. Algeria and the African Union: From National Liberation Struggle to Fight against Terrorism. In *The African Union in Light of the Arab Revolts: An Appraisal of the Foreign Policy and Security Objectives of South Africa, Ethiopia and Algeria*, eds Mikael Eriksson and Linnea Gelot, 39–58. Uppsala: Nordiska Afrikainstitutet.

6 Contested relations

Spatial ordering during conflict interventions

Introduction

The preceding chapters have shown that, during conflict interventions, actors at ECOWAS and the AU have not only employed different sets of practices to manage conflicts in their respective regions 'from afar' (Chapter 3) and 'on the ground' (Chapter 4), but also have pursued more general objectives, seeking to develop and consolidate specific regional policies (Chapter 5). Both have been intimately tied to the construction and formatting of regional spaces. An additional set of practices, so far mentioned only briefly, has been the strategic engagement of other regional and international actors, which actors at ECOWAS and the AU have employed both to directly respond to conflict situations in their respective regions as well as to contest and order relations among them. This chapter takes a detailed look at this set of practices, subsequently analyzing, first, how they have been employed 'from afar' and 'on the ground' directly towards conflict management. Second, the chapter analyzes how different actors have tried to contest and renegotiate relations among them, during conflict interventions, either arguing in spatial terms – ordering *by* space – and/or trying to establish a particular spatial order – ordering *of* space.

Taking a closer look at these dynamics, once more, a spatial perspective is helpful. While much of the interaction in and around conflict situations may be explained in terms of different national interests, hegemonic aspirations, or simply as geopolitics, I contend that all of these aspects are intimately linked to space-making. Consequently, only when paying adequate attention to space can we fully account for the ways in which these aspects (i.e., national interests, hegemony and geopolitics) are constituted, communicated and enacted. In other words, only if we take into account space can we make sense of the specific conjuncture of actors, interests and agendas during conflict intervention, as moments of dense social interaction at different sites, contributing to the construction, formatting and ordering of regional spaces and relations among them. To exemplify this point, the chapter again draws on intervention experiences of ECOWAS and AU actors in Guinea-Bissau, which despite its seeming 'marginality' has assumed central importance due to its location at the intersection of particular spatial imaginations and regional policy processes (see Chapter 5), as well as competing efforts of spatial ordering, as I explain below.[1]

Engaging other actors 'from afar'

Ever since ECOWAS and AU actors have started to engage in conflict situations in West/Africa, but increasingly so since the early/mid-2000s, their efforts and practices cannot be understood in isolation from other regional and international actors, such as the UN and the EU, as well as several Western states and occasionally also non-Western states and organizations. With overlapping interests in peace and security in Africa (see Chapter 5), and the EU and UN being influential reference points for regional organizations across the world, although not necessarily in any straightforward manner (cf. Söderbaum 2016, 7ff.), all of the described sets of practices employed by ECOWAS and the AU have involved other, 'external' actors in one way or another.

Such involvement ranges from loose inspiration to more direct and strategic participation and sometimes co-production of particular practices. While much more visible in AU than in ECOWAS processes, the field of early warning and thus the production of conflict knowledge provides a good example of the key role that 'external' actors have played in setting up and/or consolidating some intervention practices of African ROs (e.g., cf. Engel 2018).[2] However, actors at ECOWAS and the AU have also strategically engaged 'external' actors as part of their own intervention efforts and practices. In this section, I focus on this aspect as another key practice that African ROs have employed consistently over time. While existing research commonly covers such interactions in terms of (inter)dependence, hierarchical, paternalistic or asymmetrical relations (e.g., cf. Tieku and Hakak 2014; Welz 2016, 2018), more attention needs to be paid to their contested nature as well as the different ways in which these relations are actually negotiated, produced and communicated, especially during 'moments' of conflict intervention.

With regard to practices employed 'from afar', I argue that especially high-level meetings and public pronouncements play an important role. Strategic contacts may also take place on various other levels and occasions, which, however, are difficult to observe and assess (e.g., secretariat and commission staff, desk-to-desk; during information gathering and knowledge production processes). Therefore, the following focuses on how ECOWAS and AU actors have strategically engaged other regional and international actors during meetings (outside the conflict site) and through public pronouncements, and how this engagement has contributed to space-making.

During meetings

Representatives of ECOWAS and the AU, respectively, have engaged 'external' actors during meetings in several ways. First, they have invited specific actors to their own statutory meetings to observe the session or allowed them to make a statement, while not allowing them to participate during debate.[3] Conversely, they have also participated in statutory meetings of other organizations, on invitation or after requesting it, again either as observers or to deliver statements. While it is often difficult to identify actors and locate agency precisely (i.e., who exactly invites), these mutual invitations and participation have been a consistent practice, at least since the 1990s.

During 2012, for example, according to the final communiqués, representatives of the AU and UN participated as observers in all ECOWAS summits (two ordinary and four extraordinary) – except for an 'emergency mini summit' that took place on 29 March in Abidjan comprising only six ECOWAS heads of state on their way to a mission in Mali. Both UN and AU representatives, on at least one occasion, addressed the ECOWAS Authority in prepared statements (cf. ECOWAS Commission 2012a). In addition, observers included representatives of UEMOA (four times), the EU (twice) and the CPLP (once), as well as representatives of Algeria (four times), Mauritania (three times), France (twice) and Chad, Morocco, South Africa, Austria, Germany, Portugal, the United Kingdom and the US (all once). Likewise, according to ECOWAS MSC final reports, representatives of the AU and UN (at least twice), the EU, Algeria and Mauritania (at least twice), Morocco, South Africa, France and the US (all at least once) participated as observers in sessions of the MSC at ministerial level. Representatives of the AU, UN and ECOWAS 'development partners' were also present on at least one occasion during sessions of the Committee of Chiefs of Defense Staff (cf. ECOWAS CCDS 2012, para. 4).

Similarly, the AU PSC has also allowed observers to participate in its sessions, although records in that regard are not freely available. In principle, through the PSC Secretariat, the PSC may invite guests to address the meeting, but thereafter have to leave the room and may thus neither participate nor observe the debate among PSC members (AU 2002, para. 8.9–11). In practice, however, major donors of the AU (most importantly EU representatives) and some influential Western states (e.g., France and the US) are often exempted from this rule. This has repeatedly caused tensions regarding the participation of representatives of Regional Economic Communities (RECs), in particular with ECOWAS.[4] As explained in Chapter 3, ECOWAS member states are supposed to represent 'ECOWAS positions' in the AU PSC. If and to what extent they do so, however, remains subject to debate. After years of complaints on the part of ECOWAS Commission staff, efforts are underway to change the rules to allow for more inclusion of RECs as organizations (not member states) in AU PSC meetings.[5]

Illustrating mutual engagement during 2012, meeting on conflict in Guinea-Bissau, the PSC continually heard statements by representatives of ECOWAS, the CPLP and the UN, as well as on occasion by "other AU bilateral and multilateral partners" (AU PSC 2012a, para. 1). In the case of ECOWAS and the CPLP, representation primarily fell to the ambassadors to the AU of Côte d'Ivoire and Angola, both chairs of their respective organizations and members of the PSC, at the time. However, ECOWAS commission staff also went to Addis Ababa to discuss with AU PSD staff and brief the PSC on behalf of their organizations on several occasions. For example, ECOWAS Political Affairs Director at the time Abdel-Fatau Musah delivered a statement during the 340th session of the PSC, at ministerial level, on 2 November 2012 (cf. ECOWAS Commission 2012b, 1). The ECOWAS Commissioner for Political Affairs, Peace and Security, Halima Ahmed, as well as the Special Representative of the ECOWAS Commission President (SRPC), Ansoumane Ceesay, spoke at the 351st session of the PSC, at ambassadorial level, on 16 January 2013 (cf. AU PSC 2013b, para. 1).

Moreover, representatives of ECOWAS and the AU have also participated during sessions of the UN Security Council (UNSC). For example, staff of the ECOWAS Commission presented the regional position on Guinea-Bissau at the UNSC on 7 May 2012 (cf. ECOWAS MSC 2012b, 3). In addition, ECOWAS and AU actors have worked through their liaison offices in New York and conveyed messages and documents (e.g., communiqués, reports) to the UNSC through the A3, the representatives of the three African states holding non-permanent seats on the UNSC. Interestingly and a specialty in the case of Guinea-Bissau, as well as more recently regarding the conflict in the Gambia, African members of the UNSC have for the first time become 'penholders' on a specific agenda item (i.e., for Guinea-Bissau), something that until then, with few exceptions, had been reserved informally for the P3 (i.e., France, the UK and the US; cf. Security Council Report 2018). Since 2012, the penholders on Guinea-Bissau have been the delegations of Nigeria (until March 2012), Togo (March 2012 to December 2013), Nigeria (January 2014 to December 2015), Senegal (January 2016 to December 2017) and Côte d'Ivoire (since January 2018). This has allowed representatives of ECOWAS and AU member states to play an influential role in that arena.[6] In addition, ECOWAS and AU actors have also engaged EU actors, in particular through their liaison offices in Brussels and through visits at the EU headquarters. However, the available material does not allow us to assess in any detail if, how and in which meetings representatives of ECOWAS and the AU have participated, other than the consultative meetings (see below).

Second, consultative meetings have been another means to strategically engage 'external' actors, some of which take place on a regular basis, others that convene less regularly but persistently, and still others that are convened *ad hoc*. On a regular basis, the AU PSC and the EU Political and Security Council (EU PSC) meet to discuss cooperation issues and ongoing conflict situations. The same objective is behind consultative meetings between the AU PSC and the UN Security Council. Likewise, persistently but less regularly, the ECOWAS-EU Political Dialogue – ministerial meetings, sometimes also referred to as troika meetings – has also enabled mutual engagement on issues of cooperation and conflict management. For example, in 2012 and following years, conflict in Guinea-Bissau has been among the issues the

AU PSC discussed with the EU PSC and the UNSC. Similarly, the issue was also on the agenda of subsequent sessions of the ECOWAS-EU Political Dialogue (cf. ECOWAS Council of Ministers and EU Council 2013, para. 12ff.; see also ECOWAS Council of Ministers and EU Council 2017, 2018; on the 20th, cf. ECOWAS Commission President 2015). Although initially intended to become a more regular platform for mutual engagement, the AU-initiated Multinational Coordination Framework for the Stabilization of Guinea-Bissau has been rather *ad hoc*. After two meetings, in September and December 2012 in New York and Addis Ababa respectively, which failed to narrow differences between ECOWAS and CPLP representatives, this framework ceased to exist. Instead, they agreed to deploy a joint assessment mission 'on the ground' as a compromise (ECOWAS Commission President 2012, para. 11) (see below).[7]

Another consultative mechanism, regularly employed in response to specific conflicts in West/Africa, has been International Contact Groups (ICGs). On the one hand, these have met outside the conflict site, for regional and international stakeholders to share information, coordinate efforts and approaches, as well as to negotiate roles and positions (cf. Witt 2012, 212). On the other hand, they have become influential consultation fora for representatives of different intervening actors 'on the ground' (i.e., 'local ICGs'), often rather informal and involving fewer participants (see below). Examples in this regard include the ICG-Guinea (2009ff.), ICG-Madagascar (2009ff.) and ICG-Mali (2012ff.). In the example of Guinea-Bissau, an ICG-GB has been created or reconvened repeatedly since 1998. Although relatively effective in facilitating coordination earlier, in 2012 the ICG-GB collapsed, after an initial session in June 2012, due to serious tensions between representatives of ECOWAS and the CPLP. (ECOWAS Commission President 2012, para. 9). Efforts to reconvene the group in following years remained unsuccessful. Instead, it took interaction 'on the ground' to achieve some rapprochement between these organizations (see below).

Through public pronouncements

In their public pronouncements, ECOWAS and AU actors directly engage 'external' actors in at least two ways, in addition to mentioning their participation during meetings, which also contributes to conveying a specific message (see below). First, they refer to specific action taken by others (e.g., meetings, statements and missions) and relate them to their own position or action. Most commonly, they do that in a positive or diplomatic formulation (e.g., 'taking note', 'welcoming', 'expressing appreciation' or 'endorsing'). Since their creation, this has become an equally consistent practice of the AU PSC and the ECOWAS Authority.

For example, during 2012, in its communiqués on the situation in Guinea-Bissau, the AU PSC regularly mentioned statements delivered to the PSC by representatives of ECOWAS, the CPLP and others (AU PSC 2012c, para. 1,

2012a, para. 1, 2012b, para. 1, 2012d), and in one case endorsed their press releases (AU PSC 2012c, para. 1, 5 and 8).[8] The PSC also "welcomed" ECOWAS' "commitment and dynamism", simultaneously expressing appreciation to the CPLP and the UNSC, as well as the EU, and even the International Organization of the Francophonie (OIF), which has been little involved in Guinea-Bissau (e.g., AU PSC 2012a, para. 4). The PSC communiqués also sought to highlight unity among the different actors where it existed, such as, for example, with regard to the positive assessment of the first round of voting in March 2012, and to calls for the coup perpetrators to step aside (e.g., AU PSC 2012a, para. 7–8). In comparison, the pronouncements of the ECOWAS Authority, at least with regard to Guinea-Bissau, have focused much more on highlighting their own action. References to the activities of others are much less frequent, for example, "congratulating" the Angolan government on the withdrawal of MISSANG (ECOWAS Authority 2012a, para. 36), or "welcoming" initiatives to forge an international consensus (ECOWAS Authority 2012a, para. 39). Nevertheless, ECOWAS communiqués have repeatedly reaffirmed its "commitment to the close cooperation" with the AU and UN (ECOWAS Authority 2012c, para. 33; see also ECOWAS Authority 2012a, para. 39, 2012b, para. 20).

Second, both organizations issue 'calls' on other actors, communicating specific wishes or expectations regarding their action. The AU PSC, for example, has called upon AU partners, especially the UN, the EU and the CPLP, to "support the measures taken by the AU, and work together to force the perpetrators of the coup d'état and their supporters to accept the return to constitutional legality in Guinea-Bissau" (AU PSC 2012c, para. 7). At the same time, it has sought to order relations among the different actors involved, in a particular way. On the one hand, communiqués have reaffirmed the principle of "subsidiarity", the AU welcoming and supporting ECOWAS' efforts (AU PSC 2012a, para. 4). On the other hand, they have stressed the "duty of Africa" (i.e., AU and ECOWAS) to counter destabilizing actions, with the "support" of the international community (i.e., the UN, CPLP and others) (AU PSC 2012a, para. 6). In line with this, the AU PSC has requested the UNSC, as well as the EU, CPLP, OIF, the Organization of Islamic Cooperation and other "bilateral and multilateral partners", to support sanctions and measures adopted by ECOWAS and the AU (AU PSC 2012a, para. 9). However, the AU PSC also tried to assume an intermediary or facilitating position, "encouraging" ECOWAS to closely coordinate with "other relevant international actors", in particular the CPLP, AU, UN and EU, "towards the implementation of the decisions relating to the return to constitutional order in Guinea-Bissau" (AU PSC 2012b, para. 3).[9]

Similar to this, towards the end of 2012 and in early 2013, the ECOWAS Authority has called upon the AU to recognize the ECOWAS-brokered transition government and suspend its sanctions on Guinea-Bissau (ECOWAS Authority 2012b, para. 24, 2013, para. 36). Likewise, it called upon the international community to "ease sanctions imposed on the country to alleviate the suffering of the populations" (ECOWAS Authority 2012b, para. 26). Moreover, in their statements, ECOWAS heads of state have directed the ECOWAS Commission to "seek assistance" of the AU, the UN and the international community "for the implementation of the measures to be taken in Guinea-Bissau" (ECOWAS Authority 2012d, para. 28), and to "intensify consultations" with partners (ECOWAS Authority 2012a, para. 39; see also ECOWAS Authority 2012b, para. 20). In all that, ECOWAS heads of state have stressed the need for cooperation based on the "cardinal principle of subsidiarity" (ECOWAS Authority 2012c, para. 33).

Strategic engagement 'from afar' and space-making

It is perhaps no surprise that much of the direct engagement of other, 'external' actors has to do with resource mobilization. This confirms more general observations in the literature, describing especially the relationship among African ROs, the UN and the EU as hierarchical and (inter) dependent. Facing scarce financial and material resources, as well as limited personnel capacity, a main practice of ECOWAS and AU actors has been to seek 'external' support, fostering strategic 'partnerships' and alliances in order to extend scope and effectiveness of their own efforts (e.g. cf., Welz 2016). In this regard, meetings and public pronouncements facilitate the sharing of information, the communication of needs and expectations, but also the contestation of norms, principles and responsibilities. While meetings provide a closed, somewhat protected setting, public pronouncements create a certain pressure by calling specific actors out 'publicly', reminding them about 'shared' norms and principles, as well as 'responsibilities' of the international community.

Closely related to seeking material support is the objective to garner diplomatic support in order to build a strong and coordinated response. Meetings play an important role in working towards shared views about problems and possible solutions; public statements seek to demonstrate unity among the 'international community'. However, just as with material support, these statements often also seek to construct unity or foster coordination where not much existed, using public communication strategically. More generally, such communication aims to define relationships among the various international and regional actors involved in conflict management.

This aspect in particular has contributed to space-making. Strategically engaging other actors during meetings and through public pronouncements constitutes a way for ECOWAS and AU actors to construct links between different regional spaces and spatial scales, and continuously negotiate relations among them. Therefore, by establishing, negotiating and maintaining or institutionalizing links with actors representing other regional spaces, actors at ECOWAS and the AU actively seek to (re)position themselves and their regional spaces in a complex network. Thereby, they engage in spatial ordering. As explained in more detail in the following, such efforts of spatial ordering take place on different levels – 'internally' and 'externally', 'from afar' and 'on the ground'.

Engaging other actors 'on the ground'

A key characteristic of contemporary intervention settings is the simultaneous presence of a wide variety of intervening actors and organizations. Although the lack of as well as the need for coordination and cooperation is a recurring theme in existing literature, less attention has been paid to actual efforts and practices of engagement 'on the ground', and how this engagement has related to their engagement 'from afar' (see above). Staff operating 'on the ground' often have considerable room for maneuver and interpretation; decisions taken by top-level political organs do not necessarily translate into action in any automatic or mechanistic way. What is more, staff of different organizations deployed to the same conflict situation interact more frequently and directly, exchanging information and often adopting similar views of 'problems' and 'solutions' (cf. Autesserre 2014). These may diverge from official positions adopted at summits or held in headquarters. Therefore, this section examines how ECOWAS and AU actors have engaged other intervening actors 'on the ground' – most importantly through joint field missions and interaction among local representatives – and how this has related to their interaction 'from afar'. Moreover, it also reflects upon how this engagement has contributed to space-making.

Joint field missions

Complementing the more general intervention practice to deploy diplomatic field missions to conflict situations in their respective regions, ECOWAS and AU actors have also fielded joint missions, including different constellations of regional and international actors, but most importantly representatives of the UN, as well as in some cases the EU and others. These joint missions potentially play a crucial role in overcoming disagreement or opposing positions, building mutual trust, aligning assessments of the situation and eventually coordinating approaches on how to respond to a given conflict situation. Several interviewees have described this process as 'going together', from joint assessments, to joint discussions, coordinated decisions and joint statements.[10] Suffice it to say that these aspirations and potential benefits have not always fully materialized – certain differences (e.g., procedural, ideational) continue to exist. In any case, joint missions have been important moments for different organizations to interact at different levels, building and (re)negotiating relations among them. The following considerations about Joint Assessment Missions (JAMs) to Guinea-Bissau, comprising representatives of ECOWAS, the AU, CPLP, EU and UN, provide an apt example in this respect.

Following the coup d'état of April 2012, the first JAM took place in December 2012 and was the result of efforts by the AU and UN to mediate tensions and overcome opposition primarily between actors at ECOWAS and the CPLP (see also Chapter 3). At the consultative meeting in September 2012, at the margins of the UN General Assembly in New York, the idea first came up. Failing to overcome the basic differences between ECOWAS and the CPLP, the assessment mission apparently was the smallest common denominator, a compromise effort to at least do something together. ECOWAS quickly adopted it as a possible way to 'forge international consensus' around its own approach towards the crisis in Guinea-Bissau, and sought to speed up the process (see Chapter 3).

Visiting Bissau from 16 to 21 December 2012, the first JAM comprised, from the AU, PSD Director El Ghassim Wane (also coordinator of the JAM), accompanied by Matthieu Kinouani, Political Analyst at the PSD (and former Interim Head of AULO-GB, from March/April 2011 to May 2012). ECOWAS was represented by Political Affairs Director Abdel-Fatau Musah and the SRPC, Ansoumana E. Ceesay, supported by two of his advisers. The CPLP sent António P.A. Lopes (Political and Diplomatic Adviser at the CPLP Executive Secretariat and future CPLP special representative in Bissau), accompanied by Philip Baverstock (Legal Adviser). Participants from the EU included the Head of the West Africa Division of the European External Action Service, Sean Doyle, and the Head of the Political Section of the EU Delegation in Guinea-Bissau, Hannes Hauser. Last, the UN was represented by the Deputy Special Representative of the UN Secretary General to Guinea-Bissau, Gana Fofang (also Resident Coordinator of UN operational activities and UNDP Resident Representative), accompanied by Marlène S. Nzengou, Political Affairs Officer at the UN DPA, Africa II Division (cf. AU 2013, Annex II).

The mission was an important first step to jointly assess the situation "on the ground", examine underlying causes, and to "explore avenues for building consensus among the partner organizations on the way forward", and to "facilitate the formulation of a set of recommendations on how best the partner organizations can work together to assist Guinea-Bissau", as set out among the mission objectives in the terms of reference (cf. AU 2013, para. 3). All of the involved organizations welcomed the mission and considered the subsequent report (e.g., cf. ECOWAS Authority 2013, para. 35; AU PSC 2013a, para. 1). However, the joint assessment mission did not succeed in dissolving tensions between ECOWAS and CPLP actors, as even the final report of the first JAM became subject to controversy (cf. ECOWAS MSC 2013a, para. 48). Political coordination and cooperation among the participating organizations remained low.

The second JAM visited Bissau from 8 to 11 July 2013. This time representatives of the OIF also participated. Again, meeting with various representatives of the transitional authorities, political parties, civil society and ambassadors accredited to Guinea-Bissau, the mission aimed to prepare and coordinate international approaches in anticipation of the general elections. While still not able to resolve all issues among the involved organizations, the second mission contributed to a growing consensus, which the ECOWAS MSC welcomed (cf. ECOWAS MSC 2013b, para. 20 and 23.c). In their recommendations, mission participants suggested reviving the ICG-GB, including enhanced interaction at the local level in Bissau, as had been suggested on previous occasions.[11] Moreover, it was also during the second JAM that the idea emerged to create a 'follow-up mechanism' comprising the representatives of ECOWAS, the AU, EU and UN already based in Bissau, as well as representatives of the CPLP and OIF, which they would yet have to deploy (UNSG 2013, para. 22).[12] This idea subsequently developed into the framework of the Permanent Five (P5) of Guinea-Bissau created in late 2013 (see below).

By the time that the third JAM arrived in Bissau, from 15 to 19 September 2014, things had changed a lot. Mutual engagement of ECOWAS, the AU, CPLP, EU and UN in the P5 framework had helped to significantly improve relations among them and enhance coordination (see below). Moreover, the successful completion of the general elections in April and May 2014 and the subsequent lifting of sanctions against Guinea-Bissau had removed one of the main issues of contention. Thus, the P5 organizations and the OIF set out for the third JAM, aiming to consolidate the positive developments in the country. Based on a joint evaluation of the political and security situation 'on the ground', the JAM was supposed to send a signal to the new authorities and national stakeholders in Guinea-Bissau (encouragement, international attention and support), and to develop collective action of the six organizations (cf. AU et al. 2014, para. 3). The findings of the mission highlighted the need for immediate action, in order to stabilize a still precarious, fragile situation, which then would have to be followed by broad and comprehensive reforms, and a long-term economic development program (cf. AU et al. 2014, para. 7–8). The mission also considered preparations for a donors' roundtable to support the national poverty reduction strategy and the ECOWAS post-transition support and reform program (cf. AU et al. 2014, para. 9).[13]

Based on the same principle, and basically a follow-up to the first three JAMs, representatives of ECOWAS, the AU, EU, UN and CPLP, as well as the African Security Sector Network, conducted a Security Sector Joint Assessment Mission from 2 to 12 March 2015. Led by AU Special Representative of the Chairperson of the AU Commission (SRCC) Ovídio Pequeno, this mission, as with similar missions to other countries, was guided by the AU's Policy Framework on SSR (see Chapter 5). This themed joint mission focused on following up on reform needs identified during the previous JAM, assessing SSR requirements in Guinea-Bissau and making recommendations on how to support which priority areas in the immediate, medium and long-term. In addition, the mission also sought to mobilize international support, complementing existing efforts by the P5 of Guinea-Bissau (AU et al. 2015, 3). These efforts of the P5 of Guinea-Bissau have played a critical role, supporting initiatives 'on the ground'. They have provided continuity (preparation and follow-up) to those initiatives, and have continuously engaged each other in Bissau, as part of the intervention practices of ECOWAS and the AU, as well as the other three organizations (see below).

Interaction among local representatives

Being posted in the same conflict situation – as has been the case in Guinea-Bissau, but, for example, also in Côte d'Ivoire, Liberia and Mali – special representatives of ECOWAS and the AU necessarily have to engage with representatives of other organizations (or states) 'on the ground'.[14] On the one hand, this has happened occasionally and in changing constellations, for example, involving representatives of only two organizations, several of them, or including state representatives. On the other hand, in some cases, the main intervening actors have created local consultation frameworks or practices. A case in point are 'local ICGs', that is, smaller, less formal constellations of actors represented in ICGs more generally (see above). To date, such coordination frameworks in general and local ones specifically have received very little scholarly attention. An exception has been the work of Witt (2013), studying the workings of the ICGs on Guinea and Madagascar.

In the example of Guinea-Bissau, occasional interactions have been the standard until 2012 (despite recurring calls for a 'local ICG'). More regular consultation, in particular among the five main organizational actors intervening in Guinea-Bissau – the P5 of Guinea-Bissau – has been established following the coup d'état of 12 April 2012, to resolve tensions that could not be resolved during previous meetings outside the conflict site (see above), and to coordinate and harmonize approaches and positions.

Driven by the UN Secretary General (UNSG), the P5 framework emerged in late 2013. Throughout 2012 and 2013, the UNSG had repeatedly called upon international stakeholders to increase their coordination and cooperation in Guinea-Bissau. The P5 of Guinea-Bissau, subsequently, developed less as a formal structure (except for a document stating the five organizations' intention to cooperate), instead rather constituting a joint practice.[15] The AU SRCC, Pequeno, became coordinator of the framework. Seniority played a role in this decision, as did a preference by UN actors for the AU to take the lead.[16] In addition, the UN SRSG continued to be important, bringing the different actors together and coordinating the international community more generally. Its exact role, however, has depended a lot on the personality occupying the position (see also below). For example, José Ramos-Horta (formerly President of Timor-Leste and winner of the Nobel Peace Prize) was instrumental in closing gaps between actors and positions between February 2013 and May 2014.

Overall, the P5 framework helped to successfully improve relations among its members, narrowing down differences despite some remaining tensions, establishing direct channels of communication and regular interaction.[17] It has enabled them to jointly monitor, evaluate and respond to developing situations, exerting pressure on political actors in Bissau.[18] In this way, while not an ECOWAS initiative in the first place, it was through this engagement of P5 representatives *in* Bissau (as well as the joint assessment missions; see above) that ECOWAS actors managed to overcome some of the opposition from actors at the CPLP and the EU. Gradually, these aligned with the approach of the West African organization, for pragmatic reasons, requiring the actors 'on the ground' to develop more cooperative relations. AU and UN actors played a supporting role in this, although stopping short of giving in to all ECOWAS requests (see Chapters 1 and 3).

Nevertheless, from late 2013, with increasing cooperation among the P5 members 'on the ground', the group managed to work together, above everything else focusing on the transition process, to return Guinea-Bissau to 'constitutional order'. Especially ahead of the elections in early 2014, representatives of the P5 organizations interacted in Bissau almost on a daily basis.[19] They held joint meetings, undertook joint missions out of Bissau (e.g., to Côte d'Ivoire and Abuja) and issued joint statements. The representatives of the P5 in Bissau also prepared the ground and provided infrastructure and logistics for coordination among the various election observations missions (see Chapter 4). At the technical level, this included joint briefings and meetings on organizational issues. At the political level, the mission heads Sawyer and Chissano (for ECOWAS and the AU respectively) as well as then-UN SRSG Ramos-Horta met several times to share information and discuss how to jointly approach stakeholders, issuing joint press releases, occasionally also including the EU (e.g., cf. UNIOGBIS 2013, 2014d, 2014a, 2014b, 2014c; ECOWAS Commission 2014b, 2014a; AU PSC 2014, 37–8; AU Commission 2014).

After the successful elections in 2014, the P5 of Guinea-Bissau shifted their attention towards tackling structural reforms.[20] However, they quickly had to abandon any ambition in that direction when in August 2015 President Vaz dismissed Prime Minister Pereira, thereby triggering another crisis, and a political deadlock that persisted for two and a half years (see Chapter 1). During that time, interactions among the P5 of Guinea-Bissau were less frequent, also due to a less active role played by then-UN SRSG Miguel Trovoada (formerly President of São Tomé and Príncipe), appointed in July 2014. This changed again slightly when Modibo Touré took office in May 2016 (formerly Malian Minister of New Technologies, Telecommunications and Post Office, and Deputy SRSG in the Central African Republic).[21] Nevertheless, due to the frequent turnover, UN SRSGs have lacked the long-term engagement and familiarity with realities 'on the ground' – contrary, for example, to AU SRCC Pequeno, who has been in the country since 2012. The P5 of Guinea-Bissau again developed a more coherent and coordinated response in the second half of 2016, supporting ECOWAS mediation initiatives vocally and materially. These resulted in the Bissau Roadmap (of September 2016) and the Conakry Agreement (of October 2016).[22] At least publicly, the P5 organizations all pushed towards the adherence to and implementation of the Bissau Roadmap and the Conakry Agreement. Behind the scenes, however, interpretations and assessments differed and political actors in Bissau continuously sought to play on these differences between and within organizations, although in the end with limited success.[23]

Therefore, despite considerable improvement and arguably some success, interaction and cooperation among the members of the P5 of Guinea-Bissau continues to be beset by more or less visible tensions. For example, the EU delegation in Guinea-Bissau (including many Portuguese nationals) still tends to align more with the CPLP (especially the Portuguese position therein). However, since late 2016, the CPLP no longer has a special representative 'on the ground', instead being represented by the ambassadors of Portugal, Brazil and Angola in Bissau.[24] Tensions have also persisted between representatives of ECOWAS and the AU, as well as among different ECOWAS heads of state engaging 'on the ground' with conflict in Bissau (e.g., Presidents Sall versus Condé, of Senegal and Guinea respectively; see also Chapter 4).[25] Nevertheless, despite all these dynamics, in early 2018, pressure of the P5 organizations, led by ECOWAS sanctions and continuous high-level engagement, resulted in President Vaz appointing Aristides Gomes as an actual consensus Prime Minister of Guinea-Bissau, and the successful holding of parliamentary elections in March 2019 (see Chapter 1).

From the perspective of local observers, the engagement of the P5 of Guinea-Bissau has been important and to some extent successful (e.g., keeping down tensions). However, some have complained that on the one hand the P5 organizations, coming with their own approaches, did not fully understand Bissau-Guinean historical specificities. On the other hand, on occasion, they would have liked the P5 organizations to have taken stronger positions. Failing to do so, some local actors see them as co-responsible for the current situation.[26]

Mutual engagement 'on the ground' and space-making

From the above observations, it becomes clear that regional and international actors intervening 'on the ground' have increasingly sought to coordinate their efforts and cooperate where possible. As the example of Guinea-Bissau has shown, this has been despite tensions among different actors, at the level of their respective headquarters and political decision-making organs, which to some extent have also played out on the 'local' level. However, several factors influence engagement among these actors 'on the ground', changing their relationships at that level. On the one hand, a certain pragmatism requires representatives to interact with each other more cooperatively. Encountering each other in their daily operations, very different from the headquarters' level, they need to find at least some mode of co-existence. Beyond that, faced with the realities 'on the ground', to achieve their respective goals and pursue their agendas they have an increased interest in cooperating or at least not obstructing each other. If possible, different capacities, potential comparative or complementary advantages, but especially the benefit of the international community speaking with 'one voice', may provide incentives for more cooperative behavior. Of course, the extent to which this holds true depends on the particular context as well as the extent to which different actors have an interest in working more or less towards the same goal.

On the other hand, personal relationships play an important role in facilitating more or less cooperation among local representatives of different regional organizations. Therefore, the concrete individual holding a certain position matters, regarding both his competences and abilities (as perceived by his counterparts) and relationships existing prior to her or his deployment to that context (e.g., earlier cooperation, mutual acquaintances, shared professional experiences, national or regional provenience). Moreover, overlaps in social, everyday activities may bring people closer together, to work towards some degree of shared perceptions and understandings of problems as well as possible solutions and approaches. As respective mandates, rules for procedures and practices are always subject to interpretation and leave considerable leeway to adapt efforts 'on the ground' to local necessities and personal preferences (cf. Autesserre 2014, 26).

These dynamics hold interesting implications for processes of spatialization unfolding around conflict intervention, driven by different actors. First, with regard to the construction of regional spaces, the interpretation of mandates based on local necessities and personal preferences creates a certain divergence between positions and approaches adopted at different levels of the same organization, which at some point have to be reconciled again. This points to the co-constitution of agency and characteristics of ROs by various institutions and actors, working at different sites, linked through different practices and networks (i.e., ROs are not unitary actors). Consequently, regional spaces are also co-constructed simultaneously by different actors, employing different practices, at and through these different sites and networks.

Second, just as 'from afar' (e.g., at headquarters), relationships among different ROs, regional spaces and spatial scales are negotiated 'on the ground'. However, the way to do so as well as the actual outcome may differ, due to the proximity to actual conflicts as well as to representatives of other intervening organizations. However, much depends on personal or working relationships among them. For example, while good relations between the representatives of the AU and EU have resulted in close coordination and cooperation in Bissau, strained relations between the ones of ECOWAS and the EU have negatively affected their interactions (see also Chapter 4). As a consequence, the representatives of the EU in Bissau have sought to push their objectives and agenda through its representation in Abuja, and the ECOWAS headquarters (expecting the latter to instruct the ECOWAS liaison office in Bissau).[27] However, to the extent that coordination of communication and inter/action of different spatial scales is achieved 'on the ground', at least at that level, more cooperative relations emerge, as do shared visions of who should do what and how, although of course not always entirely free of tensions. Through mission reports, briefs and updates, as well as personal communication, these shared perceptions to some extent also feed back into visions and approaches at organizational headquarters (see Chapter 3).

Contesting relations, ordering *by* and *of* space

Despite considerable efforts of actors at ECOWAS and the AU to engage other regional and international actors strategically, seeking to mobilize material and political support for their interventions and to position themselves vis-à-vis others, these relations have been and continue to be very much contested. In this, conflict intervention has included moments when such contestation becomes particularly intense and visible. In the following, I argue that contestation has occurred when and *where* different agendas and political projects have intersected. Moreover, I argue that conflictive interactions, guided by particular spatial imaginations (Chapter 5), have also directly related to the ordering *by* space – using 'space' as an argument – and *of* space – aiming to establish a specific spatial order.

To explain that argument in more detail and to substantiate it empirically, this section analyzes the complex interaction among the different ROs intervening in Guinea-Bissau. In particular, it highlights three constellations of actors and spatial objectives or arguments: (i) efforts by ECOWAS and CPLP actors to spatially de/legitimize their respective interventions; (ii) the contestation and negotiation of the spatial organization of APSA around the concept of 'subsidiarity' between ECOWAS and AU actors; and (iii) the role of EU actors in formatting and ordering space in West/Africa.

Important to note at this point is that – although employing a different terminology and not all pursuing a central interest in 'space' – some aspects of the following have also been observed by other scholars studying different examples. For example, reflecting on subsequent regional and international peacekeeping missions in the Central African Republic, Welz (2016) analyzes the complex interactions between the Economic Community of Central African States, the AU and EU, shifting back and forth between cooperation and competition. Explicitly adopting a spatial perspective, Döring (2018) has studied the intense negotiations and contestations among ECOWAS, AU and EU actors (and others) surrounding interventions in response to the 2012 coup d'état in Mali, in particular the deployment of military forces through different competing frameworks (see also Döring 2019). Less concerned with space, instead focusing on contested political orders, Witt (2020) has studied the competitive interactions of actors at the South African Development Community, the Indian Ocean Commission, the AU and the EU to return Madagascar to constitutional order following the coup d'état in 2009.

In this context, the following analysis pursues the double objective of contributing a new empirical example to that literature as well as a new analytical and theoretical perspective that allows making sense of complex intervention settings, pointing to the central importance of 'space' therein.

Spatial delegitimization of conflict intervention

A key strategy of different intervening regional actors in West Africa has been to construct the legitimacy of their intervention in spatial terms or to delegitimize interventions by others spatially. Most obviously, this has related to spatial imaginations linked to specific security concerns (see Chapter 5), resulting in the securitization of specific spaces (e.g., 'Guinea-Bissau', 'West Africa', the 'Sahel'). However, it has also played an important role in the contestation and negotiation of relations between different intervening actors. In the example of Guinea-Bissau, the interaction between representatives of ECOWAS and the CPLP provides a particularly illustrative example of this strategy.

In 1998, two years after its creation, the CPLP (and specifically the foreign ministers of Portugal and Angola) started to engage in the war in Guinea-Bissau. At this point, actors at the CPLP were looking for a *raison d'être* and sought to raise the organization's international profile. Peacebuilding in Guinea-Bissau presented itself as an opportunity to do so (MacQueen 2003). However, after what appeared as initial success, ECOWAS actors quickly reacted to the involvement of the CPLP, increasingly pushing it aside and eventually deploying a military peacekeeping mission (i.e., ECOMOG III) (MacQueen 2003).[28] Ever since that time, actors at ECOWAS and the CPLP have variably competed or cooperated to varying degrees during the various crises in Guinea-Bissau.[29] Most visibly, this resulted in the process leading to the signing of the ECOWAS–CPLP–Guinea-Bissau DSSR Road Map in 2009/10. Since that time, both have tried to bring a technical-military mission into the country, against the strong opposition of the national armed forces (e.g., Herpolsheimer 2014, 53–4; see also ARB 2010).

Although the governments of Portugal and Brazil, in this context, are the more obvious actors, especially in more recent times, the Angolan government has also capitalized on imaginations of a 'Lusophone space' trying to gain a foothold in Guinea-Bissau, and West Africa more widely.[30] In early 2011, the Angolan government deployed a military-technical mission (MISSANG) officially to support national SSR efforts. However, there have been various speculations about the unofficial reasons behind that mission, creating serious tensions, and eventually leading to the withdrawal of the mission two months after the coup in April 2012.[31] Legally, the deployment of MISSANG was based on bilateral agreements between the governments of Angola and Guinea-Bissau. Interestingly, the Angolans nevertheless framed their mission in spatial terms. Whether to get approval or just to inform them, when Angolan state representatives turned to the AU PSC, they justified MISSANG as a 'CPLP mission', with the objective to help a fellow member of the Lusophone region.[32]

The mission was not well received, neither by the military of Guinea-Bissau nor by several West African heads of state. In particular, the presidents of Nigeria, Côte d'Ivoire and Senegal saw the Angolan involvement as a direct interference in their 'own' space, affecting their national and regional interests (ICG 2012; Kohl 2013). Just to give a brief indication: the Nigerian leadership saw its regional hegemonic aspirations threatened. President Ouattara of Côte d'Ivoire still remembered that the Angolans had supported his opponent, then-President Gbagbo, in the violent clashes following the 2010 elections (cf. ICG 2012; Kohl 2013). Last, the Senegalese government, on the one hand, was concerned over the implications for its fight to end conflict in the Casamance. On the other, it opposed Angolan business activities around bauxite mining, aiming to build a deep-water port in Guinea-Bissau's Buba and a railway linking it to Bamako. These infrastructure projects would have posed a direct threat to Senegalese economic interests, potentially disrupting, changing and thus re-spatializing sub-regional economic flows and power relations (e.g., diverting trade from the port of Dakar).[33]

What is interesting is how West African heads of state and foreign ministers framed their response to the 'external intrusion' by the Angolans, coming 'all the way' from Southern Africa and projecting their power way beyond their 'own' regional space.[34] First, they framed their response in regional terms, mobilizing 'ECOWAS', before they turned to the African Union, arguing that 'CPLP' was not part of 'APSA'. Since APSA had to be applied, it was for ECOWAS to deal with the situation in Guinea-Bissau and, consequently, the Angolan mission had to leave. Eventually, AU actors concurred with that position and Angolan troops had to withdraw.[35] The ECOWAS Authority quickly sent in ECOMIB to replace MISSANG, with troops from Nigeria, Senegal, Burkina Faso and Togo, and without waiting for approval or a mandate either from the AU Peace and Security Council or from the UN Security Council. While this move meant to manage conflict in Guinea-Bissau, it also aimed to pre-empt a more multilateral CPLP deployment, under consideration at the time (IRIN 2012; Security Council Report 2012b).

These considerations show how different actors, on the one hand, have imagined what they believe to be their space of influence and have taken action to assert it. On the other, it shows how they have used spatial references to enable and justify their actions, and to pursue specific interests and agendas.

'Subsidiarity' and the spatial ordering of African Peace and Security

In a similar manner, although this time 'within' APSA, ECOWAS actors have tried to fend off a more dominant AU involvement in conflicts in West Africa – once more arguing spatially, emphasizing 'proximity'. Since the West African organization was much 'closer' to conflicts in the region, with a much more intimate understanding of them (e.g., regarding society, culture and politics), ECOWAS as an organization was best positioned to be in charge of interventions in that space. Moreover, since ECOWAS member states were the first to feel the consequences of conflict, they should be leading responses. 'The AU', on the other hand, was 'far away' in Addis Ababa and should therefore rather take charge of conflicts in Eastern Africa, or in other regions that did not have ROs boasting as much capacity as ECOWAS.[36]

Up to this point, spatial de/legitimization in this story works very similarly to what I have described above concerning the ECOWAS–CPLP relationship. What makes it different, though, is the nesting of the regional spaces of ECOWAS and the AU respectively, as well as their formal inclusion and position in the ongoing process of constructing and, as I argue here, contesting of a spatial order of 'global' and 'continental peace and security' (often referred to as 'security architecture'; cf. Döring 2018). This process and respective efforts by different actors have centered on the concept of 'subsidiarity'. The meaning and interpretation of this concept has been essentially contested, in simple terms boiling down to the question of 'who is in charge of what space' within APSA.

The clash of actors at ECOWAS and the AU, following the coup d'état in April 2012 in Guinea-Bissau, illustrates this point. While in principle the stated positions of the AU and ECOWAS on the issue of UCG are not that different – basic documents of both organizations contain similar formulations and provisions – during the 2012 conflict in Guinea-Bissau a struggle over different interpretations and proper application led to serious tensions between the two African regional organizations. After an initial consensus, widely shared among international actors, which rejected any authority emanating from the coup, ECOWAS heads of state decided to break out of it, entering into negotiations with the self-appointed 'military command', thereby *de facto* legitimizing it (see Chapter 1). This largely pragmatic move, seeking to contain the situation, allowed ECOWAS representatives to renegotiate the transition agreement proposed by the 'military command' and to exert pressure on the coup-makers to accept the deployment of the ECOWAS Standby Force to Guinea-Bissau (ECOMIB). According to this deal, a transition authority was appointed, which for ECOWAS meant that 'constitutional order' was restored. The AU PSC, however, did not concur. While acknowledging ECOWAS' efforts to deal with the situation in Guinea-Bissau in principle, it did not recognize the transition authorities and kept Guinea-Bissau suspended until the elections in 2014 (see Chapter 5). This position upset ECOWAS leaders at least for two reasons. First, in line with the informal AU PSC rules, they were expecting AU actors to support whatever decision they took, since Guinea-Bissau was part of the West African region (see Chapter 3). Second, the AU's position further complicated ECOWAS' efforts to mobilize diplomatic and financial support for the transition in Guinea-Bissau as well as for ECOMIB (see Chapter 4).

Therefore, competing views of how the relationship between ECOWAS and the AU should be organized have repeatedly clashed during conflicts in West Africa – a relationship that both in principle agree to be structured around the concept of 'subsidiarity'. While it is generally agreed that ECOWAS, as the officially recognized West African REC and pillar of APSA, should be the first responder when it comes to dealing with regional conflict, what this should actually mean is much less consensual (cf. Momodu 2017; Desmidt and Hauck 2017; Döring and Herpolsheimer 2018). In Guinea-Bissau, as in various other conflict situations (e.g., in Côte d'Ivoire in 2010/11 and in Mali in 2012/13), it has become apparent that roles and relationships between RECs and the AU are continuously contested and renegotiated, despite more recent efforts to clarify and regulate their interactions. Thus, ECOWAS actors tried to assert their 'subsidiary' role as REC within APSA, leading the process in Guinea-Bissau because they saw themselves as better positioned to act (i.e., being 'closer'). AU actors, on their part, interpreted that role differently, trying to maintain and exert control over specific interpretations and coherent implementation of AU core principles linked to its UCG policy. This put both organizations into difficult positions. On the one hand, as already mentioned, it blocked financial support that actors at ECOWAS needed. On the other, actors at the AU ran the risk of further alienating ECOWAS as a powerful bloc within the AU.[37]

What is important to highlight, once more, is that, beyond a contestation of competences, the struggle between actors at ECOWAS and the AU needs to be understood as a struggle over the spatial organization of APSA – opposing an imagination of nested hierarchical scales with one of complementary blocs. Whereas the former positions the AU PSC at the very top of APSA, authorizing and directing actions taken by the RECs, the latter imagination identifies the ECOWAS security organs and mechanisms as *APSA in West Africa*, making decisions and taking action as they see fit. AU actors may – or, in fact, should – support these decisions and actions.[38] In this regard, the respective claims by ECOWAS and AU actors about what space they are in charge of (formally or *de facto*) are also tied to certain symbolic and material resources. Just to give one example, actors at the EU support the idea of a hierarchical organization of spatial scales within APSA, with the AU at its top and the RECs below. This has also translated into specific funding logics of EU support to the African Peace and Security Architecture, which I now turn to in the following section.

EU roles in constructing spatial order(s) in and beyond West Africa

As has become clear, interventions in West/Africa can hardly be understood without taking into account 'external' actors and interests. Most important in this regard have been EU actors, who have intervened in West/Africa, among other objectives pursuing specific security agendas (cf. Gegout 2017), but also to develop and consolidate their own regional policies and regional space (see Chapter 5). Consequently, it is important also to consider how EU actors have contributed to spatial ordering in West/Africa.

First, EU actors have ordered space, in West/Africa and elsewhere, through different funding instruments, which in addition to thematic logics (e.g.,

Instrument contributing to Stability and Peace, IcSP, or European Instrument for Democracy and Human Rights, EIDHR) also follow spatial, especially regional, logics. Much of the money of the European Development Fund (EDF) is dedicated to different regional indicative programs (RIPs), which include regions such as 'West Africa', but also, for example, the 'ACP', and the 'African Countries with Portuguese as an Official Language' (going by the Portuguese acronym PALOP). Guinea-Bissau, for example, has received EU money through the RIPs of all of the above, at some point.[39] Some of these RIPs have dedicated regional organizations administering their implementation. For West Africa, this has been ECOWAS and UEMOA[40] (cf. EU Commission 2015), exerting influence although not necessarily control over continuously increasing RIP budgets (cf. Piccolino and Minou 2014, 12–13), for the period 2014–20 amounting to 1.15 billion euros (cf. ECOWAS, EU and UEMOA 2014). These have included equally increasing EU support specifically to ECOWAS as an organization, building capacity at the ECOWAS Commission and supporting specific policy projects (e.g., anti-drug trafficking; see below).[41] In this way, actors at the EU directly contribute to constructing both ECOWAS as an organization and a regional space – according to a particular vision of what 'ECOWAS' should be and do, as discussed below.

At the same time that EU actors have sought to increase ECOWAS' capacity directly, and increase its ability as a regional security actor, however, they have also supported a hierarchical vision of the spatial organization of African Peace and Security (i.e., APSA, and its 'geography'; cf. Döring 2018). According to this vision, the AU (specifically the AU PSC) stands at the top, in charge of its subsidiary, sub-regional organizations and mechanisms (i.e., the RECs and Regional Mechanisms). In this regard, it has been especially the African Peace Facility (APF), also coming out of the EDF, which has funded peace support operations by African organizations, supporting the hierarchical APSA geography, and thereby affecting power relations between the RECs and the AU in favor of the latter. According to the APF rules and procedures, the AU has a certain budget that it can use as it sees fit (although EU officers still have to sign off) and that it can also forward to the RECs (e.g., for peace operations). In addition, RECs can apply directly for APF funds. However, the AU leadership has to endorse those applications.[42] In both cases, these rules and procedures strengthen AU actors as gatekeepers vis-à-vis the RECs (cf. EU Commission 2017).[43] What becomes clear at this point is that the EU's approaches to supporting African ROs and APSA have not always been coherent and coordinated.

Second, supporting the West African RO prominently and directly, EU actors have carried a particular imagination of ECOWAS – what it should be and do, covering the space of 'West Africa', and how it should relate to other spaces. This has become clearly visible in the case of Guinea-Bissau, in the clash between ECOWAS and EU actors after the coup in April 2012 (see Chapter 1), and more recently, with inverted roles since 2015. In 2012, the EU's previous, failed SSR experience in Guinea-Bissau led EU actors to respond to the coup d'état extraordinarily swiftly, suspending all support involving government institutions, very much unlike previous reactions to similar situations in the country (cf. Döring and Herpolsheimer 2016). Consequently, they were upset when ECOWAS decided to break out of the initial international consensus, openly criticizing the move (ICG 2012; Kohl 2013), and refused to support ECOWAS and ECOMIB financially through the APF. Interestingly, since 2015, EU actors (along with other international actors) have continued to push for a continuation of the mission, offering financial support, while actors at ECOWAS have seemed more and more determined to withdraw (see Chapter 4). Following the clash between the two organizations in 2012, it has been the need for a regional partner to address the situation in Mali and the Sahel that has persuaded EU actors to soften their opposition to ECOWAS' approach in Guinea-Bissau, eventually (see ICG 2012; Kohl 2013; Security Council Report 2012a, 9).

Another strategy that EU actors have applied when their imagination of 'ECOWAS' has not been met in reality – complementing the carrots-and-sticks approach – has been the 'sub-contracting' of different implementing agencies, such as, for example, the German Corporation for International Cooperation (GIZ) or the UN Office on Drugs and Crime (UNODC). In both cases, the EU Commission and/or EU member states have spent large amounts of money either to develop ECOWAS norms and capacities according to the EU's vision (e.g., as in the Support Program for the ECOWAS Commission, implemented by the GIZ; cf. GIZ 2019) or to have someone else do the job 'for' ECOWAS, maintaining the 'ECOWAS' label. For example, the latter has been the case with the ECOWAS Support Project implemented by UNODC, also known as "Support to ECOWAS Regional Action Plan on illicit drug trafficking, organized crime related to it and drug abuse in West Africa" (UNODC 2019). In both cases, framing their activities as 'regional' and tying them to 'ECOWAS' has allowed the two organizations to access significant amounts of funding.[44]

Conclusion

While actors at ECOWAS and the AU, as well as other regional actors, have tried in one way or another to manage different conflict situations – i.e., playing a role in and for those conflicts (Chapters 3 and 4) – those conflicts have also played a role for actors at ECOWAS, the AU and others. The latter has been to the extent that involvement in different conflict situations has simultaneously contributed to developing and consolidating specific regional policies (see Chapter 5). However, during conflict interventions, ECOWAS and AU actors have also tried to position themselves towards and contest their relation with other intervening actors. Therefore, this chapter has analyzed, first, how ECOWAS and AU actors have strategically engaged each other as well as other regional and international actors in order to manage conflict (e.g., coordinating, harmonizing approaches and mobilizing resources), which constitutes a consistent intervention practice employed both 'from afar' and 'on the ground'. Second, the chapter has analyzed how, at the same time, ECOWAS and AU actors have aimed to contest and negotiate their relations with other intervening actors, thereby engaging in the ordering *by* and *of* space.

In this regard, it is important to highlight that conflict interventions constitute key moments of dense social interaction at different sites, which relate to space in two interrelated ways. On the one hand, actors frequently use 'space' as an argument to achieve specific objectives, for example, claiming responsibility, competence and legitimacy, as well as de-legitimizing other actors and organizing relations among them in specific ways (i.e., ordering *by* space). On the other hand, and in practice hard to disentangle from the first, the ordering *of* space as such has also been an objective pursued by actors at ECOWAS, the AU and others during conflict interventions. In that regard, for example, the concept of 'subsidiarity', shared among the different organizations in principle, has been continuously contested and renegotiated, pitting different understandings and interpretations against each other (i.e., complementary versus hierarchical), which link to different imaginations about who should be in charge of what space and how those should relate to one another.

What becomes apparent in the above, summing up the central argument in this book, is that a spatial perspective allows us to discern and relate the different dimensions, multiple and entangled actors, sites and practices of conflict intervention by African ROs to one another. All of these contribute to the construction, formatting and ordering of regional spaces. As the seemingly 'marginal' example of Guinea-Bissau shows, the spatial perspective allows us to make sense of the conjuncture and sometimes clash of various actors in one particular conflict situation, not only pointing to different spatial imaginations and regional policy processes (see Chapter 5), but also to political projects that use 'space' for specific goals and/or actively try to order spaces. Shedding light on these dynamics complements and enhances the understanding of the role of regional organizations and their agendas in African and global peace and security dynamics.

Notes

1 I use single quotation marks to raise awareness that these terms are markers that different actors, including me as a researcher, use for different reasons and towards specific objectives, often to distinguish binary opposites (e.g., 'internal' versus 'external'; 'technical' versus 'political'). As such they are part of different discourses, knowledge–power relations and subject to socio-political contestation.

2 In addition, much of the conflict knowledge produced by ECOWAS and the AU is actually shared and co-produced by these two organizations, the UN and EU, but also different think tanks (e.g., ISS, ACCORD) (see Chapter 3).

3 Rules for such participation vary, also in how strictly they apply, and are subject to ongoing discussion. For example, ECOWAS organizational representation and participation in the AU PSC is a contested subject (cf. Interview 149, ECOWAS Officer, Addis Ababa, 28 September 2018; see also Dersso 2013).

4 Cf. Interview 149, ECOWAS Officer, Addis Ababa, 28 September 2018; Interview 163, Senior ECOWAS Officer, Department Gender and Social Affairs, Abuja, 29 October 2018.

5 Cf. Interview 149, ECOWAS Officer, Addis Ababa, 28 September 2018.

6 For more detail about their roles in the UNSC, see www.securitycouncilreport.org/guinea-bissau/page/1 (accessed 17 May 2019).

7 In addition, although difficult to account for, personal, informal meetings between representatives of different organizations, at their headquarters or at the margins of other, unrelated events (e.g., at the UN General Assembly), have also played a role. Examples in this regard include meetings of the ECOWAS MSC Chairman with the Chairman of the CPLP Council of Ministers, in September 2012 in New York, and with the Portuguese Foreign Affairs Minister, in October 2012 in Lisbon (ECOWAS MSC 2012a, para. 7), and a joint trip of the AU and UN special representatives in Bissau to Abuja, in August 2012 (ECOWAS Commission President 2012, para. 10).

8 Remarkably, the PSC also expressed its gratitude to Angola and MISSANG on two occasions (AU PSC 2012c, para. 8, 2012b, para. 4) (see also "Contesting relations, ordering by and of space").

9 Sometimes this has been in the indirect form of 'internal instructions', requesting the AUC Chairperson to engage, "initiate consultations with", "bring together" or act "in consultation" or "close cooperation with" ECOWAS, the CPLP, UN and other AU partners (e.g., AU PSC 2012c, para. 6 and 8–9, 2012a, para. 8 and 10–11, 2012d).

10 Cf. Interview 3, Diplomatic Source, Addis Ababa, 8 September 2016; Interview 7, AU Officer, Peace and Security Department, Addis Ababa, 14 September 2016; Interview 31, Senior ECOWAS Officer, Department for Political Affairs, Peace and Security, Abuja, 20 February 2017; Interview 43, ECOWAS Officer, Department for Political Affairs, Peace and Security, Abuja, 28 February 2017.

11 A similar initiative had emerged already in 2008, when it was suggested to establish a "local ICG-GB" in Bissau, in 2008 (cf. ECOWAS Commission 2008).

12 The CPLP Council of Ministers decided to appoint a special representative in July 2013; the OIF did not follow up (cf. CPLP 2014).

13 The donors' roundtable eventually took place in Brussels, in March 2015, and resulted in pledges amounting to roughly 1.2 billion euros (cf. Reuters 2015). However, due to the new crisis that started in August 2015, these pledges were never redeemed.

14 Cf. Interview 23, Senior ECOWAS Official, Ouagadougou, 29 January 2017; Interview 68; Senior AU Official, Bissau, 7 April 2017.

15 Cf. Interview 126, EU Officer, EU External Action Service, Brussels, 6 June 2018.

16 Cf. Interview 62, AU Officer, Bissau, 5 April 2017; Interview 80, Portuguese Source, Bissau, 12 April 2017; Interview 59, Senior EU Officer, Bissau, 4 April 2017.

17 Cf. Interview 7, AU Officer, Peace and Security Department, Addis Ababa, 14 September 2016; Interview 126, EU Officer, EU External Action Service, Brussels, 6 June 2018.

18 Cf. Interview 64, Senior ECOWAS Official, Bissau, 6 April 2017; Interview 78, Senior UN Official, UNIOGBIS, Bissau 12 April 2017.

19 Cf. Interview 2, Senior AU Official, Addis Ababa, 7 September 2016.

20 Cf. Interview 7, AU Officer, Peace and Security Department, Addis Ababa, 14 September 2016.

21 Cf. Interview 59, Senior EU Officer, Bissau, 4 April 2017.

22 As with previous ECOWAS documents (e.g., the DSSR Road Map of 2010, and the DSSR MoU of 2012), UNIOGBIS staff were instrumental in the drafting process, and also provided logistical support to the meetings in Bissau and Conakry (cf. Interview 79, Senior UN Officer, UNIOGBIS, Bissau, 12 April 2017).

23 Cf. Interview 80, Portuguese Source, Bissau, 12 April 2017.

24 Cf. Interview 59, Senior EU Officer, Bissau, 4 April 2017; Interview 80, Portuguese Source, Bissau, 12 April 2017.

25 Cf. Interview 59, Senior EU Officer, Bissau, 4 April 2017; Interview 79, Senior UN Officer, UNIOGBIS, Bissau, 12 April 2017.

26 Cf. Interview 72, Senior Representative of the Instituto Nacional de Estudos e Pesquisa of Guinea-Bissau, Bissau, 8 April 2017.

27 Cf. Interview 59, Senior EU Officer, Bissau, 4 April 2017.

28 However, the mission flopped. The ECOWAS military presence was unable to prevent a coup and moved out of the country only four months after deployment (for details, e.g., see Adebajo 2002; Kabia 2009).

29 For a more detailed overview of security cooperation in the CPLP, see Herpolsheimer (2014), and of its political economy as a regional security organization, see Herpolsheimer (2019).

30 On the Brazilian involvement in Guinea-Bissau, see Abdenur and Souza Neto (2014).

31 The Angolan government was perceived by many as protecting its own economic interests in Guinea-Bissau and projecting its power to West Africa. Moreover, military elites also feared that Prime Minister Gomes Junior intended to use MISSANG in order to get rid of unwanted elements in the military (ICG 2012; Kohl 2013; O'Regan and Thompson 2013; Abdenur and Souza Neto 2014). The fact that Brazil also deployed a technical-military mission to build capacities in Guinea-Bissau (April 2014), framed in CPLP terms, has received much less attention so far (Herpolsheimer 2014, 54).

32 Interview 6, Senior AU Officer, Peace and Security Department, Addis Ababa, 14 September 2016.

33 Cf. Interview 55, Senior UN Officer, UNIOGBIS, Bissau, 30 March 2017.

34 Cf. Interview 6, Senior AU Officer, Peace and Security Department, Addis Ababa, 14 September 2016.

35 Cf. Interview 6, Senior AU Officer, Peace and Security Department, Addis Ababa, 14 September 2016.

36 E.g., cf. Interview 28, Senior ECOWAS Officer, Department for Political Affairs, Peace and Security, Abuja, 16 February 2017; Interview 31, Senior ECOWAS Officer, Department for Political Affairs, Peace and Security, Abuja, 20 February 2017; Interview 13, Senior AU Officer, Peace and Security Department, Addis Ababa, 21 September 2016.

37 Interview 6, Senior AU Officer, Peace and Security Department, Addis Ababa, 14 September 2016.

38 Cf. Interview 6, Senior AU Officer, Peace and Security Department, Addis Ababa, 14 September 2016; Interview 22, Senior ECOWAS Official, Addis Ababa, 26 September 2016.

39 For an overview of EU projects funded through different RIPs, see https://ec.europa.eu/europeaid/search/site/Guinea-Bissau_en (accessed 20 May 2019).

40 UEMOA – West African Economic and Monetary Union. UEMOA comprises the Francophone member states of ECOWAS and Guinea-Bissau.

41 The EU's support to ECOWAS has been in line with its more general policy of inter-regionalism (e.g., cf. Söderbaum and van Langenhove 2005; Baert, Scaramagli and Söderbaum 2014). In pursuit of these policies, different EU actors seek to actively influence and contribute to the construction of other regionalisms, according to changing EU interests or objectives (e.g., cf. Santander 2005).

42 Cf. Interview 120, Senior EU Officer, DG DEVCO, Brussels, 4 June 2018.

43 Among EU staff, personal preferences vary, seeing either the AU or ECOWAS as more competent, able and effective, especially when it comes to African Peace and Security.

44 At the same time, actors at the EU have also pursued alternative strategies, creating new spatial frames in the process. In that regard, the EU's cocaine route program provides an interesting example (e.g., cf. Dietrich 2016).

References

Abdenur, Adriana E. and Danilo M. de Souza Neto. 2014. Rising Powers and The Security–Development Nexus: Brazil's Engagement with Guinea-Bissau. *Journal of Peacebuilding & Development* 9 (2): 1–16. doi: 10.1080/15423166.2014.950118.

Adebajo, Adekeye. 2002. *Building Peace in West Africa: Liberia, Sierra Leone, and Guinea-Bissau.* Boulder, CO: Lynne Rienner.

ARB. 2010. *Political, Social and Cultural Series* Vol. 47, No. 8, August, pp. 18495–18529.

AU. 2002. "Protocol Relating to the Establishment of the Peace and Security Council of the African Union", 1st Ordinary Session of the Assembly of the African Union, Durban, 9 July 2002.

———. 2013. "Report of the Joint ECOWAS/AU/CPLP/EU/UN Assessment Mission to Guinea-Bissau", 23 March 2013. Accessed 15 June 2019. www.peaceau.org/en/article/report-of-the-joint-ecowas-au-cplp-eu-un-assessment-mission-to-guinea-bissau.

AU, ECOWAS, CPLP and OIF, EU, UN. 2014. "Rapport de la 3ème Mission Conjointe d'Évaluation UA/CEDEAO/CPLP/OIF/UE/UN en Guinée-Bissau".

AU, ECOWAS, EU, African Security Sector Network and UN. 2015. "Report of the Joint Security Sectory Reform (SSR) Assessment Mission to Guinea-Bissau", 2–12 March 2015.

AU Commission. 2014. "Rapport Final: Mission d'Obsérvation Électorale de l'Union Africaine pour les Élections Générales du 13 avril 2014 et le Second tour de l'Élection Présidentielle du 18 mai 2014 en République de Guinée-Bissau", June 2014.

AU PSC. 2012a. "Communiqé (PSC/MIN/COMM/1. (CCCXIX))", 319th Meeting, Addis Ababa, 24 April 2012.

———. 2012b. "Communiqué (PSC/AHG/COMM.3[CCCXXVII])", 327th Meeting at the level of Heads of State and Government, Addis Ababa, 14 July 2012.

———. 2012c. "Communiqué (PSC/PR/COMM[CCCXVIII])", 318th Meeting, Addis Ababa, 17 April 2012.

———. 2012d. "Press Statement (PSC/PR/BR.2[CCCXL])", 340th Meeting, Addis Ababa, 2 November 2012.

———. 2013a. "Communiqué (PSC/PR/COMM.[CCCLXI])", 361st Meeting, Addis Ababa, 22 March 2013.

———. 2013b. "Communiqué (PSC/PR/COMM[CCCLI])", 351st Meeting, Addis Ababa, 16 January 2013.

———. 2014. "Report of the Peace and Security Council on its Activities and the State of Peace and Security in Africa (Assembly/AU/4[XXII]a)", AU Assembly, Addis Ababa, 30–31 January 2014.

Autesserre, Séverine. 2014. *Peaceland: Conflict Resolution and the Everyday Politics of International Intervention.* Cambridge: Cambridge University Press.

Baert, Francis, Tiziana Scaramagli and Fredrik Söderbaum, eds. 2014. *Intersecting Interregionalism: Regions, Global Governance and the EU.* The Netherlands: Springer.

CPLP. 2014. "Representante Especial da CPLP para a Guiné-Bissau", Nota informativa, Lisbon, 7 January 2014. Accessed 16 May 2019. www.cplp.org/id-4447.aspx?Action=1&NewsId=3078&currentPage=34&M=NewsV2&PID=10872.

Dersso, Solomon A. 2013. *Annual Review of the Peace and Security Council 2012/2013.* Pretoria: Institute for Security Studies (ISS).

Desmidt, Sophie, and Volker Hauck. 2017. *Conflict Management Under the African Peace and Security Architecture (APSA).* Discussion Paper 211. Maastrich: ECDPM.

Dietrich, Nicholas. 2016. Navigating Sovereign Territoriality: The Logic of Regionalism in International Police Cooperation. In *The New Politics of Regionalism: Perspectives from Africa, Latin America and Asia-Pacific*, eds Ulf Engel, Heidrun Zinecker, Frank Mattheis, Antje Dietze and Thomas Plötze, 175–89. Abingdon, New York: Routledge.

Döring, Katharina P.W. 2018. The Changing ASF Geography: From the Intervention Experience in Mali to the African Capacity for Immediate Response to Crises and the Nouakchott Process. *African Security* 11 (1): 32–58. doi: 10.1080/19392206.2017.1419632.

———. 2019. Making Room for War: The Spatialization of African Security Politics in the Quest for African-led Military Deployment. Unpublished doctoral thesis, Leipzig University.

Döring, Katharina P.W. and Jens Herpolsheimer. 2016. *"New Regionalisms" and Violent Conflicts in Africa: The Politics of the AU and ECOWAS in Mali and Guinea-Bissau.* SFB 1199 Working Paper Series 5. Leipzig: Leipziger Universitätsverlag.

———. 2018. The Spaces of Intervention for Mali and Guinea-Bissau. *South African Journal of International Affairs* 25 (1): 61–82. doi: 10.1080/10220461.2018.1417898.

ECOWAS, EU and UEMOA. 2014. European Union – West Africa: Regional Indicative Programme 2014–2020. Accessed 18 September 2020. https://ec.europa.eu/international-partnerships/system/files/eeas-2015-rip-west-africa_en.pdf.

ECOWAS Authority. 2012a. "Final Communiqué", 41st Ordinary Session of the Authority of Heads of State and Government, Yamoussoukro, 28–29 June 2012.

———. 2012b. "Final Communiqué", Extraordinary Session of the Authority of ECOWAS Heads of State and Government, Abuja, 11 November 2012.

———. 2012c. "Final Communiqué", Extraordinary Summit of ECOWAS Heads of State and Government, Abuja, 26 April 2012.

———. 2012d. "Final Communiqué", Extraordinary Summit of ECOWAS Heads of State and Government, Dakar, 3 May 2012.

———. 2013. "Final Communiqué", Extraordinary Session of the Authority of ECOWAS Heads of State and Government, Abidjan, 19 January 2013.

ECOWAS CCDS. 2012. "Final Report", Extraordinary Meeting of the Committee of ECOWAS Chiefs of Defence Staff (CCDS), Bamako, 13–15 August 2012.

ECOWAS Commission. 2008. "Press Release: International Contact Group Calls for Mechanism for Law Enforcement in Guinea-Bissau (N°:037/2008)", 7 May 2008.

———. 2012a. "Press Release: ECOWAS Leaders to Meet in Abidjan on Guinea Bissau, Mali Crises (N°:117/2012)", Abidjan, 25 April 2012.

———. 2012b. "Statement on Guinea-Bissau", 340th Meeting of the AU Peace and Security Council at the Ministerial Level, Addis Ababa, 2 November 2012.

———. 2014a. "Preliminary Declaration: Guinea Bissau 2014 Run-Off Presidential Election (N°: 091/2014)", Abuja, 19 May 2014.

———. 2014b. "Press Release: Heads of Election Observation Missions Appeal for Peaceful Run-Off Polls in Guinea-Bissau (N°: 089/2014)", Bissau, 17 May 2014.

ECOWAS Commission President. 2012. "Memorandum on the Situation in Guinea Bissau", Extraordinary Meeting of the Mediation and Security Council, Abuja, 9 November 2012.

———. 2015. "Memorandum on the Situation of the ECOWAS Mission in Guinea Bissau (ECOMIB)", 34th Ordinary Session of the Mediation and Security Council, Accra, May 2015.

ECOWAS Council of Ministers and EU Council. 2013. "Final Communiqué", 19th EU-ECOWAS Political Dialogue Meeting at Ministerial Level, Brussels, 16 May 2013. Accessed 17 May 2019. https://eeas.europa.eu/headquarters/headquarters-homepage/3992/node/3992_sv.

———. 2017. "Joint Communiqué", 21st ECOWAS-EU Political Dialogue Ministerial Meeting, Brussels, 4 April 2017. Accessed 17 May 2019. https://eeas.europa.eu/topics/maritime-security/24202/21st-ecowas-eu-political-dialogue-ministerial-meeting_en.

———. 2018. "Joint Statement", 22nd ECOWAS-EU Political Dialogue Meeting, Abuja, 30 November 2018. https://eeas.europa.eu/headquarters/headquarters-homepage/54800/22nd-ecowas-eu-political-dialogue-meeting_en.

ECOWAS MSC. 2012a. "Final Report", Extraordinary Session of the ECOWAS Mediation and Security Council, Abuja, 9 November 2012.

———. 2012b. "Report on the Political and Security Situations in Guinea Bissau and Mali", Extraordinary Session of Mediation and Security Council, Abidjan, 19 May 2012.

———. 2013a. "Final Report", Extraordinary Session of the Mediation and Security Council, Abidjan, 25 February 2013.

———. 2013b. "Report", 30th Meeting of the Mediation and Security Council, Abuja, 15 July 2013.

Engel, Ulf. 2018. Knowledge Production on Conflict Early Warning at the African Union. *South African Journal of International Affairs* 25 (1): 117–32. doi: 10.1080/10220461.2018.1417902.

EU Commission. 2015. European Union – West Africa Regional Indicative Programme 2014–2020. Accessed 19 January 2017. https://ec.europa.eu/europeaid/sites/devco/files/eeas-2015-rip-west-africa_en.pdf.

———. 2017. African Peace Facility. Accessed 19 January 2017. http://ec.europa.eu/europeaid/regions/africa/continental-cooperation/african-peace-facility_en.

Gegout, Catherine. 2017. *Why Europe Intervenes in Africa: Security, Prestige and the Legacy of Colonialism.* London: Hurst.

GIZ. 2019. Support Programme for the ECOWAS Commission. Accessed 23 May 2019. https://www.giz.de/en/worldwide/20759.html.

Herpolsheimer, Jens. 2014. Security Cooperation in the Community of Portuguese-Speaking Countries (CPLP). Unpublished master's thesis, Leipzig University.

———. 2019. The Finances of the Community of Portuguese-Speaking Countries (CPLP). In *The Finances of Regional Organisations in the Global South: Follow the Money*, eds Ulf Engel and Frank Mattheis, 35–50. Abingdon: Routledge.

ICG. 2012. *Beyond Turf Wars: Managing the Post-Coup Transition in Guinea-Bissau.* Africa Report 190 (17 August). Brussels: International Crisis Group.

IRIN. 2012. Division and Stasis in Guinea-Bissau (18 May). Accessed 2 May 2016. http://www.irinnews.org/report/95483/analysis-division-and-stasis-guinea-bissau.

Kabia, John M. 2009. *Humanitarian Intervention and Conflict Resolution in West Africa: From ECOMOG to ECOMIL.* Burlington, VA: Ashgate.

Kohl, Christoph. 2013. *Irrwege und Auswege: Guinea-Bissau nach dem Putsch im April 2012.* HSFK Standpunkte 1/2013. Frankfurt am Main: Hessische Stiftung Friedens- und Konfliktforschung.

MacQueen, Norrie. 2003. A Community of Illusions? Portugal, the CPLP and Peacemaking in Guiné-Bissau. *International Peacekeeping* 10 (2): 1–26. doi: 10.1080/714002450.

Momodu, Raheemat. 2017. *African Integration: Resetting the AU-REC Relationship – Policy Options Beyond the Kagame Reform.* APN Briefing Note 14. New York: African Peacebuilding Network, Social Science Research Council.

O'Regan, Davin and Peter Thompson. 2013. *Advancing Stability and Reconciliation in Guinea-Bissau: Lessons from Africa's First Narco State.* Washington, DC: Africa Center for Strategic Studies.

Piccolino, Giulia and Stephanie Minou. 2014. *The EU and Regional Integration in West Africa: Effects on Conflict Resolution and Transformation.* RegioConf Working Paper 5. Pretoria: University of Pretoria.

Reuters. 2015. Donors Pledge More than One Billion Euros for Guinea-Bissau, 25 March 2015. Accessed 16 May 2019. https://uk.reuters.com/article/uk-bissau-economy-donors/donors-pledge-more-than-one-billion-euros-for-guinea-bissau-idUKKBN0ML2CK20150325.

Santander, Sebastian. 2005. The European Partnership with Mercosur: A Relationship Based on Strategic and Neo-liberal Principles. *Journal of European Integration* 27 (3): 285–306. doi: 10.1080/07036330500190156.

Security Council Report. 2012a. December 2012 Monthly Forecast: Guinea-Bissau. Accessed 20 June 2017. www.securitycouncilreport.org/monthly-forecast/2012-12/guinea-bissau_1.php.

———. 2012b. Update Report on Guinea-Bissau (4 May). Accessed 15 August 2014. www.securitycouncilreport.org/update-report/lookup-c-glKWLeMTIsG-b-8079461.php.

———. 2018. *The Penholder System.* Research Report 3. New York: Security Council Report.

Söderbaum, Fredrik. 2016. *Rethinking Regionalism.* London, New York: Palgrave.

Söderbaum, Fredrik and Luk van Langenhove. 2005. Introduction: The EU as a Global Actor and the Role of Interregionalism. *Journal of European Integration* 27 (3): 249–62. doi: 10.1080/07036330500190073.

Tieku, Thomas K. and Tanzeel F. Hakak. 2014. A Curious Case of Hybrid Paternalism: Conceptualizing the Relationship Between the UN and AU on Peace and Security. *African Conflict and Peacebuilding Review* 4 (2): 129. doi: 10.2979/africonfpeacrevi.4.2.129.

UNIOGBIS. 2013. "Press Release: SRSG Returns from Mission to Nigeria and Côte d'Ivoire", Bissau, 13 September 2013.

———. 2014a. "Press Release: No Funding Gap for Elections", Bissau, 19 March 2014.

———. 2014b. "Press Release: Presence of International Partners is Dissuasive-SRSG Ramos-Horta", Bissau, 15 April 2014.

———. 2014c. "Press Release: Presidential Elections – 2nd Round: Free, Transparent and Fair – International Community", Bissau, 20 May 2014.

———. 2014d. "Press Release: SRSG & AU Representative Meet President Nhamajo", Bissau, 27 January 2014.

UNODC. 2019. ECOWAS Support Project. Accessed 14 November 2017. www.unodc.org/westandcentralafrica/en/newrosenwebsite/ecowasproject.html.

UNSG. 2013. "Report of the Secretary-General on the Restoration of Constitutional Order in Guinea-Bissau (S/2013/499)", New York, 21 August 2013.

Welz, Martin. 2016. Multi-Actor Peace Operations and Inter-Organizational Relations: Insights from the Central African Republic. *International Peacekeeping* 23 (4): 568–91. doi: 10.1080/13533312.2016.1178070.

———. 2018. Cooperation and Competition: United Nations-African Union Relations. In *Inter-Organisational Relations in International Security: Cooperation and Competition*, eds Stephen Aris, Aglaya Snetkov and Andreas Wenger, 54–70. London: Routledge.

Witt, Antonia. 2012. A Constructive Engagement? The European Union's Contributions to Mediating Coups d'Etat in Africa. In *New Mediation Practices in African Conflicts*, ed. Ulf Engel, 211–36. Leipzig: Leipziger Universitätsverlag.

———. 2013. Convergence on Whose Terms? Reacting to Coups d'État in Guinea and Madagascar. *African Security* 6 (3–4): 257–75. doi: 10.1080/19392206.2013.854113.

———. 2020. *Undoing Coups: The African Union and Post-Coup Intervention in Madagascar*. London: Zed Books.

7 Conclusion

Spatializing the study of African Peace and Security

Introduction

In this book, I have proposed a spatial approach to the study of African Peace and Security, combining insights from innovative approaches in International Relations (IR), International Studies and Global Studies with advances in Critical Geography. Adopting space – understood as socially constructed, relational and topological – as a central analytical category offers new empirical and theoretical perspectives on intervention practices of African regional organizations (ROs), which have been intimately tied to space-making – thereby simultaneously becoming spatializing practices. Specifically, applying this approach to ECOWAS and the AU, this book has shown that their intervention practices and 'internal' modes of operation have been diverse and interrelated, involving different actors 'within' and 'around' these and different interconnected sites. At the same time, these practices have contributed to the continuous construction, formatting and ordering of regional spaces.

The focus on concrete practices that contribute to the construction, formatting and ordering of regional spaces has allowed us to see beyond the labels commonly applied to intervention practices (e.g., 'early warning', 'mediation', 'post-conflict reconstruction and development') and to identify the concrete everyday practices underlying them, such as field visits, meetings and internal and external communication, which characterize and drive the 'internal' modes of operation of African ROs. These practices have been applied both 'on the ground' and 'from afar'. Moreover, conflict interventions have been triggered, framed and to some extent guided by particular spatial imaginations that have been tied to regional and trans-regional security concerns. Finally, beyond conflict management, actors at African ROs have simultaneously pursued other, more general objectives linked to specific spatial-political projects, linked to specific spatial imaginations. Of central importance in this regard has been to develop, establish and consolidate regional security policies (spatial formatting) as well as to contest and negotiate relations between different regional and international actors and related spaces – ordering *by* and *of* space (spatial ordering).

To conclude, this chapter summarizes the main tenets of the spatial approach proposed and applied in this book and briefly recaps the main findings. Finally, it reflects upon the book's key contributions to existing research and provides an outlook on further research on African Peace and Security from a spatial perspective.

A spatial approach to study African Peace and Security

One of the central arguments put forward in this book – following the main observation of the 'spatial turn' in the social sciences and humanities – has been that space matters and constitutes a central dimension of everyday social and political interaction. Consequently, only if space is taken into account as an analytical category is it possible to make sense of the complex processes at African ROs in the context of African peace and security dynamics.

To give direct and explicit attention to space, in this book, I have drawn on insights from Critical Geography, which have conceptualized space as *socially constructed*, resulting from continuous, open-ended social interactions and changing interrelations among different actors. Consequently, space is the temporary and always precarious outcome of multi-scalar, polycentric and intertwined processes, which are always political and often contested (Massey 2005, 9). Moreover, space is also a category of thought that allows people to make sense of the world around them, give meaning to it and act upon it. These thoughts and practices make up reality, which, in turn, impacts back on thoughts and practices (Werlen 2009, 286–7). Furthermore, saying that space is *relational* and *topological* means that, for example, 'proximity' (making presence felt) and 'distance' (placing beyond reach) are not absolute but produced by actors with the power to make the 'far near' and the 'near far' (Allen 2016, 2ff.). Chapter 2 of this book has discussed and explained this in more detail.

The 'spatial approach' presented in this book builds on three key concepts, namely 'space-making', 'spatial format' and 'spatial order'. As heuristic tools these direct attention to how different actors continuously contribute to the construction, formatting and ordering of social space, as part of everyday practices. *Space-making* refers to the ongoing, open-ended spatial organization of potentially all aspects of social life by different actors and practices, involving contestation, negotiation and unequal power relations. Influencing these processes but simultaneously resulting from them are spatial formats and spatial orders. *Spatial formats* are historically contingent, relatively stable lenses or patterns that enable actors to select, name, give meaning to and communicate specific spaces that are relevant to them. Therefore, spatial formats relate to specific material and/or discursive practices, and are tied to specific groups of actors, based on ideas about how to imagine, name, visualize and manage space (i.e., spatial formatting), as well as on ideas about what 'relevant' or 'appropriate' spatial formats are. *Spatial orders* both influence and result from such practices linked to different spatial formats. They emerge historically and relate different spatial formats to one another in specific ways, although this is achieved only temporarily and requires continuous maintenance; spatial orders are continually 'in the making'. Therefore, the processes, actors and practices need to be the main focus of research (i.e., spatial ordering).

In addition to these three key concepts, this book has utilized four supporting sensitizing tools that help to further focus academic attention and make space accessible in research. First, analyzing *spatial semantics* allows accessing particular spatial imaginations by looking at spatial terminology or references, used by different actors in different ways. Second, identifying *spatial actors* directs attention to the actual people that do the constructing, formatting and ordering of space. In that, third, they employ different *spatializing practices*, the analysis of which allows understanding and describing more concretely *how* things are done. Finally, fourth, this book has sought to identify the *sites* where intervention processes and dynamics unfold, and to understand how different sites of intervention are *connected* to one another.

While different aspects of space-making are often implicit in the existing literature on African Peace and Security, for example, with regard to 'state-building' and the implementation of regional security 'architectures', a new approach is required to capture these aspects and dynamics adequately. A spatial approach allows seeing and better understanding how particular spatial imaginations and framings have influenced conflict interventions and regional security policies, and how regions actually are being constructed, formatted and ordered during conflict interventions. African ROs and African peace and security dynamics, thereby, become discernible as complex constructs and processes (i.e., constantly 'in the making'), involving continuous contestation and negotiation, multiple and entangled actors, political projects and practices, playing out at different interconnected sites. The following sections further illustrate these points.

Spatial imaginations and framings of conflict

Sometimes implicitly or unconsciously, sometimes openly and actively, particular spatial imaginations, related to regional and transregional security concerns, have influenced (triggered, guided or framed) conflict interventions by African ROs and their regional security policies. Most importantly, this refers to imaginations about how events and dynamics in one place or area relate to other places or the regions that they are a part of. Moreover, it also refers to imaginations about how specific spaces (e.g., states or regions) should be formatted, according to which ideas, rules and norms, and how different spaces should relate to each other, according to specific (imagined) spatial orders (e.g., state systems or AU–REC relations). With regard to West Africa, two specific spatial imaginations have been most influential, one linked to security concerns about 'regional instability' and the other to trans-regional 'narco-terrorism'. Interestingly, Guinea-Bissau has assumed a prominent position in both of them, which, in turn, helps us to understand why conflicts in the country, despite its seeming marginality, have been a high priority for actors at ECOWAS and the AU, but also, at least for some time, other international and regional actors, such as the US government and the EU. Chapter 5 has discussed this in more detail.

Spatial imaginations around 'regional instability' in West Africa have, based on experiences during the 1990s, centered around concerns about potential 'spill-overs' of conflict in one state to neighboring states and the region more widely. For example, flows of refugees, weapons and fighters across state borders threaten 'regional stability'. Here different degrees and perceptions of 'proximity' (i.e., who and what is affected first) and 'interconnections' (i.e., transnational social, economic and political entanglements) play a key role. These spatial imaginations have been especially prevalent among actors of ECOWAS and the AU and have triggered policy processes and regional security cooperation mechanisms. They have also been key in contesting relations between the two organizations. In a nutshell, ECOWAS actors have argued in terms of their 'proximity' to conflicts in West Africa (i.e., being more affected and knowing the situation better) to fend off stronger engagement of AU actors in West African conflicts. They have also contested a hierarchical understanding of relations between the AU and the RECs (see below).

Spatial imaginations around 'narco-terrorism' have been prevalent especially among Western state and regional actors, most importantly the US government and the EU. AU actors, and to a much lesser extent ECOWAS actors, have also contributed to such discourses. However, this concern has been subordinate to more immediate ones, such as 'regional instability' and 'terrorism' plain and simple. Imaginations around 'narco-terrorism', first, essentially link to debates about 'weak' or 'failed states', and especially imaginations and the discursive framing of certain spaces in Africa as 'empty', 'uncontrolled' and 'ungoverned'. Second, these spaces are then linked to different kinds of transnational and trans-regional activities that are regarded as 'illicit' or 'criminal' and that might pose threats not only to those 'weak' states and their regional environment, but might affect international security at large, for example, by providing 'safe havens' and 'launch pads' for operations in Western states. In the example of Guinea-Bissau, these spatial imaginations have led EU actors to deploy a security sector reform mission to Guinea-Bissau (EU SSR-GB). This mission aimed at reforming a military that is widely believed to be complicit in the illicit drug trade, and at building state capacities to take on these issues. The decision by the EU Council authorizing the mission to Guinea-Bissau explicitly referred to the threat posed by, as well as the need to combat, drug trafficking (see Chapter 5).

Intervention/spatializing practices

Applying the spatial approach – and combining a detailed study of ECOWAS and AU conflict interventions in Guinea-Bissau with a comprehensive exploratory survey of official documents of the two organizations – in this book I have identified seven sets of basic intervention practices that ECOWAS and AU actors have applied relatively consistently over time and across different conflict situations. Three of these sets have been applied 'from afar' (e.g., organizational headquarters and meeting venues) – discussed in detail in Chapter 3; another three 'on the ground' (i.e., at the actual conflict site) – discussed in detail in Chapter 4; and one, the strategic engagement of other actors, both 'from afar' and 'on the ground' – discussed in detail in Chapter 6. While some of these intervention practices, so far, have been considered 'weak' or 'irrelevant', the spatial approach brings to the fore how important – and, in fact, essential – they have been both to regional conflict management and the construction, formatting and ordering of regional spaces. The following paragraphs briefly summarize the main sets of practices and their contribution to space-making during conflict interventions.

'From afar'

Both ROs have (i) actively and continuously contributed to producing conflict knowledge, which has enabled them to assess, frame and co-constitute reality and, eventually, to act upon conflict situations. Subsequently, the produced knowledge has formed a key ingredient for (ii) discussions, during meetings on various levels, ranging from 'technical' to different hierarchical 'political' levels. Contrary to criticism of ECOWAS and the AU as being mere 'talk shops', these meetings are in themselves an important practice. Not only are they essential in bringing different actors of the regions together to find a common outlook, as they consume a lot of resources, they also signal attention, relevance and importance. Out of these meetings, and based on the produced knowledge, the different actors and organs at ECOWAS and the AU have (iii) issued public statements, pronouncing themselves on the conflict in Guinea-Bissau – which in itself needs to be considered an important 'act'. As they selectively make some of the preceding considerations (and their functions) public, they create a certain degree of transparency and a public record.

These three sets of practices intimately link to the construction of regional spaces to the extent that they provide information and perspective and allow for the exchange of views on conflict in a specific place that is supposed to be part of the region, but which is not automatically interesting to all regional member states (i.e., 'bringing the conflict to the region'). Thereby, these practices allow ECOWAS and AU actors to function as fora or platforms that generate regional cohesion and identity. While commonly pushed by those member state representatives with the highest stakes, all members participate in the process to at least some extent and, thus, eventually come to stand behind 'regional' decisions and public pronouncements made on the issue. Moreover, these practices also apply more general regional norms and principles to specific conflict situations and communicate 'ECOWAS' and the 'AU' as legitimate actors in charge of or responsible for responding to them (i.e., 'bringing the region to the conflict'). In this way, they – initially specific member states or commission staff, in the end officially all member states – 'pull' the place within their 'reach', integrating it into their respective regional space.

At the basis of and communicated through those three sets of practices are specific spatial formats, namely the 'nation state' and the 'region'. Whereas the former is considered 'out of order' or 'threatened', the latter claims to be committed to assisting in reestablishing a 'functioning' member of the West/African state community. Thus, these practices contribute to understanding the spatial dimensions of particular conflict situations and to spatially frame them (e.g., as a threat for 'regional stability').

Another key practice, which ECOWAS and AU actors have applied 'from afar' (and 'on the ground', see below), has been to strategically engage other intervening actors, both personally during the process of knowledge production or at meetings, and impersonally via public statements. For example, they have done this by calling on them for support, be it diplomatic or financial, and by referring to statements others have made. In this way, ECOWAS and AU actors have not only communicated their own positions on specific conflict situations, but have also formulated expectations about how others should behave towards those positions, and towards the two ROs. Therefore, this practice has also been about contesting and negotiating relations among intervening actors. In this, space has played an important role as it both has been used as an argument, and has been the objective of different efforts to order space (see below).

'On the ground'

ECOWAS and AU actors have (i) dispatched various diplomatic missions to conflict sites, which have aimed to gather firsthand information talking to stakeholders 'on the ground' and to convey regional messages, negotiate with political actors and in some cases exert pressure. In addition to such short-term visits, and with similar objectives, ECOWAS and the AU have also created liaison offices in different conflict sites and appointed special representatives to head those offices. In addition, (ii) 'technical' support on the ground has sought to tackle specific issues that have been linked to conflict dynamics. For example, this has included security sector reform programs and election preparation and observation missions. Less frequently, ECOWAS and AU actors have (iii) deployed military and police peacekeeping forces to enable and accompany other practices, instead of replacing them. The deployment of the ECOWAS Standby Force (ESF) to Guinea-Bissau (ECOMIB) in May 2012 is a case in point. As the first ESF mission since the short-lived deployment to Sierra Leone in 2003/4, and self-funded by ECOWAS for three full years before the EU started to support the mission in late 2015, it testifies to the importance that ECOWAS and AU actors have accorded to conflict in Guinea-Bissau, as well as to the importance of that case for the study of African Peace and Security.

All of these practices relate directly to space-making, especially through the creation of connections and the establishment of 'physical' presence in specific conflict situations. To some extent, therefore, these practices have been the more 'material' counterparts of the important rhetoric or symbolic practices employed 'from afar'. Even more directly than public communication, the communication running through missions, delegations, special representatives and liaison offices bring the 'region' to the 'local' scale, that is, working in the opposite direction than the production of conflict knowledge at headquarters. Representatives of ECOWAS and the AU come or go, for example to Guinea-Bissau, communicating and seeking to implement regional positions and decisions as well as regional knowledge. The physical presence of individuals or groups, representing their respective regions, signals interest in and importance of 'local' affairs. It also creates popular visibility and attention for the region at the local level (e.g., local media and blogs reporting on the missions; logos on cars and flags, moving through the conflict site). At the same time, it sensitizes 'local' actors, especially elites, about their 'belonging' not only to the national but also to different regional spaces. While that may constrain their actions, it may also allow them to use them actively in order to enlarge or diversify their 'playing field'.

In all of this, specific spatial formats, such as 'nation-state' and 'region', guide action taken by ECOWAS and AU actors 'on the ground' and simultaneously are the objectives of that action. Actors within both organizations to some extent share imaginations of what states in the region should be and how they should relate to other states and the region. However, what becomes apparent 'on the ground', much less visible in actions taken 'from afar', is that while formally targeting the nation state, interventions by both ECOWAS and AU actors has largely and primarily (even though not exclusively) focused on politics and security in regional capitals. Thus, interventions commonly engage actors and institutions associated with the central state, that is, a part of the spatial format 'nation state' that is supposed to stand in for the whole national territory.

As mentioned above, actors at ECOWAS and the AU have also engaged other intervening actors 'on the ground'. However, on that level, coordination and cooperation among different regional and international actors may differ from interaction at the level of headquarters ('from afar'). On the one hand, a certain pragmatism requires representatives to interact with others more frequently and cooperatively. On the other hand, personal relationships play an important role in facilitating more or less cooperation among local representatives of different ROs (see Chapter 6).

These dynamics hold interesting implications for processes of spatialization. First, with regard to the construction of regional spaces, the interpretation of mandates based on local necessities and personal preferences creates a certain divergence between positions and approaches adopted at the different levels of one and the same (African) RO. This points to the co-constitution of agency and characteristics of ROs by various 'internal' and 'external' actors, self-identified 'African' and 'non-African' actors, working at different sites, linked through different networks. Consequently, regional spaces are constructed simultaneously at and through these different sites and networks. Second, to the extent that coordination of communication and inter/action of different spatial scales is achieved at the 'ground level', at least when perceived at that level, different scales increasingly overlap. This does not mean that hierarchies and/or imbalances among them disappear, but cooperative relations may emerge, as do shared visions of who should do what and how – even though most likely never entirely free of tensions.

Political-spatial projects pursued during conflict intervention

During conflict interventions, as moments of dense social interaction, actors at ECOWAS, the AU and other regional organizations have not only sought to manage conflict in that country. Instead, through the same practices, they have simultaneously pursued several additional objectives linked to specific political-spatial projects. Among these have been, on the one hand, to develop, implement and consolidate specific regional security policies (spatial formatting, discussed in Chapter 5) and, on the other, the ordering by and of space (spatial ordering, discussed in Chapter 6).

'Internal' and 'external' formatting of space

Actors at both ECOWAS and the AU, as well as at the EU, have adopted different conflict situations as items to their agenda in relation to specific security policies. In that sense, these organizations have not only been relevant for these conflict situations, but these conflicts have also been relevant *for* actors at these organizations and the 'internal' and 'external' formatting of regional spaces. Most importantly, this has related to policy processes at ECOWAS and the AU aiming to develop and implement coherent approaches in response to 'unconstitutional changes of government' (UCGs). Building on the principle of 'zero tolerance' for coups d'état, or any other unconstitutional means to access state power, both organizations have increasingly sought, since the 1990s, to take a firm and consistent stance, and implement their respective policy scripts (codified in text and/or practice). From that perspective, the ambition is to respond to every situation according to the same principles, practices and procedures. While both ECOWAS and AU actors share this objective, in principle, interpretations and approaches to implementation have differed, repeatedly leading to clashes between the two organizations. Other examples include regional policies of ECOWAS and the AU on security sector reform (SSR) and post-conflict reconstruction and development (PCRD), which staff at both organizations have sought to fill with life and content.

Following a slightly different logic, EU actors have engaged in 'external' spatial formatting, adopting West/African conflict situations as a deployment site for their SSR missions under the EU's Common Security and the Defense Policy and testing the 'consultation procedure' according to Article 96 of the Cotonou Agreement. Both have, on the one hand, aimed to format certain spaces according to the spatial format 'nation state'. These spaces are 'external' to the EU's 'own' regional space, but for different reasons have been identified as relevant and to some extent interconnected with European security and economic interests. On the other hand, applying these policies has also been about consolidating them, as an objective in itself, and about performing a specific self-image, both of which has intimately linked to the formatting of European spaces (see Chapter 5).

Ordering by *and* of *space*

In addition to pursuing specific regional security policies, and sometimes related to that, actors at African ROs, as well as other regional and international actors, have also tried to contest and negotiate relations among them referring to space, using it as an argument for their goals and/or in their efforts to establish a particular spatial order – i.e., ordering *by* and/or *of* space. In this book, I have argued that these interactions occur where different political-spatial projects have intersected and often link to particular spatial imaginations (see above). To explain that argument in more detail and to substantiate it empirically, I have referred to the complex interaction among different intervening actors in Guinea-Bissau. In particular, I have highlighted three constellations of actors and interrelated spatial objectives or strategies, all of which have pointed to the central importance of space to understand the relations and interaction among African ROs and different regional and international actors during conflict intervention.

First, actors at ECOWAS and the Community of Portuguese-Speaking Countries (CPLP) have tried to spatially legitimize or delegitimize their interventions in Guinea-Bissau. In 2011/12, the Angolan government legitimated its military presence in the country by referring to the regional framework of the CPLP, helping a fellow member state of the Lusophone space. In response to that, the governments of several ECOWAS member states (in particular, Senegal, Nigeria and Côte d'Ivoire) rejected the involvement of a power 'all the way' from Southern Africa in what they framed as their 'own', West African, space. Subsequently, they mobilized ECOWAS and referred to APSA, which only recognizes the West African REC (and not the CPLP) as one of its pillars and in charge of peace and security in that part of Africa.

Second, tensions between different representatives of ECOWAS and the AU, during 2012 and 2013 in Guinea-Bissau, have been an expression of the continual contestation and negotiation of the spatial organization of APSA around the concept of 'subsidiarity'. While ECOWAS is the recognized APSA pillar in West Africa, both organizations have proposed different interpretations of what that would mean exactly for their relationship. Whereas actors at ECOWAS emphasized the aspect of 'complementarity', putting ECOWAS in charge of peace and security in West Africa, actors at the AU favored a hierarchical understanding with the AU at the top, as the ultimate authority to decide how to respond to conflict in all parts of Africa.

Third, in line with a more general policy of interregionalism, EU actors have sought to actively influence and contribute to the construction of other regions, according to (changing) interests and objectives. However, EU approaches have not always been coherent and coordinated. For example, although to a large degree funding and supporting the hierarchical APSA geography with the AU Peace and Security Council at the top and decision making organs of the RECs below, it also supports RECs directly, thereby undermining the position of the AU. That EU actors have a more or less clear imagination of 'ECOWAS' (i.e., what it should be or do) has been clearly visible in the example of interventions in Guinea-Bissau, especially following the coup of April 2012, when EU actors first refused to support ECOMIB, but later pushed ECOWAS not to withdraw the mission (see Chapter 6).

Contribution and outlook

Highlighting the intimate connection between conflict interventions by African ROs and space-making, this book points to the elevated importance of space as an analytical category and the benefit of a spatial approach. Such an approach helps capturing, understanding and theorizing 'internal' modes of operation of African ROs as well as the complexity of their conflict interventions and African peace and security dynamics more generally. These involve multiple, entangled actors, practices and sites of conflict intervention, and are intimately linked to specific spatial imaginations, as well as the continuous construction, formatting and ordering of regional spaces. In this way, this book contributes to the 'spatial turn' in the partly overlapping academic fields of IR, International Studies and Global Studies, productively linking them to advances in Critical Geography. Empirically, this book has presented a detailed study of ECOWAS and AU conflict interventions in Guinea-Bissau, as well as a comprehensive exploratory mapping of intervention practices of the two organizations over time and across different conflict situations. Based on this, and applying the spatial approach it has identified and described different basic sets of intervention practices of ECOWAS and the AU, underlying different efforts to foster peace and security in West/Africa.

Moreover, to IR, International Studies and Global Studies, and in particular, however, to the interdisciplinary research field of African Peace and Security, this book offers a new methodological and theoretical approach that, among the things already mentioned, emphasizes African agency, countering eurocentric perspectives and further nuancing the role of African actors in regional and international politics. In this way, it also contributes to debates about African/International Relations (cf. Abrahamsen 2017) and Comparative Regionalism (cf. Börzel and Risse 2016). In that regard, the book offers new insights on how different actors at African ROs actively construct, format and order regional spaces – i.e., *how* exactly regions are actually made and remade – as well as trans-regional and international relations. At the same time, the spatial approach also allows us to critically question some established terms, categories and concepts (e.g., 'state', 'region', 'geopolitics', 'internal' and 'external') and point to their continuous construction, negotiation and contestation, highlighting the politics involved therein.

While this book constitutes an important first step towards a better understanding of intervention practices of African ROs and their 'internal' modes of operation in the context of African peace and security dynamics, more research will be required in order to overcome some of the limitations resulting from the difficulties of doing research at African ROs (see Chapter 1). In particular, more detailed and long-term research will have to further study meeting practices at African ROs, based on interviews and, where possible, participant observation. Once meetings are established as important – and, in fact, essential – practice at any international or regional organization, research will have to work towards an in-depth understanding of dynamics during meetings of different organs and constellations of actors. The same applies to external communication practices of African ROs and the actual workings of diplomatic field missions, as well as local coordination frameworks. All of this will eventually contribute to a more complete picture of how African ROs 'come together' from multiple actors, sites and practices.

References

Abrahamsen, Rita. 2017. Africa and International Relations: Assembling Africa, Studying the World. *African Affairs* 116 (462): 125–39. doi: 10.1093/afraf/adw071.

Allen, John. 2016. *Topologies of Power: Beyond Territory and Networks.* London, New York: Routledge.

Börzel, Tanja A. and Thomas Risse, eds. 2016. *The Oxford Handbook of Comparative Regionalism.* Oxford: Oxford University Press.

Massey, Doreen B. 2005. *For Space.* Los Angeles, CA: SAGE.

Werlen, Benno. 2009. Regionalisations, Everyday. In *The International Encyclopedia of Human Geography*, eds Rob Kitchin and Nigel Thrift, 286–93. Oxford: Oxford University Press.

Appendix

No.	Interview partner	Affiliation	Place	Date
1	Senior CPLP Official	Executive Secretariat	Lisbon	19.11.2015
2	Senior AU Official	---	Addis Ababa	07.09.2016
3	Diplomatic Source	---	Addis Ababa	08.09.2016
4	Senior Government Official of Guinea-Bissau	---	Addis Ababa	08.09.2016
5	Senior Government Official of Guinea-Bissau	---	Addis Ababa	08.09.2016
6	Senior AU Officer	Peace and Security Department	Addis Ababa	14.09.2016
7	AU Officer	Peace and Security Department	Addis Ababa	14.09.2016
8	Senior AU Officer	Department of Political Affairs	Addis Ababa	14.09.2016
9	AU Officer	Department of Political Affairs	Addis Ababa	14.09.2016
10	Senior AU Officer	Peace and Security Department	Addis Ababa	16.09.2016
11	AU Officer	Peace and Security Department	Addis Ababa	16.09.2016
12	ECOWAS Officer	---	Addis Ababa	20.09.2016
13	Senior AU Officer	Peace and Security Department	Addis Ababa	21.09.2016
14	AU Officer	Department of Social Affairs	Addis Ababa	21.09.2016
15	Senior AU Officer	Peace and Security Department	Addis Ababa	22.09.2016
16	AU Officer	Peace and Security Department	Addis Ababa	22.09.2016
17	EU Officer	EU Delegation to the AU	Addis Ababa	22.09.2016
18	EU Official	EU Delegation to the AU	Addis Ababa	22.09.2016
19	AU Officer	Peace and Security Department	Addis Ababa	23.09.2016

No.	*Interview partner*	*Affiliation*	*Place*	*Date*
20	AU Officer	Peace and Security Department	Addis Ababa	23.09.2016
21	UN Officer	UN Office to the AU	Addis Ababa	23.09.2016
22	Senior ECOWAS Official	---	Addis Ababa	26.09.2016
23	Senior ECOWAS Official	---	Ouagadougou	29.01.2017
24	Senior Consultant	---	Ouagadougou	29.01.2017
25	Senior ECOWAS Officer	Department for Political Affairs, Peace and Security	Abuja	14.02.2017
26	ECOWAS Officer	Department for Political Affairs, Peace and Security	Abuja	15.02.2017
27	ECOWAS Officer	Department for Political Affairs, Peace and Security	Abuja	15.02.2017
28	Senior ECOWAS Officer	Department for Political Affairs, Peace and Security	Abuja	16.02.2017
29	Senior ECOWAS Officer	Department for Political Affairs, Peace and Security	Abuja	16.02.2017
30	Senior ECOWAS Officer	Department for Political Affairs, Peace and Security	Abuja	20.02.2017
31	Senior ECOWAS Officer	Department for Political Affairs, Peace and Security	Abuja	20.02.2017
32	Senior ECOWAS Officer	Department for Political Affairs, Peace and Security	Abuja	21.02.2017
33	ECOWAS Officer	Department for Political Affairs, Peace and Security	Abuja	21.02.2017
34	ECOWAS Officer	Office of the Vice President of the ECOWAS Commission	Abuja	21.02.2017
35	Senior ECOWAS Officer	Department for Political Affairs, Peace and Security	Abuja	23.02.2017
36	ECOWAS Officer	Department for Political Affairs, Peace and Security	Abuja	23.02.2017
37	ECOWAS Officer	Department for Political Affairs, Peace and Security	Abuja	24.02.2017
38	Senior ECOWAS Officer	Department for Political Affairs, Peace and Security	Abuja	24.02.2017

No.	*Interview partner*	*Affiliation*	*Place*	*Date*
39	EU Officer	EU Delegation to Nigeria (and ECOWAS)	Abuja	24.02.2017
40	Senior GIZ Officer	GIZ Office Abuja	Abuja	24.02.2017
41	Senior ECOWAS Officer	Department for Social Affairs and Gender	Abuja	27.02.2017
42	ECOWAS Officer	Department for Social Affairs and Gender	Abuja	27.02.2017
43	Senior ECOWAS Officer	Department for Political Affairs, Peace and Security	Abuja	28.02.2017
44	Senior UN Officer	UN House Abuja	Abuja	28.02.2017
45	ECOWAS Officer	Department for Political Affairs, Peace and Security	Abuja	01.03.2017
46	Military Advisor	Department for Political Affairs, Peace and Security	Abuja	01.03.2017
47	Military Advisor	Department for Political Affairs, Peace and Security	Abuja	01.03.2017
48	Senior EU Official	EU Delegation to Nigeria (and ECOWAS)	Abuja	01.03.2017
49	Senior ECOWAS Officer	Department for Political Affairs, Peace and Security	Abuja	02.03.2017
50	International Advisor	Department for Political Affairs, Peace and Security	Abuja	02.03.2017
51	Senior WANEP Officer	---	Abuja	02.03.2017
52	Senior GIZ Officer	GIZ Office Abuja	Abuja	02.03.2017
53	Senior ECOWAS Officer	Department for Political Affairs, Peace and Security	Abuja	03.03.2017
54	Senior ECOWAS Officer	Department for Political Affairs, Peace and Security	Abuja	03.03.2017
55	Senior UN Officer	UNIOGBIS	Bissau	30.03.2017
56	UN Officer	UNIOGBIS	Bissau	30.03.2017
57	NGO Representative	---	Bissau	01.04.2017
58	UN Officer	UNIOGBIS	Bissau	03.04.2017
59	Senior EU Officer	EU Delegation to Guinea-Bissau	Bissau	04.04.2017
60	Senior UN Officer	UNIOGBIS	Bissau	04.04.2017
61	Senior UN Officer	UNIOGBIS	Bissau	04.04.2017
62	AU Officer	---	Bissau	05.04.2017
63	Senior AU Officer	---	Bissau	05.04.2017
64	Senior ECOWAS Official	---	Bissau	06.04.2017

No.	*Interview partner*	*Affiliation*	*Place*	*Date*
65	EU Officer	EU Delegation to Guinea-Bissau	Bissau	06.04.2017
66	Senior Police Official	Public Order Police	Bissau	06.04.2017
67	Senior Police Officer of Guinea-Bissau	---	Bissau	06.04.2017
68	Senior AU Official	---	Bissau	07.04.2017
69	Researcher	National Defense Institute of Guinea-Bissau	Bissau	07.04.2017
70	Senior Police Officer of Guinea-Bissau	---	Bissau	07.04.2017
71	NGO Representative	---	Bissau	08.04.2017
72	Senior Representative	National Study and Research Institute (INEP)	Bissau	08.04.2017
73	Teacher	Amílcar Cabral University	Bissau	08.04.2017
74	Diplomatic Source	---	Bissau	10.04.2017
75	Senior Government Official	Ministry of Defense	Bissau	11.04.2017
76	Local NGO Representative	---	Bissau	11.04.2017
77	Local NGO Representative	---	Bissau	11.04.2017
78	Senior UN Official	UNIOGBIS	Bissau	12.04.2017
79	Senior UN Officer	UNIOGBIS	Bissau	12.04.2017
80	Portuguese Source	---	Bissau	12.04.2017
81	Businessman and Former Politician of Guinea-Bissau	---	Bissau	13.04.2017
82	Senior Researcher and Former Politician of Guinea-Bissau	---	Bissau	13.04.2017
83	Diplomatic Source	---	Bissau	13.04.2017
84	US Officer	---	Bissau	13.04.2017
85	Senior Analyst, Lecturer and Former Politician of Guinea-Bissau	---	Bissau	14.04.2017
86	Angolan Source	---	Bissau	15.04.2017
87	Senior EU Officer	EU Delegation to Senegal	Dakar	21.04.2017
88	US Source	---	Dakar	21.04.2017
89	Senior ECOWAS Officer	---	Dakar	24.04.2017
90	UN Officer	UN Office on Drugs and Crime Dakar	Dakar	25.04.2017
91	UN Officer	UN Office on Drugs and Crime Dakar	Dakar	25.04.2017

No.	*Interview partner*	*Affiliation*	*Place*	*Date*
92	UN Officer	UN Office on Drugs and Crime Dakar	Dakar	25.04.2017
93	UN Officer	UN Office on Drugs and Crime Dakar	Dakar	25.04.2017
94	UN Officer	UN Office on Drugs and Crime Dakar	Dakar	25.04.2017
95	UN Officer	UN Office for West Africa and the Sahel	Dakar	26.04.2017
96	UN Officer	UN Office for West Africa and the Sahel	Dakar	26.04.2017
97	UN Officer	UN Office on Drugs and Crime	Dakar	27.04.2017
98	UN Officer	UN Office for West Africa and the Sahel	Dakar	01.05.2017
99	Senior UN Official	UN Office on Drugs and Crime Dakar	Dakar	02.05.2017
100	UN Officer	UN Office on Drugs and Crime Dakar	Dakar	02.05.2017
101	Diplomatic Source	---	Dakar	02.05.2017
102	Senior UN Officer	UN Office for West Africa and the Sahel	Dakar	03.05.2017
103	Senior UN Officer	UN Office for West Africa and the Sahel	Dakar	03.05.2017
104	Senior Representative	ISS Dakar	Dakar	03.05.2017
105	Researcher	ISS Dakar	Dakar	03.05.2017
106	EU Official	EU Delegation to Senegal	Dakar	04.05.2017
107	Senior EU Officer	EU Delegation to Senegal	Dakar	04.05.2017
108	UN Officer	UN Office on Drugs and Crime Dakar	Dakar	04.05.2017
109	Bissau-Guinean Source	---	Dakar	04.05.2017
110	Nigerian Source	---	Dakar	05.05.2017
111	UN Officer	UN Department of Political Affairs	New York	07.11.2017
112	Senior ECOWAS Official	---	New York	08.11.2017
113	UN Officer	UN Department of Political Affairs	New York	09.11.2017
114	UN Officer	UN Department of Political Affairs	New York	09.11.2017
115	Senior UN Officer	UN Peacebuilding Support Office	New York	10.11.2017
116	Nigerian Diplomatic Source	---	New York	10.11.2017
117	Nigerian Diplomatic Source	---	New York	10.11.2017
118	Nigerian Diplomatic Source	---	New York	10.11.2017

No.	*Interview partner*	*Affiliation*	*Place*	*Date*
119	Nigerian Diplomatic Source	---	New York	10.11.2017
120	Senior EU Officer	DG DEVCO	Brussels	04.06.2018
121	Senior EU Officer	EU External Action Service	Brussels	05.06.2018
122	EU Officer	EU External Action Service	Brussels	05.06.2018
123	EU Officer	EU External Action Service	Brussels	05.06.2018
124	EU Officer	EU External Action Service	Brussels	05.06.2018
125	EU Officer	DG DEVCO	Brussels	06.06.2018
126	EU Officer	EU External Action Service	Brussels	06.06.2018
127	EU Officer	DG DEVCO	Brussels	08.06.2018
128	AU Officer	Peace and Security Department	Addis Ababa	19.09.2018
129	Senior Researcher	ISS Addis Ababa	Addis Ababa	20.09.2018
130	AU Officer	Peace and Security Department	Addis Ababa	21.09.2018
131	AU Officer	Directorate of Strategic Planning, Policy, Monitoring, Evaluation and Resource Mobilization	Addis Ababa	21.09.2018
132	AU Officer	---	Addis Ababa	22.09.2018
133	Senior AU Officer	Peace and Security Department	Addis Ababa	24.09.2018
134	AU Officer	Peace and Security Department	Addis Ababa	24.09.2018
135	International Advisor	Peace and Security Department	Addis Ababa	24.09.2018
136	Researcher, PSC Report Program	ISS Addis Ababa	Addis Ababa	24.09.2018
137	Senior AU Officer	Department of Political Affairs	Addis Ababa	25.09.2018
138	Senior EU Officer	EU Delegation to the AU	Addis Ababa	25.09.2018
139	EU Officer	EU Delegation to the AU	Addis Ababa	25.09.2018
140	Researcher, PSC Report Program	ISS Addis Ababa	Addis Ababa	25.09.2018
141	AU Officer	Peace and Security Department	Addis Ababa	26.09.2018
142	AU Officer	Peace and Security Department	Addis Ababa	27.09.2018
143	Freelance Consultant	---	Addis Ababa	27.09.2018
144	Senior AU Officer	Peace and Security Department	Addis Ababa	28.09.2018
145	AU Officer	Peace and Security Department	Addis Ababa	28.09.2018

No.	*Interview partner*	*Affiliation*	*Place*	*Date*
146	AU Officer	Peace and Security Department	Addis Ababa	28.09.2018
147	AU Officer	Peace and Security Department	Addis Ababa	28.09.2018
148	Senior ECOWAS Official	---	Addis Ababa	28.09.2018
149	ECOWAS Officer	---	Addis Ababa	28.09.2018
150	US Officer	---	Addis Ababa	01.10.2018
151	Senior ECOWAS Officer	Department for Political Affairs, Peace and Security	Abuja	22.10.2018
152	Military Advisor	Department for Political Affairs, Peace and Security	Abuja	22.10.2018
153	Senior ECOWAS Officer	Department for Political Affairs, Peace and Security	Abuja	23.10.2018
154	Senior ECOWAS Officer	Department for Political Affairs, Peace and Security	Abuja	23.10.2018
155	Senior ECOWAS Officer	Department for Political Affairs, Peace and Security	Abuja	24.10.2018
156	Senior ECOWAS Officer	Department for Political Affairs, Peace and Security	Abuja	24.10.2018
157	ECOWAS Officer	Office of the Vice President of the ECOWAS Commission	Abuja	24.10.2018
158	Senior ECOWAS Officer	Office of the Vice President of the ECOWAS Commission	Abuja	25.10.2018
159	Senior ECOWAS Officer	Department for Political Affairs, Peace and Security	Abuja	26.10.2018
160	ECOWAS Officer	Department for Political Affairs, Peace and Security	Abuja	26.10.2018
161	Senior ECOWAS Officer	Department for Political Affairs, Peace and Security	Abuja	29.10.2018
162	ECOWAS Officer	Department for Political Affairs, Peace and Security	Abuja	29.10.2018
163	Senior ECOWAS Officer	Department for Social Affairs and Gender	Abuja	29.10.2018
164	Senior ECOWAS Officer	Department for Political Affairs, Peace and Security	Abuja	30.10.2018

No.	Interview partner	Affiliation	Place	Date
165	Senior ECOWAS Officer	Department for Political Affairs, Peace and Security	Abuja	31.10.2018
166	Senior ECOWAS Officer	Department for Political Affairs, Peace and Security	Abuja	01.11.2018
167	Senior ECOWAS Officer	Department for Political Affairs, Peace and Security	Abuja	01.11.2018
168	UN Officer	UN Department of Political Affairs	New York	04.12.2018
169	Senior UN Officer	UN Department of Political Affairs	New York	06.12.2018
170	Senior ECOWAS Official	---	New York	07.12.2018

Index

Abidjan (Côte d'Ivoire) 78, 85, 175; *see also* sites, interconnected
Abrahamsen, Rita 39–41
Abuja (Nigeria) 52, 74, 78, 84, 85, 115, 155, 184, 186; *see also* sites, interconnected
actors: complex collective 3, 34, 52–3, 63, 208–9, 186; local 20–1, 36–7, 115, 116, 123, 185, 208; unitary actors 3–4, 6, 51, 52, 186
Addis Ababa (Ethiopia) 52, 70, 87, 109, 111, 148, 154, 156, 176, 177, 190; *see also* sites, interconnected
Adler, Emanuel 38–9
African Charter on Democracy Elections and Governance (ACDEG) 118, 152
African Peace and Security Architecture (APSA) 2, 52, 111, 154, 189–92, 210–11
African Peace and Security: research field 2, 3–8, 13, 20, 34–43, 211–12; spatial approach to *see* space; spatial ordering of 189–93
African Peace Facility (APF) 128, 192–3
agency 36, 38, 39, 40, 63, 73, 76, 175; African 3, 16, 42, 73, 76, 111, 149, 152, 211; co-constitution of 186, 208–9; *see also* actors
Allen, John 43, 47–8
Angola 17, 18, 71, 79, 86, 87–8, 124, 128, 175–6, 178, 185, 188–9, 210; *see also* CPLP; MISSANG
AU Assembly 66, 70–1, 73, 78, 83, 114, 152, 156; Chair 86
AU Commission 73, 80, 87, 114, 119, 125, 152–4, 156; Chairperson *see* Chairperson of the AU Commission; research on 7; staff 14, 20, 65–7, 73, 76, 79–80, 82–3, 115, 149, 153–4, 156–7, 161, 176
AU Commissioner for Peace and Security 65, 73, 79, 163n7
AU Committee of Intelligence and Security Services of Africa (CISSA) 64–5
AU Conflict Management and Post-Conflict Reconstruction Division (CMPCRD) 65, 66, 153–5; *see also* post-conflict reconstruction and development (PCRD)
AU Conflict Prevention and Early Warning Division (CPEWD) 64
AU Continental Early Warning System (CEWS) 64, 66
AU Defense and Security Division (DSD) 153, 156
AU Democracy and Electoral Assistance Unit (DEAU) 118, 156
AU Department of Political Affairs (DPA) 156
AU Executive Council 71, 83, 154
AU liaison office 111–12, 115; in Guinea-Bissau (AULO-GB) 87, 109, 114–16
AU Peace and Security Council (PSC) 66, 71–3, 78–80, 83–3, 87–9, 107, 109, 111, 125, 152–3, 175–8, 190–2; Chair 71, 73, 76
AU Peace and Security Department (PSD) 64, 65, 71, 73, 82, 92, 111, 115, 153–5, 176; Director 181
AU Permanent Representatives Committee (PRC) 70
AU-REC relations 2, 16, 51–2, 153, 175, 191, 192, 205, 210–11; *see also* African Peace and Security Architecture;

African Peace and Security: spatial ordering of
Autesserre, Séverine 37

Banjul (Gambia) 84, 108, 154; *see also* sites, interconnected
Bissau Roadmap 184–5
Brazil 185, 188; *see also* CPLP
Brussels (Belgium) 52, 111, 176; *see also* sites, interconnected
Bueger, Christian 38–9
Burkina Faso 108, 110, 126, 128, 189

Ceesay, Ansoumana E. 113, 176, 181; *see also* Special Representative of the President of the ECOWAS Commission (SRPC)
Central African Republic (CAR) 154, 156, 160; *see also* ECCAS
Chairperson of the AU Commission (AUC Chairperson) 65, 67, 79, 82, 86–9, 107, 109, 111, 114, 119
Chergui, Smaïl 73; *see also* AU Commissioner for Peace and Security
Conakry (Guinea-Conakry) *see* Conakry Agreement; *see also* sites, interconnected
Conakry Agreement 20, 113, 127, 184–5
Condé, Alpha 78, 88, 109, 185; *see also* Guinea-Conakry
connections 9, 40, 44, 47–8, 52, 92, 103, 115, 116, 129, 208
consensual prime minister (of Guinea-Bissau) 20, 108, 113–14, 185
constitutional order, return to 18–19, 67, 79, 84–9, 107–8, 117, 152–3, 160, 178, 184, 187, 190
Constitutive Act of the African Union 70, 73
Côte d'Ivoire 77–9, 107, 108, 147, 176, 189, 210
Cotonou Agreement: Article 96 of the 159–61, 210
CPLP (Community of Portuguese-Speaking Countries) 17, 19, 77, 79, 88, 89, 115, 121, 175–7, 181–2, 185, 188–9, 210; *see also* Angola; DSSR Roadmap; Portugal
Critical Geography 43–8, 203; *see also* space; space-making
cross-border: cooperation 147; crimes 147; *see also* transnational

Dakar (Senegal) 84, 96n40, 148, 189; *see also* sites, interconnected
de Souza, Marcel Alain 114; *see also* President of the ECOWAS Commission
de- and re-territorialization 42, 47, 48; *see also* re-spatialization; spatialization
defense and security sector reform (DSSR) 67, 84–8, 124–5, 130; ECOWAS policy framework on 120–1, 155–6; in Guinea-Bissau 120–3, 182, 188; *see also* DSSR Roadmap; EU SSR-GB
Delegation of the European Union to Guinea-Bissau 181, 185
Dlamini-Zuma, Nkosazana 79, 87; *see also* Chairperson of the AU Commission (AUC Chairperson)
drug trafficking 15–16, 17, 67–9, 87, 114, 149–50; ECOWAS action plan on 85
DSSR Roadmap: ECOWAS 121; ECOWAS-CPLP 88, 121, 188

ECCAS (Economic Community of Central African States) 187
ECOMIB 16, 19, 85–6, 113; and DSSR 121–2; and space-making 129–30; deployment of 84–6, 108, 124–8; funding 128–9; mandate 124–8; withdrawal of 68, 122, 127
ECOMOG 16, 104, 147, 188; research on 4; *see also* ECOWAS Standby Force (ESF)
ECOWARN 64
ECOWAS Authority 9, 19, 62, 66, 74–6, 78, 84–6, 113, 124, 125, 127, 175, 177–9, 189; Chair 84, 107, 127
ECOWAS Commission 64, 74, 83–5, 112–13, 119, 126–9; research on 7; staff 65–6, 76, 82–3, 92, 125, 149, 174–6; *see also* President of the ECOWAS Commission
ECOWAS Commissioner for Political Affairs, Peace and Security (CPAPS) 85, 108, 176
ECOWAS Committee of Chiefs of Defense Staff (CCDS) 76–8, 108, 125–7, 175; Chair 78, 108
ECOWAS Conflict Prevention Framework (ECPF) 74, 118, 120, 155

ECOWAS Department of Political Affairs, Peace and Security (DPAPS) 64, 65, 82, 115–16, 125
ECOWAS Director of Political Affairs 176, 181
ECOWAS Early Warning Directorate (EWD) 64
ECOWAS liaison office 110–12; in Guinea-Bissau 113, 115–16, 186
ECOWAS Mediation and Security Council (MSC) 74–80, 82, 85, 110, 113, 119, 124, 126–7, 175; *see also* ECOWAS Authority
ECOWAS Protocol Relating to the Mechanism for Conflict Prevention, Management, Resolution, Peacekeeping and Security (1999 Mechanism) 64, 74, 76, 104, 110–11, 124, 147, 155
ECOWAS Regional Security Division (RSD) 155–6
ECOWAS Standby Force (ESF) 16, 19, 85–6, 103, 124; and space-making 129–30; research on 4; *see also* ECOMIB
election observation: missions (EOMs) 109–10, 118–20; AU policy 118, 156; ECOWAS policy 107, 118, 155
EU Commission 19, 128–9, 158–60, 193
EU Common Defense and Security Policy (CSDP) 121, 157–9
EU Council 19, 158–60, 205
EU SSR-GB 158–60, 205
European Development Fund (EDF) 158, 192
expertise 63, 66, 83, 91, 110, 118

France 147, 158, 175, 176

Gadinger, Frank 38–9
Gambia 16, 79, 84, 103, 108, 155, 156, 176
geopolitics 51, 162n2, 173, 212; Critical Geopolitics 46–7
Germany 193; GIZ (Corporation for International Cooperation) 193
Global Studies 2, 3, 20, 42, 211–12
Gomes Junior, Carlos 18–19, 85, 86, 88, 119; *see also* Guinea-Bissau
Gomes, Aristides 20, 185; *see also* Guinea-Bissau
Guinea-Bissau: Bissalanca attack 86, 89; capital of 17, 116–17, 128, 130, 151; Chief of the Armed Forces of 18, 78, 160; coup of 12 April (2012) 18; double assassination (2009) 78, 79, 121; elections in 18, 19, 20, 83–4, 112, 118–20, 124, 126, 185; external dependency 17; Interim President of 18, 85, 86, 108; memorandum of understanding (MoU) on DSSR 108, 121; military of 17–18; post-colonial state of 16–17, 126; President of 19–20, 68, 78, 79, 112–14, 120, 121, 127, 184, 185; Prime Minister of 18–19, 85, 86, 112, 161, 184; territorial control 17, 130, 208; *see also* Bissau Roadmap; Conakry Agreement; transition arrangement; consensual prime minister; political instability

heads of state (and government) 51, 66, 70–1, 73, 74, 76, 78–80, 82, 85–6, 104, 108, 113, 114, 124, 127, 147, 148, 156, 175, 178–9, 185, 189

'in the making' 52, 153, 204
Indjai, António 18, 160; *see also* Guinea-Bissau
Institute for Security Studies (ISS) 154
international contact group (ICG) 77, 177; local 183; for Guinea-Bissau (ICG-GB) 77, 88, 177, 182
International Organization of the Francophonie (OIF) 17, 19, 178, 181–2
International Relations (IR) 2, 3, 211–12; approaches 3–6, 35–41
International Studies 2, 3, 20, 211–12; approaches 35–41
intervention practices 2–3, 5–6, 8–12, 15, 20–2, 62–3, 103, 202, 205–9; conflict knowledge 63–8; engaging other actors 173–9, 180–5; field missions 103–10; liaison offices 110–16; meetings 69–80; peacekeeping forces 123–9; pronouncements 81–90; research on 7; 'technical' support 117–23
interviews 12–14, 212
ISSAT (International Security Sector Advisory Team) 155, 156

Jammeh, Yahya 84; *see also* Gambia
joint assessment mission (JAM) 86, 89, 109, 115, 154–6, 180–3; on SSR 156, 182–3

Jonathan, Goodluck 78, 84, 109; *see also* Nigeria

legitimacy 63, 69, 90–1, 188, 194

Mac Ginty, Roger 36
Madagascar 112, 123, 153, 156, 160, 177, 183, 187; *see also* SADC
Mali 19, 77, 83, 84, 88, 117, 130, 156, 175, 177, 187, 191, 193
Massey, Doreen 34–5, 43–6
Mauretania 153
Mbeki, Thabo 148; *see also* South Africa
member states 65–9, 76, 80, 82, 91–2, 176, 207: AU 73, 125, 152, 156; AU PSC 70–1, 73, 79, 175–6; CPLP 115; EU 157, 159, 161, 193; ECOWAS 74, 76, 85, 108, 115, 120, 126, 128, 175–6, 189–90, 210
methodology 8–9, 13–15; *see also* space: spatial approach
methods 12–13
MISSANG (Angolan Security Mission in Guinea-Bissau) 18, 19, 85, 86, 88, 124, 178, 188, 189; *see also* Angola
Modibo Touré 184; *see also* Special Representative of the UN Secretary General (SRSG)

'narco-state' 15, 67, 149–50, 159; *see also* spatial imaginations
'narco-terrorism' 16, 21, 150–1, 159, 204–5; *see also* spatial imaginations
NaTchuto, Bubo 15–16
New York (USA) 52, 89, 109, 111, 176, 177, 181; *see also* sites, interconnected
Nigeria 71, 73, 78, 107–8, 109, 113, 126, 128, 176, 189, 210
non-state actors 7, 20, 51, 80

Ó Tuathail, Gearóid (Gerard Toal) 43, 46–7
Obasanjo, Olusegun 109, 113, 148; *see also* Nigeria
Organization of African Unity (OAU) 17, 51, 107, 109, 118, 148; Assembly 148, 152; Central Organ 111; Mechanism for Conflict Prevention, Management and Resolution (1993) 107, 111; Secretary General 107, 109, 148
organs of regional organizations: 'political' and 'technical' 20, 65, 70–1, 74, 76, 82–3, 152, 180, 191, 211; research on 7
Ouédraogo, Kadré Désiré 78, 83–4, 107, 108, 113, 121, 126; *see also* President of the ECOWAS Commission

P5 of Guinea-Bissau 182, 183–5
PAIGC 17, 18, 19, 68, 89, 108
Pequeno, Ovídio 87, 109, 114–15, 182–4; *see also* Special Representative of the Chairperson of the AU Commission (SRCC)
Pereira, Domingos Simões 19–20, 113, 161, 184; *see also* Guinea-Bissau
Pereira, Raimundo 18–19, 85, 86, 88; *see also* Guinea-Bissau
Ping, Jean 79, 86–7, 109, 114; *see also* Chairperson of the AU Commission (AUC Chairperson)
policy: agendas 118–19, 120–1, 151–7, 157–61; implementation 20–1, 89–90, 151–7, 157–61; processes 21, 149, 151–61, 173–4, 205, 209–10; script 87, 151–2, 209; *see also* post-conflict reconstruction and development (PCRD); election observation; security sector reform (SSR); spatial-political projects; unconstitutional changes of government (UCG)
'political instability' (in Guinea-Bissau) 17, 67–9, 87, 112, 150; *see also* spatial imaginations
portals of globalization 42; *see also* sites, interconnected
Portugal 17, 158, 175, 185, 188; *see also* CPLP
post-conflict reconstruction and development (PCRD) 114, 153, 209; AU Interdepartmental Task Force on (ITF-PCRD) 154–5; AU policy on 153–5; ECOWAS practice 155; *see also* AU Conflict Management and Post-Conflict Reconstruction Division (CMPCRD)
Pouliot, Vincent 38–9
power 2, 36, 40–1, 45–8, 70, 189, 203; (unequal) power relations 36, 46, 48–50, 53–4, 129, 189, 192, 203; power-geometries 45; power-knowledge 46, 48–9, 53
practices 15, 37, 40–1; communities of practice 38–9; definition 38; international practices 38–9;

spatializing practices 2, 8–12, 20–2, 35, 44–6, 48–53, 68–9, 80–1, 90–3, 116–17, 123, 129–32, 149, 179–80, 185–7, 202, 204–9; *see also* intervention practices; spatial format / formatting; spatial order/ordering
presence, physical 47, 103ff., 110–11, 116, 129–31, 180, 203, 208
President of the ECOWAS Commission 65, 78, 82–5, 104, 107–8, 110–11, 113–14, 121, 126
PSC Protocol 64, 70, 107, 111, 152, 153–4

Ramos-Horta, José 120, 183, 184; *see also* Special Representative of the UN Secretary General (SRSG)
re-spatialization 48, 49, 53
'reach' 17, 47, 54, 62ff., 90, 203, 207
Regional Contact Group for Guinea-Bissau (RCG-GB) 78, 85, 86, 109, 126; Chair 78, 108, 109; meetings and missions 77, 84, 108
Regional Economic Communities (RECs) 2, 16, 51–2, 153, 156, 175, 191, 192, 205, 211
Regional Indicative Program (RIP) 192
'regional in/stability' 69, 131, 146–51, 205; *see also* 'political instability'
responsibility 63, 69, 90, 91, 129, 148, 149, 194
Richmond, Oliver 36

SADC (South African Development Community) 153, 187
Salim, Salim Ahmed 109, 148
Sall, Macky 109, 127, 185; *see also* Senegal
sanctions (imposed on Guinea-Bissau): AU 19, 86–8, 178–9; ECOWAS 19, 84–6, 108, 178–9; EU 19, 160, 178–9; lifting of 19, 79, 125, 152–3, 182; UN 19
Secretariat 175; *see also* PSC Protocol
security sector reform (SSR) 112, 114, 122, 151, 156–60, 209–10; AU policy framework on 156; in Guinea-Bissau 120–3, 182, 188; *see also* AU Defense and Security Division (DSD); EU SSR-GB
Senegal 108, 109, 126–8, 147, 176, 185, 189, 210
Shields, Rob 43, 45, 47–8
sites, interconnected 3, 8, 37, 42, 45, 52, 91, 131, 202; 'from afar' 62ff., 206–7; 'on the ground' 103ff., 207–9
South Africa 71, 73, 79, 107, 148, 175
space-making 2–3, 8–9, 20–2, 48–9, 52, 173, 208–9; and conflict knowledge 68–9; and field missions 116–17; and meetings 80–1; and military deployments 129–30; and public pronouncements 90–1; and power 46–9; and strategic engagement 179–80; 185–7; and 'technical' support 123–4; definition 49–50, 203; *see also* geopolitics; Critical Geography; actors; practices; spatial imaginations
space: and politics 45–7, 203; as analytical dimension 2, 7, 20, 34–5, 43–4, 203; relational 2, 44–5, 203; spatial turn 43; spatial approach 48–53, 203–4; topological 47–8, 203
spatial format / formatting 50–2, 145–6, 202, 203–4, 209–10; 'external' 157–61, 210; 'internal' 151–7, 209; 'nation-state' 69, 91, 116–17, 123, 130, 131, 146, 151, 159, 161, 207, 208, 210; 'region' 69, 90–2, 116, 129, 131, 207, 208
spatial imaginations 16, 21, 34, 46, 50–2, 64, 68, 90, 146–151, 157, 158, 173–4, 188, 194, 202, 204–5; *see also* 'narco-state'; 'narco-terrorism'; 'regional in/stability'
spatial order / ordering 3, 8, 20–2, 42, 45, 50–2, 91, 161, 173–4, 179–80, 187–94, 210–11
spatial semantics 50–2, 204
spatial-political projects 45, 145, 149, 151, 187–8, 209–11; *see also* spatial format / formatting; spatial order / ordering
spatialization 45, 47, 49, 55n24; processes of 50, 53, 186, 208
Special Representative of the Chairperson of the AU Commission (SRCC) 87, 109, 111, 114–16, 182–4
Special Representative of the President of the ECOWAS Commission (SRPC) 110–11, 113–14, 176, 181
Special Representative of the UN Secretary General (SRSG) 115, 120, 182–4; *see also* UNIOGBIS
state capitals 52, 116–17, 130

subsidiarity 85, 87, 88, 130, 178, 179, 194; and spatial order 189–91, 210–11
Supplementary Protocol on Democracy and Good Governance (2001 Supplementary Protocol) 74, 85, 107, 118, 120, 124, 149, 152, 155

Togo 108, 126, 128, 160, 176, 189
Training for Peace 154
trans-regional: ordering 3, 91; threats / security concerns 21, 68, 149–51, 202, 204–5; *see also* space-making; spatial imaginations
transition arrangement (in Guinea-Bissau) 18, 19, 78, 79, 86–7, 125, 153, 178, 181, 190; rejection of 19, 84, 85, 87, 88, 108–8
transnational: linkages 5–6, 205; 'organized crime' 68, 149–51, 205; 'terrorism' 148–51; threats 68; *see also* cross-border
troop/police contributing countries (T/PCCs) 126, 128, 189
Trovoada, Miguel 184; *see also* Special Representative of the UN Secretary General (SRSG)

UEMOA (West African Economic and Monetary Union) 175, 192
UN Office on Drugs and Crime (UNODC) 149–50, 163n8, 193
UN Secretary General (UNSG) 88, 183
UN Security Council 17, 19, 88, 89, 125, 176, 189
unconstitutional change of government (UCG) 79, 151–3, 190–1, 209; AU policy on 87, 152; ECOWAS policy on 152; *see also* constitutional order, return to
UNIOGBIS (UN Integrated Peacebuilding Office in Guinea-Bissau) 17, 112, 123, 182; *see also* Special Representative of the UN Secretary General (SRSG)
United Kingdom (UK) 158
United Nations (UN): actors 62, 65, 68, 77, 82, 109, 114, 119, 120, 130, 174, 175, 180, 181, 184; and post-conflict reconstruction and development 153–4; and security sector reform 155–6; peacekeeping 1, 3, 124, 146–7; Secretariat 1, 42; UN-AU-RO relations 4, 5, 179, 183; *see also* UNIOGBIS
United States (US) 85, 146, 150, 175, 205; US Agency for International Development (USAID) 12, 64; Drug Enforcement Agency (DEA) 15–16

Vaz, José Mario 19–20, 113–14, 120, 127, 184, 185; *see also* Guinea-Bissau

West African Network for Peacebuilding (WANEP) 64
Williams, Michael 39–41
Witt, Antonia 37, 183, 187

Yamoussoukro (Côte d'Ivoire) 78; *see also* sites, interconnected

For Product Safety Concerns and Information please contact our EU representative GPSR@taylorandfrancis.com
Taylor & Francis Verlag GmbH, Kaufingerstraße 24, 80331 München, Germany

www.ingramcontent.com/pod-product-compliance
Lightning Source LLC
LaVergne TN
LVHW021125300926
849160LV00010B/867

* 9 7 8 0 3 6 7 6 1 8 0 7 0 *